Environmentally Responsible Design

Environmentally Responsible Design

GREEN AND SUSTAINABLE DESIGN FOR
INTERIOR DESIGNERS

Edited by Dr. Louise Jones
LEED AP, IDEC, ASID, IIDA

WILEY

John Wiley & Sons, Inc.

*This book is dedicated to my friend and mentor
Elizabeth King, who started me on this journey.*

Contents

PART THREE: Evaluation of Interior Finishes and Furnishings

PART FOUR: Case Studies

Louise Jones, ArchD, LEED AP, IDEC, ASID, IIDA,
    Eastern Michigan University

Preface

The goal of environmentally responsible design is to transform the building industry such that the design and construction of the built environment enhances the health and well-being of both the current and future generations who live, work, and play in the designed environment and of the planet that sustains them.

Interior designers are responsible for the interior environments of homes, workplaces, and public buildings. Only in the past 25 years have designers come to understand the complexities of their role and the comprehensive consequences of their decisions. The designed environment and the natural environment are interrelated in complex ways that are not yet fully understood. The decisions made by the designer affect the health and well-being of both current and future generations and the planet on which they live, work, and play.

The terms *green design, ecological design, sustainable design, environmentally conscious design, green architecture,* and *environmentally responsible design* are often used interchangeably. However, there can be a subtle differences; for example, *green* products can be specified for a *sustainable* project. *Green design* often implies a micro perspective, with protection of people's health, safety, and well-being as the foundation for design decisions (e.g., safer environments for people with allergies, asthma, emphysema, or multiple chemical sensitivity). *Sustainable design* often implies a macro perspective, with enhancement of the global environment and protection of the world's ecosystems as the underpinning for design decisions (e.g., concern for natural resource depletion). *Environmentally responsible design* implies an interest in both green and sustainable design.

The resources available to the interior designer do not currently support the full scope of their role in the creation of the designed environment. An abundance of resources are available regarding the use of sustainable design practices and specification of environmentally responsible construction materials in the design and construction of buildings, but very few resources are available that focus on the design of the interiors of these buildings. This primer provides a foundation for environmentally responsible interior design. It opens with a broad perspective on the problems that threaten life as we know it on planet Earth and then focuses more narrowly on the issues within the purview of an interior designer. An understanding of the content of this book will lead the reader to a shift in the paradigm that supports the work of the interior design student or practitioner. No longer will design decisions be made with consideration of only aesthetics and functional requirements—decisions regarding the design of the interior environment will be approached through a filter of environmental responsibility.

Every project has, by definition, a starting point. This introduction to *environmentally responsible interior design* has as its starting point the Native American axiom: "We don't inherit the earth from our ancestors, we borrow it from our children." This canon serves as the philosophical grounding for this investigation of green and sustainable design precepts.

Acknowledgments

This book was written with the generous assistance, encouragement, and support of many people; I regret being able to recognize only a few who contributed most significantly to this project. First, I acknowledge my parents, Glen and Betty Jones, who instilled in me the love of and respect for nature and a passion for learning.

This book could not have been written without the continuing love and support of my husband, Henry, who assumed the responsibilities of our daily lives so that I could focus on the task at hand. I am grateful for the patience of my children, Rob, Katrisha, and Scott, and of their children, who granted me the countless hours spent away from them, working on this project.

I am indebted to my colleagues who contributed segments of the book: Dorothy Fowles, Amanda Gale, Anna Marshall-Baker, Jeanne Mercer-Ballard, Helena Moussatche, and Linda Nussbaumer. They worked diligently to bring this project to a successful completion. The depth and breadth of the discussion is due to their willingness to share their knowledge and expertise with students and designers who are interested in environmentally responsible design.

Special thanks to Bob Lahidji and the faculty, staff, and interior design graduate students at Eastern Michigan University for their encouragement when I was overwhelmed by the enormity of the endeavor.

Finally, thank you to Paul Drougas, and his associates at John Wiley & Sons, for guiding me throughout the project.

PART ONE

Environmentally Responsible Interior Design

Will we be able to face our children and assure them that we did not lack the courage to face these difficult questions, did not lack the stamina to pursue the correct solutions?
—Pierre Elliot Trudeau

CHAPTER ONE

Global Sustainability: The Macro Perspective

The earth belongs to each . . . generation during its course, fully and in its own right. The second generation receives it clear of debts and encumbrances of the first, the third of the second, and so on. For if the first could charge it with debt, then the earth would belong to the dead and not the living generation.
—Thomas Jefferson (1789)

Good Design by Any Other Name

ENVIRONMENTALLY RESPONSIBLE DESIGN

In 1987 the United Nations provided the definition of sustainable development that is used most often: "meeting the needs of the present without compromising the ability of future generations to meet their needs" (UN World Commission on Environment and Development 1987, 54). This mandates a macro perspective that juxtaposes current human behavior with prospects for the long-term survival of the human race at the level of its current manifestation in developed countries. Two fundamental concepts are identified in the United Nations' definition: (1) the fair and just intergenerational allocation and use of natural resources and (2) the preservation of ecosystems across time. Both are deemed necessary if the needs of both present and future generations are to be met.

Sustainable design suggests a macro perspective on environmental responsibility—protection of the health and welfare of global ecosystems for current and future generations. *Green design* suggests a micro perspective—protection of people's health and welfare in the built environment. *Environmentally responsible design* (ERD), a combination of green and sustainable design, has far-reaching benefits for planet Earth and its inhabitants.

DEFINITIONS OF TERMS

Environmentally responsible design (ERD): A comprehensive perspective that addresses both the health and well-being of people in the built environment and the health and well-being of the global ecosystems that support life for both current and future generations.

Green design: A micro perspective that addresses the health, safety, and well-being of people in the built environment.

Sustainable design: A macro perspective that addresses the health and well-being of the global ecosystems that support life for both current and future generations.

Sustainable development: "An approach to progress that meets the needs of the present without compromising the ability of future generations to meet their needs" (UN World Commission on Environment and Development 1987, 54).

A Paradigm Shift

The *paradigm shift* from environmental irresponsibility to environmental responsibility will challenge the range of professionals responsible for the design and construction of the *built environment*. Decisions made regarding the built environment affect the health and well-being of people and of planet Earth. The built environment does not exist in isolation; it impacts and is impacted by the natural environment. Design, construction, operation, use, and maintenance of buildings are now recognized as interdependent activities.

The paradigm shift from *unsustainable* to *sustainable* design and construction is challenging those who are responsible for the built environment. Ultimately, environmentally responsible design and construction will be the joint endeavor of government officials, professional planners, developers, financiers, architects, engineers, interior designers, construction managers, code officials, landscape architects, and facility managers, as well as the tradespeople responsible for the systems that support the infrastructure and the interconnections of the elements of the built environment. There is increasing recognition that ERD, a combination of *green* and *sustainable design*, has a positive impact on the natural environment, the global economy, and the people who live, work, and play in the built environment.

PRINCIPLES OF SUSTAINABLE DESIGN

Principle 1, Respect for the Wisdom of Natural Systems

Sustainable design respects nature and natural systems; nature should be used as a mentor and model for design in a process Janine Benyus (2002) called *biomimicry*.

Principle 2, Respect for People

Sustainable design endeavors to create healthy habitats for all people without diminishing the ability of nature to provide nourishing places for all of creation as well as for our own species in the future.

Principle 3, Respect for Place

Sustainable design honors the differences that exist between places, both on the macro level (e.g., with climate change) and on the micro level (e.g., with biological differences). Buildings should respond to place in fundamental ways.

Principles 4, Respect for the Cycle of Life

Sustainable design respects the natural cycle of life and centers on the concept that in nature all waste products are useful to other organisms— "waste equals food." The goal is a safe environment "for all people for all time" (William McDonough). The choices made today will have consequences for all creatures yet to be born.

Principle 5, Respect for Energy and Natural Resources

Sustainable design recognizes that all natural resources have intrinsic value in their natural state. Conservation and renewable resources are the canon of a finite world.

Principle 6, Respect for Process

Sustainable design is more than the sum of the whole; to change the result, the process that leads to the result must change. Only through holistic thinking, collaboration, and interdisciplinary communication can a sustainable future be built.

Source: ADAPTED FROM MCLENNAN (2004).

Environmental Impact of Human Behavior

INTERACTION OF ECONOMIC, SOCIAL, AND ECOLOGICAL SYSTEMS

An investigation of environmentally responsible design is complex, as it involves a wide range of diverse subjects and must be undertaken within the context of economic, social, and ecological systems. Creation of the built environment involves resource issues, potential environmental degradation, human-health issues, building economics, community development, and other issues intertwined in and among economic, social, and ecological systems. A macro perspective of sustainability is the focus of this chapter.

Ecosystem: An interconnected and symbiotic grouping of animals, plants, and microorganisms that functions as an interdependent unit to sustain life through biological, geological, and chemical activity.

Paradigm shift: Acceptance by the majority of people in a changed belief, attitude, or way of doing things; a fundamental change in people's worldview.

Built environment: Human-made surroundings that provide the settings for human activity; in developed countries the vast majority of the environment is human made, and these artificial surroundings are so extensive and cohesive that they function as a system that affects the way people live, work, and play.

Unsustainable: Meets an immediate need but, with time, depletes or damages natural resources such that it cannot continue.

Sustainable: Provides ongoing benefits without degrading the environment.

Market economy: An economy in which the greater part of production, distribution, and exchange is controlled by individuals and privately owned corporations rather than by the government.

ENERGY CONSUMPTION COMPARISONS

In 2006 the building sector accounted for 39 percent of the total U.S. consumption of energy—more than transportation or industry. Buildings consumed 71 percent of the U.S. electricity production (Stewart 2007). However, it is ultimately nature that provides all of the energy and raw materials needed to create the built environment. Each minute in 1999 the global economy burned an amount of energy (mostly fossil fuels) that the planet took 10,000 minutes to produce through solar-energy collection and photosynthesis (Hawken 1999).

Economic Systems

The built environment is a major component of the U.S. economy. The creation, production, maintenance, renovation, and exchange of elements of the built environment have a major impact on the *market economy*. The construction industry comprised 8.3 percent of the United States' gross domestic product (GDP) in 2004 (U.S. Department of Census, Bureau of Economic Affairs).

Social Systems

The creation of the built environment requires a healthy social system to make decisions for the good of the general populace. The social system involves the relationship between planners, developers, building owners, architects, engineers, interior designers, landscape architects, contractors, and tradespeople. Creation and operation of buildings is directly related to power generation; connection of water, natural gas, and other utilities; solid waste processing; wastewater and storm-water processing and disposal; automobile use; public transportation; and other human-made systems that interact with *ecological systems*. Potential problems involving the destruction of plants and wildlife habitat; disposal of solid waste; release of toxic materials; alteration of natural drainage systems; and pollution of water and air must be identified and avoided. The social systems that govern the community must function in harmony with the economic and ecological systems that determine its destiny. The current use of land, energy, water, and materials is not sustainable and must end if earth is to be inhabitable by future generations—this is the mandate of the social system.

Ecological Systems

Nature provides all of the energy and raw materials needed to create the built environment, the land on which the buildings are located; the fuel to power the construction and run the resulting structures; the water for the occupants; and the mechanisms for absorbing, assimilating, and processing waste. In short, without healthy ecological systems, there would be no resources for a built environment or

THE PROBLEM WITH BUILDINGS

Buildings have a major influence on many of the environmental problems facing the global society. According to the Worldwatch Institute, about 10 percent of the global economy involves the construction, furnishing, and operation of buildings, thereby using as much as 50 percent of the world's natural resources. Conventional design and construction methods have been linked to environmental damage, including depletion of natural resources, air and water pollution, toxic wastes, and global warming. In the United States, buildings consume 65 percent of the annual electricity production, 25 percent of the timber harvest, and 42 percent of the potable water. Buildings produce 30 percent of the annual greenhouse gas emissions, and building materials account for 40 percent of landfill waste (Guidry 2004).

for the community in which it exists. Ecological interactions provide the milieu for development of the built environment (Kibert 1999).

Environmentally responsible design decisions are based on an assessment of the global environmental impact of human behavior. This assessment has two components. First, scale must be calculated, which can be done using arithmetic and statistics. From electricity consumption per square foot to solid-waste production per household per annum, any parameter can be estimated and scaled to give global averages and then extrapolated backward and forward in time. Second, the importance of the outcome must be calculated and weight must be assigned in order to make comparisons among the potential outcomes (Kibert 1999). Bamboo and red oak can both be used as hard-surface flooring in residential projects. Which is the most environmentally responsible choice? Bamboo is a grass that is rapidly renewable (4 to 8 years), but it must be shipped by freighter from China. Red oak is harvested from a sustainably managed forest within 500 miles of the building site; however, it will take 20 to 40 years to regenerate. Disagreements in assessing the scale can be resolved, but finding consensus regarding the relative importance and future effects of any human activity is much more difficult, as demonstrated at the Kyoto and Johannesburg World Summits on Sustainable Development.

Recognition of the interconnectedness of the built environment, the people in the buildings, and the community in which the buildings exist is essential for the creation of an environmentally responsible built environment. Planners, owners, architects, interior designers, and the people who live, work, and play in the buildings must all be engaged in the conception of an environmentally responsible built environment. It is the inclusion of all stakeholders and interdisciplinary teamwork that are the prerequisites for the successful creation of a built environment that supports the health and well-being of all living things and the planet they call home.

Population Explosion

WORLD POPULATION GROWTH

The rapid growth of the world population is a recent phenomenon. The population 2,000 years ago was about 300 million. For a long time the population did not grow significantly, with periods of growth followed by periods of decline. It took until 1600 AD for the world population to double to 600 million; it was 1804 before it reached 1 billion. However, the twentieth century witnessed extraordinary population growth—world population increased from 1.65 billion in 1900 to 6 billion in 1999. This century experienced both the highest rate of population growth (averaging 2.04 percent per year in the late 1960s) and the largest annual increment to world population (86 million persons per year in the late 1980s). The world population growth rate has fallen from its peak of 2.04 percent to 1.3 percent in 2000; nonetheless, world population will continue to show substantial growth during the twenty-first century, increasing to 9.46 billion in 2100—more than double the population in 1985 (4.76 billion). However, the twenty-first century is expected to be one of comparatively slower population growth than the previous century and to be characterized by declining fertility rates and the aging of the population. United Nations projections (using the medium fertility scenario) indicate that the world population will stabilize at just above 10 billion persons after the year 2200 (United Nations 1999).

WORLD POPULATION MILESTONES

Population	Year	Time Elapsed	Population	Year	Time Elapsed
½ billion	1500		6 billion	1999	12 years later
1 billion	1804	304 years later	7 billion	2013	14 years later
2 billion	1927	123 years later	8 billion	2028	15 years later
3 billion	1960	33 years later	9 billion	2054	26 years later
4 billion	1974	14 years later	10 billion	2183	129 years later
5 billion	1987	13 years later	Stabilization achieved at ~10 billion		

Source: UNITED NATIONS SECRETARIAT, POPULATION DIVISION, DEPARTMENT OF ECONOMIC AND SOCIAL AFFAIRS (1999).

Ninety-five percent of population growth is in the developing world. China and India account for more than one-third of total population growth. More than half of the world's population lives in Asia—4 out of every 10 people are Chinese or Indian. By 2050, India is expected to surpass China in population and to account for more than 30 percent of the people in the world. Despite Asia's high population, Africa continues to have the highest growth rate, increasing by 2.2 percent every year. By 2050, Africa will have more than twice the number of people it had in 2006, almost 2 billion people (United Nations 2007).

GLOBAL POPULATION COMPARISON 1950–2050 (IN MILLIONS)

Geographic Area	Population			Population Projections 2050		
	1950	*1975*	*2007*	*Low*	*Medium*	*High*
World	2,535	4,076	6,671	7,792	9,191	10,756
Africa	224	416	965	1,718	1,998	2,302
Asia	1,411	2,394	4,030	4,444	5,266	6,189
Europe	548	676	731	566	664	777
Northern America	172	243	339	382	445	517

Source: UNITED NATIONS SECRETARIAT, POPULATION DIVISION OF THE DEPARTMENT OF ECONOMIC AND SOCIAL AFFAIRS (2007).

Degradation and Pollution of Air, Land, and Water

AIR POLLUTION

A few common air pollutants are found all over the United States. These pollutants can injure people's health, harm the environment, and cause property damage. Air pollution affects *indoor air quality* (IAQ), which can cause an itchy, irritated throat, burning eyes and/or nose, and trouble breathing. Air pollution can cause *sick building syndrome* (SBS) and *building-related illness* (BRI). Some chemicals found in polluted air cause cancer, birth defects, brain and nerve damage, and long-term injury to people's lungs and breathing passages. Some air pollutants are so dangerous that accidental releases can cause serious injury or even death.

Air pollution can cause environmental damage, negatively impacting animals, vegetation, and bodies of water. Air pollutants have thinned the protective ozone layer above the Earth. This loss of ozone is causing changes in the environment (i.e., global warming), as well as increased incidence of skin cancer and cataracts (eye damage that can lead to blindness if not treated). Air pollution damages property: carbon deposits soil buildings and other structures and create chemicals that can erode stone, thereby damaging buildings, monuments, and statues. Air pollution can cause haze, reducing visibility on the ground and interfering with aviation.

Smog and Other Criteria Air Pollutants

The Environmental Protection Agency refers to pollutants that are found all over the United States as *criteria air pollutants* because the agency has regulated them by first developing health-based criteria (i.e., science-based guidelines) as the foundation for setting permissible levels. One set of limits (i.e., the primary standard) protects health; another set of limits (i.e., the secondary standard) prevents environmental and property damage. A geographic area that meets or does better than the primary standard is called an *attainment area*; areas that do not meet the primary

Indoor air quality (IAQ): ASHRAE (American Society of Heating, Refrigerating and Air-Conditioning Engineers, Inc.) defines acceptable indoor air quality as air in which there are no known contaminants at harmful concentrations as determined by cognizant authorities and with which 80 percent or more people who are exposed express no dissatisfaction.

Sick building syndrome (SBS): A building whose occupants experience acute health and/or comfort affects (e.g., headache; runny nose; inflamed, itchy eyes; cough, etc.) that appear to be linked to time spent therein but where no specific illness or cause can be identified. Complaints may be localized in a particular room or zone or may spread throughout the building; symptoms diminish or abate on leaving the building.

Building-related illness (BRI): A diagnosable disease or health problem whose cause and symptoms can be directly attributed to a specific pollutant source within a building (e.g., Legionnaire's disease). Symptoms do not diminish or abate on leaving the building.

Criteria air pollutants: Air pollutants for which the U.S. Environmental Protection Agency (EPA) used health-based guidelines as the basis for regulations regarding permissible levels in the atmosphere.

Attainment area: A geographic area that meets or does better than the EPA 1990 Clean Air Act primary standard, which protects people's health; areas that do not meet the primary standard are called nonattainment areas. The secondary standard protects property and the environment.

Smog: A dense, discolored fog containing large quantities of soot, ash, and gaseous pollutants, such as sulfur dioxide and carbon dioxide. Responsible for human respiratory ailments.

Ozone (O3): A naturally occurring, highly reactive, irritating gas, formed by recombination of oxygen in the presence of ultraviolet radiation. This gas accumulates in the lower atmosphere as smog pollution, while in the upper atmosphere it forms a protective layer that shields the earth and its inhabitants from excessive exposure to damaging ultraviolet radiation.

Volatile organic compounds (VOCs): Highly evaporative, carbon-based chemical substances that produce noxious fumes; found in many paints, caulks, stains, and adhesives.

standard are called *nonattainment* areas. Although the EPA has been regulating criteria air pollutants since the 1970 Clean Air Act was passed, many urban areas are classified as nonattainment areas for at least one criteria air pollutant. An estimated 90 million Americans live in nonattainment areas (U.S. EPA 2006a).

What is typically called smog is primarily ground-level ozone. Ozone can be good or bad, depending on where it is located. Ozone in the stratosphere protects human health and the environment, but ground-level ozone is the primary harmful ingredient in smog. Ground-level ozone is produced by the combination of pollutants from many sources, including industrial smokestacks, automobiles, alkyd- and oil-based paints, and solvents. When an automobile burns gasoline or a painter uses alkyd-based paint, smog-forming pollutants are released. Often, wind blows smog-forming pollutants away from their sources. Therefore, smog is often more intense miles away from the source of smog-forming pollutants. The smog-forming chemical reactions take place during the time pollutants are being blown through the air. The pollutants literally cook in the sky, and when it is hot and sunny, smog forms more easily. It takes time to create smog; it often takes several hours from the time pollutants get into the air until the smog becomes severe.

Weather and geography determine where smog goes and how severe it is. When temperature inversions occur (i.e., when warm air stays near the ground instead of rising and winds are calm), smog may stay in place for days at a time. As traffic and other sources add more pollutants to the air, the smog gets worse. Smog travels across county and state lines; when a metropolitan area covers more than one state (e.g., the New York City metropolitan area includes parts of New York, New Jersey, and Connecticut), their governments and air-pollution control agencies must cooperate in a multistate effort to reduce the smog problem (U.S. EPA 2006).

In late October 1948, a heavy fog blanketed Donora, an industrial town snuggled between the hills of western Pennsylvania. As the days passed, the fog turned

Figure 1-1
The emissions from the petroleum refinery camouflage the facility and create dangerous conditions for those who work there.

into a toxic smog when an atmospheric inversion held the town's 12,000 citizens under a cloud of sulfur dioxide from US Steel's Donora Zinc Works. When the furnaces were finally turned off, 20 people were dead and 6,000 more were ill; perhaps smog was more than a nuisance? Later in the day, rain cleared the air; the next day, the Zinc Works reopened. Public outcry over the incident forced the federal government to begin studying air pollution, its causes, effects, and control mechanisms. This led to the Air Pollution Control Act of 1955, the ancestor of the Clear Air Act of 1970.

> For a report on current air quality in your local area go to http://airnow.gov/.

1990 Clean Air Act

The 1990 *Clean Air Act* (CAA) was a revision of the CAA first passed in 1970. The 1990 amendments made major changes in the CAA. This summary covers the most important of the provisions of the 1990 Clean Air Act.

- *Federal and state governments' roles.* Although the 1990 Clean Air Act is a federal law covering the entire country, states enforce the act, because pollution-control problems often require special understanding of local industries, geography, housing patterns, etc.; for example, a state would hold a hearing regarding a permit application by a power plant. The United States government, through the EPA, assists states by providing scientific research, expert studies, engineering design, and money to support clean air programs. Under the CAA, the EPA sets limits on how much of a pollutant can be in the air anywhere in the United States; therefore, all Americans have the same basic health and environmental protections. The EPA sets national air-quality standards for six principal air pollutants (also called the criteria pollutants): nitrogen dioxide (NO_2), ozone (O_3), sulfur dioxide (SO_2), particulate matter (PM), carbon monoxide (CO), and lead (Pb). The act allows individual states to have stronger pollution controls (e.g., to regulate more pollutants or to allow lower quantities of a given pollutant), but they cannot have weaker pollution controls than the federal regulations.

  Air pollution often travels from its source in one state to another state. In many metropolitan areas, people live in one state and work, play, and/or shop in another; vehicular air pollution can spread throughout the interstate area. The 1990 CAA mandated interstate commissions to develop regional strategies for addressing air pollution. Air pollution also moves across national borders. The 1990 CAA covered pollution that originates in Mexico or Canada and drifts into the United States, as well as pollution from the United States that reaches Canada or Mexico.

- *Hazardous air pollutants (HAPs) or air toxics.* Some air pollutants can cause cancer, reproductive problems, and other very serious illnesses, as well as environmental damage. *Volatile organic compounds (VOCs)*, smog-forming chemicals deemed carcinogenic by the EPA, are criteria pollutants found in gasoline and many construction products, from aerosol sprays to particle board and plastic packaging.

Air toxics have killed people swiftly when large quantities were released; the 1984 release of methyl isocyanate at a pesticide-manufacturing plant in Bhopal, India, killed approximately 4,000 people and injured more than 200,000. HAPs are released from large stationary sources (e.g., incinerators) and from small stationary sources (e.g., gasoline heaters at construction sites). The 1990 CAA included a list of 189 HAPs selected by Congress on the basis of potential health and/or environmental hazards that the EPA must regulate. The EPA was given the authority to add new chemicals to the list as they were identified.

- *Nonattainment areas.* The EPA and states cooperated to identify a nonattainment area for each criteria air pollutant. The EPA classified these nonattainment areas according to the severity of the pollution, ranging from marginal (relatively easy to clean up quickly) to extreme (requiring a lot of work and a long time to clean up). This classification system was used to develop cleanup requirements and to set realistic deadlines. States with nonattainment areas were required to show the EPA that they were

AIR POLLUTION PRODUCTION OF A COAL-BURNING POWER PLANT

Number of late-model cars it takes to generate 10,000 tons of nitrogen oxide (NO_x), the principal constituent of lung-inflaming smog, in one year	500,000
Number of average-sized coal-burning power plants it takes to generate the same amount of NO_x	1
Number of coal-burning electric power plants it took to release 17.5 million tons of carbon dioxide (CO_2), the principal global-warming gas, in the town of Monroe, Michigan, in one year	1
Number of trees that would have to be cut down or burned to add that amount of CO_2 to the atmosphere	761,000,000
Approximate number of Americans who died in the aftermath of the first Iraq War	300
Number likely to die each year, as a result of diseases caused by the Monroe, Michigan, coal-burning plant—where George W. Bush announced his new energy policy, giving high priority to building new coal-burning power plants	300
Tons of sulfur dioxide (SO_2), the principal cause of acid rain, emitted per year by a typical gas or oil power plant	44
Tons of SO_2 emitted per year by a coal-burning power plant of equal capacity	30,000

Source: WORLD WATCH MAGAZINE (2004).

making "reasonable progress." There are cleanup programs for smog, carbon monoxide, and particulate matter. Getting rid of particulates (e.g., soot, dust, smoke) requires pollution controls on power plants and restrictions on smaller sources, such as particulates from wood fires at building sites to manage solid waste or dust from construction sites.

- *Market approaches and economic incentives for reducing air pollution.* The 1990 CAA had many features designed to clean up air pollution as efficiently and inexpensively as possible. One innovative feature was to allow businesses to make choices about the best way to reach pollution-cleanup goals. These flexible programs are called *market* or *market-based* approaches. For example, the acid rain–cleanup program offered businesses choices as to how they reached their pollution reduction goals and included pollution allowances that could be traded, bought, and sold.

  If an operator of a major pollutant source wants to release more of a criteria air pollutant, an offset (a reduction of the criteria air pollutant by an amount greater than the planned increase) must be obtained somewhere else so that permit minimum requirements are met and the nonattainment area keeps moving toward attainment. An increase in a criteria air pollutant can be offset with a reduction of the pollutant from another source at the same site, at another site owned by the same company, or a site owned by another company in the nonattainment geographic area. Since total pollution continues to decrease when offsets are used, trading, buying, and selling among companies is allowed. This is one of the market approaches to cleaning up air pollution in the Clean Air Act.

  One of the major breakthroughs of the 1990 CAA legislation was a permit program for large sources of air pollution. The CAA requires permits in order to release pollutants into the atmosphere and into lakes, rivers, or other waterways, thereby creating a national permit system that replaced individual state systems. The permit includes information on which pollutants will be released, how much will be released, and the steps the source's owner or operator will take to reduce and control pollution, including plans to monitor the pollution.

- *Enforcement and changes to the CAA.* The 1990 CAA gave the EPA important new enforcement powers, including the ability to levy fines. Other parts of the CAA brought enforcement powers in line with other environmental laws. The EPA routinely reviews air quality standards (e.g., standards for smog, carbon monoxide, and particulate matter) and, based on new scientific evidence, makes revisions to the standards. It has also developed a program to control regional haze, which is largely caused by particulate matter.

ACIDIC DEPOSITION

Acid rain is a serious environmental problem that affects large parts of the United States and Canada. It is particularly damaging to lakes, streams, and forests, as well as the plants and animals that live in these ecosystems. Acid rain is a broad term referring to a mixture of wet and dry materials, deposited from the atmosphere, that contain higher than normal amounts of nitric and sulfuric acids. Acidic precipitation may be in the form of acid rain, snow, fog or mist, gas, or dust. The precursors of acidic precipitation are from both natural sources (such as volcanoes and decaying vegetation) and man-made sources (primarily emissions of sulfur dioxide [SO_2] and nitrogen oxides [NO_x], by-products of fossil-fueled combustion). In the United States, roughly two-thirds of all SO_2 and one-quarter of all NO_x come from electric power generation that relies on burning fossil fuels, primarily coal. When sulfur dioxide and nitrogen oxides are released from power plants and other sources, prevailing winds can blow these compounds over hundreds of miles, across state and national borders. Acid rain occurs when these gases react in the

EARTH DAY 2004 FACT SHEET

Environmental Progress Since the First Earth Day 1970

Air quality: Since 1970 aggregate emissions of the six principal air pollutants tracked nationally have been cut by 25 percent.

- During that same time period, the U.S. GDP increased 161 percent, while energy consumption increased 42 percent. Vehicle miles traveled have increased 149 percent.
- National air quality levels measured at thousands of monitoring stations across the country have shown improvements over the past 20 years for all six principal pollutants.
- Over the past 20 years, monitored levels of nitrogen dioxide (NO_2) have decreased 24 percent. All areas of the United States that once were in violation of national air quality standards for NO_2 now meet that standard.
- Sulfur dioxide emissions decreased 25 percent from 1981 to 2001, while the 2001 ambient average carbon monoxide concentration is almost 62 percent lower than that for 1982. The lowest recorded measurement in the last 20 years was in 2001.

Acid rain: The Environmental Protection Agency's market-based emissions trading program to reduce acid rain has successfully reduced these air pollutants from 16 million tons in 1990 to 11.2 million tons in 2000. . . .

Energy efficiency: "Energy consumption per dollar of GDP has declined at an average annual rate of 1.7 percent during the last 25 years," according to the U.S. Energy Information Administration. "Similarly, per-capita energy use grew 61 percent in the 25 years from 1949 to 1974, but grew only 2 percent in the 25 years since then," according to the Pacific Research Institute's Index of Leading Environmental Indicators 2001.

Source: REPRINTED FROM EARTH DAY INFORMATION CENTER (2004).

Figure 1-2
Acid rain is eroding the sculpture on a cathedral in Germany. Photo by Nicole Crow.

atmosphere with water, oxygen, and other chemicals to form various acidic compounds. The result is a mild solution of sulfuric acid and/or nitric acid (EPA 2007a).

Effects of Acid Rain

Acid rain causes acidification of lakes and streams and contributes to the damage of many sensitive forest soils and of trees at high elevations. (Red spruce trees at high altitudes appear to be especially sensitive to acid rain.) It accelerates the decay of building materials, including irreplaceable buildings, statues, and sculptures that are part of our nation's heritage.

Acid rain looks, feels, and tastes just like pure water. There is no direct harm to people from acid rain. However, the pollutants that cause acid rain—sulfur dioxide (SO_2) and nitrogen oxides (NO_x)—do damage human health. These gases interact in the atmosphere to form fine sulfate and nitrate particulates that can be transported long distances by winds and then inhaled deep into people's lungs. Fine particles can be carried indoors during routine HVAC (heating, ventilating, and air-conditioning) air exchanges. Many scientific studies have shown a relationship between elevated levels of fine particles and increased illness and premature death from heart and lung disorders, such as asthma and bronchitis.

Based on health concerns, SO_2 and NO_x are controlled under the Clean Air Act, through the Acid Rain Program. By lowering SO_2 and NO_x emissions from

Acid rain: The result of sulfur dioxide (SO_2) and nitrogen oxides (NO_x) reacting in the atmosphere with water and returning to earth as rain, fog, or snow. Broadly used to include both wet and dry deposition.

Allowance: A tradable permit to emit a specific amount of a pollutant. Under the Acid Rain Program, one allowance permits the emissions of one ton of sulfur dioxide (SO_2).

Acidification: A reduction of something's pH, making it more acidic.

Deposition: The processes by which chemical constituents move from the atmosphere to the earth's surface. These processes include precipitation (wet deposition, such as rain or cloud fog) as well as particle and gas deposition (dry deposition).

Eutrophication: A reduction in the amount of oxygen dissolved in water. Symptoms of eutrophication include declines in the health of fish and shellfish, loss of coral reefs, and ecological changes in food webs.

Nitrogen oxides (NO$_x$): A group of gases that cause acid rain and other environmental problems, such as smog and eutrophication of coastal waters.

pH: A scale that denotes how acidic or basic a substance is. Pure water has a pH of 7.0 and is neither acidic nor basic.

Sulfur dioxide (SO$_2$): A gas that causes acid rain, which is released in the burning of fossil fuels.

Source: Environmental Protection Agency (n.d.)

power plants, the reduced levels of fine sulfate and nitrate particles cause fewer and less severe health problems. In 2010, when fully implemented, the public health benefits of the Acid Rain Program are projected to be $50 billion annually, due to decreased mortality, hospital admissions, and emergency-room visits. Decreases in NO$_x$ emissions are also expected to have a positive impact on human health by reducing the nitrogen oxides that react with volatile organic compounds to form ozone. Ozone can cause lung inflammation, including asthma and emphysema (EPA 2007a).

Reducing Acid Rain

To preserve the integrity of natural habitats as well as to reduce damage to man-made structures, *acid rain* must be reduced in the United States and Canada and throughout the world. There are several ways to reduce acid rain—more properly called acidic deposition—that range in scale from government intervention to individual action. The EPA has taken steps to limit the amount of NO$_x$ and SO$_2$ emitted into the atmosphere, because they are the main contributors to acid rain.

- *Clean up smokestacks.* Most of the electrical power in the United States comes from burning fossil fuels such as coal, natural gas, and oil. Nitrogen oxides are formed when any fossil fuel is burned, whereas coal accounts for most SO$_2$ emissions as well as a large portion of NO$_x$ emissions. Sulfur dioxide emissions can be reduced by using coal containing less sulfur or by chemically removing the SO$_2$ before the gases leave the smokestack. Power plants can burn natural gas that creates much less SO$_2$ than coal. Finally, power can be generated using renewable resources, such as hydropower or wind power.

- *Use alternative energy sources.* There are other sources of electricity besides fossil fuels, including nuclear power; hydropower; and wind, geothermal,

MOTOR VEHICLES AND AIR POLLUTION

Today's motor vehicles produce 60 to 80 percent less pollution than motor vehicles produced in the 1960s. Despite this progress, most types of air pollution from mobile sources have not improved significantly. In the United States:

- Motor vehicles are responsible for up to half of the smog-forming VOCs and NO$_x$.
- Motor vehicles release more than 50 percent of the hazardous air pollutants.
- Motor vehicles release up to 90 percent of the carbon monoxide found in urban air.

Source: ACID RAIN EPA (2006).

and solar energy. In the United States, coal, nuclear, and hydropower are the least expensive and most widely used, while wind, solar, and geothermal energy are just beginning to be harnessed on a large enough scale, due to advancements in technologies and regulatory developments, to make them economically feasible alternatives. Interior designers can specify heat-pump furnaces that operate on geothermal principles, use solar energy to supply hot water and to heat the building, and explore *off-the-grid power* installations.

- *Conserve energy.* Like many environmental problems, acid deposition is caused by the cumulative actions of millions of people. Each individual could reduce their contribution to the problem and thereby become part of the solution. Conservation of energy is the most effective action, because energy production causes the largest portion of acid deposition. People can turn off lights and appliances when not in use; set the thermostat at 74°F in the summer and 68°F in the winter; and use *setback thermostats* to reduce indoor temperature at night, or when the building is not occupied, to reduce power consumption. Using public transportation or car pools, even bicycling or walking, will reduce consumption of gasoline, as will using automobiles that provide higher miles per gallon of gasoline. Interior designers can specify higher *R values* for insulation, specify *Energy Star* appliances and equipment, plan for daylighting, and manage heat gain and loss associated with window glazing.

CLEAN WATER RESOURCES

Clean Drinking Water

On a global scale, water resources are abundant: 330 million cubic miles, which would form a cube with each edge 695 miles long (Interfaith Broadcasting Commission 2006). There are even adequate supplies of freshwater: 36 million cubic miles. However, it is not uniformly distributed: one-fifth of the global population—one in twenty people—does not have access to safe drinking water. Furthermore, the total quantity of freshwater is diminishing; Earth replenishes the freshwater supply with rain and snow, but it is being consumed 20 percent faster than it will be replenished. Water scarcity affects every continent and 40 percent of the global population. This situation is made more acute by population growth, urbanization (which frequently pollutes freshwater supplies), and the increase in domestic and industrial water use in developing countries.

Water for Irrigation

By 2030 the world will need 55 percent more food, based on predicted population growth. However, irrigation already claims 70 percent of all the water that is consumed for human use (UN Joint Monitoring Programme 2006). Only 20 percent of the world's cropland is irrigated, but it produces 40 percent of the total

Off-the-grid power: Electric power generated by solar or wind sources for residential applications when connecting to the utility company power grid is not feasible or desirable.

Setback thermostats: Controls that can be programmed to set the temperature for specified periods so as to use less power for heating and cooling.

Insulation R values: A measure of the resistance of an insulating or building material to heat flow (e.g., R11, R20); the higher the number, the greater the resistance to heat flow.

Energy Star: A federal government program that labels appliances on their energy efficiency, measured in dollars per year.

Today one in six people in underdeveloped countries, does not have access to safe drinking water (Barrett 2007).

Average annual, per capita, freshwater consumption in North America is 1,851,170 liters, more than 7.5 times what it is in Africa, where consumption is 245,944 liters (Global Ministries 2007).

food production. The Ogalalla aquifer is the largest single source of water in the United States; but 220,000 wells are drawing 13 million gallons a minute from this aquifer to irrigate farmland—14 times faster than it can be replenished (Interfaith Broadcasting Commission 2006). The Earth Policy Institute reports that 3.3 billion people live in countries that are overpumping aquifers. Finding ways to produce more food with less water is critical to the survival of the human race.

"As population grows and development needs call for increased allocations of water for cities, agriculture and industries, the pressure on water resources intensifies, leading to tensions, conflicts among users, and excessive strain on the environment," said Food and Agriculture Organization director-general, Dr. Jacques Diouf (UN Food and Agriculture Organization 2007). Climate change is intensifying the situation at an unparalleled rate. Global warming has been blamed for more frequent droughts, further reducing the aquifer-replenishment rate. Climate change has also intensified storms and flooding, which destroy crops and irrigation systems, contaminate freshwater, and damage the facilities used to store and carry that water.

Water stressed: Less than 1,700 cubic meters of water available per person, per year, for agriculture, industry, domestic purposes, energy, and the environment.

The Clean Water Act

The Clean Water Act (CWA) is the cornerstone of surface water–quality protection in the United States. The statute employs a variety of regulatory and nonregulatory tools to control direct pollutant discharges into waterways, finance municipal wastewater-treatment facilities, and manage polluted runoff. This achieves the broader goal of restoring and maintaining the "chemical, physical, and biological integrity" of the nation's waters for "the protection and propagation of fish, shellfish, and wildlife, and recreation in and on the water" (U.S. EPA 1972). For many years following the passage of CWA in 1972, the focus was on maintaining chemical integrity. More recently attention has been given to physical and biological integrity. In the early decades of the act's implementation, efforts focused on regulating discharges from traditional sources, such as municipal sewage plants and industrial facilities, with little attention paid to runoff from streets, construction sites, farms, and other wet-weather sources. Starting in the late 1980s, efforts to address polluted runoff increased significantly. For nonpoint runoff, voluntary programs, including cost sharing with landowners, have been effective. For wet-weather point sources, like urban storm-sewer systems and construction sites, a regulatory approach has been effective (U.S. EPA 1972).

Evolution of CWA programs has shifted from a program-by-program, source-by-source, or pollutant-by-pollutant approach to more comprehensive watershed-based strategies. Under the watershed approach, equal emphasis is placed on protecting healthy waters and restoring impaired ones. A full array of issues are addressed, not just those subject to CWA regulatory authority. Involvement of stakeholder groups in the development and implementation of strategies for achieving and maintaining water quality and other environmental goals is a hallmark of this approach.

Five percent of the world's population survives on one percent of its water in the Middle East (Global Ministries 2007).

DESERTIFICATION

Extensive research is being done to identify the factors contributing to *desertification* and the practical measures necessary to combat it and to mitigate the effects of drought. The United Nations Environment Programme (2006) is doing much to educate the public regarding desertification and the potential outcomes of different responses to the phenomenon. Desertification became well known in the 1930s, when parts of the Great Plains in the United States turned into the dust bowl as a result of drought and poor farming practices. During the dust bowl period, millions of people were forced to abandon their farms and livelihoods. Greatly improved methods of agriculture, as well as land and water management in the Great Plains, have prevented that disaster from recurring; however, desertification affects millions of people on almost every continent. This degradation of formerly productive land is a complex process that has multiple causes and proceeds at varying rates in different climates. Desertification may intensify a general climatic trend toward greater aridity, or it may initiate a change in local climate. Desertification does not occur in linear, easily mapped patterns. Deserts advance erratically, forming patches on their borders. Areas far from natural deserts can degrade quickly to barren soil, rock, or sand through poor land management. The presence of a nearby desert has no direct relationship to desertification (U.S. Geological Service 1998).

Salinization: A global environmental phenomenon wherein water-quality degradation is caused by the addition of salt to water or soil, making it unusable for agriculture or human consumption.

Desertification: The transformation of land once suitable for agriculture into desert; the process can result from climate change or from human practices such as deforestation and overgrazing.

Paleodeserts: Sand deposits from the Paleozoic era 543 to 248 million years ago.

Figure 1-3
Camels are used for transportation in the desert fringe area outside of a major city in the United Arab Emirates.

Droughts are common in arid and semiarid lands, but well-managed lands can recover from drought when the rains return. Continued land abuse during droughts, however, increases land degradation. In the Sahel (in West Africa), a five-year drought, which began in 1968, combined with regional land-use practices, caused the deaths of 100,000 to 250,000 people and more than 12 million cattle, the disruption of millions of lives, and the collapse of the agricultural bases of five countries, as well as the disruption of social organizations from small villages to the national governments (UN Environment Programme 2006).

Figure 1-4
Turned-over treetops are witnesses of the droughts in the Sahel of West Africa. Photo by David Haberlah.

GLOBAL LAND-USE COMPARISONS (IN SQUARE KILOMETERS)

Area of land planted in cotton, worldwide	330,000
Area of land that is flooded by dams, worldwide	400,000
Area of land planted in potatoes, worldwide	180,000
Area of land that turns to desert each year, worldwide	200,000
Area of land planted in orange groves, worldwide	48,000
Area of land burned by fires between 1997–1998	87,000

Source: UN FOOD AND AGRICULTURE ORGANIZATION (1998).

While desertification has received tremendous publicity by politicians and the news media, there are still many things that are not known about the degradation of productive lands and the expansion of deserts. Contrary to many popular reports, desertification is actually a subtle and complex process of deterioration that may often be reversible. In northeastern China, a "Green Wall" that will eventually stretch more than 5,700 kilometers in length, much longer than the famous Great Wall, is being planted to protect sandy land—deserts believed to have been created by human activity (UN Environment Programme 2006).

More efficient use of existing water resources and control of *salinization* are other effective tools for improving arid lands. New ways are being sought to use surface-water resources such as harvesting rainwater or irrigating with seasonal runoff from adjacent highlands. New ways are being sought to find and tap groundwater resources and to develop more effective ways of irrigating arid and semiarid lands. Research on the reclamation of deserts is also focusing on discovering proper crop rotation to protect the fragile soil, on understanding how sand-fixing plants can be adapted to local environments, and on developing the effective use (and not overuse) of grazing lands and water resources (UN Environment Programme 2006). Interior designers who collaborate with landscape architects to create outdoor extensions of interior spaces will need to consider vegetation water needs and appropriate erosion-prevention ground covers.

Renewable vs Nonrenewable Resources

DEFORESTATION

Most deforestation occurs when forests are cleared for agriculture or building, when wood is harvested for fuel or lumber, or when land is cleared to build roads and urban areas. Although deforestation addresses some needs, it has profound, sometimes devastating, consequences, including social conflict, extinction of plants and animals, and climate change. Although tropical forests cover only about 7 percent of the Earth's dry land, they harbor about half of all the species on Earth. Many species are so specialized to microhabitats within the forests that they can only be found in small areas, making them vulnerable to extinction (NASA Earth Observatory 2007).

Agricultural expansion is the single most important cause of forest loss; in a 2001 study, agriculture was the primary cause in 96 percent of 152 cases of deforestation going back to 1880 (Geist and Lambin 2001). Indirect factors also lead to deforestation, such as poverty, economic growth, government policies, technological change, and cultural factors. Worldwide, from 2000 to 2005, forested areas contracted by 36.6 million hectares, just under 1 percent, a continuation of the decades-long trend of forest loss in much of the world. Total losses were actually 65 million hectares over the five-year period, but these losses were partially offset by expansion of plantation forests and the regrowth of natural forests.

Globally, the area of forest that is certified as sustainably managed continues to expand. The Forest Stewardship Council (FSC) reported that the certified forests covered 68 million hectares in 66 countries in January 2006, a 45 percent increase in just one year. However, the total certified area amounts to less than 2 percent of total global forested area (Forest Stewardship Council 2006). There is an ever-increasing global market for products that depend on sustainable harvesting: latex, bamboo, cork, fruit, nuts, timber, fibers, spices, natural oils and resins, and medicines. Beyond their commercial value, forests provide incalculable ecological services, including habitat for diverse species, erosion control, and regulation of the hydrological cycle (Millennium Ecosystem Assessment 2005a). They are an important tool in the battle to stabilize the climate in that they act as sponges for atmospheric carbon. As forested areas contracted from 1990 to 2005, the carbon storage capacity of the world's forests declined by more than 5 percent (UN Food and Agriculture Organization 2005c). However, forests can be an important source of carbon emissions—rotting branches, trees, and other debris give off carbon dioxide. The UN Food and Agriculture Organization (FAO) concludes that deforestation accounts for 25 percent of the annual emissions of carbon caused by human activity (2005b).

Strategies for preserving tropical forests range from local to international. Governments and nongovernmental organizations (NGOs) are working with local communities to encourage low-impact agricultural activities, such as shade farming, as well as the sustainable harvesting of non-wood-forest products such as rubber, cork, produce, or medicinal plants. Parks and protected areas can be marketed to attract tourists (e.g., ecotourism), providing employment for the local population as well as stimulating local service-sector economies. There is an increasing demand in the global marketplace for products, such as timber, beef, coffee, and soy, that are certified as sustainably produced or harvested. This can provide incentives for landowners to adopt more forest-friendly practices and for governments to create and enforce forest-preservation policies. According to the NASA Earth Observatory (2007), "Direct payments for the ecosystem services that intact forests provide, particularly for carbon storage to offset greenhouse gas emissions, are likely to become an important international mechanism for sustaining tropical forests as more countries begin to seriously tackle the problem of global warming."

LOSS OF BIODIVERSITY

Biodiversity is besieged: the diversity of life on Earth faces a crisis of historical and planetary proportions. Unsustainable consumption in many northern countries and crushing poverty south of the equator are fueling the extinction of native flora and fauna species. Extinction is the gravest aspect of the biodiversity crisis—it is, by definition, irreversible. Native plants and animals face a number of dire threats. Perhaps the most ominous of these is habitat loss due to conversion of forest to other land uses and habitat fragmentation due to road construction and other infrastructural developments. Accelerating anthropogenic climate change will undoubtedly magnify the effects of

Figure 1-5
Dried fish can be marketed far from the shores of the sea where they were caught; but overfishing stresses indigenous species, threatening the survival of this important food source.

habitat destruction and fragmentation. Direct exploitation of species for food, medicine, and the pet trade is a serious threat. Native animal species in Africa and Asia, including but not limited to elephants and rhinoceros, are being hunted to extinction. Wild meat is particularly important in Africa, while the medicinal aspect is especially important in Asia.

Predatory invasive species have had a devastating impact. Introduction of exotic plant species, particularly Mediterranean-type vegetation, is also having massive ecosystem effects. Another grave concern is the severe decline of amphibians worldwide, the cause of which remains unknown. While extinction is a natural process, human impacts have elevated the rate of extinction by at least one thousand, possibly several thousand, times the natural rate. Mass extinctions of this magnitude have only occurred five times in the history of the planet; the last brought the end of the dinosaur age (Biodiversity Hotspots 2007a).

Biodiversity: The variety of plants, animals, and other living things in a particular area or region. Biodiversity is important because plant and animal species interact and depend upon one another for food, shelter, oxygen, and soil enrichment.

Extinction: The disappearance of a species from the Earth.

Endemic species: The species is restricted to a particular geographic region and found nowhere else in the world.

Biodiversity hotspot: A geographic location that contains at least 1,500 endemic plant species and has lost at least 70 percent of its original habitat (natural vegetation).

Scientists estimate that 67 million birds die in the United States each year after exposure to agricultural pesticides (Youth 2002).

To learn more, search the Biodiversity Hotspots Database: www. biodiversityhotspots.org/xp/ Hotspots/search/.

Biodiversity "Hotspots"

British ecologist Norman Myers defined *biodiversity hotspot* in 1988 to address the pressing question that conservationists face: what areas require immediate attention in order to conserve biodiversity? There are 34 regions worldwide where 75 percent of the planet's most threatened mammals, birds, and amphibians survive within habitat covering just 2.3 percent of the Earth's surface (Mittermeier, Gil, and Hoffman 2005). These biodiversity hotspots hold especially high numbers of endemic species and face extreme threats. To qualify as a hotspot, a region must meet two strict criteria: it must contain at least 1,500 species of vascular plants as endemics, and it has to have lost at least 70 percent of its original habitat (natural vegetation) (Myers et al. 2000).

Since endemic species cannot be found anywhere else, the area where an endemic species lives is wholly irreplaceable. "The biodiversity hotspots are the environmental emergency rooms of our planet," according to R. A. Mittermeier, president of Conservation International. "We must now act decisively to avoid losing these irreplaceable storehouses of Earth's life forms" (2007). Hotspots provide a real measure of the conservation challenge. If this small fraction of the planet's land area cannot be conserved, more than half the planet's natural heritage will be lost.

Conservation International uses a two-pronged strategy for global conservation prioritization, simultaneously focusing on the irreplaceable and threatened biodiversity hotspots and on the five high-biodiversity wilderness areas, which are irreplaceable but still largely intact. However, pinpointing hotspots is not the only system devised for assessing global conservation priorities. Bird Life International, for instance, has identified 218 "endemic bird areas," each of which hold two or more bird species found nowhere else. The World Wildlife Fund (WWF) has derived a system called the "Global 200 Ecoregions," the aim of which is to select priority ecoregions for conservation within each of 14 terrestrial, 3 freshwater, and 4 marine habitat types. They were chosen for their species richness, endemism, taxonomic uniqueness, unusual ecological or evolutionary phenomena, and global rarity. All hotspots contain at least one Global 200 Ecoregion, and all but three contain at least one endemic bird area. Sixty percent of Global 200 Terrestrial Ecoregions and 78 percent of endemic bird areas overlap with known hotspots (Mace, Balmford, and Ginsberg 1999).

Red List of Threatened Species

As a global-prioritization system, hotspots are extremely important in informing the flow of conservation resources. However, they are not a direct measure of the threat of extinction of an individual species. The Red List of Threatened Species, compiled by the Species Survival Commission of the World Conservation Union, classifies species that have a high probability of extinction in the medium-term future as: critically endangered, endangered, or vulnerable. Assessments of the distribution and the conservation status of mammals, birds, and amphibians have been conducted, and the

Figure 1-6
Tea plantation in the Western Ghats of India. Deforestation to create agricultural land poses serious threats to biodiversity in this hotspot. Photo by Dr. T. N. Khan, Maulana Azad College.

probability of extension of these species can be measured with a high level of accuracy. The Global Reptile Assessment is currently underway, and equivalent data for threatened reptile species should be available in a few years.

Some species are threatened by species-specific threats such as hunting, exploitation, disease, and predation by invasive species. Responses to these threats must be implemented one species at a time; these typically involve incentives and legislation to reduce the threats leading to extinction and to support captive breeding, propagation, and reintroduction. These intensive conservation tactics are expensive; it is not possible to conserve all threatened species one-by-one. However, most threatened species are in danger of extinction due to the degradation and destruction of their habitat. The primary response to the biodiversity crisis must therefore be the establishment and effective management of protected areas by programs such as the Forest Stewardship Council's FSC Wood Certification Program. Many residents of the most biodiverse areas are extremely poor, often living on less than a dollar a day. In addition, a large portion of the sites with remaining biodiversity are in indigenous people's traditional homeland. Therefore, species loss represents not only a loss of global biodiversity but of cultural heritage as well (Biodiversity Hotspots 2007b).

MANUFACTURING

Manufacturers have traditionally used, and must now move away from the unsustainable, *open-loop, cradle-to-grave* model wherein a product's life cycle is measured from creation to disposal. In the sustainable, *closed-loop model,* identified

Open loop, cradle to grave: A term used in life-cycle analysis to describe the entire life of a component or product from creation through disposal (often before the end of its defined life) with no consideration of environmental responsibility.

Closed loop, cradle to cradle: A term used in life-cycle analysis to describe the entire life of a component or product extending from sourcing raw materials to recycling into raw materials at the end of its defined life. This concept of "no waste," modeled after nature, was introduced by architect William McDonough.

Environmental footprint:
A company's environmental impact is its footprint, and this is determined by the amount of depletable raw materials and nonrenewable resources it consumes to make its products and the quantity of wastes and emissions that are generated in the process. Traditionally, for a company to grow, the footprint had to become larger.

Throwaway society:
A societal propensity to dispose of items rather than to reuse or recycle them. The problem is that there is no "away." Unless the intent is to transport waste to other solar systems, the first law of physics is that matter can be neither created nor destroyed.

as *cradle to cradle* by William McDonough (see Chapter 4), a product's life cycle is infinite. When the product is no longer useful, it is reclaimed as the source of raw material for the next iteration of the product (e.g., aluminum table base) or as the raw material for the natural life cycle (e.g., compost). For example, carpeting has traditionally been made from virgin nylon, installed, and, when replaced, sent to a landfill—cradle to grave. In the new model, the carpeting is manufactured, installed, and, when replaced, returned to the mill to be regenerated as the raw material for new carpeting—cradle to cradle. However, adoption of the cradle-to-cradle model alone is not sufficient to sustain life on this planet for future generations. Current consumption and production patterns are projected to be 25 percent greater than the earth's ecological capacity. A simultaneous focus on dematerialization, de-energization, decarbonization, and detoxification must be an inherent part of the production of material goods in order to maintain and revivify global ecosystems.

WASTE MANAGEMENT

Solid Waste

Materials resulting from human and animal activities that are useless, unwanted, or hazardous are considered solid waste or refuse. They can be classified as garbage (i.e., decomposable waste from food) or rubbish (i.e., nondecomposable waste); rubbish is further classified as either combustible (such as paper) or noncombustible (such as glass). In 2005, U.S. residents, businesses, and institutions produced more than 245 million tons of solid waste, which is approximately 4.5 pounds of waste per person per day (U.S. EPA 2007a). The most environmentally sound management of municipal solid waste is achieved when EPA guidelines are followed: source reduction first, recycling and composting second, and disposal in landfills or waste incinerators last. In the United States, 32 percent of solid waste was recovered and recycled or composted in 2006; 14 percent was burned at combustion facilities; and the remaining 54 percent was disposed of in landfills (U.S. EPA 2007d). Source reduction can be a successful method of reducing waste generation. Practices such as grass cycling, backyard composting, two-sided photocopying, and packaging reduction by industry have yielded substantial benefits. Source reduction has many environmental benefits. It prevents emissions of many greenhouse gases, reduces pollutants, saves energy, conserves resources, and reduces the need for new landfills and incinerators.

Landfills

Under the Resource Conservation and Recovery Act (RCRA), landfills are primarily regulated by state, tribal, and local governments; however, the EPA is responsible for national standards for landfills. Paper and paperboard products comprise 40 percent of all municipal solid waste, newspapers alone constitute 13 percent. Each ton of paper that is recycled saves more than 3 cubic yards of landfill space (EPA 2006).

Landfills are referred to as "dry tombs," because they restrict exposure of the waste to air and water, thereby slowing biodegradation and increasing the time required for landfill stabilization. Stabilization occurs when liquid produced by the waste is no longer a pollution hazard to the groundwater below, gas production is negligible, and the majority of waste settlement has occurred. However, landfills remain a contamination risk for decades, therefore, severely limiting land reuse options—federal regulations require monitoring and maintenance of landfills for a minimum of 30 years following their closure (Lawrence Berkeley Laboratory 2002).

Incinerators

Burning solid wastes can generate energy while reducing the amount of waste by up to 90 percent in volume and 75 percent in weight (EPA 2007). When the walls of the combustion chamber are lined with boiler tubes, through which water circulates, the heat is absorbed to produce steam, which can be used for power generation (Hiang 2007). Combustion is 85 to 90 percent complete for the combustible materials. However, the products of incineration include water and carbon dioxide—as well as sulfur and nitrogen oxides, other gaseous pollutants, ash, and unburned solid residue. The EPA's Office of Air and Radiation is responsible for regulating incinerators, because air emissions pose significant environmental concerns (EPA 2007).

Recycling

Increasingly, municipalities are requiring solid waste be separated from bottles, cans, newspapers, cardboard, and other recyclable Items. Recycling, including composting, diverted 79 million tons of material in 2005, up from 15 million tons in 1980, when the recycle rate was just 10 percent. Harvesting, extracting, and processing the raw materials that are required to manufacture new products is an energy-intensive activity. Reducing or nearly eliminating the need for these processes, therefore, results in enormous energy savings when compared to production using virgin materials.

- Each ton of recycled paper saves 17 trees when compared to virgin paper.
- Construction of each ton of recycled paper requires 7,000 fewer gallons of water and 4100 kWh less energy.
- Manufacturing recycled paper results in 74 percent less air pollution and 35 percent less water pollution.
- Manufacturing with recycled copper scrap saves 85 percent of energy required to make the same amount of copper from copper ore.
- Manufacturing with recycled aluminum scrap saves 95 percent of the energy required to make the same amount of aluminum from its virgin source, bauxite (EPA 2006).

U.S. RECYCLING RATES FOR CONSUMER GOODS IN 2005

Newspapers:	88.9 percent	Magazines:	38.5 percent
Steel cans:	62.9 percent	Scrap tires:	35.6 percent
Yard trimmings:	56.3 percent	Plastic soft drink bottles:	34.1 percent
Corrugated cardboard boxes:	71.5 percent	Plastic milk and water bottles:	28.8 percent
Aluminum beer and soda cans:	44.8 percent	Glass containers:	25.3 percent

Source: EPA (2006).

Recycling prevents the emission of water pollutants, saves energy, supplies valuable raw materials to industry, creates jobs, stimulates the development of greener technologies, conserves resources for future generations, and reduces the need for new landfills and combustors. Recycling also reduces greenhouse gas emissions that affect global climate change. In 2005, the national recycling rate of 32 percent prevented the release of approximately 49 million metric tons of carbon into the air—roughly the amount emitted annually by 39 million cars—and saved energy equivalent to 11 billion gallons of gasoline (EPA 2007).

Hazardous Waste

Hazardous waste has been defined by the EPA as waste that poses a potential hazard to humans or other living organisms for one or more of the following reasons: the waste is nondegradable or persistent in nature; its effects can be magnified by organisms in the environment; it can be lethal; or it can cause detrimental cumulative effects. General categories of hazardous waste include toxic chemicals and flammable, radioactive, or biological substances (EPA 2006). Management of hazardous waste is subject to both federal and state regulation. However, no satisfactory method has yet been demonstrated for permanent disposal of radioactive waste.

Wastewater Treatment

A typical metropolitan area handles a volume of wastewater equal to 60 to 80 percent of its total daily water requirements, the remainder used for activities such as washing cars, watering lawns, and manufacturing processes. Domestic sewage results from people's day-to-day activities (such as bathing, body elimination, food preparation, and recreation), averaging about 60 gallons per person daily (Huang 2007). The quantity and character of industrial wastewater is highly varied, depending on the type of industry, the management of its water usage, and

SOLID WASTE STATISTICS

- In 1960 the United States generated 88.1 million tons of municipal solid waste; by 1990 the figure was 205.2 million; by 2000 it was 231 million.
- In 1960 each person in the United States generated 2.7 pounds of solid waste; by 1990 the figure had risen to 4.5 pounds. In the next decade, progress was made by standing still; total waste was still at 4.5 pounds per person in 2000.

Source: LAWRENCE BERKLEY LABS (2002).

the degree of treatment the wastewater receives before it is discharged (U.S. EPA 2007c). Wastewater is transported from its source to a treatment facility through pipe systems that are classified according to the type of wastewater they carry. Older systems carry both sewage and storm water; however, most municipalities now provide separate systems for sewage and storm water. This arrangement excludes the voluminous storm water from the treatment plant, permitting efficiency in the operation of the plant. This also prevents the pollution overflow that occurs when the sewer is not big enough to transport both sewage and storm water. After being processed at the treatment center, direct discharge into a receiving stream or lake is the most commonly practiced means of disposal of wastewater. In areas faced with shortages of water for both domestic and industrial purposes, appropriately treated wastewater is being reused for groundwater recharge, irrigation of nonedible crops, industrial processing, recreation, and other uses.

GREEN POWER

The EPA introduced the *Green Power Partnership* to highlight the value of on-site energy production. The Partnership encourages organizations to buy green power as a way to lessen the environmental impacts associated with conventional electricity use; using conventional fossil-fueled electricity is typically an organization's worst environmental impact. Renewable energy resources used to generate green power include solar, wind, geothermal, biogas, biomass, and low-impact hydro. A green-power resource produces electricity with zero anthropogenic (caused by humans) emissions, has a superior environmental profile when compared to conventional power generation, and has been put in operation after January 1, 1997 (U.S. EPA 2007b).

The Partnership was created to provide technical assistance and marketing opportunities to both public and private organizations that want to use green power for at least part of their power supply. The program is similar in strategy to the Energy Star program in that labeling will ultimately guide the consumer to the most efficient products on the market, subsequently driving the market to higher efficiency standards on its own, rather than through legislation or other stimulus.

The EPA is challenging Fortune 500 companies to roughly double their current level of green-power purchasing. The goal is to exceed 5 billion kilowatt hours (kWh) of green-power purchasing among participating companies by the end of 2007, which would be enough electricity to power more than 400,000 average American homes annually. Achieving this goal will avoid the equivalent CO_2 emissions associated with more than 680,000 passenger cars each year (U.S. EPA 2007b).

Ozone Depletion, Global Warming, Climate Change

OZONE DEPLETION

When ozone is in the troposphere, it acts as a greenhouse gas that contributes to global warming. However, the ozone layer in the stratosphere protects humans, animals, and plants from damaging shortwave ultraviolet (UV) radiation. Ozone is produced in the upper stratosphere by the interaction of shortwave solar UV radiation with oxygen. It is destroyed by reactions with certain compounds (ozone-depleting substances) in the presence of somewhat longer wavelength UV radiation. The dynamic balance between production and destruction determines the concentration and total amount of ozone in the stratosphere or the "thickness" of the ozone layer. Anthropogenic emissions of ozone depleting substances that contain chlorine and bromine disturb this balance. A single chlorine or bromine atom can destroy thousands of ozone molecules before being removed from the atmosphere (WMO 2006a).

The dramatic depletion of stratospheric ozone, which is observed in polar regions (e.g., the ozone hole over Antarctica), is caused by a combination of anthropogenic emissions of ozone-depleting substances, stable circulation patterns, extremely low temperatures, and solar radiation. The major cause of ozone depletion is high levels of chlorine and bromine compounds in the stratosphere. Compounds that cause significant ozone depletion include chlorofluorocarbons (CFCs), carbon tetrachloride, methyl chloroform, halons, hydrochlorofluorocarbons (HCFCs), hydrobromofluorocarbons (HBFCs), and methyl bromide. Other factors that affect the ozone layer include natural emissions, large volcanic eruptions, climate change, and the greenhouse gases methane and nitrous oxide (WMO 2006a).

In 1987, the UN Montreal Protocol on Substances that Deplete the Ozone Layer, ratified by 162 parties, called for a 50 percent reduction in 1986 CFC consumption levels by 2000. Production, sales, and consumption of ozone depleting substances has fallen significantly. However, these ozone-depleting substances have a very long lifetime in the stratosphere. Therefore, over the polar regions, extensive ozone depletion will continue to be observed in the spring for many decades—the ozone hole over the Antarctic was larger than it has ever been, twice as large as Europe, at the end of September 2007 (EUMETSAT 2007). Complete recovery is not expected until after 2050 (UNEP 2007).

Climate change and depletion of the ozone layer are two separate issues, however; ozone absorbs solar radiation and is a greenhouse gas, and therefore ozone changes and climate change are linked in important ways. Both stratospheric ozone depletion and increases in global tropospheric ozone contribute to climate change. Ozone-depleting substances, and their replacement compounds, are greenhouse gasses with long atmospheric lifetimes, and they will, therefore, contribute to climate change for many years to come (European Environment Agency 2007).

GLOBAL WARMING

The global warming problem is related to changes in the concentration of the greenhouse gases (water vapor, CO_2, CH4 [methane], N_2O [nitrous oxide], and CFCs that trap infrared radiation from the Earth's surface, thereby causing the greenhouse effect and warming the atmosphere. This effect is a natural phenomenon that helps maintain a stable temperature and climate on Earth. However, human activities have led to an increase in the concentration of greenhouse gases. Carbon dioxide accounts for 60 percent of the greenhouse gases; currently, atmospheric levels of carbon dioxide are rising by over 10 percent every 20 years. Consequently, more infrared radiation has been captured in the atmosphere, which causes changes in the air temperature, precipitation patterns, sea level, and melting of glaciers. Global warming has momentum; it will continue to affect the earth's natural systems for hundreds of years, even after greenhouse gas emissions are reduced and atmospheric levels stop rising.

The United Nations Framework Convention on Climate Change (UNFCCC) was adopted on May 9, 1992, in New York, and signed at the 1992 UN Earth Summit in Rio de Janeiro by more than 150 countries. An addition to the treaty, the Kyoto Protocol, an international and legally binding agreement to reduce greenhouse gases emissions worldwide, was approved at the 1997 UN Earth Summit in Kyoto, Japan, and entered into force on February 16, 2005, with 175 signatures. The ultimate objective of the Protocol is the "stabilization of greenhouse gas concentrations in the atmosphere at a level that would prevent dangerous anthropogenic interference with the climate system." Under the UNFCCC, the included parties agreed to return greenhouse gas emissions, which are not controlled by the Montreal Protocol, to 1990 levels by the year 2000. Unfortunately, this goal was not met.

CLIMATE CHANGE

Climate change in its broadest sense refers to "any change in climate over time, whether due to natural variability or as a result of human activity" (Intergovernmental Panel for Climate Change 2007). This differs from the UNFCCC praxis, which defines climate change as "a change of climate which is attributed directly or indirectly to human activity that alters the composition of the global atmosphere and which is in addition to natural climate variability observed over comparable time periods" (UNFCCC 1992, 4).

The Intergovernmental Panel for Climate Change (IPCC) is widely regarded as the most authoritative international voice on the science and impacts of climate change. Established under the auspices of the World Meteorological Organization (WMO) and UN Environment Programme (UNEP) in 1988, the IPCC produces

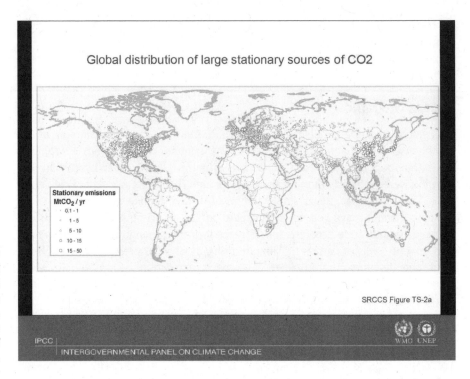

Figure 1-7
The Intergovernmental Panel on Climate Change, under the auspices of the United Nations Environment Programme, tracks concentrations of carbon dioxide (CO_2), the principal global warming gas.

reports every five years reflecting the state of knowledge on climate change. This research review of scientific literature represents international consensus among the more than 2,000 scientists involved in the preparation of the report. The summary report, *Climate Change 2007,* provided solid, scientific evidence that human activity is affecting climate change through global warming. (Their most important findings are highlighted below.)

Radiative forcing:
A "measure of the influence that a factor has in altering the balance of incoming and outgoing energy in the Earth-atmosphere system and . . . an index of the importance of the factor as a potential climate change mechanism. Positive forcing tends to warm the surface while negative forcing tends to cool it" (IPCC 2007, 2).

Anthropogenic factors:
Human activity that changes the environment and influences Earth's climate.

FINDINGS FROM *CLIMATE CHANGE 2007*

"Changes in the atmospheric abundance of greenhouse gases and aerosols, in solar radiation and in land surface properties alter the energy balance of the climate system. These changes are expressed in terms of radiative forcing, which is used to compare how a range of human and natural factors drive warming or cooling influences on global climate. . . .

Global atmospheric concentrations of carbon dioxide, methane and nitrous oxide have increased markedly as a result of human activities since 1750 and now far exceed pre-industrial values determined from ice cores spanning many thousands of years The global increases in carbon dioxide concentration are due primarily to fossil fuel use and land-use change, while those of methane and nitrous oxide are primarily due to agriculture. . . .

Eleven of the last twelve years (1995–2006) rank among the 12 warmest years in the instrumental record of global surface temperature (since 1850). . . . The linear warming trend over the last 50 years is nearly twice that for the last 100 years (+0.74). . . . Paleoclimate information supports the interpretation that the warmth of the last half century is unusual in at least the previous 1300 years. The last time the polar regions were significantly warmer than present for an extended period (about 125,000 years ago), reductions in polar ice volume led to 4 to 6 meters of sea level rise. . . . Most of the observed increase in globally averaged temperatures since the mid-20th century is very likely due to the observed increase in anthropogenic greenhouse gas concentrations. . . .

At continental, regional, and ocean basin scales, numerous long-term changes in climate have been observed. These include changes in Arctic temperatures and ice, widespread changes in precipitation amounts, ocean salinity, wind patterns and aspects of extreme weather including droughts, heavy precipitation, heat waves and the intensity of tropical cyclones. . . . Furthermore anthropogenic warming and sea level rise would continue for centuries due to the timescales associated with climate processes and feedbacks, even if greenhouse gas concentrations were to be stabilized." (IPCC 2007, 2–18)

Climate change was inevitable because of past and current emissions. The problem causing the greatest concern is the increase in CO_2 levels due to the emissions from fossil-fueled combustion. Other anthropogenic factors, including land use, ozone depletion, animal agriculture, CO_2 emissions related to cement production, and deforestation, also affect climate change. It should be noted that the increase in aerosols (i.e., particulate matter in the atmosphere), which reduces air quality, exerts a cooling effect (IPCC 2007). The Kyoto Protocol under the UNFCCC during its first commitment period was only a first step in addressing climate change. Strong mitigation measures must be implemented that will substantially reduce global greenhouse-gas emissions. Global emissions will have to be reduced by up to 50 percent by 2050 to limit temperature increases to a maximum of 2°C above preindustrial levels, the target proposed by the European Union as necessary to avoid unacceptable climate change impacts in the future (European Environment Agency 2007).

The World's Ecological Footprint

The Millennium Ecosystem Assessment (MEA), a comprehensive analysis produced by 1,360 scientists in 2005, concluded that the health of the world's ecosystems was at significant risk: "Human activity is putting such strain on the natural functions

Ecological footprint: A measure of natural resource consumption; it also shows that humans are putting exorbitant pressure on Earth. The footprint can be used to calculate the total amount of land countries need to produce the resources that they use—the biocapacity (Global Footprint Network 2007).

of Earth that the ability of the planet's ecosystems to sustain future generations can no longer be taken for granted" (MEA 2005b, 5). The ecological footprint, a measure of natural resource consumption, also shows that humans are putting exorbitant pressure on Earth. The footprint can be used to calculate the total amount of land countries need to produce the resources that they use—the biocapacity. Humanity used about one-half the planet's biocapacity in 1961; in 2003 the biocapacity was overdrawn by 25 percent! The ecological footprint shows that humanity has been living beyond its means since 1987, drawing down the resources that are the basis for the continued health of the planet (Global Footprint Network 2007). Some countries use far more biocapacity than others. If everyone were to consume at the 2003 level for high-income countries, another 2.5 planets would be needed (Global Footprint Network 2006). If everyone consumed at this level, Earth could sustain only 1.8 billion people—not the 6.5 billion people living on Earth in 2007. If every country had U.S. consumption levels, the planet could support only 1.2 billion people! With world population projected to be more than 9 billion in 2050, with rapid economic growth in developing economies, such as China and India, and with continued high-consumption rates in developed countries, the MEA scientists' conclusion could well become reality if people and their governments do not find the will to make significant changes.

References

Barrett, K. 2007. *Fresh water in limited supply* (March 22). Alexandria, VA: Conservation International.

Benyus, J. 2002. *Biomimicry: Innovation inspired by nature*. New York: Harper Collins.

Biodiversity Hotspots. 2007a. *Hotspots science*. Retrieved March 22, 2007, from Biodiversity Hotspots Web site: http://www.biodiversityhotspots.org/xp/Hotspots/hotspotsScience/.

———. 2007b. The most remarkable places on earth are also the most threatened. Retrieved March 22, 2007, from Biodiversity Hotspots Web site: http://www.biodiversityhotspots.org/xp/Hotspots/.

Blamire, J. n.d. *Biodiversity 911: Saving life on earth* (World Wildlife Fund traveling exhibit). Retrieved January 12, 2007, from Biodiversity 911 Web site: http://www.biodiversity911.org/default.html.

Chestnut, L. G., and D. Mills. 2005. A fresh look at the benefits and cost of the U.S. Acid Rain Program. *Journal of Environmental Management* 77 (3): 252–266.

Earth Day Information Center. Earth Day 2004 Fact Sheet: Environmental Progress Since the First Earth Day. Washington, DC: Earth Day Information Center, 2004. Retrieved January 11, 2008, from Earth Day Information Center Web site: http://www.nationalcenter.org/EarthDay04Progress.html.

Earth Policy Institute. n.d. *Population in overpumping countries.* Washington, DC: Earth Policy Institute.

European Environmental Agency (EEA). 2003. Stratospheric Ozone Depletion. *Europe's environment: The third assessment.* Retrieved October 20, 2007, from EEA Web site: http://reports.eea.europa.eu/environmental_assessment_report_2003_10/en/kiev_chapt_04.pdf.

————. 2007. Climate change. *Europe's environment: The fourth assessment.* Retrieved October 20, 2007, from EEA Web site: http://www.eea.europa.eu/pan-european/fourth-assessment/climate-change.

European Organization for the Exploitation of Meteorological Satellites (EUMETSAT). 2007, *EUMETSAT satellite measures ozone hole.* Retrieved October 20, 2007, from The Ozone Hole Web site: http://www.theozonehole.com/metop.htm.

Forest Stewardship Council (FSC). 2006. *Information on certified forest sites endorsed by Forest Stewardship Council.* Retrieved October 19, 2007, from FSC Web site: www.certified-forests.org.

Geist, H. J., and E. F. Lambin. 2001. *What drives tropical deforestation?* (Land Use and Land Cover Change Project, LUCC Project Report Series No. 4). Louvain-la-Neuve, Belgium. Retrieved October 19, 2007, from http://www.geo.ucl.ac.be/LUCC/lucc.html.

Global Footprint Network (GFN). 2006. *Ecological footprint and biocapacity: 2006 edition.* Retrieved October 18, 2007, from GFN Web site: http://www.footprintnetwork.org/gfn_sub.php?content=datamethods.

————. 2007. *Humanity's footprint.* Retrieved October 18, 2007, from GFN Web site: http://www.footprintnetwork.org/gfn_sub.php?content=global_footprint.

Global Ministries. 2007. *Water wars.* Retrieved April 4, 2007, from Global Ministries Web site: http://www.globalministries.org/index.php?option=com_content&task=view&id=1123&Itemid=32.

Guidry, K. (2004). How green is your building? An appraiser's guide to sustainable design. *The Appraisal Journal* 72 (1): 57–69.

Hawken, P. 1999. *Ecology of commerce: A declaration of sustainability.* New York: Harper Collins.

Health and Safety Commission, Great Britain. n.d. *Icmesa chemical company, Seveso, Italy.* Health and Safety Evaluation, 2007. Retrieved February 20, 2007, from Health and Safety Evaluation Web site: http://www.hse.gov.uk/comah/sragtech/caseseveso76.htm.

Huang, J. 2007. *Sewage disposal.* Retrieved October 18, 2007, from Encarta Web site: http://encarta.msn.com.

Humke, J. 2007. MacArthur Foundation to assess climate change threats and fund responses. Retrieved March 25, 2007, from World Conservation Union (IUNC) Web site: http://www.iucn.org/en/news/archive/2007/02/13_climate_change.pdf.

Interfaith Broadcasting Commission. 2006. *Troubled waters* (documentary). Cleveland, OH: Interfaith Broadcasting Commission by the United Church of Christ.

Intergovernmental Panel on Climate Change (IPCC). 2007. *Climate change 2007: The physical science basis (Summary report for policymakers).* Geneva, Switzerland: IPCC. Retrieved February 24, 2007, from IPCC Web site: http://www.ipcc.ch/SPM2feb07.pdf.

Kibert, C. J. 1999. *Reshaping the built environment.* Washington, DC: Island Press.

Lamoreux, J., and G. A. B. da Fonseca. 2005. *Hotspots revisited: Earth's biologically richest and most threatened terrestrial.* Vol. III. Alexandria, VA: Conservation International.

Lanki, T., P. Tiittanen, P. P. Aalto, K. Koskentalo, et al. 2007. Even low levels of fine particle pollution increase stroke risk. *Stroke: Journal of the American Heart Association,* February 15. Retrieved February 24, 2007, from American Heart Association Web site: http://www.americanheart.org/presenter.jhtml?identifier=3045419.

Mace, G. M., A. Balmford, and R. Ginsberg. 1999. *Conservation in a changing world.* Cambridge: Cambridge University Press.

McLennana, J. 2004. *The Philosophy of Sustainable Design.* Kansas City, Mo: Ecotone.

Melnick, D. 2002. Investing in science and technology: Strategies for successful sustainable development. *World Summit on Sustainable Development in Johannesburg, Africa.* Retrieved January 14, 2007, from Earth Institute Web site: http://www.earthinstitute.columbia.edu/cudkv/wssd/biodiversity.html.

Millennium Ecosystem Assessment (MEA). 2005a. *Ecosystems and human well-being: Current state and trends.* Washington, DC: Island Press.

———. 2005b. *Living beyond our means: Natural assets and human well-being* (Statement from the Board). Washington, DC: World Resources Institute.

Mittermeier, R. A. 2007. *Hotspots science: Key findings.* Retrieved March 22, 2007, from Biodiversity Hotspots Web site: http://www.biodiversityhotspots.org/ xp/Hotspots/hotspotsScience/key_findings/.

Mittermeier, R. A., P. R., Gil, M., Hoffman, et al. 2005. *Hotspots revisited: Earth's biologically richest and most endangered terrestrial ecoregions.* Chicago and Alexandria, VA: Distributed by University of Chicago Press for Conservation International.

Mumma, T. 1995. Reducing the embodied energy of buildings. *Home Energy Magazine Online* (January/February 2006). Retrieved February 14, 2006, from Home Energy Web site: http://www.homeenergy.org/archive/hem.dis.anl.gov/eehem/95/950109.html.

Myers, N., R. A. Mittermeier, C. G. Mittermeier, G. A. B. da Fonseca, and J. Kent. 2000. Biodiversity hotspots for conservation priorities. *Nature* 403: 853–858.

NASA Earth Observatory. 2007. *Tropical deforestation*. Retrieved October 19, 2007, from Earth Observatory Web site: http://earthobservatory. nasa.gov/Library/Deforestation/deforestation_update5.html.

Stewart, R. K. 2007. *Energy efficient federal buildings.* Testimony before the U.S. Senate Energy and Natural Resources Committee, February 12. Retrieved March 15, 2007, from U.S. Senate Web site: http://energy. senate.gov/public/_files/RKStewartatSenateEnergyFebruary82007 FINAL.pdf.

Templeton, D. 1998. Cleaner air is legacy left by Donora's killer 1948 smog. *Pittsburgh Post-Gazette,* October 29. Retrieved July 22, 2006, from Donora Fire Department Web site: http://www.donora.fire-dept. net/1948smog.htm.

UN Environment Programme (UNEP). 2006. *Facts about deserts and deser- tification.* Retrieved March 25, 2007, from UNEP Web site: http:// www.unep.org/wed/2006/downloads/PDF/FactSheetWED2006_ eng.pdf

UN Food and Agriculture Organization (FAO). 1998. *FAOSTAT Statistics Database.* Retrieved February 20, 2007, from FAO Web site: http:// faostat.fao.org/

———. 2005a. Change in extent of forest and other wooded land, 1990–2005. *Global Forest Resources Assessment.* Retrieved October 19, 2007, from FAO Web site: http://www.fao.org/forestry/site/ 32033/en/

———. 2005b. *Incentives to curb deforestation needed to counter climate change.* (Press release: December 9). Retrieved October 19, 2007, from FAO Web site: http://www.fao.org/newsroom/en/news/2005/1000176/ index.html

———. 2005c. Key Findings—Forest and climate change. *Global Forest Resources Assessment.* Retrieved October 19, 2007, from FAO Web site: http://www.fao.org/forestry/site/32250/en/.

———. 2007. *United Nations World Water Day.* (Brochure). Retrieved February 20, 2007, from UN-Water Web site: http://www.unwater. org/wwd07/downloads/documents/wwd07brochure.pdf.

UN Framework Convention on Climate Change (UNFCCC). 1992. *Kyoto Protocol to the United Nations Framework Convention on Climate Change,* article 1, definition 2, 4. New York: United Nations. Retrieved January 13, 2007, from UNFCC Web site: http://unfccc.int/essential_ background/kyoto_protocol/items/1678.php.

UN Joint Monitoring Programme. 2006. *Water a shared responsibility: The United Nations world water development.* (Report 2.) Retrieved February 20, 2007, from World Water Assessment Program Web site: http://www.unesco.org/water/wwap/wwdr2/index.shtml.

UN Ozone Secretariat, Environment Programme (UNEP). 2007. *Montreal Protocol: Celebrating 20 years of progress in 2007.* Retrieved October 20, 2007, from UNEP Web site: http://ozone.unep.org/.

UN Secretariat, Population Division, Department of Economic and Social Affairs. 1999. *The world at six billion*. Retrieved October 18, from United Nations Web site: http://www.un.org/esa/population/publications/wpp2006/English.pdf.

———. 2007. *World population prospects: The 2006 revision*. Retrieved October 18, 2007, from United Nations Web site: http://www.un.org/esa/population/publications/wpp2006/English.pdf.

UN World Commission on Environment and Development. 1987. *Our common future*. New York: Oxford University Press. Retrieved January 13, 2008, from ANPED Web site: http://anped.org/index.php? part=176.

U.S. Department of Census, Bureau of Economic Affairs. 2005. *Gross domestic product and corporate profits* (August 31). Washington, DC: Department of Census. Retrieved February 20, 2005, from Bureau of Economic Affairs Web site: http://www.bea.gov/bea/newsreel/gdnewsrelaease.htm.

U.S. Environmental Protection Agency (EPA), Office of Air Quality. n.d. *Latest findings on national air quality: Status and trends—Acid rain*. Washington, DC: EPA 2007.

U.S. Environmental Protection Agency (EPA). 1972. *Clean Water Act*. Washington, DC: EPA. Retrieved from EPA Web site: http://www.epa.gov/watertrain/cwa.

———. 2006a. *Acid rain*. Retrieved February 20, 2007, from EPA Web site: http://www.epa.gov/air/oaqps/peg_caa/pegcaa05.html.

———. 2006b. *Acid rain glossary*. Retrieved February 20, 2007, from EPA Web page: http://www.epa.gov/acidrain/glossary.html.

———. 2006c. *Cleaning up air pollution: The programs in the 1990 Clean Air Act*. Retrieved February 20, 2007, from EPA Web site: http://www.epa.gov/air/oaqps/peg_caa/pegcaa03.html.

———. 2006d. *Municipal solid waste: Frequently asked questions*. Retrieved October 18, 2007, from EPA Web site: http://www.epa.gov/epaoswer/non-hw/muncpl/faq.htm#4.

———. 2006e. *The plain English guide to the 1990 Clean Air Act*. Retrieved February 20, 2007, from EPA Web site: http://www.epa.gov/air/oaqps/peg_caa/pegcaa01.html.

———. 2007a. *Acid rain program*. Retrieved from EPA Air Markets Web site: http://www.epa.gov/airmarkets/progsregs/arp/index.html.

———. 2007b. *Green power partnership: National top 25*. Washington, DC: EPA. Retrieved April 6, 2007, from EPA Web site: http://www.epa.gov/greenpower/toplists/top25.htm.

———. 2007c. *Municipal solid waste: Basic Facts*. Retrieved October 18, 2007, from EPA Web site: http://www.epa.gov/epaoswer/non-hw/muncpl/facts.htm/

———. 2007d. *Ozone: Good up high, bad nearby.* Retrieved March 27, 2007, from http://www.epa.gov/epahome/ozone.htm.

U.S. Geological Service (USGS). 1998. *Desertification.* Washington, DC: USGS. Retrieved March 25, 2007, from USGS Web site: http://pubs.usgs.gov/gip/deserts/desertification.

World Conservation Union (IUCN). 2007. *MacArthur Foundation to assess climate change threats and fund responses* (news release). Retrieved October 18, 2007, from IUCN Web site: http://www.iucn.org/en/news/archive/2007/02/13_climate_change.pdf.

World Meteorological Organization (WMO). 2006a. *Twenty questions and answers about the ozone layer.* Geneva, Switzerland: WMO. Retrieved October 20, 2007, from Earth Systems Research Laboratory (ESRL), National Oceanic and Atmospheric Administration (NOAA) Web site: http://www.esrl.noaa.gov/csd/assessments/2006/twentyquestions.html.

———. 2006b. *Scientific assessment of ozone depletion: 2006. Global Ozone Research and Monitoring Project.* Geneva, Switzerland: World Meteorological Organization.

Worldwatch Institute. 2004. Matters of scale: Coal facts. *World Watch Magazine* 13, 1 (January/February). Retrieved February 14, 2007, from Worldwatch Institute Web site: http://www.worldwatch.org/node/796.

Youth, H. 2002. The Plight of Birds. *World Watch Magazine* 15, 3 (1 May): 18–29.

CHAPTER TWO

A Timeline of Human and Environmental Interactions

Louise Jones, ArchD, LEED AP, IDEC, ASID, IIDA

Society is a partnership, not only between those who are living, but between those who are living, those who are dead, and those who are to be born.
      —Edmund Burke

Humankind and the Natural Environment

At the beginning of the twenty-first century, the building industry in the United States is slowly but consistently developing and piloting protocols for environmentally responsible design. Interior designers are being asked to create spaces that protect the health, safety, and well-being of the people who live, work, and play in the interior environments that they design and the health, safety, and well-being of the global ecosystems that support life on planet Earth. The relationship of humankind and the natural environment is rooted in prehistory and intertwined through time. This reciprocal relationship can be traced, using geological, anthropological, and archeological milestones, to more fully understand and implement environmentally responsible design precepts.

180 to 2 Million Years Ago

- *180 million years ago:* The supercontinent Pangea began to break up into several land masses. The largest was Gondwana, the areas that are now

Figure 2-1
Some two million years ago, all land masses were connected, forming one large area known as Pangea, which broke apart to form Laurasia (now North America, Europe, and Asia) and Gondwana (now Africa, Antarctica, Australia, India, and South America).

Africa, Antarctica, Australia, India, and South America. Antarctica, was still a land of forests. North America and Eurasia were still joined, forming the northern supercontinent of Laurasia.

- *15 million years ago:* Apes migrated from Africa to Eurasia to become gibbons and orangutans. Humans' ancestors speciated from the ancestors of the gibbon.

- *13 million years ago:* Humans' ancestors speciated from the ancestors of the orangutans.

- *5 million years ago:* Humans' ancestors speciated from the ancestors of the chimpanzees. Chimpanzees and humans share 98 percent of their DNA. Biochemical similarities are so numerous that their hemoglobin molecules differ by only one amino acid.

2,000,000 to 5,500 Years Ago: The Stone Age

- *2 million years ago: Homo habilis* ("handy man"), who were meat-eating, used primitive stone tools in Tanzania.

- *1.8 million years ago: Homo erectus* evolved in Africa and migrated to other continents, primarily South Asia.

- *1.75 million years ago: Homo georgicus,* with both *H. erectus* and *H. habilis* characteristics, traveled from Africa to Georgia in Asia. Several skulls were found between 1991 and 2001, culminating in the discovery of a skeleton—Dmanisis man—with implements and animal bones found alongside the ancient hominid remains. Fossil records suggest that *H. georgicus* cared for the sick and elderly in their group.

- *500,000 years ago:* *H. erectus,* in China, used charcoal to control fire, although it is not clear that they knew how to start a fire.

- *355,000 years ago:* In southern Italy, three *Homo heidelbergensis* left the earliest known *Homo* footprints, which were preserved when they were buried by powdery volcanic ash that solidified.

- *195,000 years ago:* The craniums of Omo 1 and Omo 2, dating from this time, have been excavated in the Omo River area in Ethiopia. They are the earliest known *Homosapiens*.

- *160,000 years ago:* *H. sapiens* in Herto village in Ethiopia butchered large mammals and practiced mortuary rituals. The village was preserved when it was covered with volcanic ash, which has made radioisotope dating possible.

- *150,000 years ago:* Mitochondrial Eve, who lived in Africa, is thought to be the last female ancestor common to all mitochondrial lineages in humans alive today.

- *130,000 years ago:* Neanderthal man *(Homo neanderthalensis),* who evolved from *H. heidelbergensis,* lived in Europe and the Middle East. They buried the dead, cared for the sick, and used spears, probably for stabbing rather than throwing.

- *100,000 years ago:* The first anatomically modern humans *(H. sapiens),* who were derived from *H. heidelbergensis,* appeared in Africa. They lived in South Africa and Israel, probably alongside Neanderthals. Modern humans entered Asia via two routes: one north through the Middle East and another farther south from Ethiopia, via the Red Sea and southern Arabia. Mutation caused skin color changes that allowed optimal absorption of ultraviolet (UV) light in different geographical latitudes; modern "race" formation began.

- *74,000 years ago:* A super volcano in Sumatra, Indonesia, caused the *H. sapien* population to crash to 2,000. Volcanic ash up to 16 feet deep covered India and Pakistan. Six years without a summer were followed by a 1,000-year ice age.

- *70,000 years ago:* *H. sapiens* in the Blombos cave in South Africa made tools from bones and showed symbolic thinking by creating ochre cave paintings and the earliest three-dimensional art. Pieces of ochre were scraped and ground to create flat surfaces, then early artists decorated the stones with a complex, geometric array of carved lines. These findings suggest that early *H. sapiens* were able to think abstractly, behaving like modern humans much earlier than was previously believed. The geometric rather than representational quality of the carvings hints at the development of written, symbolic language.

- *60,000 years ago:* Y-chromosomal Adam lived in Africa. He is thought to be the male ancestor from whom all current human Y-chromosomes are descended.

- *50,000 years ago:* Modern humans expanded from Asia to Europe and Australia.

- *40,000 years ago:* Cro-Magnon humans hunted and painted mammoths in France. They had extraordinary cognitive powers, equivalent to modern humans, that enabled them to become predators at the top of the food chain. Extinction of marsupials in Australia, probably due to human activity, resulted in the lack of domesticated animals, contributing to the relatively primitive lifestyle of the humans there, as compared to the rest of the world. This is the first known instance of humankind negatively affecting the future of the species because of the interactions with the natural environment.

- *30,000 years ago:* Modern humans moved into Japan. Bows and arrows were used in the Saharan Africa grassland. Fired ceramic animal forms were made in Moravia (Czech Republic). Modern humans entered North America from Siberia in numerous waves. Later waves crossed the Bering land bridge; but early waves probably island-hopped across the Aleutian Islands. By the time Europeans arrived, by crossing the Atlantic Ocean, at least two of the first waves were extinct, leaving no genetic descendants among South or North Americans.

- *27,000 years ago:* Neanderthals died out leaving *H. sapiens* and *H. floresiensis* as the only living species of the genus *Homo*. Although totally dependent on the environment for survival, they began to manipulate natural elements to improve their quality of life. Humans in Moravia invented textiles and pressed weaving patterns into pieces of clay before firing them.

- *23,000 years ago:* Artifacts suggest that the surviving *Homo* species began to modify materials found in their environment to support evolving abstract concepts. The Venus of Willendorf, a small sculpture of a female figure, was excavated near Willendorf, Austria, in 1908. The 4½-inch figure is carved from an oolitic limestone that is not local to the region and tinted with red ochre. The sculpture is not a realistic portrait but rather an idealization of the female figure. The lack of a face has prompted some archaeologists to view the Venus as a "universal mother." The credibility of this view is enhanced by other signs of fertility such as her breasts, swollen belly, and vulva, suggesting that there may have been some concept of a godlike higher authority that controlled what humans could not.

- *20,000 years ago:* Humans continue using natural materials in their environment to improve their quality of life. Oil lamps, made from burning animal fat on shells, were used in caves in Grotte de la Mouthe, France.

Figure 2-2
As early as 23,000 years ago,
Homos *modified materials in their*
immediate environment to portray
abstract concepts. The Venus of
Willendorf is thought to be a repre-
sentation of the ideal female form,
perhaps a universal mother figure
suggesting an early understanding
of the dependence of human life on
the benevolence of Mother Nature.
Photo by João Granja Correia.

The *Homo shandingdong* (Upper Cave Man), found in widespread sites in China, used bone needles to sew animal hides. Mammoth bones were used to build houses in Russia.

■ *18,000 years ago: H. floresiensis* has recently been identified as a species in the genus *Homo*. Discovered in 2003, it is remarkable for its small body, small brain, and survival until relatively recent times. The type specimen for the species, found in the Liang Bua limestone cave on the remote Indonesian island of Flores, is a fairly complete skeleton of a thirty-year-old female, about 3 feet in height, that has been nicknamed Little Lady of Flores or Flo. The discoverers have associated *H. floresiensis* with advanced behaviors. There is evidence of the use of fire for cooking and stone tools, apparently used in cooperative hunting. The other remarkable aspect of this find is that this species is thought to have survived on Flores until at least as recently as 12,000 years ago. This makes it the longest-lasting nonmodern human, surviving long past the Neanderthals and coexisting for a long time with modern humans, although there is no evidence that they interacted. Local geology suggests that a volcanic eruption on Flores was responsible for the demise of *H. floresiensis* in the part of the island under study (Wong 2005). It is interesting that in the mythology of the island, there were common references to small furry men called Ebu Gogo, persisting even into the nineteenth century. Some scientists wonder if the Ebu Gogo might be descendents of Flo who are living in parts of the island as yet unexplored. Could there be *H. floresiensis* living on remote, as yet unexplored islands, using only what nature provides to survive?

- *15,000 years ago:* The last ice age ended and previously glaciated land became habitable again; sea levels rose, flooding many coastal areas and separating former mainland areas into islands. Japan separated from Asia; Siberia separated from Alaska; Tasmania separated from Australia; and Malaysia and Indonesia separated.

- *12,000 years ago:* The cave paintings of Lascaux, France, and Altamira, Spain, portray humans' complete dependence on the natural environment for food and shelter. The use of charcoal in the drawings suggests knowledge of fire. The drawings provide evidence that these hunters used stone tools. Unexpectedly, the paintings suggest the artists had sufficient time and intellectual development to draw the images in perspective.

- *10,000 to 3,000 years ago:* Mesolithic Europeans were the first to alter the natural environment through fire to create a more predictable environment. They created a mosaic of woodlands and open land that supported food gathering and hunting.

- *8,000 to 2,000 years ago:* A group of humans in the Middle East's Fertile Crescent developed agriculture, and their success brought permanent

Figure 2-3
Cave paintings in Lascaux, France, dating to about 12,000 years ago, illustrate a lifestyle completely dependent upon the natural environment for survival. However, anthropologists cannot fully explain the images; these early hunters were not thought to have the intellectual development or time to create perspective drawings.

settlements. Then cities appeared, first in what is now Iraq. This process of food production, coupled later with the domestication of available animals, caused a massive increase in the human population that has continued to the present.

- *7,500 years ago:* Desertification of north Africa began, which ultimately led to the creation of the Sahara Desert. This process probably led to migration of some western African natives to the region of the Nile in the east, thereby laying the groundwork for the rise of Egyptian civilization.

RELATIONSHIP OF HUMANS AND NATURE IN THE ANCIENT WORLD

In much of the ancient world, nature was regarded with awe and fear; people were thought to be helpless in the face of its power. Architecture in ancient cities was, by its very nature, environmentally responsible. Construction technology was based on manual labor, working with regionally available materials that satisfied the demands of climate and topography. The hand-built dwellings in China, Egypt, Babylonia, Greece, and Italy dematerialized back into the natural environment when no longer required for shelter.

However, the need to honor the gods, which were believed to control daily life, and the quest for eternal life, established a mandate for buildings with exceptional durability. Using stone, contemporaneous building technology (not all of which is fully understood in the twenty-first century), and available resources, including slave labor, temples and palaces were built to be indestructible. The architectural ruins of these ancient societies are evidence of their attempt to control their environment beyond their own existence, to delay dematerialization of structures back into the natural elements from which they came. With the design and construction of buildings that had an extended lifetime, they manipulated the environment to create artifacts that were in continued use for multiple generations. The aesthetic design and construction methods evidenced by the Egyptian pyramids, Chinese palaces, Greek temples, Roman baths, and Byzantine cathedrals have been studied in detail and elements copied for more than 5,000 years. However, all are now showing damage from not only time but also acid rain and other pollutants created by people's use (and misuse) of natural materials.

These ancient societies were not always at one with nature. Plato agonized over the loss of forests that surrounded ancient Athens as a result of deforestation for shipbuilding and fuel. The once fertile Mediterranean basin had become a man-made desert. Prosperous ports were abandoned as the harbors filled with silt, and the peripheral towns around Athens became landlocked (Wines 2000).

5,500 to 2,500 Years Ago: Iron and Bronze Ages

- *3500 BC:* Humans began using iron tools.[1]
- *3000 to 2000 BC:* Hinduism, Taoism, and Confucianism provided explanations for the patterns of nature and taught reverence for them.

Figure 2-4
As early as 5,000 years ago, cedar was timbered in Phoenicia (Lebanon) for export to Egypt and Sumeria. India may also have been involved in the production of commercial timber during this period, demonstrating an awareness that the natural environment could be a source of income as well as provide the essentials for life on Earth. Photo by Charles Roffey.

[1]The timekeeping system conventionally used with the Julian and Gregorian calendars was developed to demark time based on the Christian era, using BC (for "before Christ," that is, before the birth of Jesus of Nazareth, the Christ child) and AD (anno Domini, from the Latin, "in the Year of the Lord"), with 0 BC/AD a theoretical point in time marking the birth of the Christ child. Using this system, 3000 BC is equivalent to 5,000 years ago (3,000 years before birth of Christ and 2,000 years after the birth of Christ). Anno Domini is sometimes referred to as CE, the Common Era: the period of time "before the Common Era" is then referred to as BCE. This terminology is often preferred by those who desire religiously neutral terms.

- *2600 BC:* Large-scale commercial timbering of cedars took place in Phoenicia (Lebanon) for export to Egypt and Sumeria. Similar commercial timbering occurred in South India.

- *2150 BC:* Some of the first laws protecting the remaining forests were decreed in Ur, a city in ancient Sumeria.

- *2100 BC:* In Sumeria, soil erosion and salt buildup devastated agriculture. One Sumerian wrote that the "earth turned white." Civilization moved north to Babylonia and Assyria. Again, deforestation became a factor in the rise and subsequent fall of these civilizations.

- *1500 BC:* Soil erosion was both a consequence of growth and a cause of collapse of Central American city-states.

- *1450 BC:* Minoan civilization in the Mediterranean declined, but scholars are divided on the cause. Possibly a volcanic eruption was the source of a catastrophe. On the other hand, gradual deforestation may have led to materials shortages in manufacturing and shipping.

- *600 to 350 BC, Babylonian and Persian periods:* Egyptian, Sumerian, and Babylonian civilizations had extensive and intricate links between nature and the divine. Humankind was expected to respect nature as the link between earth and the kingdoms of the gods.

500 BC to 600 AD: Classical Greek and Ancient Roman Periods

- *500 BC:* Greek coastal cities became landlocked after deforestation caused extensive soil erosion. The resulting silt filled the bays and mouths of rivers.

- *500 BC:* Cloaca Maxima (big sewer) was built in Rome by the Etruscan dynasty. As Rome grew, networks of cloacae (sewers) and aqueducts were built.

- *450 BC:* Hippocrates, a Greek physician who is considered the father of medicine, noted the effect of food, occupation, and climate in causing disease. One of his books, *Air, Waters, and Places*, is the earliest work on human ecology.

- *350 BC:* Aristotle and other Greek philosophers saw nature as the key to understanding life. Whereas Aristotle's teacher, Plato, had located ultimate reality in ideas or eternal forms, knowable only through reflection and reason, Aristotle saw ultimate reality in physical objects, knowable through experience. Objects, including organisms, were composed of a potential, *matter*, and of a reality, *form*. In living creatures, form was identified with the soul; plants had the lowest kinds of souls; animals had higher souls capable of feelings; humans alone had rational, reasoning souls.

- *250 BC:* Ashoka the Great reigned over most of South Asia and beyond, from present-day Afghanistan to Bengal and as far south as Mysore.

Figure 2-5
Entrance to the Cloaca Maxima, which is part of the system of aqueducts and cloacae (sewers) built in Rome during the Etruscan dynasty (500 BC), demonstrating the ability to modify the natural environment to improve the quality of life. Photo by Patrick MacNeil.

He pursued an official policy of nonviolence (i.e., ahimsa). Even the unnecessary slaughter or mutilation of animals was abolished. Wildlife was protected by the king's law against sport hunting and branding. Limited hunting was permitted for consumption, but Ashoka also promoted the concept of vegetarianism. He is acclaimed for constructing hospitals for animals.

- *1 AD:* Human population reached 150 million.

- *100 AD:* Occupational disease was well known in ancient Rome. Vitruvius wrote of workers in lead and mercury mines and smelters who suffered from severe health problems (both are neurotoxins). Lead fallout from smelting operations was so widespread that it was found in ice cores from Greenland glaciers 2,000 years later. Romans were aware of the pollution (i.e., *gravioris caeli*) in what had become the largest city in the world. Odors and run-off from garbage, sewage, smelting, and tanning fouled both air and water. However, the Romans set a new standard for public health. Aqueducts carried clean water to gymnasiums and public baths. Many areas of the city had sewage systems or used reservoirs to store water that was used to sweep streets clean. A similar level of public health would not return to Europe until the mid-eighteenth century.

■ *100 AD to 600 AD:* Lead poisoning may have contributed to the decline of the Roman Empire. Analysis of the bones of the aristocracy show high levels of lead. The direct consumption of lead-sweetened wine and foods created serious and widespread lead poisoning among upper-class Romans. An aristocrat with a sweet tooth might have eaten as much as a gram of lead a day, causing gout, sterility, and insanity.

■ *535 AD:* Roman emperor Justinian's legal code (*Book II, The Division of Things*) included protection for the environment: "By the law of nature these things are common to mankind—the air, running water, the sea, and consequently the shores of the sea."

■ *550 AD*: The collapse of ancient Rome is sometimes dated from the destruction of its magnificent array of aqueducts by sixth-century invaders, who controlled Europe until the twelfth century.

1200 to 1400 AD: The Middle Ages

■ *1150 to 1250:* British queens fled London to escape heavy wood smoke.

■ *1275:* Marco Polo returned from his journey through China with "black rocks that burned" (i.e., coal).

■ *1306:* Edward I forbid coal burning in London when Parliament was in session; as was true for most laws limiting the burning of coal, it had little effect.

■ *1347 to 1350s:* In the Middle Ages, Romans depended on wells and cisterns for water; only the poor dipped their water from the yellow waters of the Tiber River. The bubonic plague decimated Europe, creating the first attempts to enforce public health laws that linked abuse of the environment (e.g., water pollution) to human disease.

■ *1366:* Butchers in Paris were forced to dispose of animal wastes outside the city; similar laws would be disputed in Philadelphia and New York nearly 400 years later.

■ *1388:* The English Parliament passed an act forbidding the throwing of filth and garbage into ditches, rivers, and waters. Cambridge passed the first urban sanitary laws in England.

Fifteenth Century

■ *1450:* Within the city of Rome, Pope Nicholas V introduced the fresh spirit of the Renaissance. His first directives were practical: reinforcing the city's fortifications, cleaning and even paving some of the primary streets, and restoring the water supply. The Aqua Virgo aqueduct, originally constructed by Agrippa, was restored by Pope Nicholas. It emptied into a simple basin that Leon Battista Alberti designed, which was the predecessor of the Trevi Fountain. Alberti, in his chapter on drains and sewers in *De Re Aedificatoria,* distinguishes between drains that carry away "the filth into some river, lake, or sea" and those leading to "a deep hole dug in the ground."

Sixteenth Century

- *1556:* Italian city-states passed laws against mining because of its effects on woodlands, fields, vineyards, and olive groves.
- *1560 to 1600:* Rapid industrialization in England led to heavy deforestation and increasing substitution of coal for wood.
- *1590:* Queen Elizabeth I forbid coal burning in the vicinity of Westminster Palace. She was "greatly grieved and annoyed" by coal smoke in the Palace.

Seventeenth Century

- *1603:* James I ordered coal burned in his London household; but rather than smoky bituminous coal, he used hard, cleaner-burning, anthracite coal from Scotland.
- *1640:* Isaac Walton wrote *The Compleat Angler,* the first monograph on conservation.
- *1661:* Industrial emissions blew across the English Channel between England and France, harming plants and people—an early record of what is now considered long-range air pollution. John Evelyn, an English country gentleman, was the author of some thirty books, including his diary, which is considered an invaluable source of information on the social, cultural, religious, and political life of seventeenth-century England. In 1661 he wrote of his impression of the city of London: it "resembles the suburbs of Hell [rather] than an assembly of rational creatures." In 1684 he wrote of the city's severe smoke: "Hardly could one see across the street, and this filling the lungs with its gross particles exceedingly obstructed the breast, so as one would scarce breathe." He proposed remedies for London's air pollution problem that included large public parks with abundant flowers.
- *1666:* Japan's shogun warned against the dangers of erosion, stream siltation, and flooding caused by deforestation. He issued a proclamation urging people to plant tree seedlings. This and additional measures led to an elaborate system of woodland management by 1700.
- *1690:* Colonial Governor William Penn required Pennsylvania settlers to preserve one acre of trees for every five acres cleared.

JEFFERSON'S DECLARATION OF ENVIRONMENTAL RESPONSIBILITY

When the United States was first colonized in the 1600s, the natural environment was viewed as something to be tamed and civilized. However, in 1789, Thomas Jefferson expressed a sentiment that was not widely shared and would not be given widespread credibility for 200 years. "The earth belongs to each generation during its course, fully and in its own right. The second generation receives it clear of debts and encumbrances, the third of the second, and so on . . . for if the first could change it with debt, then the earth would belong to the dead and not the living generations" (U.S. EPA 2004).

- *1690s:* Paris became first European city since ancient Rome with an extensive sewer system.

Eighteenth Century

- *1711:* Jonathan Swift, an Anglo-Irish priest, satirist, essayist, political pamphleteer, and poet, noted the contents of London's gutters: "sweepings from butchers' stalls, dung, guts and blood, drowned puppies, stinking sprats [oily fish], all drenched in mud" ("Poem: A Description of a City Shower," 1710).
- *1739:* Benjamin Franklin petitioned the Pennsylvania Assembly to stop waste dumping and to remove tanneries from Philadelphia's commercial district. He cited foul smell, lower property values, disease, and interference with firefighting. The industries complained that their rights were being violated, but Franklin argued for the "public's rights." Franklin and the environmentalists won a symbolic battle (but the dumping continued).
- *1762:* Benjamin Franklin chaired a committee that attempted to regulate waste disposal and water pollution in Philadelphia.

Nineteenth Century

- *1820:* World population reached 1 billion.
- *1845:* Henry David Thoreau moved to Walden Pond "to live deliberately." His time there, slightly over two years, demonstrated the natural harmony that was possible in a reciprocal relationship with nature. His reputation as a prophet for ecological thought and the value of wilderness was born at Walden Pond. In 1862, Thoreau wrote "Walking," an essay in which he describes "wildness" as a "treasure to be preserved, rather than a resource to be plundered . . . in wildness is the preservation of the world."

Figure 2-6
A replica of Henry David Thoreau's cabin near Walden Pond, where he lived in isolation to demonstrate the natural harmony that was possible in a reciprocal relationship with nature. Thoreau wrote that nature was a "treasure to be preserved, rather than a resource to be plundered" ("Walking," 1862). Photo by Aaron Yates.

- *1849:* Establishment of the U.S. Department of Interior. A department for domestic concerns was considered by the First Congress in 1789, but those duties were placed in the Department of State. In 1849, land and natural resource management, Native American affairs, wildlife conservation, and territorial affairs were assigned to the Department of the Interior.

- *1850:* John Burroughs was known as the Hudson River Valley naturalist and the father of the American nature essay. Burroughs began promoting the protection of nature in the 1850s, when there were neither national parks nor conservation movements. Concerned about the exploitation and destruction caused by rapid expansion and industrialization, he wanted to share the beauty he saw in nature. In an effort to save America's wilderness resources, "John Burroughs did perhaps more than any one else to open our eyes to the beauty of nature" (Fisher 1931). His greatest contribution was his writing: a million and a half copies of his twenty-three volumes of essays were published, extolling nature and encouraging people to experience the natural world.

- *1852:* Chemist Robert Angus Smith, in the course of his research on air pollution in and around Manchester, England, discovered and coined the term *acid rain,* noting that the sulphuric acid in city air damaged fabrics and metals.

- *1854:* Henry David Thoreau published *Walden: Life in the Woods,* which became one of the best-known nonfiction books written by an American. The message that came through most clearly was the idea that humans are part of nature and function best, whether as individuals or societies, when conscious of that fact. More than a century later, Walden remains a touchstone for Americans seeking to "get in touch with nature" and is a major cultural icon.

- *1864:* George Perkins Marsh, American diplomat and philologist, is considered by some to be America's first environmentalist. He wrote *The Earth as Modified by Human Action,* the first systematic analysis of humanity's destructive impact on the environment. Marsh's book became the fountain head of the conservation movement.

Ecology: A branch of science concerned with the interrelationship of organisms and their environment.

- *1866:* The word *ecology* was coined by the German biologist Ernst Haeckel. *Ecology* was derived from the Greek *oikos,* meaning house or dwelling, and *logos,* meaning discourse or study of a thing.

- *1872:* First annual Arbor Day in the United States was celebrated on the last Friday in April.

- *1872:* U.S. President Ulysses S. Grant signed a congressional bill to create the first national wildlife preserve in the world, Yellowstone National Park, which was the first national park in the United States.

- *1873:* First of a series of killer fogs in London. Over 1,150 died in three days from severe air pollution created by burning coal.

- *1874:* Othmar Zeider, a German graduate student, developed the chemical formula for the potent insecticide DDT (dichloro-diphenyl-trichloroethane).

A MARKET ECONOMY

"The bourgeoisie, by the rapid improvement of all instruments of production, by the immensely facilitated means of communication, draws all, even the most barbarian nations, into civilisation . . . It compels all nations, on the pain of extinction, to adopt the bourgeois mode of production; it compels them to introduce what it calls civilisation into their midst, i.e., to become bourgeois themselves. In one word, it creates a world after its own image" (Marx and Engels 1848, 7).

By the mid-1800s, the life of the bourgeoisie was emulated by the emerging middle class. In the market economy that emerged, natural resources seemed inexhaustible, and societies developed with few environmental constraints (Dresner 2002).

THE INDUSTRIAL REVOLUTION

By the mid 1800s, the Industrial Revolution had changed the relationship of the natural and human environments—machines were developed that used natural resources to create an economy based on acquisition of the symbols of wealth. The Modern Age brought the "subjection of Nature's forces to man . . . machinery [and the] application of chemistry to industry and agriculture, steam navigation, railways, electric telegraphs, clearing of whole continents for cultivation, and the canalization of rivers" (Marx and Engels 1848, 7).

- *1876:* The British River Pollution Control Act made it illegal in England to dump sewage into a stream.
- *1885:* In Germany, Karl Benz built the first successful gasoline-driven automobile.
- *1886:* The Audubon Society was founded. Its mission is to "conserve and restore natural ecosystems, focusing on birds, other wildlife, and their habitats for the benefit of humanity and the earth's biological diversity." Their national network of community-based nature centers and chapters, scientific and educational programs, and advocacy on behalf of areas sustaining important bird populations, engage millions of people of all ages and backgrounds in positive conservation experiences.
- *1892:* John Muir founded the Sierra Club to preserve and make accessible the Sierra Nevada.

THE SIERRA CLUB

The Sierra Club was founded as the "guardian of the environment" on May 28, 1892. It was the first major organization in the world committed to achieving a vision of humanity living in harmony with nature. The 182 charter members elected John Muir as president. The club, with more than 750,000 members working together to explore, enjoy, and protect the planet, is America's oldest, largest, and most influential grassroots environmental organization. The modern ecology movement has its origin in the Sierra Club's conservation campaigns.

"Our generation owes much to John Muir . . . His was a dauntless soul . . . He was what few nature-lovers are—a man able to influence contemporary thought and action on the subjects to which he had devoted his life . . . so as to secure the preservation of those great natural phenomena—wonderful canyons, giant trees, slopes of flower-spangled hillsides [of Yosemite]" (Theodore Roosevelt 1903, in *Outlook,* January 16, 1915, 127–128).

Twentieth Century

- *1908:* The first continuous chlorination system in North America began operating in Jersey City, New Jersey, starting a trend in drinking water disinfection intended to stop the ravages of cholera, typhoid, and other diseases caused by water polluted by sewage discharges.
- *1909:* President Theodore Roosevelt convened the North American Conservation Conference in Washington, DC.
- *1916:* Congress created the National Park Service with Stephen Mather as president.
- *1927:* Great Mississippi Flood. The U.S. Army Corps of Engineers had designed and built a levee system to confine the Mississippi River. The levies represented man's power over nature. On Good Friday morning, the rain began, setting all-time records for scope and intensity. As the waters rose, the Corps increased the height of the levees, from 2 feet to as much as 38 feet. But the levees failed. The flood was the second most destructive river flood in U.S. history (see Table 2-1 for a comparison to the 1993 Mississippi River Flood). It caused over $400 million in damages in seven states, killed 246 people, and displaced more than 700,000.

THE 1927 GREAT MISSISSIPPI FLOOD

The stage was set for the flood when heavy rains pounded the central basin of the Mississippi in the summer of 1926. John Barry tells the story in his award-winning book, *Rising Tide: The Great Mississippi Flood and How It Changed America* (1997). In the winter of 1926–1997, the rains were so heavy that on the tributaries of the Mississippi the water overflowed the banks, causing floods to the west in Oklahoma and Kansas and to the east in Illinois and Kentucky.

On Good Friday, April 15, 1927, the *Memphis Commercial Appeal* warned: "The roaring Mississippi River, bank and levee full from St. Louis to New Orleans, is believed to be on its mightiest rampage . . . All along the Mississippi considerable fear is felt over the prospects for the greatest flood in history." The rain continued, setting all-time records.

Several hundred thousand square miles were covered, including much or all of the states of Missouri, Illinois, Arkansas, Mississippi, Texas, and Louisiana. The Mississippi River broke out of its levee system in 145 places and flooded 27,000 square miles—where nearly one million people lived—up to a depth of 30 feet. By May of 1927, the Mississippi River below Memphis, Tennessee, reached a width of 60 miles. By July 1, even as the flood began to recede, 1.5 million acres were underwater and the river was 70 miles wide.

- *1930:* World population reached 2 billion.

- *1934–1937:* The Dust Bowl drought of the U.S. plains region caused harsh economic and social conditions. The environmental and economic damage sparked a series of water-management and soil-conservation measures. It has also led to wide-scale irrigation, with underground water often pumped faster than it can be replaced.

- *1945:* The first atomic explosions began. Over the next couple of decades, nuclear fallout, including radioactive iodine and strontium 90, descended over large expanses of the planet. The fallout was found in milk thousands of miles from nuclear test sites.

- *1948:* The World Conservation Union (i.e., International Union for the Conservation of Nature and Natural Resources, or IUCN) was founded and headquartered in Gland, Switzerland. The international organization is dedicated to natural resource conservation.

- *1948:* In late October a heavy fog blanketed Donora, an industrial town snuggled between the hills of Western Pennsylvania. As the days passed, the fog turned into a toxic smog when an atmospheric inversion held the town's 12,000 citizens under a cloud of gas from the Donora Zinc Works. On October 31, when the furnaces were finally turned off, only hours before rain cleared the air, 20 people were dead and thousands more were ill. Public outcry over the incident forced the federal government to begin studying air pollution, its causes, effects, and control mechanisms. This led to the Air Pollution Control Act of 1955, the ancestor of the Clear Air Act of 1970.

Figure 2-7
A combination of low rainfall, high winds, light soil, and poor land-conservation methods created conditions that spawned massive dust clouds that caused ecological devastation in the 1930s in the American plains. In addition to the erosion that ruined crop and pasture land, the "black blizzards" that turned day to night were a severe health hazard. Courtesy of Library of Congress.

- *1949:* The United Nations Scientific Conference on the Conservation and Utilization of Resources, held in New York, was the first major United Nations meeting on natural resource problems.

- *1951:* The Nature Conservancy, an environmental organization, was founded in the United States.

- *1952:* The infamous London smog killed 4,000. A year later, a New York smog killed 200.

- *1955:* The Air Pollution Control Act, the ancestor of the Clear Air Act of 1970, took effect.

- *1956:* Widespread mercury poisoning was discovered in a Japanese village. Industrial discharges entered the food chain through fish, a staple food for Minamata Bay dwellers. The poisoning caused more than 100 deaths and several hundred cases of illness, including brain damage and birth defects. This experience caused concern when mercury was later found in some fish in the Great Lakes and nearby lakes and rivers.

- *1960:* World population reached 3 billion.

- *1960:* Concerns about nuclear fallout and chemical pollution triggered the beginning of the modern environmental movement, with protests against nuclear weapons and chemical pollution. Acid rain was identified as a serious problem in Scandinavia, while Lake Erie was said to be "dying" from excessive phosphorus pollution. Chemicals such as DDT and PCBs (polychlorinated biphenyls) were found in wildlife. A series of major oil spills aroused public alarm.

- *1961:* The World Wildlife Fund (WWF), now the World Wide Fund for Nature, was created in Switzerland; it has become a leading nongovernmental agent for international conservation.

- *1962:* Rachel Carson introduced the term *ecosystem* to the general public. Before *Silent Spring* (see page 58), nearly all Americans believed that science was a force for good. Her work demonstrated that DDT and other chemicals used to enhance agricultural productivity were poisoning lakes, rivers, oceans, and humankind. Thanks to her, the destruction of nature could no longer be called progress.

- *1963:* Britain, the United States, and the Soviet Union signed the Limited Atmospheric Nuclear Test Ban Treaty.

- *1964:* The Wilderness Act was passed, establishing a process for permanently protecting designated land from development.

- *1965:* To protect its soldiers during the Vietnam War, the United States sprayed massive amounts of a defoliant known as Agent Orange, which was later found to be contaminated with dioxin, a highly dangerous chemical associated with cancer and birth defects in animals. This led to reports of health problems by both U.S. veterans and Vietnamese citizens.

Ecosystem: An interconnected and symbiotic grouping of animals, plants, fungi, and microorganisms that sustains life through biological, geological, and chemical activity.

RACHEL CARSON'S *SILENT SPRING*

In 1962 Rachel Carson's *Silent Spring* brought to public attention the results of the indiscriminate use of DDT (dichloro-diphenyl-trichloroethane) and other pesticides. Popularly viewed as a miracle of modern technology, DDT had been used successfully in World War II to kill fleas, mosquitoes, and other insects that spread deadly diseases. However, by midcentury, biologists had begun to compile evidence of the rise of DDT-resistant strains of insects and of the harmful side effects of DDT on other species. The U.S. Department of Agriculture—and the manufacturers of DDT and similar pesticides—nonetheless continued to strongly support the use of these substances (Chemical Heritage Foundation 2005). But Carson's compelling accounts of ecological disasters were based on meticulous research and use of scientific literature. A single application on a crop killed insects for months, not only the targeted insects but countless more, and the residue remained toxic in the environment even after it was diluted by rainwater. Carson detailed the pathway by which DDT entered the food chain and accumulated in the fatty tissues of animals, including human beings, causing cancer and genetic damage. She criticized industrial society for abusing the natural environment, eloquently questioning humanity's faith in technological progress, and she set the stage for the environmental movement. "The 'control of nature' is a phrase conceived in arrogance, born of the Neanderthal age of biology and philosophy, when it was supposed that nature exists for the convenience of man."

Perhaps the most important legacy of *Silent Spring* was a new public awareness that nature was vulnerable to human intervention. Rachel Carson had made a radical proposal—at times, technological progress is so fundamentally at odds with natural processes that it must be curtailed. Conservation had never captured the public's interest; few people really worried about the disappearance of wilderness. But the threats Carson had outlined—the contamination of the food chain, cancer, genetic damage, the deaths of entire species—were too frightening to ignore. *Silent Spring* transformed the nation's consciousness and launched a revolution in attitudes at all levels of society—from schoolchildren to leaders of government and industry. For the first time, the need to regulate industry in order to protect the environment became widely accepted, and environmentalism was born (National Resources Defense Council 1997).

Eutrophication: The process by which a body of water becomes enriched with dissolved nutrients (e.g., phosphates), which stimulate the growth of aquatic plant life, usually resulting in the depletion of dissolved oxygen.

- *1966:* The U.S. Lunar Orbiter took the first photographs of "Spaceship Earth," revealing the finite and frail nature of the biosphere. People saw the planet as a small oasis of life in a hostile solar environment. The pictures became a powerful new symbol for the ecology movement.

Figure 2-8
The U.S. Lunar Orbiter took the first photographs of "Spaceship Earth" during the Apollo missions.

- *1966:* The Environmental Defense Fund (EDF) was formed to pursue legal solutions to environmental damage. The Fund went to court to stop the Mosquito Control Commission from spraying DDT on Long Island, New York.

- *1968:* Paul Ehrlich published *The Population Bomb,* which described the ecological threats of a rapidly growing human population and triggered an ongoing debate about population, consumption, and the relative impacts on developed and developing nations.

- *1968:* The National Environmental Policy Act (NEPA) was passed. NEPA is considered to be the basic "national charter" for protection of the environment.

- *1968:* The Intergovernmental Conference of Experts on the Scientific Basis for Rational Use and Conservation of the Resources of the Biosphere was held in Paris. It was a turning point in the emergence of an environmental perspective in the community of international organizations.

- *1969:* Humans walk on the moon.

Figure 2-9   *On July 20, 1969, Neil Armstrong became the first human to walk on the moon, a "giant leap for mankind." For a short period, the possibility of setting up colonies beyond planet Earth seemed more than a science fiction adventure story.*

Figure 2-10   *Neil Armstrong and Buzz Aldrin spent 2.5 hours exploring the lunar surface, leaving the American flag a testament to humankind's first visit to the moon.*

- *1969:* Friends of the Earth was formed as an advocacy organization dedicated to the prevention of environmental degradation, the preservation of diversity, and the role of citizens in decision making.
- *1969:* A fire on the surface of the Cuyahoga River in downtown Cleveland, Ohio, awakened the public to the extent of river pollution.

NATIONAL ENVIRONMENTAL POLICY ACT

It was not until 1969 that policies mandating environmental responsibility were first established in the United States with the passage of the National Environmental Policy Act (NEPA). The purpose was to "foster and promote the general welfare, to create and maintain conditions under which man and nature can exist in productive harmony and fulfill the social, economic, and other requirements of present and future generations" The United States was one of the first countries to establish a national legislative framework to protect the environment. It set the basis for environmental impact assessment throughout the world (U.S. EPA 2006).

- *1970:* The first Earth Day was celebrated on March 21. UN Secretary General U Thant, in late 1970, proclaimed Earth Day a global holiday that was to be celebrated each year on the March equinox the first day of spring in the Northern Hemisphere. He called on people of all creeds and cultures to observe a few moments of silence, to take time to consider their role in the nurturing of Earth and their commitment to its care. It has been celebrated each year thereafter at the United Nations, bringing attention to its original purpose: peace, justice, and the care of Earth. The highlight of each ceremony has been the ringing of the peace bell.

- *1970:* Responding to widespread environmental problems, Gaylord Nelson, a U. S. senator from Wisconsin, called for an environmental teach-in, or Earth Day, to be held on April 22, 1970. Over 20 million people participated that year, and Earth Day is now observed each year by more than 500 million people and national governments in 175 countries on April 22.

- *1970:* The Environmental Protection Agency (EPA) was created. In this, the first major U.S. environmental legislation, Congress declared "that it is the continuing policy of the Federal Government, in cooperation with State and local governments, and other concerned public and private organizations, to use all practicable means and measures, including financial and technical assistance, in a manner calculated to foster and promote the general welfare, to create and maintain conditions under which man and nature can exist in productive harmony, and fulfill the social, economic, and other requirements of present and future generations of Americans."

- *1970:* The Resource Recovery Act provided the EPA with funding for resource recovery programs. In 1976 Congress enacted the Resource Conservation and Recovery Act, establishing a system for managing nonhazardous and hazardous solid wastes in an environmentally sound manner. Specifically, it provides for the management of hazardous wastes from the point of origin to the point of final disposal (i.e., "cradle to grave").

- *1970:* The Natural Resources Defense Council (NRDC) was formed to use law, science, and the support of 1.2 million members to protect and to ensure a safe and healthy environment for all living things. The council's mission is to safeguard the Earth, its people, its plants, animals, and the natural systems on which all life depends; to restore the integrity of the elements that sustain life (air, land, and water); to defend endangered natural places; and to establish sustainability and good stewardship of the Earth as central ethical imperatives of human society.

- *1970:* The Clean Air Act was passed, greatly expanding protection that began with the Air Pollution Control Act of 1955 and the first Clean Air Act of 1963. (See "1990 Clean Air Act," Chapter 1, page 10.)

- *1971:* Greenpeace, an international environmental organization, launched an aggressive agenda to stop environmental damage through civil protests

EARTH DAY CELEBRATION

The celebration of Earth Day has helped to make environmental protection a major national issue in the United States by focusing attention on environmental responsibility for one day a year. The first Earth Day to be celebrated in the United States was held on the first day of spring in the Northern Hemisphere, March 21, 1970 (the autumnal equinox in the Southern Hemisphere), when the sun crosses the celestial equator, causing the length of day and night to be equal—a state of equilibrium throughout the Earth. The first day of spring, a day that historically has been celebrated by people of every creed and culture, is an appropriate day to recognize the reciprocal relationship of humankind and the planet Earth. Nature provided the marker, the equinox, as a billion-year symbol of unity and balance.

> May there only be peaceful and cheerful Earth Days to come for our beautiful *Spaceship Earth* as it continues to spin and circle in frigid space with its warm and fragile cargo of animate life—United Nations Secretary General U Thant, March 21, 1971.

In 1975 the U.S. Congress passed a resolution and President Gerald Ford proclaimed the observance of Earth Day on the March equinox: "The earth will continue to regenerate its life sources only as long as we and all the peoples of the world do our part to conserve its natural resources. It is a responsibility which every human being shares."

Margaret Mead in 1997 spoke of the significance of the celebration:

> Earth Day reminds the people of the world of the need for continuing care which is vital to Earth's safety. Earth Day draws on astronomical phenomena in a new way; using the vernal equinox, the time when the Sun crosses the equator making night and day of equal length in all parts of the Earth. The selection of the March equinox makes planetary observance of a shared event possible. The vernal equinox calls on all mankind to recognize and respect Earth's beautiful systems of balance, between the presence of animals on land, the fish in the sea, birds in the air, mankind, water, air, and land. Most importantly there must always be awareness of the actions by people that can disturb this precious balance.

For many, this date marks the beginning of the modern American environmental movement (Earth Day Network 2005).

Figure 2-11
The Earth Flag, which is flown at the United Nations, Spaceship Mir, and the North and South poles, is a symbol of global and environmental awareness. "The Earth Flag is my symbol of the task before us all. Only in the last quarter of my life have we come to know what it means to be custodians of the future of the Earth—to know that unless we care, unless we check the rapacious exploitations of our Earth and protect it, we are endangering the future of our children and our children's children" (Margaret Mead, Earth Day address to the UN, March 22, 1977)

and nonviolent interference. In 2006 Greenpeace had national and regional offices in 41 countries worldwide.

- *1971:* The International Institute for Environmental Affairs, later known as the International Institute for Environment and Development (IIED), was created to promote sustainable patterns of world development through collaborative research, policy studies, networking, and information dissemination.

- *1971:* United Nations Environmental Programme (UNEP) was founded to provide leadership and encourage partnership in caring for the environment by inspiring, informing, and enabling nations and peoples to improve their quality of life without compromising that of future generations.

ENVIRONMENTAL PROTECTION AGENCY ESTABLISHED

In 1970 President Richard Nixon submitted to Congress a reorganization plan proposing the establishment of the U.S. Environmental Protection Agency (EPA) as an independent unit in the executive branch of the federal government. Born in the wake of elevated concern about environmental pollution, the EPA was established on December 2, 1970, "to consolidate in one agency a variety of federal research, monitoring, standard-setting and enforcement activities to ensure environmental protection. EPA's mission is to protect human health and to safeguard the natural environment—air, water, and land—upon which life depends."

- *1972:* The Clean Water Act became the primary federal law in the United States governing water pollution. It was originally passed over President Nixon's veto as the Pollution Control Act. The final vote tally was overwhelming: 52 to 12 in the Senate, 247 to 23 in the House. It was amended in 1977 and 1987 to establish the symbolic goals of eliminating releases to water of toxic substances, ensuring that surface waters would meet standards necessary for human sports and recreation by 1983 and eliminating additional water pollution by 1985.

- *1972:* The production and distribution of DDT is banned in the United States.

- *1972:* Researchers documented that most of the acid rain falling on Sweden resulted from air pollution coming from industrial nations to the south, in Europe, highlighting the problem of the long-range transport of air pollution.

- *1973:* The Endangered Species Act was passed in the United States, one of the first countries to implement legal protections for fish, wildlife, and plants. It has become one of the most powerful tools in the continuing effort to protect the environment.

- *1973:* The Organization of Petroleum Exporting Countries (OPEC) announced an oil embargo against United States. This created a world energy crisis and drove up oil prices, sparking the largest round of energy conservation measures in North America since the World War II. Sales of small cars soared; thermostats were turned down; insulation was added to buildings; lights were turned off when not in use, darkening skylines; and governments invested in energy conservation.

- *1974:* World population reached 4 billion.

- *1974:* The World Watch Institute, an independent research organization that works for an environmentally sustainable and socially just society, was formed in the United States to raise public awareness of global environmental threats and to catalyze effective policy responses; annual publication of the *State of the World* report began in 1984.

- *1974:* The Cocoyoc Declaration was the outcome of a symposium in Cocoyoc, Mexico, organized by UN Environment Programme (UNEP) and the UN Commission on Trade and Development (UNCTAD). The symposium fostered the idea that misdistribution of resources was a key factor in environmental degradation.

- *1975:* U.S. Energy Policy and Conservation Act (EPAC) was passed after the Arab oil embargoes. The EPCA authorized three primary programs: United States involvement in the International Energy Agency, the Strategic Petroleum Reserve (SPR), and efforts to "reduce vulnerability through several energy efficiency and renewable energy and conservation programs."

■ *1976:* Habitat for Humanity International was founded in Georgia to address issues of affordable housing. This ecumenical organization seeks to eliminate poor housing and homelessness from the world and to make decent shelter a matter of conscience and action. Habitat invites people to work together to build houses for families in need of safe, decent, and affordable shelter. Through volunteer labor and donations of money and materials, Habitat builds and renovates houses in partnership with the families who will be the new homeowners. The houses are sold at no profit and are financed with affordable mortgages. Habitat has built about 200,000 houses around the world, providing homes for some one million people in more than 3,000 communities.

■ *1977:* The EPA banned the discharge of PCBs (polychlorinated biphenyls) into the environment when they were identified as a significant source of toxic environmental pollution. More than 1.5 billion pounds of these very stable compounds, which resist decomposition by natural processes, were manufactured and distributed in the United States before their production was banned by the EPA in 1979. However, a significant quantity of PCBs remained in use; moreover, the environment remained contaminated by PCBs that had been discharged before the ban or that had been dumped illegally or accidentally spilled after the ban.

■ *1978:* Love Canal became the biggest pollution story in North American history. Chemicals seeped from an old toxic waste dump in Niagara Falls, New York, into neighborhood basements and bubbled up onto the ground beside the elementary school. New York declared a state of emergency, closed the school, and evacuated infants and pregnant women. Eventually 255 families were evacuated. The chemicals, including *dioxin,* also drained into the Niagara River and Lake Ontario.

UNITED NATIONS ENVIRONMENTAL PROGRAMME

In 1971, at the United Nations Conference on the Human Environment, in Stockholm, Sweden, the concept of sustainable development was shaped. As a result of this conference, the United Nations Environmental Programme (UNEP) was initiated to promote the idea of environmentally sound development. Prime Minister Indira Ghandi said poverty is the greatest polluter—i.e., the poor have to exploit the environment to meet immediate needs. This made a strong link between environment and development issues, helping to set the scene for the sustainable development concept. In 1972, the UNEP launched the International Environmental Education Program (IEEP).

■ *1980: The World Conservation Strategy*, released by the World Conservation Union (i.e., the IUCN), United Nations Environment Programme, and World Wildlife Foundation, proposed that environmental protection was in the self-interest of the human species. It warned that the destruction of natural resources eliminated future sources of food, medicines, and industrial products. It encouraged sustainable forms of development and the conservation of essential life processes for the benefit of humanity as well as other species. It was another major step in launching the public debate about sustainable development.

■ *1980:* The widely publicized *Global 2000 Report to the President* by the Council on Environmental Quality, commissioned by U.S. president, Jimmy Carter, projected what the world might be like if current trends continued and called for "vigorous and determined new initiatives" to deal with environmental deterioration of "alarming proportions." The report recognized biodiversity for the first time as critical to the proper functioning of the planetary ecosystems, which are weakened by species extinction.

■ *1980:* The U.S. Congress passed the Superfund Law, creating a fund to clean up abandoned toxic-waste sites.

■ *1982:* The United States, Canada, Sweden, and Norway banned most aerosol uses of *chlorofluorocarbons.*

■ *1983:* A study by the U.S. Environmental Protection Agency and the U.S. National Academy of Sciences resulted in front-page stories that launched the public debate about what was then known as the *greenhouse effect,* later defined as *global warming* and, finally, *climate change.*

Chlorofluorocarbons (CFCs): Stable, artificially created chemical compounds, containing carbon, chlorine, fluorine, and sometimes hydrogen, they are found in both products and manufacturing processes (e.g., aerosol cans, foam upholstery cushions, cooling units in refrigerators and air conditioners). These CFCs are believed to be responsible for depleting the stratospheric ozone layer that protects the Earth and its inhabitants from excessive ultraviolet radiation.

EARLY ENVIRONMENTALISTS IN THE UNITED STATES

The 1970s marked the beginning of America's conscientious relationship with the environment. Bicycling, recycling, vegetarian diets, and composting became part of the social fabric. Communes provided community support for alternative lifestyles that were seen as at one with nature (Speer 1997). Passive solar designs that used thermal mass to store heat from the sun, as well as active solar designs, such as solar roof panels to heat the water piped through them, were developed as alternative heat sources during the energy shortage of the early 1970s.

However, the environmentalists' "confrontational rhetoric portrayed the government and industry as greed-driven and irresponsible conspirators, destroying people and plant life for their own nefarious ends" (Speer 1997). This early environmental movement never really succeeded in influencing government or the general public. The hostile accusations were interpreted by many mainstream Americans as threatening to their lifestyles and requiring personal sacrifices to save animals and trees.

- *1984:* In Bhopal, India, an accident at a pesticide plant released tons of methyl isocyanate, a lethal gas used in making insecticides. The toxic cloud killed more than 3,000 people quickly. Thousands more died in following years, while tens of thousands suffered health effects from the world's worst industrial accident.

- *1985:* Discovery by British scientists of an *ozone hole* over the Antarctic spurred action to regulate ozone-destroying chlorofluorocarbons. The Vienna Convention for the Protection of the Ozone Layer was the first step in a long series of agreements to eliminate the pollution that destroys the ozone layer.

- *1986:* An explosion and fire in a nuclear reactor at Chernobyl, in Ukraine, ejected seven tons of radioactive material into the atmosphere, causing the world's worst nuclear accident. Radiation circled the world in 11 days, and fallout contaminated food in parts of Europe.

- *1987:* World population reaches 5 billion, doubling in 40 years.

- *1987:* Gro Harlem Brundtland, the prime minister of Norway, was asked by the secretary general of the United Nations to chair the World Commission on Environment and Development (WCED). The charge was to reexamine critical environment and development problems and formulate realistic proposals to address them. In 1987 *The Brundtland Report: Our Common Future* provided the groundwork for a global sustainability movement. *Sustainable development* was defined as "an approach to progress that meets the needs of the present without compromising the ability of future generations to meet their needs" (54).

- *1987:* Twenty-four nations signed the Montreal Protocol to control substances that deplete the ozone layer, the first step in a global atmospheric-protection

Greenhouse effect: (1) The warming of the Earth's surface and lower atmosphere as a result of carbon dioxide and water vapor in the atmosphere, which absorb and reradiate infrared radiation. (2) An intensification of this warming effect brought about by increased levels of carbon dioxide in the atmosphere, resulting from the burning of fossil fuels.

Global warming: A process that raises the air temperature in the lower atmosphere due to heat trapped by greenhouse gases, such as carbon dioxide, methane, nitrous oxide, CFCs, and ozone. It can occur as the result of natural influences, but the term is most often applied to the warming predicted to occur as a result of human activities (i.e., emissions of greenhouse gases).

Climate change: Sometimes used to refer to all forms of climatic inconsistency, but the term is more properly used to imply a significant change from one climatic condition to another. *Climate change* has been used synonymously with the term *global warming*; scientists, however, tend to use the former in the wider sense to also include natural changes in climate.

TEACH THE CHILDREN

By the early 1980s, the energy shortage had been temporarily resolved. In the United States, sustainable home design (perceived by most as straw-bale construction, with concrete for thermal mass and water barrels to capture rainwater runoff) was considered by the majority to be unattractive. There was a social stigma associated with the "green movement." It was associated with being a nonshaving, Volkswagen bus–driving, unemployed vegetarian, generally a person living a "hippie" lifestyle (Hawthorne 2001). Cheap oil was once again readily available; therefore, most Americans turned their backs on sustainable lifestyles. But the seeds of a revolution were being planted and nurtured—in their school classrooms, children were learning about recycling and protecting the environment. Not only did they carry the message home to their parents, but they carried it into their own adulthood as cultural norms.

Ozone hole: The ozone layer in the stratosphere prevents most harmful UVB wavelengths (270–315 nm) of ultraviolet light from reaching Earth. Ozone depletion describes two distinct, but related conditions: the steady decline in the total amount of ozone in Earth's stratosphere since 1980, and a much larger seasonal decrease in ozone over Earth's polar regions that has created what is is commonly referred to as the ozone hole. Both conditions are created by catalytic destruction of ozone by atomic chlorine and bromine that are emitted at the earth's surface as CFCs and halons.

Dioxin: A synthetic chemical by-product formed during the manufacture of other chemicals and during incineration. Studies show that dioxin is one of the most potent carcinogens ever tested, as well as the cause of severe weight loss, liver problems, kidney problems, birth defects, and death.

Sustainable development: An approach to progress that meets the needs of the present without compromising the ability of future generations to meet their needs (UN World Commission on Environment and Development 1987).

agreement. It was important because the negotiations involved industry and began the phaseout of chlorofluorocarbons (CFCs) and related chemicals that deplete the ozone layer of the stratosphere.

- *1988:* The Intergovernmental Panel on Climate Change (IPCC) was established by two United Nations organizations, the World Meteorological Organization (WMO), and the United Nations Environment Programme (UNEP) to assess the "risk of human-induced climate change."

- *1989:* The Exxon Valdez tanker ran onto a reef in Alaska's Prince William Sound, dumping 76,000 tons of crude oil. The spill, the largest ever in the United States, covered more than 8,000 miles of pristine coastline with oil and killed more than 250,000 birds.

- *1989:* The Montreal Protocol to ban substances that deplete the ozone layer entered into force on January 1. Since then, it has undergone five revisions— in 1990 (London), 1992 (Copenhagen), 1995 (Vienna), 1997 (Montreal), and 1999 (Beijing).

- *1990:* The National Environmental Education Act required the EPA to provide national leadership to increase environmental literacy by awarding grants to develop environmental education curricula and to provide professional development for teachers.

- *1990:* The Clean Air Act set limits on how much of a pollutant can be in the air anywhere in the United States. This ensured that all Americans had the same basic health and environmental protections. The law allows individual states to have stronger pollution controls, but states are not allowed to have weaker pollution controls than those set for the whole country. The act gave important new enforcement powers to the EPA that were in line with enforcement of other federal environmental laws.

- *1990:* The Intergovernmental Panel on Climate Change's first assessment report was completed and served as the basis of the United Nations Framework Convention on Climate Change (UNFCCC).

- *1991:* The Gulf War led to the world's largest oil spill, as Iraqis retreating from Kuwait set fire to hundreds of oil wells. Soot fell as far away as the Himalayas.

- *1992:* The Earth Summit, held in Rio de Janeiro, was attended by the largest number of government leaders ever to assemble at one site. International conventions were developed on global climate change, *biodiversity*, and forest-management principles. *The Rio Declaration* contained 27 principles that defined the rights and responsibilities of nations as they pursue human development and well-being, as well as a detailed plan of action called *Agenda 21*, which was a blueprint for development that is socially, economically, and environmentally sustainable. The Earth Summit marked the peak of government proclamations. It was followed by a decline in interest caused by a severe recession and a lack of direction as to implementation promises for more sustainable development.

UNITED NATION'S DEFINITION OF SUSTAINABILITY

The World Commission on Environment and Development (WCED) issued its report, *Our Common Future* (UNWCED 1987, 54). The Commission, created by the United Nations and chaired by Norwegian prime minister Gro Harlem Brundtland, defined sustainable development: "Humanity has the ability to make development sustainable—to ensure that it meets the needs of the present without comprising the ability of future generations to meet their own needs." It said that development must "be environmentally, economically and socially sustainable." This report marked one of the most important turning points in modern environmental history. The debate began to shift from identifying crises and demanding new laws to punish polluters (react and cure) to trying to design development so as to be less harmful to the environment (anticipate and prevent). This brought industry into the environmental debate, not just to defend its actions but to try to find long-term solutions.

Biodiversity: A large number and wide range of species of animals, plants, fungi, and microorganisms. Ecologically, wide biodiversity is conducive to the development of all species.

- *1992:* In *Changing Course,* the World Business Council for Sustainable Development (WBCSD) provided an extensive analysis of how the business community can adapt and contribute to the crucial goal of sustainable development; it combines the objectives of environmental protection and economic growth. The WBCSD coined the term *eco-efficiency,* which has become synonymous with a management philosophy geared toward creating more value with less environmental impact.

- *1992:* The American Institute of Architects (AIA) Committee on the Environment (COTE), with funding from the Environmental Protection Agency, developed a guide to building products based on life-cycle analyses, the first such assessment to be conducted in the United States. The individual product evaluations were compiled in the AIA Environmental Resource Guide (ERG), which encouraged numerous building product manufacturers to make their products more environmentally responsible.

Eco-efficiency: A process to reduce the ecological impacts of production throughout the life cycle by using fewer resources and creating less waste and pollution to produce competitively priced goods and services.

- *1993:* President Bill Clinton initiated the Greening of the White House program with an energy audit of the 200-year-old building by the Department of Energy and an environmental audit by the Environmental Protection Agency. Improvements led to $300,000 in annual energy and water savings, landscaping expenses, and solid-waste costs, while reducing atmospheric emissions from the White House by 845 tons of carbon per year. The success of the project led to the greening of other properties in the vast federal portfolio, including the Pentagon, the Presidio, and the Department of Energy headquarters, as well as three national parks: Grand Canyon, Yellowstone, and Denali.

- *1993*: The Mississippi River Flood was the second most devastating flood in United States history. Residents along the Mississippi River were no strangers to overflows and flooding. Since the early eighteenth century, people have built levees and floodwalls along the 2,000-mile-long waterway to control it. However, in years with record-breaking rainfall, taming the river becomes impossible.

MISSISSIPPI RIVER FLOOD OF 1993

The Mississippi River begins at Lake Itasca in Minnesota and flows south more than 2,000 miles to the Gulf of Mexico. The flood of 1993 was an unusual and significant hydrometeorological event that devastated the Midwest. It was distinctive from other record floods in terms of its magnitude, severity, the resulting damage, and the season in which it occurred. The flooding resulted in the deaths of 52 people and caused between $15 to $20 billion in damages. Seventy thousand people were displaced, some never to return to their homes. At least 50,000 homes were damaged; 10,000 were totally destroyed; and hundreds of towns were impacted, with about 75 towns totally and completely under flood waters. At least 15 million acres of farmland in nine states were inundated. Over 1,000 of the 1,300 levees were topped.

At Saint Louis, Missouri, the river crested at 49.6 feet—19 plus feet above flood stage and more than 6 feet above the record set in 1973. The Mississippi River remained over flood stage at Saint Louis for over two months. As Mark Twain said a hundred years ago, the Mississippi River "cannot be tamed, curbed or confined, you cannot bar its path with an obstruction which it will not tear down, dance over and laugh at" (*Life on the Mississippi*, 1883).

Table 2-1   Statistical Comparison of the 1927 and 1993 Mississippi River Floods

	1927 Flood	*1993 Flood*
Loss of human life	246	47
Displaced people	700,000	74,000
Financial loss	$347 million in 1927 = $4.4 billion in 1993	$7.5 billion
Structural damage	137,000 buildings destroyed or damaged	47,650 buildings destroyed or damaged
Flooded area	27,000 square miles	15,600 square miles
River volume	2.5 million cubic feet of water per second	1 million cubic feet of water per second (USGS)

Data from the U.S. Army Corps of Engineers except where noted.

FINITE RESOURCES

By the mid 1900s, a perception was evolving that natural resources, which were once considered boundless, had limits. There was a dawning recognition by much of the population in developed countries that the traditional ways of doing things might not be indefinitely sustainable (McDonough and Braungart 1998).

- *1994:* The World Conservation Union (i.e., IUCN) published a revised *Red List* of endangered and threatened species, creating a world standard for gauging threats to biodiversity. One in four mammal species and one in eight bird species face high risk of extinction in the near future.

- *1994:* Canada, the United States, and Mexico signed both the North American Free Trade Agreement (NAFTA), which lowered tariff barriers, and the North American Agreement for Environmental Cooperation (NAAEC), which provided mechanisms for collaboration among the three nations and a forum for citizens to hold governments accountable for the enforcement of environmental laws.

- *1995:* The Intergovernmental Panel on Climate Change, a group of hundreds of prominent climate scientists assembled by the UN, released a report concluding that "the balance of evidence suggests that there is a discernible human influence on global climate." It warned of social, economic, and environmental consequences unless there was a large reduction in greenhouse gas emissions.

- *1996: Our Stolen Future* raised concerns regarding endocrine disrupting chemicals. It warned of reproductive threats from the release of billions of pounds of synthetic chemicals, some of which mimic naturally occurring hormones necessary for reproduction. The authors—Colborn, Dumanoski, and Myers, who are all well known and respected scientists—worked from a database of over 4,000 scientific publications. They cautioned that the worldwide exposure to endocrine disruption has thrust everyone into a large-scale, unplanned, unintended experiment with their health, the outcome of which may not be known for generations.

- *1996:* The International Organization for Standardization (ISO) introduced the ISO 14000 Standard for Environmental Management Systems, which refers to a series of voluntary standards in the environmental field, including environmental auditing, environmental-performance evaluation, environmental labeling, and life-cycle assessment. All of the ISO standards were developed through a voluntary, consensus-based approach.

- *1997:* The U.S. Navy initiated development of the *Whole Building Design Guide*, an online resource that incorporated sustainability requirements into mainstream specifications and guidelines. The project is now managed by the National Institute of Building Sciences.

THE FIRST ENVIRONDESIGN CONFERENCE

In 1997 the first annual EnvironDesign Conference was held to focus attention on environmentally responsible design issues. Each year, educational sessions, tours of sustainable-design exemplars, and a tradeshow provide learning and networking opportunities. EnvironDesign 10 (2006), which was held in Toronto, Canada, moved beyond the geographic confines of the United States. It was marketed as a "forum for today's environmental leaders: Redefining Global Leadership in Sustainable Design." In 2007 they introduced EnvironDesign "webinars," which can be viewed by anyone with an Internet connection, to help design professionals demystify the green products selection process and ensure maximum impact on green building projects. http://www.environdesign.com/

- *1997:* The Kyoto Protocol was negotiated as an amendment to the United Nations Framework Convention on Climate Change. Countries that ratified this protocol committed to reduction of their emissions of carbon dioxide and five other greenhouse gases.
- *1998:* The ozone hole over Antarctica grew from 3 million square kilometers in 1993 to 25 million square kilometers in 1998, an area twice the size of Canada.

KYOTO PROTOCOL'S IMPACT ON GLOBAL WARMING

The Kyoto Protocol, an agreement under which industrialized countries would reduce emissions of greenhouse gases was negotiated in Kyoto, Japan, in 1997, although it was not in effect until 2005. The protocol is an amendment to the United Nations Framework Convention on Climate Change, which was adopted at the Earth Summit in Rio de Janeiro in 1992. With the notable exception of the United States and Australia, 156 countries ratified the agreement, representing the source of over 61 percent of global emissions. Countries that ratified this protocol committed to reducing their emissions of greenhouse gases including carbon dioxide, methane, nitrous oxide, sulfur hexafluoride HFCs (hydrofluorocarbons), and PFCs (perfluorocarbons) or engaging in emissions trading if they maintained or increased emissions of these gases. The objective was the stabilization of greenhouse-gas concentrations in the atmosphere at a level that would prevent dangerous anthropogenic interference with the climate system. The United States, although a signatory to the protocol, has neither ratified nor withdrawn from the protocol. The protocol is nonbinding for the United States until ratified (United Nations 2005).

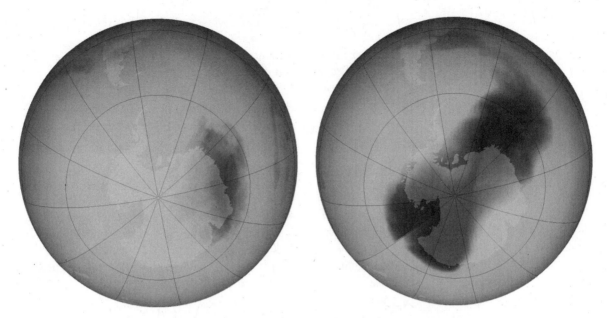

Figures 2-12a and 2-12b *Change in the ozone hole over Antarctica, from 1985 (a) to 2006 (b).*

- *1998:* President Clinton issued three "greening" executive orders (EO): EO 13101 called upon the federal government to improve its use of recycled and environmentally preferred products (including building products). EO 12123 encouraged government agencies to improve energy management and reduce emissions in federal buildings through better design, construction, and operation. EO 13148 charged federal agencies to integrate environmental accountability into day-to-day decision making and long-term planning.

- *1999:* The President's Council on Sustainable Development sponsored the U.S. National Summit on Sustainable Development in Detroit, Michigan. It catalyzed a national movement toward sustainability by showcasing ideas, technologies, and best practices.

INTERIOR DESIGNERS' PERCEPTIONS OF ENVIRONMENTALLY RESPONSIBLE DESIGN

In 1999 the International Interior Design Association (IIDA), in partnership with Collins & Aikman Floor Coverings, conducted a study regarding environmentally responsible interior design. They found major differences between designers' perceptions and their actions. Although 83 percent of the designers surveyed felt they had a moral responsibility to offer sustainable design options to a client, only 37 percent actually did so. However, 75 percent of the designers surveyed cited a lack of consistent and credible information as a key obstacle in implementing sustainable design concepts (Coleman 2000).

- *1999:* Paul Hawken, Amory Lovins, and Hunter Lovins published *Natural Capitalism: Creating the Next Industrial Revolution,* which suggests a transformation of commerce and societal institutions by redesigning industry on biological models with closed loops and zero waste, thereby reinvesting in the natural capital that is the basis of future prosperity.
- *1999:* The Dow Jones Sustainability Indexes group is launched, giving more credibility to companies and funds with a sustainability perspective.

Early Twenty-First Century

- *2000:* World population is just over 6 billion.
- *2000:* The UN Millennium Summit was the largest gathering of world leaders to date; they agreed to a set of time-bound and measurable goals for combating poverty, hunger, disease, illiteracy, environmental degradation, and discrimination against women. Now known as the Millennium Development Goals, they are to be achieved by 2015.
- *2001:* President George W. Bush rejected the Kyoto Protocol with a statement that it would be detrimental to U.S. business interests.
- *2001:* The United Nations reported that tropical countries lose more than 15 million hectares of forests per year to agriculture, logging, and other threats.
- *2001:* The World Trade Organization (WTO) issued a mandate to ensure that environmental issues were addressed in world trade talks.
- *2001:* The Intergovernmental Panel on Climate Change (IPCC) published the *IPCC Third Assessment Report: Climate Change 2001* stating that the global temperature was rising and there was "new and stronger evidence that most of the warming observed over the last 50 years is attributable to human activities."

USGBC'S INTRODUCTION OF THE LEED GREEN BUILDING RATING SYSTEM

- The U.S. Green Building Council (USGBC) launched the LEED® Green Building Rating System in 2000. The USGBC is "the nation's foremost coalition of leaders from across the building industry, working to promote buildings that are environmentally responsible, profitable, and healthy places to live and work" (USGBC 2005). The LEED (Leadership in Energy and Environmental Design) program is a voluntary, consensus-based, national standard for developing high-performance, sustainable buildings.

In July of 2007 the 1000th building received LEED certification, and more than 16,000 projects, located in all 50 states and in 41 countries, were in the process of becoming LEED certified.

Source: USGBC PRESS RELEASE

DESIGN COMMUNITY SURVEY

At the beginning of the new century there was an evolving recognition of the fragile balance between human behavior and the environment in which it occurs. In 2002 *Metropolis* magazine sponsored a survey of 550 interior designers, architects, and product designers. The vast majority (93 percent) indicated that they were interested in sustainable design, and 52 percent believed that their clients were interested. They were also asked, "How often is sustainable design desirable on projects you apply for or perform?" Seventy-eight percent replied always or sometimes desirable. Although 39 percent indicated sustainable design was required for their projects, 60 percent had no formal education regarding sustainable design. In addition, the designers and architects were also asked: "When will all design need to incorporate sustainable practices to be considered 'good design'?" Sixty-four percent replied that it would be within the next five years.

- *2002:* The United Nations warns that a three-kilometer-deep smog layer stretching across South Asia is modifying weather patterns, damaging agriculture, and endangering health.

- *2002:* The United Nations held a World Summit on Sustainable Development (WSSD) in Johannesburg, South Africa, to assess the progress made in implementing international agreements adopted at the 1972 UN Conference on the Human Environment in Stockholm, Sweden, and at the 1991 Rio conference in Brazil. Some of the 104 world leaders and the thousands of delegates who attended saw Johannesburg as the "empty summit," one without concrete results, because agreement was achieved on only a limited plan to reduce poverty and protect the environment.

- *2002:* Biologist E. O. Wilson of Harvard University, in *The Future of Life*, estimated that at current rates of human destruction of the biosphere, one-half of all species of life will be extinct in 100 years.

- *2003:* Amazon deforestation increased 40 percent compared with 2001.

- *2004:* The European Union issued its first-ever pollution register—representing a landmark event in public provision of environmental information.

- *2005:* The Kyoto Protocol came into effect. Almost all developed countries in the world, with the notable exception of the United States, pledged to reduce the emission of gases that contribute to global warming.

- *2005:* Hurricanes Katrina, Rita, and Wilma caused widespread destruction and environmental damage to coastal communities in the U.S. Gulf Coast region. This sparked discussion regarding the effect of global warming on the size and frequency of hurricanes.

AMERICAN RESPONSE TO INACTION

The executive director of the Izaak Walton League expressed the frustration much of the populace was experiencing:

> While many of today's Republican leaders seem to be out of step with the American public, and much of their own party, when it comes to environmental conservation, the tactics of some environmentalists also play a significant role in creating the political polarization and stalemate that have caused gridlock for more than a decade on environmental policy. (Hansen 2005)

INCREASING URBANIZATION

On World Environment Day in 2005, the *United Nation's Plan for the Planet* gave voice to the challenge of population movement to urban areas. Although cities use only 2 percent of the Earth's land surface, they use 75 percent of the Earth's resources.

> In 1950 fewer than one person in three lived in a town or city. . . . In 2005, for the first time in human history, more people will live in urban areas than in rural areas. This transformation has already had a huge impact on the planet's resources, as well as an impact on our perspective of nature and the environment. No prior human experience offers a guide on how to feed, house, and sustain so many people in so many cities. (Williams, 2005)

- *2006:* The Holocene extinction event continues with the observed rate of extinction rising dramatically in the previous 50 years. Most biologists believe this is the beginning of a tremendously accelerated anthropogenic mass extinction.

- *2006:* The Stern Review, commissioned by the British Government, presented a robust economic case that the costs of inaction regarding climate change would be up to 20 times greater than the measures required to address the issue immediately.

- *2006:* NASA reported continuing recovery of the ozone layer, due in part to reduced concentrations of CFCs, which were phased out under the Montreal Protocol.

- *2007:* On October 8, 2007, global population was just over 6.6 billion (6,623,213,982), and the U.S. population was just over 303 million (303,071,742). For current figure see: http://www.census.gov/main/www/popclock.html/popclock

- *2007:* Former U.S. Vice President Al Gore's documentary about climate change, *An Inconvenient Truth,* which received two Academy Awards, raised public awareness of climate change.
- *2007:* Al Gore and the UN Intergovernmental Panel on Climate Change were awarded the Nobel Peace Prize for their wide-reaching efforts to draw the world's attention to the connection between human activities and global warming, the inherent danger of climate change, and the actions that need to be taken to counteract these changes.

Timeline Sources

American Society for Environmental History. 2006. http://www.hnet.org/~environ/ASEH/home.html

An Environment and Sustainability Chronology for the Great Lakes. 2001. http://www.sustreport.org/lakes/timeline.htm

An Environment and Sustainability Chronology. 2002. http://www.sustreport.org/resource/es_timeline.htm

Art History. 2002. http://www.accessexcellence.org/WN/SU/caveart.html

Atlas of the Human Journey. 2005. https://www3.nationalgeographic.com/genographic/atlas.html

Building Design and Construction. 1993. White paper on sustainability. http://www.bdcmag.com

Earth Day 2005 Fact Sheet. 2005. http://www.nationalcenter.org/EarthDay05History.html

Ecology Hall of Fame. 2003. http://www.ecotopia.org/ehof/index.html

Environmental History Timeline. 2000. http://www.radford.edu/~wkovarik/envhist/1ancient.html

Environmental Milestones: A World Watch Retrospective Timeline. 2004. http://www.worldwatch.org/brain/images/pubs/timeline/tl2004lg.jpg

Environmental Movement Timeline. 2002. http://ecotopia.org/ehof/timeline.html

Government of Canada: Sustainable Development Historical Path. 2002.

Great archaeological sites. 2005. http://www.culture.gouv.fr/culture/arcnat/en/index.html

H-Environment. 2006. http://www.h-net.org/~environ/

History Cooperative. 2005. http://www.historycooperative.org/ehindex.html

History. 2000. http://www.channel4.com/history/

International Institute for Sustainable Development. (2006). The IISD Timeline. http://www.iisd.org/pdf/2006/sd_timeline_2006.pdf

Landmark events in protecting the global environment: 1945-Present. 2002. http://www.interenvironment.org/wd1intro/events.htm

List of archaeological periods. 2006. http://en.wikipedia.org/wiki/List_of_archaeological_periods

Modern World. 2005. http://en.wikipedia.org/wiki/Modern_world

Rand Corporation. 2003. Our Future – Our Environment. http://www.rand.org/scitech/stpi/ourfuture

The Earth Times. 2006. http://www.earthtimes.org

The Sustainability Report. An Environment and Sustainability Chronology. 2002. http://www.sustreport.org/resource/es_timeline.htm

Timeline of Environmental Events. 2005. http://en.wikipedia.org/wiki/Timeline_of_environmental_events

Timeline of Evolution. 2006. http://en.wikipedia.org/wiki/Evolutionary_timeline

UN Population Division. 2006. Source of historical population figures. http://www.census.gov/ipc/www/popclockworld.html

U.S. Environmental Protection Agency. 2007. Environmental Progress. Retrieved September 15, 2007, from http://www.epa.gov/earthday/history.htm

World Watch Institute. 2005. http://www.WorldWatch.org

References

Barry, J. M. 1997. *Rising Tide: the great Mississippi flood and how it changed America.* New York: Simon and Schuster.

———. 2002. The 1927 Mississippi river flood and its impact on US society and flood management strategy. Paper presented at the Annual Meeting of the Geological Society of America (October 27–30, 2002), Denver, CO. Retrieved February 15, 2006 from National Geologic Society Web site: http://gsa.confex.com/gsa/2002AM/finalprogram/abstract_44272.htm

Chemical Heritage Foundation. 2005. Chemical achievers: The human face of the chemical sciences. Retrieved November 21, 2005, from Chemical Heritage Foundation Web site: http://www.chemheritage.org/classroom/chemach/environment/carson.html

Carson, R. 1962. *Silent spring.* Boston: Houghton Mifflin; Cambridge, MA: Riverside Press.

Cohen, M. P. 1988. *Sierra Club history: Origins and early outings.* Retrieved February 14, 2006, from the Sierra Club Web site: http://www.sierraclub.org

Coleman, C. 2000. Interior design. Assessing the future of green design. *Interior Design Magazine,* 71(1): 66. Retrieved October 22, 2004, from First Search database.

Dresner, S. 2002. *The principles of sustainability.* London: Earthscan Ltd.

Earth Day Network. 2005. *2005 Annual Report.* Washington, DC: Author. Retrieved February 9, 2006, from Earth Day Network Web site: http://www.earthday.net

European Society for Environmental History. 2005. *Environmental history bibliography*. Retrieved February 10, 2006, from European Society for Environmental History Web site: http://eseh.org/resources/bibliography/

Fisher, C. 1931. With John Burroughs at Slabsides: Recollections of the famous poet-naturalist and his mountain retreat near Riverby. *Natural History Magazine*, 31(5): 510. Retrieved October 8, 2007, from EcoTopia/USA Web site: http://www.ecotopia.org/ehof/burroughs/apprec.html

Gould, K. 2002. Teaching green: The full survey report. *Metropolis Magazine*, 20 (November). Retrieved September 23, 2004, from http://www.metropolismag.com/html/content_1102/sup/index.html

Hansen, P. W. 2005. *Earth Day quotations*. Retrieved February 2, 2006, from The National Center for Public Policy Research Web site: http://www.nationalcenter.org/EarthDay05Quotes.html

Hawthorne, C. 2001. The case for a green aesthetic. *Metropolis Magazine*, 19 (October): 112–125. Retrieved September 23, 2004, from http://www.metropolismag.com/html/content_1102/sup/index.html

Henshilwood, C., F. d'Errico, R. Yates, Z. Jacobs, C. Tribolo, G. A. Duller, et al. 2002. Emergence of modern human behavior: Middle Stone Age engravings from South Africa. *Science*, 295(February 15): 1278–1280. Retrieved October 20, 2006, from First Search database.

Lawrence, L., and J. McConnell. 1999. *Earth Day past, present, and future*. Retrieved January 29, 2006, from Environmental Protection Agency Web site: http://www.epa.gov/earthday/history.htm

Kibert, C. J. 2005. Sustainable construction: Green building design and delivery. Hoboken, NJ: John Wiley & Sons.

Marx, K., and F. Engels. 1848. The communist manifesto. Oxford, England: Oxford University Press.

McDonough, W., and M. Braungart. 1998. The next industrial revolution. *Atlantic Monthly*, 282 (October): 82–92. Retrieved October 20, 2006, from First Search database.

National Resources Defense Council. 1997. The story of silent spring. Retrieved December 29, 2005, from National Resources Defense Council Web site: http://www.nrdc.org/health/pesticides/hcarson.asp

Neuzil, M., and W. Kovari. 1996. Mass media and environmental conflict. Thousand Oaks, CA: Sage Publications.

Speer, T. 1997. Growing the green market. American Demographics, 19(August): 45–49. Retrieved October 20, 2006, from First Search database.

U Thant. 1971a. Earth Day Proclamation. United Nations Press Release SG/1749 — February 26, 1971. Retrieved September 10, 2007, from International Earth Day Web site: http://www.earthsite.org/mc-lee.htm

———— 1971b. Peace Bell Rings. Retrieved September 10, 2007, from International Earth Day Web site: http://www.earthsite.org/mc-lee.htm

United Nations Conference of the Parties. 1997. *Kyoto Protocol*. Retrieved December 10, 2005, from United Nations Framework Convention on Climate Change Web site: http://unfccc.int/kyoto_protocol/items/2830.php

United Nations World Commission on Environment and Development. 1987. *The Brundtland Report: Our common future*. Oxford, England: Oxford University Press.

U.S. Environmental Protection Agency (EPA). 2004. *Sources of indoor air pollution—formaldehyde*. Retrieved July 15, 2005, from EPA Web site: http://www.epa.gov/Iaq/formalde.html

————. 2006. *History of sustainability*. Retrieved July 15, 2005, from EPA Web site: http://www.epa.gov/ebtpages/envihistory.html

U.S. Green Building Council (USGBC). 2005. *Meet the US Green Building Council*. Retrieved December 5, 2005, from USGBC Web site: http://www.usgbc.org

————. 2006. *Greenbuild*. Retrieved January 3, 2006, from USGBC Web site: http://www.usgbc.org

Williams, K. 2005. Worldwide green building councils achieve natural balance as change agents. *Environmental Design + Construction,* 8(11): 28. Retrieved from First Search Database.

Wines, J. 2000. *Green architecture*. New York: Taschen.

Wong, K. 2005. The littlest human. *Scientific American*, February: 40–49. Retrieved October 20, 2004, from First Search database.

CHAPTER THREE

Environmentally Responsible Interior Design

Louise Jones, ArchD, LEED AP, IDEC, ASID, IIDA

We must do what we conceive to be right and not bother our heads or burden our souls with whether we'll be successful. Because if we don't do the right thing, we'll do the wrong thing and we'll be part of the disease and not part of the cure.
   —E.F. (Fritz) Schumacher

The Context for Environmentally Responsible Interior Design

Recognition of the interconnectedness of the buildings, people, and community is essential for the creation of an environmentally responsible built environment. Government officials, urban planners, developers, building owners, architects, engineers, interior designers, construction managers, code officials, contractors, tradespeople, landscape architects, facility managers, and the people who live, work, and play in the buildings must all be engaged. The inclusion of all stakeholders and interdisciplinary teamwork are prerequisites for the successful creation of a built environment that supports the health and well-being of both the populace and the planet it calls home. A recent Roper survey (2002) found that the top reason Americans cite for taking care of the environment is to protect human health; 78 percent felt that people are at increased risk due to poor environmental conditions. Native American ideology maintains that "we do not inherit the earth from our ancestors, we borrow it from our children." Extending the influence of this canon, the World Commission on Environment and Development (1987) defines sustainable development as "meeting the needs of the present without compromising the ability of future generations to meet their own needs" (p. 54).

In *The Hanover Principles: Design for Sustainability* (1992), written to guide the planning of the Expo 2000 World's Fair, William McDonough defines *environmental intelligence* as the process of using natural resources, energy, and technology, efficiently and appropriately, in a closed-loop manufacturing cycle, to ensure that damage to the environment is avoided when bringing products for the built environment to the market. Specification of furnishings, finishes, and equipment (FF&E) that are green (i.e., protect people's health and well-being) and sustainable (i.e., protect Earth's health and well being) reflects environmental responsibility. However, although there are several groups disseminating information regarding green and sustainable building construction methods and materials (e.g., the U.S. Green Building Council), no one is concentrating on a comprehensive understanding of environmentally responsible FF&E. This lack of focus on interiors has created an information void for architects, interior designers, and facility managers who want to specify environmentally responsible FF&E for interior environments.

Increasingly, the purveyors of the products that designers specify offer environmentally responsible alternatives, because they recognize that it makes good

Figure 3-1
Midtown Lofts, Minneapolis, Minnesota. Lander Group Urban Development Corporation. Built on a former industrial site in 2002, the project used many green technologies, including large high-performance windows and doors with low-emittance (low-e) insulated glass to maximize daylighting; low-VOC paints and finishes and fresh air supply for each unit to improve IAQ; bamboo and recycled rubber flooring; as well as sheetrock with recycled flyash content and materials purchased locally to minimize energy required for transportation.

Figure 3-2
The Midtown Lofts' kitchens feature Energy Star–rated appliances, water-efficient faucets, granite countertops, and fluorescent lamps on dimmer switches. The cabinets are made of 100 percent formaldehyde-free ResinCore, with 100 percent post-industrial recycled content, and feature FSC-certified maple veneer door surfaces with a UV-cured finish.

business sense for them to do so. A survey by Arthur D. Little, a consulting firm, indicated that 83 percent of North American and European business leaders believed they can derive real business value from incorporating environmental responsibility into their business strategy and operations. However, in their fervor to market their products, some manufacturers indulge in *greenwashing*—exaggerating the green or sustainable characteristics of their products—thereby creating additional problems for designers who want to practice environmental responsibility.

INTEREST IN ENVIRONMENTAL RESPONSIBILITY

Although the practice of environmentally responsible interior design (ERID) has only come to the foreground in the past 5 to 8 years, a 1999 survey of 100 nonresidential interior designers showed that 83 percent believed they had a moral obligation to offer environmentally responsible solutions to their clients; however, only 37 percent indicated that they did so (Beecher 2003). The primary obstacle, according to these designers, was lack of information. However, misinformation was also a problem. Some mistakenly believed that environmentally responsible design decisions would inherently compromise their standards, that somehow it would involve a sacrifice in color, performance, or cost. Many designers also mistakenly believed that sustainability was a low priority with clients. However, a survey by American Demographics found that as early as 1996, approximately 50 percent of American consumers looked for environmental labeling and actually switched brands based on environmental friendliness (Speer 1997).

Greenwashing: Purposeful dispersion of false or exaggerated information so as to present an environmentally responsible image. Greenwashing creates problems by causing confusion for designers and their clients (Greenpeace 2003).

Sustainable development: "An approach to progress that meets the needs of the present without compromising the ability of future generations to meet their needs" (World Commission on Environment and Development 1987, 54).

Green design: A micro perspective that addresses the health, safety, and well-being of the people who live, work, and play in the built environment.

Sustainable design: A macro perspective that addresses the health and well-being of the global ecosystems that support life for both current and future generations.

Environmentally responsible design (EDR): A comprehensive perspective that addresses both the health and well-being of people in the built environment and the health and well-being of the global ecosystems that support life for current and future generations.

INTEREST IN ENVIRONMENTALLY RESPONSIBLE BUILDING PRODUCTS

A number of factors have led to a significant increase in interest, specification, and purchasing of green building products over the last five years. These include a greater awareness of and sensitivity to the world's limited natural resources; a growing demand for healthier, more energy-efficient and environmentally responsible homes and work places; the establishment of the USGBC and its efforts to promote policies and programs for the implementation of green building projects, such as the LEED rating system; municipalities offering incentives to go green, such as tax credits for the construction of buildings that are environmentally responsible; and the EPA taking on more of a leadership role in actively mandating greener building policies.

—Laura Dodge, Director of Marketing and Communications, Dodge-Regupol, Inc.

GREEN + SUSTAINABLE DESIGN

Often the terms *green design* and *sustainable design* are used interchangeably. However, there is an important difference. *Green design* focuses on people's issues—their health, safety, and welfare; whereas *sustainable design* encompasses a more global approach—the health, safety, and welfare of the planet, so that it is possible for this generation to meet their needs without jeopardizing the ability of future generations to meet their needs. The term *environmentally responsible interior design* (ERID) encompasses both concepts (Green Design Education Initiative 2003). It is the responsibility of those who are charged with creating interior spaces in the built environment to implement environmentally responsible design in both new construction and in renovation of existing buildings.

Environmentally responsible interior design addresses the interrelationships of the designed environment, human behavior, and environmental responsibility. Design practitioners who practice ERID plan, specify, and execute interior environments that reflect their concern for the users' quality of life and the world's ecology. They use a process in which environmental attributes are treated as design objectives (Office of Technology Assessment 1992).

ERID'S ROLE IN ENHANCING ORGANIZATIONAL PERFORMANCE

An investigation of environmentally responsible interior design is complex, as it involves a wide range of diverse elements and must be undertaken within the context of economic, ecological, and social systems. Creation of an environmentally

Figure 3-3
*Los Manos Bed and Breakfast,
Buena Vista, Colorado. Pamm
McFadden, architect, Boulder,
Colorado. Los Manos Bed and
Breakfast exemplifies post-and-
beam construction with straw-
bale infill, an indigenous form of
architecture in Colorado. All of the
electricity used to build and run
the house comes from solar panels
installed on-site before construction began, although a wind generator has recently been installed
for supplemental power.*

responsible built environment involves resource issues, environmental interactions, human health and well-being, economics, community development, and other issues that are intertwined in the economic, ecological, and social systems.

Early leaders in environmentally responsible design have shown that it is possible to build high-quality, high-performance buildings on budget and on time. What started as a small, charismatic community focusing on environmentally responsible design has matured into an established sector of the construction industry. Now the business community is exploring the potential relationship between environmentally responsible interior design and the potential for improved organizational performance by looking at issues ranging from resale value to quality of employees' worklife. These include:

Financial outcomes
- Operation and maintenance costs,
- Cost of building-related litigation,
- Rental and resale value of property,
- Costs of churn,
- Costs of absenteeism,
- Costs of turnover;

Figure 3-4
The 1,200-square-foot Los Manos house's exterior finish consists of several inches of stucco. The interior was created with 45 tons of native clay dug from the front yard to form adobe walls and floors that retain heat in the winter and remain cool in the summer. In addition to the locally sourced straw and logs, the builders reused windows and unique architectural items, such as headboards, a chandelier, and living room furniture, thereby salvaging them before they were sent to the landfill. Photos courtesy of Los Manos Bed and Breakfast, www.lasmanosbandb.com.

Stakeholder relations
- Public image and reputation,
- Customer satisfaction,
- Community outreach and education,
- Knowledge transfer,
- Local economic impact, and
- Community livability;

Human capital development
- Quality of work life,
- Work satisfaction,
- Personal productivity,

- Social and psychological well-being,
- Ability to attract and retain high-quality workers, and
- Absenteeism (Heerwagen 2002).

In 2004, nearly 1,800 transnational corporations filed reports on issues of corporate responsibility, up from virtually zero in the early 1990s. In 2005, by midyear, more than 1,600 reports had been filed. These reports, sometimes referred to as nonfinancial reports, include everything from the impact on local communities to greenhouse gas emissions. The majority of the reports are being filed by European corporations. Between 2001 and 2005, 54 percent came from Europe, 25 percent from Asia and Australia, 17 percent from North America, and 2 percent from South America, Africa, and the Middle East, respectively (World Watch Institute 2006).

A Paradigm Shift

The creation of interior environments, the renovation of existing spaces, and the replacement of the components of the designed environment are undertaken within the context of economic, ecological, and social systems. The production of FF&E depends almost entirely on nature for both energy and raw materials. However, the current use of land, energy, water, and natural resources is not sustainable and must end if Earth is to be inhabitable by future generations.

Various laws supporting environmentally responsible design and construction (ERDC) are already in place. In some European countries, new technology and audits of materials at demolition sites result in the use of recycled products during construction. Manufacturers are required to take responsibility for recycling and reusing the materials that they produce for the designed environment. Legislation mandates energy efficiency and the extensive use of daylighting as the primary light source (Eiserman 2004). In the United States, extra up-front costs associated with green and sustainable buildings sometimes result in limited acceptance by the public sector. However, any additional up-front costs would quickly be recouped through maintenance and replacement cost-savings (e.g., life-cycle cost of linoleum compared to the life-cycle cost of vinyl flooring) and through energy cost reductions of 25 to 40 percent. Research has shown that construction costs for ERDC can now equal the costs for conventional buildings when an integrative process is used (Gack and Green 2003). To meet this goal, interior environments must be planned, designed, and constructed through the collaboration of all members of the design and construction team.

The paradigm shift from environmental irresponsibility to ERDC is challenging those who are responsible for the built environment. Ultimately, ERDC will become the joint endeavor of government officials, urban planners, developers, architects, building owners, engineers, interior designers, construction managers, code officials, contractors, tradespeople, landscape architects, and facility managers, as well as the people responsible for the systems that support both the infrastructure and the interconnections of the elements of the built environment.

HALLMARKS OF THE PRODUCTIVE WORKPLACE

A world-class workplace is one that goes beyond function and aesthetics to become a strategic business tool. It is the result of an integrated, sustainable approach to develop workplaces that reflects the GSA's seven hallmarks of the productive workplace:

1. Spatial fairness: Design the workplace to meet the functional needs of the users by accommodating the tasks to be undertaken without compromising individual access to privacy, daylight, outside views, and aesthetics.
2. Healthfulness: Create workplaces with a clean, healthy building environment free of harmful contaminants and excessive noise, with access to clean air, light, and water.
3. Flexibility: Choose workplace configuration components that can be easily adapted to organizational or work process changes, and can be readily restructured to accommodate key functional changes with a minimum of time, effort, and waste.
4. Comfort: Distribute workplace services, systems, and components that allow occupants to adjust thermal, lighting, acoustic, and furniture systems to meet personal and group comfort levels.
5. Technological connectivity: Enable full communication and simultaneous access to data among distributed coworkers for both on-site workplaces (including individual workstations, team space, conference/multimedia space, hoteling space, etc.) and off-site workplaces (including telework or commuting center, home office, travel venues, etc.)
6. Reliability: Support the workplace with efficient, state-of-the-art heating, ventilating, air conditioning (HVAC), lighting, power, security, and telecommunication systems and equipment that require little maintenance and are designed with battery and/or greater back-up capabilities to ensure minimal loss of service or downtime.
7. Sense of place: Endow the workplace with a unique character, appropriate image, and business identity to enable a sense of pride, purpose, and dedication among both the individual and the workplace community.

Source: U.S. GOVERNMENT SERVICES ADMINISTRATION (GSA). 2005. LEADING BY EXAMPLE: A DEMONSTRATION TOOLKIT FOR CREATING A WORLD CLASS WORKPLACE. RETRIEVED OCTOBER 30, 2007, FROM GSA WEB SITE: HTTP://WWW.GSA.GOV/GSA/CM_ATTACHMENTS/GSA_DOCUMENT/ LEADINGBYEXAMPLE_R2-Y-AA-E_0Z5RDZ-I34K-PR.PDF

Specification of Environmentally Responsible Design

THE 3 Rs: REDUCE, REUSE, RECYCLE

As early as the 1970s, environmentalists were urging Americans to reduce, reuse, and recycle in order to preserve the natural environment. Schoolchildren urged their parents to recycle cans, bottles, and paper. Although distrustful of environmentalists, in general, the generation that had lived through the Great Depression was already practicing the *3Rs:* reduce, reuse, recycle. During the 1973 oil crisis, it appeared that the United States was ready to adopt an environmentally responsible lifestyle. But by the end of the twentieth century, the "throw-away" generation was rejecting reduce and reuse in favor of rampant consumerism. Waste management is a difficult problem that is rapidly becoming more evident. Nationwide, almost 4 billion pounds of carpet are being sent to landfills every year. In the United States, thirty-two truckloads of waste are created for every truckload of goods produced. Within one year, 90 percent of everything made in the United States is "thrown away" (Bonda 2003). However, the reality is that unless waste is to be transported off of planet Earth, there is no "away"!

The 15 percent of the world's population living in high-income countries (i.e., "minority countries"), account for 56 percent of the world's total consumption, while the poorest 40 percent (i.e., "majority countries") account for only

---

ENVIRONMENTAL IMPACT OF BUILDINGS

Buildings fundamentally impact people's lives and the health of the planet. In the United States, buildings use more than one-third of our total energy, more than two-thirds of the electricity, and one-eighth of the water, and they transform land that provides valuable ecological services. Atmospheric emissions from the use of energy leads to acid rain, ground-level ozone (i.e., smog), and global climate change. Buildings are responsible for:

- 68 percent of total U.S. electricity consumption;
- 39 percent of total U.S. energy use;
- 38 percent of total U.S. greenhouse gas emissions;
- 136 million tons of construction and demolition waste (approx. 2.8 lbs per person per day)—60 percent of the total nonindustrial waste generated in the U.S.;
- 12 percent of potable water used in the United States; and
- 40 percent (3 billion tons annually) of raw materials used globally.

Source: U.S. ENVIRONMENTAL PROTECTION AGENCY GREEN BUILDING WORKGROUP. 2004. BUILDINGS AND THE ENVIRONMENT: A STATISTICAL SUMMARY. (DECEMBER 20). RETRIEVED OCTOBER 30, 2007, FROM EPA WEB SITE: HTTP://EPA. GOV/GREENBUILDING/PUBS/GBSTATS.PDF (FOR MORE INFORMATION, SEE EPA'S GREEN BUILDING WEBSITE AT HTTP://WWW.EPA.GOV/GREENBUILDING/)

Off-gassing: Process of evaporation or chemical decomposition through which vapors are released from materials, also referred to as *out-gassing.*

Open-loop, cradle-to-grave model: Concept used in life-cycle analysis to describe the entire life of a material or product from creation through disposal (often before the end of defined life with no consideration of environmental responsibility).

Closed-loop, cradle-to-cradle model: Concept used in life-cycle analysis to describe a material or product that is recycled into a new product at the end of its defined life; this concept of "no waste," modeled after nature, was introduced by architect William McDonough.

Sustainable practices: Practices that provide ongoing economic and social benefits without degrading the environment (Learner.org 2007).

Unsustainable practices: Practices that meet an immediate need but over time deplete or damage natural resources (Learner. org 2007).

11 percent of consumption (UNDESA 2003). The U.S. Green Building Council reports that the built environment is growing globally at a rate three times faster than the growth rate of the population. When American Institute of Architects (AIA) president, R. K. Stewart, spoke before the U.S. Senate Energy and Natural Resources Committee (February 12, 2007), he reported that buildings were the most overlooked sector in the greenhouse gas debate. Buildings produce 30 to 40 percent of the atmospheric emissions in the United States and 9 percent of the carbon dioxide worldwide.

If everyone in the world were to live like an average person in the minority, high-income countries, an additional 2.5 planet Earths would be required (computed by Global Footprint Network 2007 using United Nations statistics). Even current consumption and production levels appear to be 25 percent greater than the Earth's carrying capacity (UN Department of Economic and Social Affairs 2003).

Not until the beginning of the twenty-first century did the 3Rs regain favor with a significant percentage of the population. There are currently many proposals for a fourth R—including refurbish, rethink, and redesign. Julie Stewart-Pollack and Lauren Pillote, both interior design educators, prefer seven Rs (7Rs): rethink, redesign, reduce, reuse, renew, refurbish, and recycle, but note that with appropriate use of the first six, there would be little need to recycle. Whether a splitter (7Rs) or a lumper (3Rs), it is the designer's responsibility to reduce the quantity of materials used, to reuse materials whenever possible, and to recycle in order to produce zero waste.

SUSTAINABILITY IN CONTRACT CARPETS

There is a relatively new and growing dimension to the design, production and promotion of contract carpets. Some call it recycling. Those closest to the cutting edge call it sustainability. In a nutshell, it's a concept that ultimately results in a cradle-to-cradle loop of technical nutrients that can flow endlessly in a continuous cycle of rebirth. Recycling isn't new to the carpet industry. Internal waste reduction and resource conservation programs have been around for 15 years or more. Most sources agree that 4.5 billion pounds of post-consumer carpet go to landfills annually. This year the industry in total will divert only 150 to 200 million pounds from those landfills. Most carpets were never made to be recycled. Carpets are made of layers of dissimilar materials that are assembled to provide maximum performance, appearance retention, and value. Two nylons are used in contract carpet face fiber: type 6,6 and type 6. They perform equally well in properly constructed contract carpets. But nylon 6 currently has a small and growing advantage. It's made of one plastic component and water. Technology exists to break it down in post-consumer carpets and use it to make more nylon 6 carpet fiber, cradle-to-cradle. None of these materials and processes mean much if manufacturers and other stakeholders do not develop the infrastructure to return these products to a recycling point at the end of the carpet's useful life. No one, as yet, has the capacity to take back everything they make. Even if we build it, carpet users must use it for the system to work. Cradle-to-cradle demands a closing of the loop by returning material to the carpet manufacturing process.

Claims of recycled content in any product can be clouded by a legal practice called "mass balance." Every pound of recycled material that comes into a mill becomes a "credit" to be claimed in any component that would technically include some recycled content. As long as a company claims no more pounds leaving its shipping docks than the total pounds received into the manufacturing process, the claim is allowed per FTC guidelines. However, this does not speak to the spirit of recycled content. Ask manufacturers for the annual total pounds of recycled material received and the total pounds of all raw material, virgin and recycled, received. The numbers may give you a different perspective on percentage of recycled content.

Another common misconception is in the reporting of a manufacturer's environmental footprint and reductions in impacts. Many specialized contract carpet manufacturers do not extrude, spin, or dye their own yarns. They buy yarn from other companies, precolored and ready to tuft. The carpet producer does not report the environmental impacts of the yarn producer. This devalues the effort and investment of large integrated manufacturers, who take responsibility for some of the more environmentally difficult tasks associated with improving sustainable practices. The market will determine the future of sustainable carpet products and processes. In contract carpet, specifiers perform a crucial role in promoting sustainability. If specifiers, interior designers, and end users do not reward manufacturers that invest in cradle-to-cradle technologies, put real solutions on the floor, and do far more than talk about a better future, then that future will be cradle-to-grave not cradle-to-cradle.

—Steven L. Bradfield, vice president, Environmental Development, Shaw Contract Group

Source: S. L. BRADFIELD. 2002. PERSPECTIVES ON SUSTAINABLE DESIGN, ENVIRONMENTAL DESIGN & CONSTRUCTION. (NOVEMBER 21). RETRIEVED OCTOBER 30, 2007, FROM ED&C WEB SITE: HTTP://WWW.EDCMAG. COM/CDA/ARCHIVES/6736A2C01A697010VGNVCM100000F932A8C0

LIFE-CYCLE ANALYSIS

Green building standards set by such rating systems as LEED (Leadership in Energy and Environmental Design) are encouraging the industry to look at buildings as long-term investments. A new whole-building perspective that bases costs on the entire life cycle of a building is replacing an approach that is based solely on initial construction costs. In the new perspective, small investments at the beginning of a project that go toward better efficiency are rewarded—sometimes tenfold—through significant operational savings that are realized over the life of the building (Craig 2004). For interior designers, a life-cycle approach requires the analysis of interior furnishings and finishes from the specification of raw materials to the end of useful life. Designers must identify and analyze the raw materials, manufacturing methods, transportation, installation, use, maintenance, and disposal of all the FF&E specified for an interior space. Reduce, reuse, and recycle are the guiding principles. When disposal at the end of useful life becomes reuse, manufacturing has become a closed-loop process, the ultimate goal for products and materials (McDonough and Braungart 2003).

The life-cycle analysis (LCA) process is the analytical basis for design decisions that are environmentally responsible. It is currently the most effective measure of sustainability—effective use of LCA can determine how the design affects the health and welfare of global ecosystems. Several tools—including ATHENA (from Athena Sustainable Materials Institute), BEES (Building for Environmental and Economic Sustainability), LEED, and MSDG (Minnesota Sustainable Design Guide; now Minnesota Sustainable Building Guidelines, or MSBG)—have been developed to assist designers in preparing a detailed life-cycle assessment of each design decision to ensure environmentally responsible programming and space planning, as well as specification and installation of environmentally responsible FF&E. All of the LCA systems are computer based and easily accessible to design teams. (See Chapter 8 for a broader discussion of certification and evaluation tools.)

In manufacturing, the LCA process is governed under ISO 14000, a series of international standards addressing environmental management. This assessment pertains to the manufacturing process rather than to the actual product being manufactured; the standards enable organizations to minimize the negative effects of their operations on air, water, or land. When designers can ascertain that a potential supplier is ISO 14000 certified, they can be assured that the manufacturer understands the company's role in environmentally responsible design and construction. (For a more detailed discussion of the LCA process, see Montgomery 2003.)

INDOOR AIR QUALITY

Because it can impact people's health, comfort, well-being, and productivity, indoor air quality (IAQ) is a major concern. Most Americans spend up to 90 percent of their time indoors, and many spend most of their working hours in an office environment (EPA 2007). Studies conducted by the U.S. Environmental Protection Agency (EPA) and others show that indoor environments sometimes can have levels of pollutants that are actually higher than levels found outside (EPA 2007). People exposed to indoor air pollutants for the longest periods of time are often those most susceptible to the negative effects of indoor air pollution. Such groups include but are not limited to children, elders, and people who are chronically ill, especially those suffering from cardiovascular diseases, respiratory diseases (including allergies and asthma), or multiple chemical sensitivity (MCS).

Environmentally responsible interior design addresses the interrelationships of design, human health and welfare, and ecology. Designers who practice green design plan, specify, and execute interior environments that reflect their concern for the users' quality of life. Careful specification of FF&E identifies and eliminates materials that off-gas noxious or toxic vapors to protect indoor air quality. Chapter 5, "Indoor Air Quality," explores the scope of the IAQ problem and the designer's responsibilities regarding IAQ, as a member of the design team. One of the most distinguished scholars of *indoor environmental quality* (IEQ) research, William J. Fisk, PhD, of the Indoor Environment Department at Lawrence Berkeley National Laboratory, has projected the estimated potential annual savings and productivity gains from improved indoor air quality at $6 to $14 billion from reduced respiratory disease, $1 to $4 billion from reduced allergies and asthma, $10 to $30 billion from reduced SBS-related illness, and $20 to $160 billion from direct improvements in worker performance unrelated to health. Fisk and his colleague, A. H. Rosenfeld, have put a value of $12 to $125 billion annually in worker-performance gains from thermal and lighting improvements (Fisk 2000).

Figure 3-5
Interface Showroom and Offices, Atlanta, Georgia. Holder Construction, Atlanta. Steve Clem and Carlie Bullock-Jones, LEED AP, TVS Interiors, Atlanta. The Interface Showroom, a retail and commercial showroom tenant space in the Centergy Building, Atlanta, was awarded the first LEED-CI Platinum certification. The designers created a classic, minimalist backdrop to showcase the Interface products, using the original concrete flooring, floating the gypsum wallboard, and using large lampshade, metal halide fixtures below an exposed ceiling. The open design reduced material use and simplified the disassembly required for future adaptability. At least 60 percent of the existing walls, doors, flooring, and ceiling systems were retained, and 85 percent of the construction waste was diverted from the landfill.

Figure 3-6
In the Interface Showroom, extensive daylighting and efficient electrical lighting (both fluorescent and metal halide lamps were used) reduced energy consumption. To further enhance efficient use of energy, photovoltaic cells, occupancy sensors to monitor daylighting and adjust the electrical lighting accordingly, and an astronomical timer to drop lighting levels after work hours were used. Employees have individual control of lighting, temperature, and ventilation in the offices.

Environmentally Responsible Interior Design

ERID PRECEPTS

The creation of an environmentally responsible interior environment involves the relationships among all of the stakeholders: government officials, urban planners, developers, building owners, architects, engineers, interior designers, construction managers, code officials, contractors, tradespeople, landscape architects, facility managers, and the people who live, work, and play in the built environment. The interior designer must be engaged in creative and critical thinking to ensure that the design solutions rise from a platform of environmental responsibility. Each design project is unique and must be grounded in its contextual setting. There are, however, a few broad precepts that can guide the designer through the design process.

- *Develop flexible space plans,* that are adaptable for multiple uses and/or different user groups and that can be easily reconfigured when requirements change (e.g., divide spaces with demountable partitions).
- *Support closed loop manufacturing* (e.g., recycle "pulled" carpet through CARE, the Carpet America Recovery Effort). See Chapter 4, "Nature as a Model for Design."

- *Specify FF&E that do not off-gas volatile organic compounds (VOCs) or formaldehyde,* both of which are known carcinogens; select composite wood and agrifiber products that do not contain urea-formaldehyde resin; require GreenGuard IAQ certification. See Chapter 5 Indoor Air Quality.

- *Do not specify FF&E made with PVC plastic* (polyvinyl chloride), a known carcinogen. See Chapter 5, "Indoor Air Quality."

- *Protect materials from moisture during construction* to prevent mold growth; comply with any state or local mold legislation. See Chapter 5, "Indoor Air Quality."

- *Require a flush-out period prior to occupancy* to evacuate off-gassed toxins and other allergens. See Chapter 5, "Indoor Air Quality."

- *Monitor IAQ* with continuous testing and adjust the ventilation as needed. See Chapter 5, "Indoor Air Quality."

- *Inform client of document-cleaning and maintenance procedures* that are environmentally responsible. See Chapter 5, "Indoor Air Quality."

- *Design an energy-efficient, effective lighting plan* (e.g., evaluate the luminaires, lamps, ballasts, and controls). See Chapter 6, "Environmentally Responsible Lighting Design."

- *Specify plumbing fixtures that reduce water use* (e.g., waterless urinals) and investigate water reuse systems. See Chapter 7, "Energy, HVAC, and Water."

- *Recommend energy-efficient electrical equipment* that is Energy Star rated. See Chapter 7, "Energy, HVAC, and Water."

- *Only use FSC certified wood* that is from managed forests with chain of custody documentation. See Chapter 8, "Certification Programs and Evaluation Instruments."

- *Plan for zero waste* by recycling demolition materials on-site or at another location (e.g., reuse of architectural detailing) and investigating end-of-useful-life options for new materials (e.g., wood flooring that can be removed and reinstalled at a different location). See Chapter 9, "United States Green Building Council and LEED Certification."

- *Use recycled materials* to reduce the use of raw materials and to divert material from landfills. Make virgin, petroleum-based materials, the rare exception to the rule, not the standard (e.g., use polyester fabric made from recycled soda pop bottles). See Chapter 9, "United States Green Building Council and LEED Certification."

- *Use refurbished materials* to reduce the use of raw materials and to divert material from landfills (e.g. refinish original wood flooring rather than installing new flooring). See Chapter 9, "United States Green Building Council and LEED Certification."

- *Use rapidly renewable materials* (e.g., bamboo flooring, which is harder than oak, although it is a grass that regrows when cut, without being

Material safety data sheet: Product-information literature that identifies hazardous chemicals and health hazards, including exposure limits and precautions for workers who come into contact with these chemicals.

Flush-out period: Designated period of time after construction ends (typically two weeks) when air exchange rate is increased, using 100 percent outside air and new filtration media, to remove toxins and allergens from indoor air prior to occupancy.

Zero waste: Design principle that seeks to change the flow of resources through implementation of cradle-to-cradle design and production. The goal is to ensure that, at the end of useful life, all products are reused or recycled safely as natural or technological nutrients in a closed-loop process.

replanted). See Chapter 9, "United States Green Building Council and LEED Certification."

- *Maximize daylighting and provide views to the outdoors* from all occupied spaces. See Chapter 9, "United States Green Building Council and LEED Certification."

- *Reduce embodied energy by buying local* (within 500 miles) to minimize fuel load whenever possible; ship materials using reusable packing materials and the most fuel efficient method. See Chapter 9, "United States Green Building Council and LEED Certification."

- *Plan for recycling* by specifying recyclable materials, recycling during construction, and planning for recycling on-site when the project is completed (e.g., specify recycle containers and allocate storage space for recycled materials). See Chapter 9, "United States Green Building Council and LEED Certification."

- *Research FF&E specifications carefully, documenting life-cycle analysis.* See Chapter 10, "Specification of Products for Environmentally Responsible Interior Design."

- *Require submission of a Material Safety Data Sheet* (MSDS) whenever there is a concern about toxicity (e.g., mercury and lead are toxic and cannot be used in paints and coatings in the United States, but may be a concern in other countries). See Chapter 10, "Specification of Products for Environmentally Responsible Interior Design."

- *Select products and materials with minimal or no packaging*, whenever possible (e.g., blanket wrapped furnishings). See Chapter 10, "Specification of Products for Environmentally Responsible Interior Design."

Nadav Malin, editor of *Environmental Building News*, identifies "creative tensions" (i.e., the sensation of being pulled in all directions when trying to reach an environmentally responsible design decision) as one of the most important issues facing the environmental design community. He suggests that it is critical to document which decisions work and which do not. This requires measuring and tracking design decisions and comparing the outcomes to local, national, and global benchmarks. Although some design decisions, and subsequent outcomes, cannot yet be measured effectively, it is important to document what can be measured and to develop instruments for what cannot (Ketcham 2004). A myriad of ideas comes together in an environmentally responsible design project; research, both quantitative and qualitative, can serve as a foundation upon which to develop better solutions that have environmentally responsible design as the nexus.

A PHILOSOPHY FOR PROBLEM SOLVING

The 2006 Design Giants Survey by *Interior Design* magazine found that 20 percent preferred to hire someone who could design spaces that would qualify for LEED certification from the U.S. Green Building Council (Davidsen, Leung, and

> **THE ROLE OF THE INTERIOR DESIGNER**
>
> I do not believe that the process of human life on this globe has degenerated to a point of no return. I do believe, however, that we are fast approaching that point and we must redirect and correct our course in life to ensure health and a good life for the seventh generation coming. This legacy is passed down not to ensure the present, but to guarantee the future. Thinking of future generations is an·enormous responsibility that requires vision.
>
> —Chief Oren Lyons, in Foster et al. 2006.
>
> Interior designers and architects share the responsibility for interpreting Chief Lyons' vision in the design of the built environment. They have the power to create a new future. Designers know that there is never one right way to resolve a design problem. Searching for new answers, creatively adapting what is known into what is needed in order to resolve design problems, is what designers do. By adopting an environmentally responsible interior design filter, they can show their clients how to see the world from a green and sustainable point of view.
>
> BONDA, P., 2003. WHY GREEN DESIGN MATTERS, *ASID ICON MAGAZINE.* (MAY)

Girmscheid 2007). The Council for Interior Design Accreditation (CIDA), the accrediting body for interior design programs, requires that student work demonstrate an understanding of environmentally responsible design. It would appear that the interior design profession recognizes not only that ERID is a moral mandate, but also that it makes good business sense for interior designers to practice environmentally responsible interior design. James Ludwig, director of design at Steelcase said: "Environmental sustainability is more than a corporate responsibility. It inspires innovation and offers a unique opportunity to redefine quality. We believe that's how design professionals look at it, too. I think most designers consider their work to be a social contract with the user. . . . We'd all prefer to use sustainable products. . . . It's a philosophical approach, a way of solving design problems . . . it's about sustainable behavior, and that's the way we should approach things as designers" (Steelcase 2006).

References

Annenberg Media. 2007. *The habitable planet: A systems approach to environmental science.* Retrieved October 25, 2007, from the Learner.org Web site: http://learner.org/channel/courses/envsci/index.html

Beecher, M. A. 2003. What's new? What's now? What's next? *Interiors & Sources.* (January/February). Retrieved September 25, 2007, from *Interiors & Sources Magazine* Web site: http://www.interiorsandsources. com/articles/detail.aspx?contentID=3776

Bonda, P. 2003. Waste not, America. *Interiors & Sources.* (January/ February). Retrieved September 25, 2007, from *Interiors & Sources Magazine* Website:http://www.interiorsandsources.com/articles/detail. aspx?contentID=3965

Cassidy, R. 2003. White paper on sustainability. *Building Design and Construction.* (November): 35–36.

Craig, B. 2004. Reduce. Reuse. Recycle. Rethink. *Midwest Real Estate News.* 20, 1: 16–18.

Davidsen, J., W. Leung, and L. Girmscheid. 2007. They just got even bigger. *Interior Design.* (January). Retrieved September 25, 2007, from *Interior Design Magazine* Web site: http://www.interiordesign. net/id_article/CA6411097/id

Eiserman, R. 2004. Down to earth: It's time to embrace sustainable design and devise innovative, inclusive processes that consume fewer resources. *Design Week.* 19, 4: 14–16.

EPA (U.S. Environmental Protection Agency). 1998. *An office building occupant's guide to indoor air quality.* Retrieved March 13, 2004, from EPA Air and Radiation Web site: http://www.epa.gov/iaq/pubs/ occupgd.html

EPA (U.S. Environmental Protection Agency). 2007. *The inside story: A guide to indoor air quality* (#402-K-93-007, 1995, updated 2007). Retrieved October 25, 2007 from EPA Office of Radiation and Indoor AirWeb site: http://www.epa.gov/iaq/pubs/insidest.html#Intro1

Fisk, W. J. 2000. Health and productivity gains from better indoor environments and their relationship with building energy efficiency. *Annual Review of Energy and the Environment.* 25, (November): 537–566.

Foster, K., A. Stelmack, and D. Hindman. 2006. *Sustainable residential interiors.* Hoboken, NJ: Wiley.

Gack, J., and J. Greene. 2003. A guide to cost-effective green design for public building owners. *Environmental Design & Construction.* 6, 6: 62–64. Retrieved March 11, 2004, from ProQuest.

Global Footprint Network. 2007. *Ecological footprint.* Retrieved October 25, 2007, from Footprint Network News Web site: http://www.footprintnetwork.org/gfn_sub.php?content=global_footprint

Grahl, C. L. 2001. Perspectives on sustainable design. *Environmental Design and Construction.* 4, 6: 10–15.

Green Design Education Initiative. (n.d.) Green/Sustainable interiors: Frequently asked questions. Retrieved March 1, 2004, from Interior Design Educators Council Web site: http://www.idec.org/greendesign/home.html

Heerwagen, J. 2002. Sustainable design can be an asset to the bottom line. Environmental Design & Construction. 5, 4: 35–40. Retrieved October 25, 2007, from First Search.

Ketcham, T. 2004. Interview with Nadav Malin. *GreenMoney Journal.* 12, 3. Retrieved February 20, 2004, from *GreenMoney Journal* Web site: http://www.greenmoneyjournal.com/article.mpl?newsletterid=24&articleid=252

McDonough, W. 1992. *The Hannover principles: Design for sustainability.* New York: William McDonough Architects.

McDonough, W., and M. Braungart. 2003. Towards a sustaining architecture for the 21st century: The promise of cradle-to-cradle design. *Industry and Environment* 26, 2/3: 13–16. Retrieved October 25, 2007, from William McDonough's Web site: http://www.mcdonough.com/writings/towards_a_sustaining.htm

Montgomery, M. 2003. Life cycle assessment tools. *ArchitectureWeek: Environment.* (August, 13): E2.1. Retrieved February 20, 2004, from *ArchitectureWeek* Web site: http://www.architectureweek.com/2003/0813/environment_2-1.html

Office of Technology Assessment. 1992. *Green products by design: Choices for a greener environment.* (#OTA-E-541). Washington, DC: U.S. Government Printing Office.

Roper ASW. 2002. Roper's Green Gauge Report shows that Americans are adopting environmentally sound habits. *Green@Work.* 18, (September/October).

Ryan, A. 2005. Experts disagree on whether green construction costs more. *Daily Journal of Commerce.* (October 11).

Speer, T. 1997. Growing the green market. *American Demographics.* 19, (August): 45–49. Retrieved October 26, 2007, from First Search database.

Steelcase Incorporated. 2006. Cradle-to-cradle design. *360 Magazine.* (December). Retrieved September 25, 2007, from Steelcase Web site: http://www.360steelcase.com/e_000152534000035897.cfm?x=b11,0,w

Thorp, A. 2003. Why the marketplace is ready to embrace sustainable design. *Design Week.* 18, 22: 16–18.

UNDESA (UN Department of Economic and Social Affairs). 2003. Sustainable production and consumption: Fact sheet. Retrieved November 2, 2006, from United Nations Division for Sustainable Development Web site: http://www.un.org/esa/susdev/sdissues/consumption/Marrakech.htm

UNWCED (UN World Commission on Environment and Development). 1987. *The Brundtland report: Our common future.* New York: Oxford University Press.

World Watch Institute. 2006. Corporate responsibility reports take root. *Trends in Vital Signs 2006–2007.* Retrieved July 18, 2007, from World Watch Institute Web site: http://www.worldwatch.org/node/4268

CHAPTER FOUR

Nature as a Model for Design

Anna Marshall-Baker, PhD, IDEC

Think about it: you may be referred to as a consumer, but there is very little that you actually consume—some food, some liquids. Everything else is designed for you to throw away when you are finished with it. But where is "away"? Of course, "away" does not really exist. "Away" has gone away.
    —William McDonough

An Ecologically Intelligent Framework

In 2002, William McDonough and Michael Braungart published *Cradle to Cradle: Remaking the Way We Make Things,* articulating a message they have been practicing and disseminating for more than a decade. The message extends beyond green design or sustainable design to espouse environmental responsibility and to embrace a shift in the way human beings view their place in and their use of the world. McDonough (2004c) describes this new condition, cradle-to-cradle design, as "an ecologically intelligent framework in which the safe, regenerative productivity of nature provides models for wholly positive human designs. Within that framework, every material is designed to provide a wide spectrum of renewable assets. . . . [The consequence is] . . . redesign [of] the very foundations of architecture and industry, creating systems that purify the air, land, and water; use current income and generate no toxic waste, and use only safe, regenerative materials." The purpose of this chapter is to articulate the meaning of cradle-to-cradle design, illustrating its concepts with examples of materials and substances, interior and industrial design, architecture, and landscape. And regardless of the scale, cradle-to-cradle design begins with nature.

TREES BREATHING

Charles David Keeling began measuring levels of carbon dioxide in the earth's atmosphere almost 50 years ago. The question driving his quest was whether greenhouse gases such as carbon dioxide (CO_2) accumulated in the atmosphere or were absorbed by the oceans and vegetative areas of the earth. Placing sensors away from cities and urban areas that *produce* carbon dioxide but also away from vegetation that *absorbs* carbon dioxide, Keeling discovered that the concentration of CO_2 rose in some months of the year and dropped in others. Specifically, he observed that the concentration dropped in the period between May and September, and then concentrations began to rise again. He determined that what he was recording was vegetation breathing in the spring and summer when plants were blooming, growing, pulling carbon dioxide from the air. In the fall and winter, when the plants not only were not growing but decaying, the level of carbon dioxide in the atmosphere rose again. In other words, what Keeling had uncovered was Earth's respiration, a remarkable cycle that organizes all life on the planet (Scripps Institute of Oceanography 2005; Palfreman 2000).

Yet discovering that the earth has a respiratory cycle should not be surprising, because we are immersed in nature's cycles: the rotation of the earth, the revolution of the earth around the sun, the rise and fall of tides, seasonal changes, and so on. Ancient civilizations were so in awe of these natural occurrences that their citizens worshipped spirits or gods believed to be in control of these events. We also might not be surprised to realize that events that are not cyclical but linear

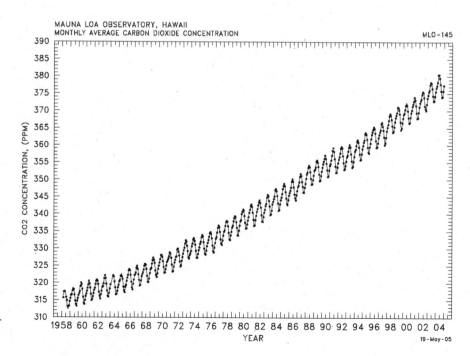

Figure 4-1
Keeling's Curve revealing increasing levels of CO_2. Courtesy of Scripps Institute of Oceanography.

and contrary to the model provided us by nature are problematic. In fact, they are destructive. Keeling's work also reveals the framework for this destruction.

INDUSTRIAL ACTIVITY

Keeling produced what some have described as the "single most important data set taken in the 20th century" (Scripps Institute of Oceanography 2005). Before documenting the Earth's cycle of respiration, little was known regarding the increasing amounts of carbon dioxide released into the atmosphere from domestic and industrial activity. What we see in Keeling's work is a steady rise of concentrations of CO_2 within the last 50 years. In other words, the earth's "inhale" is not strong enough to balance the amount of carbon dioxide produced with the amount consumed by the oceans and vegetation. The cycle of each inhale and exhale continues, but the curve in the data reflecting the residual amounts of carbon dioxide grows steeper, elevating the seasonal fluctuations of the earth's respiration higher and higher on the graph. These data that form "Keeling's Curve" represent an accumulation of carbon dioxide that is consistent with the findings of other investigators who are measuring the earth's atmosphere in ice cores.

Layers of snow across time compress to form the ice sheet that we know as Antarctica. Because low temperatures at this base of the earth assure that the ice does not melt, the ice conserves a record of atmospheric conditions from which its snows formed and then fell to the earth. Once on the ground (the ice), air collects between the frozen water crystals that are snowflakes. With the accumulation of more snow and its weight, the crystals merge to form masses of ice, and the air trapped between them becomes bubbles, archives of atmospheric activity thousands of years old. Drills pull long cores of ice that reveal properties of the snow and air captured in a chronological record. When the core samples from Law Dome, Antarctica, for example, are studied for carbon dioxide, they tell a story of gentle fluctuations from a thousand years ago but significant increases in CO_2

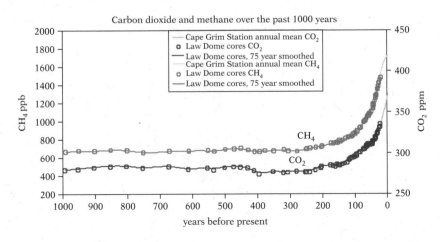

Figure 4-2
Analyses of ice cores show increasing levels of CO_2. Natural and anthropogenic changes in atmospheric CO_2 over the last 1,000 years from air in Antarctic ice and firn. ©CSIRO Marine and Atmospheric Research. From Etheridge et al., Journal of Geophysical Research *101, D2 (1996): 4115–4128. This material is not to be reproduced in any other publications without separate written permission from CSIRO.*

during the nineteenth and twentieth centuries. Perhaps more importantly, these data reveal increases in carbon dioxide that parallel Keeling's Curve during the second half of the last century (Jacka 1993).

Collectively, studies like these tell the same story: that levels of CO_2 have risen consistently in the last century and risen significantly in the last 50 years. When we look at human activity during this time, we see a period of industrial growth unlike any other, a period we call the Industrial Revolution. Generally, this period may be described as a time in which humankind began to view nature as a tool, a convenient market of "resources" to be harnessed and manufactured to produce the necessities of late nineteenth- and early twentieth-century living. A metaphor of this industrial age, of the first Industrial Revolution, may be the *Titanic* (McDonough and Braungart 2002c), a vast human-built object weighing 66,000 tons and filled with every luxuriance of the day (*Titanic and...* 2005).

Manufacturing of the *Titanic* required massive quantities of materials pulled from the earth, a brutal application of force to these materials to mold, make, and produce objects, products, and fuel. All the while and during the ship's brief life (and death), it contaminated water, air, and soil. A result of industrial processes typical of the day, the *Titanic* was believed to be invincible to the forces of nature, much as our approach to our industrialized culture currently is viewed.

Nature is believed or assumed to be subservient to the ingenuity of humankind, existing as the source of materials necessary for us to fashion our environment. "Raw" materials such as oil, coal, ore, wood, and water, whether renewable or nonrenewable, are viewed as "natural capital" (e.g., Daly 2000). They are harvested as "income" necessary for the development of products, a practice that vastly underestimates their value. Importantly, these materials are not "raw," lying in wait to be called into some form of useful service. They are parts of active systems that provide the foundation for "clean air and water, climate stabilization, rainfall, ocean productivity, fertile soil, watersheds, and...processing waste" (McDonough and Braungart 2002g). Nonetheless, this view of nature as a marketplace for industrial activity has been widely accepted, perhaps subconsciously, since the late 1800s. And this approach to industrial activity has changed the world in significant ways. It has enabled modes of transportation, means of communication, improvements in health and hygiene, conveniences of service in homes and businesses, and advances in information technologies. Yet accompanying these achievements are unintended negative consequences that include:

- release of toxic materials into the air, soil, and water;
- production of dangerous materials such as nuclear waste;
- deposits of valuable materials after a useful life into material graves;
- regulations articulating lawful and unlawful amounts of pollution; and
- erosion of diversity among species and cultures (McDonough and Braungart 2002c).

Having turned from nature as a model to nature as a tool, we concocted a linear material flow that produces waste and fouls the planet. McDonough and

Braungart (2002c) describe this scenario as *"cradle to grave,"* succinctly known as *"take-make-waste."* Sadly ironic, this cradle-to-grave scenario was exactly the path of the *Titanic*, a mantle of the first Industrial Revolution.

Cradle to Grave

A cradle-to-grave design scenario is characterized by an end point for nearly all materials that is typically a landfill, incinerator, or other form of material grave (McDonough and Braungart 2002c; 2004). The largest majority of items that we "consume" actually are not "consumed" but "discarded": in the trash, in the land-fill, in the incinerator.

We are described, for example, as "consumers" whenever we purchase some-thing such as a computer. But the computer is never consumed. We use it, but we do not consume it. When it (quickly) becomes antiquated and we are ready to purchase a new computer, the existing one is materially the same as when we bought it: same size, same components, original materials and substances, and so on. Nothing has been consumed. But its useful life now over, it heads toward a material grave of some sort. We assume that because our outdated computers are out of our sight, they are somehow "gone" or "away." But they are not gone. They simply have arrived at various destinations where an undervalued employee, for example, may remove small amounts of metals at great risk to human and environmental health and then discard

Figure 4-3
Partial view of the amount of household waste collected each day in a landfill in Greensboro, North Carolina.

the remains of the computer (McDonough and Braungart 2004). Or the computer may be tossed in its entirety into a material grave such as a landfill.

Landfills are made up of "consumed" products such as sofas, bicycles, televisions, and carpet, where they are left to deteriorate. But a plastic soda bottle, for example, may take a century to degrade—we have not been throwing plastic away long enough to know exactly how long it takes to decompose. Other materials that we throw away, like nuclear waste, will take many centuries to degrade, and because it is so toxic to human and environmental health, it is "thrown away" in guarded tombs. In all instances, materials and products reflecting enormous investments of time, money, and energy are discarded and abandoned. Rather than contributing to the development and maintenance of a healthy environment, the only activity associated with these materials at this point is the regulation and control of substances that may destroy or degrade the quality of air, soil, and water, a process that requires even more resources to maintain. This take-make-waste approach characteristic of cradle-to-grave design reflects a scenario that McDonough and Braungart (2002c) refer to as a "strategy of tragedy."

WASTE IN MAKING

Waste is not only in the materials and goods that live brief lives as items to be consumed or used and then live long lives as discarded items. A second type of waste results from the manufacture of objects and products, another form of ecological tragedy. In many parts of the world, such as Peru and Guyana, for example, local residents are challenging long-held industrial practices, such as mining, that destroy (waste) the landscape to retrieve small amounts of natural capital from a larger environmental context (Sanders 2005). Gold nuggets, for example, no longer are plucked from screen-bottomed pans used by miners to swish sparkling water across river rock and stream pebbles. Current gold mining uses a process called heap-leaching, in which tons of ore (dirt and rock) are extracted from the earth, "heaped," and then chemically sifted, using a liquid cyanide solution that dissolves and removes microscopic amounts of gold. An interview with the general manager of the world's largest gold mine, located in Peru, reveals that 30 tons of rock and dirt must be displaced to recover 1 ounce of gold using heap-leaching (Heeter and Tuller 2005). Once the gold is removed, the dirt and rock remain displaced (wasted), and the cyanide solution is stored in open, lined ponds.

Mining also illustrates a third tragedy of cradle-to-grave design: unintended by-products of industrial processes. As the cyanide solution dissolves and separates the gold from the ore, for example, it also separates silver, platinum, and mercury (Heeter and Tuller 2005). Silver and platinum, like gold, are recovered for use; mercury, however, is a neurotoxin that must be safely removed from the site. Although its use is banned in some countries, mercury still is used in some health-care and industrial applications. Yet this by-product of gold mining is known to negatively affect the nervous system, liver, and kidneys, and it is associated with developmental delays, lowered IQ scores, and cancer (Zadorozhnaja et al. 2000). A spill in Choropampa, Peru, in 2000 sickened more than 1,000 villagers who were treated for mercury poisoning, although the health effects are expected to last for years (Bergman and Perlez 2005). Thus, another unintended consequence of a cradle-to-grave industrial process is the production of materials and substances that are harmful to human and environmental health, substances that require additional resources to contain, manage, and secure.

WASTE IN MAKING, USING, DISCARDING

Unwanted materials—or "waste"—and other substances are not always in liquid or solid forms; they also may be gases. Polyvinyl chloride (PVC) is an example of a material that is associated with toxic gases at each stage of its life cycle: production, use, and end of life. Common household products, such as vinyl flooring and shower curtains, are made of a material produced from a manufacturing process that includes chlorine gas, hydrochloric acid, ethylene, vinyl chloride, vinyl acetate, and dioxin (Steinbrager 2005).

These substances are separately or collectively carcinogenic, explosive, deadly, or outlawed as weapons. Though meant to be a closed system of production, manufacturing facilities of PVC rank among the top polluters in the country, with reports of one particular plant releasing from 31,000 to 45,000 pounds of vinyl chloride or vinyl acetate into the atmosphere in 2001 and 2002.

Yet the toxicity of PVC is not limited to its production. Once in use in seemingly benign everyday products such as garden hoses and phone cords, PVC off-gasses the substances of which it is made, causing at best respiratory illness and at worst cancer (Ackerman and Massey 2003).

The problems with PVC persist at the end of its useful life. When PVC is discarded in a landfill, it leaches substances that degrade air, soil, and water quality. But PVC also has been incinerated routinely. Popular for its flexibility, durability, and maintenance, PVC has many applications in health care. When the dangers of throwing biologically contaminated waste into material graves became known in the 1980s, hospitals began burning or incinerating waste, including PVC. But heated PVC releases hydrochloric acid and dioxin into the air, gases that threaten human health, even at extremely low levels (Ackerman and Massey 2003). And PVC is only one of many products that manifest the toxic effects of a material from its component parts, through its manufacture and use to the end of its useful life.

In summary, a cradle-to-grave scenario consumes large amounts of time, energy, and material to produce or manufacture objects and products that typically end their useful lives, no matter how long or short, in a material grave. This approach to the design of objects is typically harmful to human and environmental health in numerous stages of harvest, production, use, and deterioration. Recognizing the destruction of this "strategy of tragedy," citizens in the United States have been encouraged in recent years to "reduce, reuse, recycle" in an effort to slow the negative effects through waste prevention and source reduction (e.g., U.S. EPA 2005). Because reducing and reusing clearly only prolong the inevitable descent to a material grave, recycling may be the only possible saving grace of a cradle-to-grave design scenario.

Figure 4-4
The future of PVC?

RECYCLING

Recycling is meant to recover valuable materials in existing products, preparing them for another useful life. Yet much of *recycling* is actually *down*-cycling, which causes the material value to fall over time (McDonough and Braungart 2002c; 2002h). Melting plastics from beverage containers such as milk or water, for example, often mixes a variety of different polymers. The consequence is a lower quality material that can only be used in a product of lower quality such as planks for decking or park benches. When this product, this plastic plank, has reached the end

Figure 4-5
*Recycled newspaper in
Greensboro, North Carolina.*

of its useful life, even down-cycling to a less valuable material is not probable and the product, and the material, ultimately, is discarded in a material grave.

Metals also are typically down-cycled (McDonough and Braungart 2002c). Although the high-quality steel used in the manufacture of cars and other motor vehicles could be used again, fully recycled, this does not happen because the steel is often painted or coated with plastics. Processes do not currently exist that can separate successfully and economically the coating from the steel, causing the steel to be melted with other components that lessen its quality and prevent its use in other high-tensile conditions. Further degrading the recycle process for metals are the emissions released during the recycling process. The paints and plastic coatings that burn off during a melting process release toxic chemicals such as dioxin and furan into the atmosphere. A similar situation occurs with aluminum. Processes to remove the painted or screened inks from aluminum cans are either nonexistent or expensive; thus, those inks are burned off during the aluminum recovery process, releasing toxic substances into the air. Complicating recycling of aluminum cans, also, is the use of two different grades of aluminum—one for the top and another for the sides and bottom. These two grades are seldom separated but mixed together in a recycling process that produces a lower-grade aluminum.

Recycling, then, although seemingly describing a process of productive reuse of a material, often produces material of an inferior quality, while simultaneously creating conditions that are hazardous to human and environmental health. And any condition that is potentially hazardous to human and environmental health must be regulated.

REGULATING

Many of the processes in place that currently degrade the quality of air, water, and soil and harm human and environmental health were well developed before the risks to the public were acknowledged. They often have been the unintended effects of entrepreneurs and industrialists who were trying to make life better, safer, and more productive (McDonough and Braungart 2002b). Monoculture, for example, was a practice developed during the early part of the twentieth century in an attempt to make farming more efficient by working a single, primary crop. Yet, as Janine Benyus describes in *Biomimicry* (1997), farming a single crop (monoculture) not only removed the diversity of plants, animals, and insects that controlled pests and other natural threats such as molds and fungi but also provided a veritable feast for insects that fed on a particular crop, now the only plant for acres and acres. The chemical industry, thus, became prolific in its development of herbicides and pesticides. And agriculturalists and farmers, thus, became prolific in their use of these chemicals to control weeds and pests that threatened their crops. Not until the publication of Rachel Carson's *Silent Spring* (1962) were the dangers of unquestioned practices such as large-scale spraying of agricultural products revealed to the public and to lawmakers. Carson is recognized as a pioneer of the environmental movement, as someone whose work helped set the stage for successive passage of federal legislation that included clean air and water acts as well as creation of the Environmental Protection Agency (EPA). The consequence of such legislation, however, was regulation rather than elimination of substances that are harmful to human and environmental health. Companies, for example, are required to report to the EPA the amount of pollutants that they release into the environment. They are not required to eliminate pollutants from their emissions. And if the reported amount exceeds the level determined to be acceptable by the EPA, the company will be fined and, perhaps, forced to clean up the site. The purpose of regulation, then, is only to determine the level to which pollution is acceptable. McDonough and Braungart (2002c; 2004) describe this regulatory process as a "signal of design failure."

Design failure occurs when a product, for example, in any stage of its life, creates a condition that is harmful to human or environmental health. A regulatory process that only requires compliance with low levels of emissions does not foster examination of the fundamental design flaws that created pollutants initially. That is, if a company can restrict the flow of pollutants that leave its plant, then it is in regulatory compliance with little (or no) incentive to examine or redesign the process to prevent the development of harmful substances. Regulations, then, only assure practice that is "less bad" (McDonough and Braungart 2002c). And being "less bad" is not the same as being good. Recently, even this practice of "less bad" through regulation is being challenged by reports that previously acceptable (low) levels of pollution also are significantly harmful to human and environmental health (Waldman 2005).

The consequence of efforts to reduce, reuse, recycle, and regulate (see McDonough and Braungart 2002c) may be described best as "take less, make (and use) less, waste less" (GreenBlue 2005). We may take less material if we reuse. We may make (and use) less material if we reduce. We may waste less if we recycle. We may experience fewer health-related issues if we poison more slowly through regulation. In other words, if we become more efficient in our use of materials, more efficient in our production, then the impact upon human and environmental

Figure 4-6
Gordon Turner, grandfather of the author, in his stand of soybeans in Gretna, Virginia, 1967.

health will be narrowed. Yet this type of efficiency, known as "eco-efficiency" (McDonough and Braungart 2002c), is a weak attempt to manage the conflict between the environment and industrial activity. Further, eco-efficiency serves only to slow industry as well as to curb economic growth as companies try to do the same or more with less. And slowing industry and curbing growth are unacceptable strategies in an industrial age (McDonough and Braungart 2002g).

In summary, a confluence of conditions and events that began in the latter part of the nineteenth century and persists into the twenty-first century are realized in a destructive, linear, cradle-to-grave design scenario characterized by:

- industrial processes that strip the earth of materials;
- one-time use of materials that are engorged with inherent value including time, money, and energy;
- increasing use of fossil fuels that emit carbon dioxide to sustain industrial activity in an industrial age;
- a steady increase in the concentration of carbon dioxide that is changing the composition of the earth's atmosphere;
- rising levels of greenhouse gases that lead to global warming; and
- pervasive signals of design failure such as material graves, down-cycling, and regulations to control acceptable levels of harm to human and environmental health.

Collectively, these conditions describe a "strategy of tragedy." Although perhaps an unintended outcome of an unintended strategy, the consequence is nonetheless tragic. The survival of the planet, our survival, is dependent upon a strategy of change. McDonough (2003a) describes the new design strategy this way: "By design, we can create a new world, a world of sustaining prosperity in which materials are nutritious, growth is good, and human activity supports all life." This alternative strategy is cradle-to-cradle design.

Cradle to Cradle

Cradle-to-cradle design, in contrast with cradle-to-grave design, does not use nature as a tool but, rather, as a model (McDonough and Braungart 2002c). As a consequence, cradle-to-cradle design is not linear but cyclic, inspired by the cycles of the natural world and modeled after them. Cradle-to-cradle design is characterized by flows of energy and nutrients—the life-giving energy of the sun, organisms that feed other organisms, closed-loop cycles in which the waste of one process becomes fuel for another. This approach to design celebrates the diversity of components that characterize healthy systems and may result from either natural or human activity. Cradle-to-cradle design also involves stewardship—of the planet; of product design, engineering, and manufacturing; and of those who make the product and those who use it. The intention of cradle-to-cradle design is to apply design intelligence and ecological intelligence to the development of products or facilities, and to the processes necessary for their manufacture. To do so generates designs that are of economic, ecologic, and social value and affirms a healthy relationship between human activity and the natural world (McDonough 2002; McDonough and Braungart 2002e). The basis of cradle-to-cradle design is expressed in three key principles of natural systems: waste equals food, solar income, and diversity (McDonough and Braungart 2002c; McDonough et al. 2003).

WASTE EQUALS FOOD: BIOLOGICAL METABOLISM

Regenerative cycles of nature occur because its products, its objects, are composed of organic compounds that contribute continuously to the health of the ecosystem (e.g., McDonough and Braungart 2002c; 2002g). This is a cycle with which we are very familiar. A deer, for example, may eat an apple from the limb of a tree but drop part of the core to the ground. Other smaller animals, insects, organisms, and microorganisms feed on the fruit from the tree that is now on the ground. Whatever is left eventually biodegrades, deteriorating into nutrients that provide fuel (fertilizer) that supports the life of the tree. *Waste* generated at any point along this continuum becomes nourishment for other organisms and for the tree. McDonough and Braungart (2002c) describe this cycle of growth and deterioration as a "biological metabolism." Products of a biological metabolism are viewed as products of consumption because at the end of their useful life they are consumed in a manner that provides food for another process—the tree produced the fruit that ultimately provided nourishment to the tree to produce more fruit. But biological nutrients do not have to be only products of nature. Biological nutrients may also be products of industrial activity.

McDonough and Braungart (e.g., 2002c) describe the experience of working with a textile company to develop a fabric that is a biological nutrient, one that can be discarded into a compost pile and consumed by the many organisms and microorganisms in the natural environment. The company had recently been informed by its government that the trimmings from the fabric were toxic to the environment. (Interestingly, the fabric inside the trimmings, which was sold and distributed to consumers for use in upholstery, was not flagged as toxic because it was not discarded by the factory and, thus, not measured by the government.) After an investigation of all materials and substances used in the manufacturing and dyeing processes, fibers and chemicals were chosen not only because of the toxic qualities they did *not* possess but because of the positive ones they *did* possess. Pesticide-free wool and ramie, for example, were chosen because of their nontoxic properties but also because the combination of the fibers would make a fabric that was strong and would wick moisture and permit air to move through the fabric (allowing it to "breathe"). The 8,000 chemicals typically used in the manufacture of textiles were eliminated from consideration, and the 38 that were considered "nutritious" were used in the creation of the entire fabric line. The results were manifold: the fabric was beautiful and strong; the need for regulation was eliminated; factory workers no longer wore gloves and masks necessary to protect them from toxins associated previously with the fabrics; space at the factory for storing hazardous

Figure 4-7
Rohmer textile that is a biological nutrient. Courtesy of William McDonough.

chemicals was freed for recreational use and work space; and at the end of the fabric's useful life as upholstery, it could be taken from the furniture and used as compost or fertilizer.

WASTE EQUALS FOOD: TECHNICAL METABOLISM

Similarly to the regenerative, closed-loop cycles of the biological metabolism is the technical metabolism that is fueled by processes of industrial activity (see McDonough and Braungart 2002c; 2002g). Synthetic materials such as nylons and mineral resources, including gold, circulate continuously within a technical cycle, providing "food" for successive, high-value products. Critical to the technical metabolism is production, use, recovery, and remanufacture of valuable materials (McDonough, Braungart, et al. 2003). Contrary to down-cycling, which reduces the value of a material in a cradle-to-grave scenario, "up-cycling" is a process in cradle-to-cradle design that makes a material more valuable. A particular nylon fiber used in carpet, for example, may be retrieved and transformed into a more valuable material, a fiber that is "inherently stain resistant, inherently colorfast, and infinitely recyclable" (McDonough and Braungart 2001). In this way, the fiber is not *de-* but *re-*materialized, bringing with it the time, energy, money, and materials used to generate it initially, and providing a *raw* material that is fully prepared for remanufacture.

Figure 4-8
Shaw carpet, a technical nutrient.
Courtesy of William McDonough.

Because materials in a technical metabolism are never consumed, products of a technical metabolism are meant to continuously circulate. McDonough and Braungart (2002c) refer to these as "products of service." Designed as technical nutrients in a closed-loop cycle, products of service conceivably could be taken back by the company that manufactured them, and their material reclaimed (McDonough and Braungart 2002c). Some manufacturers in the carpet industry, for example, have programs in which they take back carpet from consumers when the carpet is worn and at the end of its first useful life (McDonough and Braungart 2003b). With an effective reclamation system, carpet may be separated from its backing and the fiber and backing remanufactured into a new carpet product. This type of reclamation system enables "material banks" or "pools" of materials that companies own and maintain, never losing their investment in the initial or subsequent development of materials nor constantly investing time, energy, and money to generate new material (McDonough and Braungart 2003a). In addition to this financial gain from material banks, companies would further profit from the cost of services their products offer. That is, companies would not sell the carpet, losing forever their investment in its initial development. Companies would "lease" the carpet, profiting from its service as a floor covering.

These principles of maintaining material pools and "leasing" products apply also to design for disassembly, a system that enables reclamation of parts to be used in the next iteration of products (McDonough and Braungart 2003a). This is a reality for some furniture manufacturers, taking back chairs, for example, that become worn and reusing the component parts in the making of new chairs (McDonough and Braungart 2002e). Design for disassembly is being pursued also in the automobile industry and is the law in some parts of Europe (McDonough and Braungart 2002h).

These closed-loop cycles describe the continuous flow of natural or synthetic nutrients into their respective biological and technical metabolisms. Their cyclic processes are built upon the smallest component parts of the systems: molecules and microorganisms. But cradle-to-cradle design encompasses natural flows far beyond the microlevel of materials and substances, extending to the level of the planet.

SOLAR INCOME

The second principle of natural systems that forms the foundation for cradle-to-cradle design regards the use of solar income (McDonough and Braungart 2002c). At one level, this is as obvious as it appears: harvesting the energy of the sun, using active or passive solar processes to generate heat, energy, and lighting. In Boulder (Colorado) Community Foothills Hospital, for example, daylighting is used primarily to light the central, two-story entry space. But solar income is not limited to immediate solar gain.

Figure 4-9
Upper foyer of Boulder Community Foothills Hospital, Boulder, Colorado.

The warmth of the sun also interacts with the geology of the surface of the earth to generate geothermal energy, which can be used a source of power, heat, or hot water (U.S. Department of Energy 2001). Wind energy also is a form of solar energy generated by the heat of the sun, which creates reliable circulation patterns in the earth's atmosphere, and these natural flows also may be harvested by windmills as sources of energy. Other forms of renewable energy impacted by solar income are biomass generated by plant material that has been fueled by the sun and hydrogen, which can be produced from renewable energy resources such as solar radiation (President's National Science and Technology Council 1993).

Figure 4-10
Nature and the built environment in Tivoli, Italy.

Figure 4-11
Overhangs at Boulder (Colorado)
Community Foothills Hospital
prepared to receive or deflect
the sun.

These energy systems are characterized by relationships among flows of sun and wind against an array of landforms, hydrology, and vegetation. From these components, we have the strength of solar income and currents of air and water, and we have changes in landscape and vegetation. These are discrete and diverse, but collectively they contribute to a system that is regenerative. The interdependent, reciprocal effects of components characterize natural systems that can serve as models by which to consider the relationship between the environment and human activity and human habitation. If solar heat and wind complement each other, for example, then so should the environment and human habitation. Organism and environment complement each other or "fit" when the relationships between the diversity of forms in the system are regenerative.

Figure 4-12
Regional materials used inside and out of Boulder Community Foothills Hospital.

CELEBRATE DIVERSITY

The third design principle of natural systems that is central to cradle-to-cradle design is diversity (McDonough and Braungart 2002c; McDonough, Braungart, et al. 2003). Clearly, ecosystems survive and healthy ecosystems thrive because of the unique industries of the resident organisms, which complement the work of other living organisms within the natural community. Without diversity, as we have seen, for example, in the agricultural industry (Benyus 1997), crops are vulnerable to unchecked invasion of plants and insects as well as to weather conditions that uproot or flatten plants, revealing the weaknesses of mono-root systems, which are precluded from intertwining with other types of plant systems.

In the built environment, diversity is realized when knowledge of a place, its natural flows and distinctive landscape, is understood and incorporated into the decisions regarding human habitation. This suggests, for example, positioning a

Figure 4-13
*Eco-effectiveness. Courtesy of
William McDonough.*

structure to take advantage of sun, wind, water, and vegetation. It suggests careful selection of materials that are not only safe and restorative but local, thereby assuring the fit of the organism within the environment (McDonough et al. 2003). Inclusion of such a structure is to give a sense of nativeness to a place, a condition that engages inhabitants and materials in a dialogue with a natural world (McDonough and Braungart 2002b). The resulting community not only sustains and enhances the qualities of the landscape but enjoys an environment that is healthy for human inhabitants and the natural world. This is ecologically intelligent design.

ECO-EFFECTIVENESS

Fundamental to ecological intelligence is recognizing the interdependence of natural systems and processes (see McDonough and Braungart 2002b). Through recognition, we become informed via the language of the landscape, its terrain, its climate, its inhabitants, its natural flows—and we cannot help but see its effectiveness. There is no waste. There are no power lines. There are abundant flows of nutrients and energies. There is a plethora of animals and plants, copious numbers of organisms that have yet to be "discovered," such an abundance of life forms that it is difficult to comprehend (McDonough and Braungart 2002g). But such fecundity suggests inefficiency—so many animals, so many trees, so many types of ants. But efficiency is not a condition of natural systems and processes—effectiveness is. McDonough and Braungart (2002g) use a cherry tree to illustrate this principle:

Each spring [the cherry tree] produces thousands of blossoms, only a few of which germinate, take root and grow. Who would see cherry blossoms piling

Figure 4-14
Constructed wetland at Boulder Community Foothills Hospital.

up on the ground and think, "How inefficient and wasteful"? The tree's abundance is useful and safe. After falling to the ground, the blossoms return to the soil and become nutrients for the surrounding environment. Every last particle contributes in some way to the health of a thriving ecosystem. Waste that stays waste does not exist. Instead, waste nourishes; waste equals food.

McDonough and Braungart describe the effectiveness of natural systems and processes such as those characteristic of the cherry tree as "eco-effective design." Eco-effectiveness is a cradle-to-cradle design strategy directed toward products, whether buildings or fabrics, for example, that have safe and regenerative impacts on the environment (McDonough and Braungart 2002b). In contrast to eco-effectiveness is eco-efficiency, a strategy discussed previously that manages only to slow the negative effects of cradle-to-grave design through reducing, reusing, recycling, and regulating—in other words, being efficient. Designs that are eco-effective create an abundance of nutrients, biological and technical, that provide continuously valuable materials, as does nature. Eco-effectiveness is a design strategy based on the idea that "nothing exceeds the effectiveness of the earth's natural cycles" (McDonough and Braungart 2002f).

Products and buildings modeled after naturally occurring effective systems enable us to experience the reemergence of nature in our daily lives and to celebrate responsive, fruitful relationships with our surroundings (McDonough and Braungart 2001). For example, when planners of the Boulder Community Foothills Hospital realized that a wetland would be impacted by placement of the facility, they created a wetland that was eight times as large in another part of the site. Native water plants and animals have since inhabited the wetland. In another area of the same site, a prairie dog colony was relocated rather than destroyed, and existing colonies were preserved. And as the prairie dogs maintained their community, they provided frolicking entertainment for the patients recovering in their rooms.

Thus, using nature as a model, cradle-to-cradle design acknowledges the interdependence of component parts of healthy natural systems such as wetland and animal habitats, prairie dog and human habitats. Importantly, this practice of eco-effectiveness applies not only to organisms in natural ecosystems but also to the component parts of business and industry. McDonough and Braungart (2002c; 2002d) represent three commercial interests—economy, ecology, and social equity—in a "fractal triangle" that is based on eco-effectiveness.

ECONOMY, ECOLOGY, EQUITY

Concerns regarding economy (such as company profits) and ecology (the environment) are often in opposition. In other instances, economy might conflict with social equity or social equity conflict with environmental interests. As a design strategy, eco-effectiveness values the interdependence of natural systems as well as that of economy, ecology, and equity (McDonough and Braungart 2002a; 2002d). To illustrate, an economic interest that is achieved at the expense of environmental or social concerns might damage the human and natural resources necessary to make the economic interest viable. An example of this might be heap-leach mining, in which the economic interest of retrieving an ounce of gold destroys the landscape and sickens the local population because of air, soil, and water contamination incurred by the mining process (Heeter and Tuller 2005; Sanders 2005). To achieve an eco-effective approach that celebrates commerce while nurturing human and natural resources requires an exercise that assesses the interests of one sector with the interests the others.

If my interests as a corporate official are purely economic, the questions that I would bring to the design process would primarily concern wealth such as

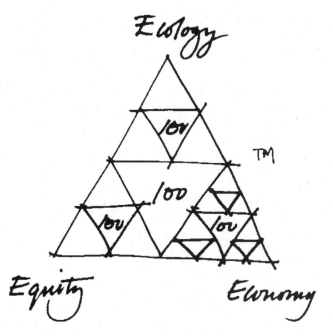

Figure 4-15
Fractal triangle by William McDonough and Michael Braungart. Courtesy of William McDonough.

company profits, the value of company shares, and the bottom-line costs of operations. I might ask, for example: how much money are we making from the gold we are mining? But when I balance interest in one sector against another, such as economy and equity, the questions shift to concerns of money and fairness—whether employees are earning a wage on which they can live or support a family, for example, or whether men and women were paid equitably.

If my interests were focused on equity or social justice and fairness, decisions about my company's business practices might concern primarily whether my employees and people of the community were treated respectfully. Issues of racism, sexism, and age discrimination would be paramount in our decision making. But when I balance concerns of equity with those of the environment, questions shift, for example, to whether I am exposing my employees or the community to toxic emissions within or outside the workplace environment. I would consider also the long-term effects of the product I was manufacturing: Will it poison future generations? Does it pollute groundwater? Is it fair to do so? Will it end its brief albeit useful life in a landfill? Incinerator? Sealed earthen tomb?

Purely ecological interests would reflect whether I had followed nature's laws, for example, and whether my practice was sustainable to current and future generations of all living organisms, no matter how large or small, complex or simple. Financial concerns enter the picture when I consider ecology and economy: Does my practice enable healthy financial and environmental systems? Do I have a product that is profitable, fruitful for my business interests and that cultivates a healthy environment?

An eco-effective approach to decision making regarding business or practice honors economy, ecology, and equity equally. Rather than searching for a balance or compromise between these three sectors, an eco-effective approach recognizes the value of the interdependence among the sectors that collectively enriches opportunities that are at once economic, ecologic, and equitable. A consequence of this process is a "world of commercial productivity, cultural wealth, and ecological intelligence" (McDonough 2003b). A product of an eco-effective approach is the River Rouge plant in Detroit, Michigan.

ECO-EFFECTIVE DESIGN

In May 1999 the Ford Motor Company began the process of renovating one of its largest manufacturing plants; antiquated, dilapidated, and deteriorating (see McDonough and Braungart 2002d), it was described as "ground zero" for the First Industrial Revolution (Louv 2005). The design process for the River Rouge plant used the fractal triangle to explore the plant's economic, ecologic, and equitable value (McDonough and Braungart 2002d). The result is a 450,000-square-foot manufacturing facility that profitably produces Ford F-150 pickup trucks under the largest green roof on record. Native birds have claimed their stake on the roof, and employees of the plant, some on break from assembly lines, have taken to birdcalling (Braungart and McDonough 2004). The roof not only provides habitat for native plants and animals but insulates the building and filters rainwater

Figure 4-16
Green roof at the River Rouge plant of Ford Motor Company in Detroit, Michigan. Courtesy of William McDonough.

Figure 4-17
Nesting at the River Rouge plant.
Courtesy of William McDonough.

while making oxygen and sequestering carbon—in other words, it is regenerative. Rainwater not collected in the green roof combines with water that has filtered through the porous pavement in the parking lots and is used in other parts of the facility. The grounds are planted with thousands of flowers, shrubs, and trees, and vines are expected to one day completely cover the exterior walls. The interior of. the plant, which is flooded with daylight, boasts wider aisles for employees in the assembly area and includes features such as platforms that raise and lower the trucks to reduce stretching and fatigue (Hammonds 2004).

The River Rouge plant illustrates a design process that resulted in prosperity in terms of commerce, the environment, and the social community, which includes those who work in the plant and those who live with the plant. Critics note that this plant, beneath a green roof, produces trucks not known for fuel efficiency. And criticism extends to the designers who work within such a hypocritical condition. Yet McDonough and Braungart reply that industry such as one based on fossil fuels is exactly the kind of industry with which they should be working. And Ford Motor Company maintains that this building and related changes in the production process indicate a shift by the company toward more responsible stewardship (Hammonds 2004). Not coincidentally, Ford recently introduced a hybrid SUV.

The renovation of the River Rouge plant is an example of a business generating revenue in all three sectors: economy, ecology, and equity. It is an example of eco-effective design that illustrates application of ecological intelligence in a condition that utilizes closed-loop metabolisms and solar income and that honors diversity and life. It is cradle-to-cradle design.

Conclusion

Human activity and ingenuity enabled a form of industrial "progress" that separated us from nature. From an assumption that nature provided capital for our use in the development of substances and materials forged into objects to serve our whims and needs, we developed a linear, one-way flow that was contrary to nature and harmful in many ways to human and environmental health. In contrast, the cyclic flow of energy and nutrients characteristic of a cradle-to-cradle scenario mimics the regenerative processes of nature and provides a strategy for change, a strategy for hope. McDonough (2005) describes it this way: "We seek a delightfully diverse, safe, healthy, and just world: with clean air, soil, water, and power; economically, ecologically, and elegantly enjoyed. Period." To help us accomplish this, McDonough (2004c) leaves us with a new design assignment, one that will:

- introduce no hazardous materials into the air, water, or soil;
- measure prosperity by how much we enhance the positive effects of the human footprint;
- measure productivity by how many people are gainfully and meaningfully employed;
- measure progress by how many buildings have no smokestacks or dangerous effluents;
- not require regulations whose purpose is to stop us from killing ourselves too quickly;
- produce nothing that will require future generations to maintain constant vigilance;
- generate more energy than is consumed;
- make every building a life-support system; and
- celebrate the abundance of biological and cultural diversity and renewable energy.

This assignment generates the Next Industrial Revolution.

THE HANNOVER PRINCIPLES

The following sustainable principles were presented at Expo 2000, the World's Fair in Hannover, Germany, celebrating the dawning of the millennium.
The principles articulate the foundation for cradle-to-cradle design and compile, collectively, a living document intended to evolve with new ideas and practices.

1. *Insist on the right of humanity and nature to co-exist* in a healthy, supportive, diverse, and sustainable condition.

2. *Recognize interdependence.* The elements of human design interact with and depend upon the natural world, with broad and diverse implications at every scale. Expand design considerations to recognize even distant effects.

3. *Respect relationships between spirit and matter.* Consider all aspects of human settlement, including community, dwelling, industry, and trade, in terms of existing and evolving connections between spiritual and material consciousness.

4. *Accept responsibility for the consequences of design decisions* upon human well-being, the viability of natural systems, and their right to co-exist.

5. *Create safe objects of long-term value.* Do not burden future generations with requirements for maintenance or vigilant administration of potential dangers due to the careless creation of products, processes, or standards.

6. *Eliminate the concept of waste.* Evaluate and optimize the full life cycle of products and processes to approach the state of natural systems, in which there is no waste.

7. *Rely on natural energy flows.* Human designs should, like the living world, derive their creative force from perpetual solar income. Incorporate this energy efficiently and safely for responsible use.

8. *Understand the limitations of design.* No human creation lasts forever, and design does not solve all problems. Those who create and plan should practice humility in the face of nature. Treat nature as a model and mentor, not as an inconvenience to be evaded or controlled.

9. *Seek constant improvement by the sharing of knowledge.* Encourage direct and open communication between colleagues, patrons, manufacturers, and users to link long-term sustainable considerations with ethical responsibility and to reestablish the integral relationship between natural processes and human activity.

Source: MCDONOUGH (2004A).

References

Ackerman and Massey. 2003. *The Economics of Phasing Out PVC.* Report to the Global Development and Environment Institute at Tufts University, Somerville, MA.

Benyus, J. 1997. *Biomimicry: Innovation inspired by nature.* New York: HarperCollins.

Bergman, L., and J. Perlez (reporters). 2005. *Peru: The curse of Inca gold.* Produced by Nelli Black. New York: A Frontline/World Co-Production with *The New York Times.*

Braungart, M., and W. McDonough. 2004. *World of Abundance* (keynote address). EnvrionDesign8, April 2004, Minneapolis, MN.

Carson, R. 1962. *Silent spring.* Boston: Houghton Mifflin.

Daly, H. 2000. *Farewell speech.* Whirled Bank Group.

GreenBlue. 2005. *Introduction to cradle to cradle design.* Pre-conference workshop presented to the Interior Design Educators Council, Savannah, GA.

Hammonds, D. 2004. Greener, literally: Ford's better ideas for newest plant include grass-covered roof, pollution-eating plants. *Post-Gazette.*

Heeter, C., and D. Tuller. 2005. *The toxic shimmer of gold* (documentary). New York: PBS/Frontline.

Jacka, T. H. 1993. *Antarctic ice cores and environmental damage.* Australian Antarctic Division

Louv, R. 2005. "Revolution II saves Earth." *San Diego Union-Tribune*

McDonough, W. 2002. *Buildings like trees, cities like forests.*

———. 2003a. *Celebrating human artifice.*

———. 2003b. *Toward a future of energy effectiveness.*

———. 2004a. Principles, practices, and sustainable design: Toward a new context for building codes. Retrieved November 8, 2005 from W. McDonough's Web site: http://www.mcdonough.com/writings/ principles_practices_and.htm.

———. 2004b. "Teaching design that goes from cradle to cradle." *Chronicle of Higher Education*

———. 2004c. *Twenty-first century design.*

———. 2005. *Thinking big and small: Designing the next industrial revolution.* San Francisco: Sierra Club.

McDonough, W., and M. Braungart. 2001. Five steps towards reinventing the world: Step four: Entering the realm of true eco-effectiveness. Green@work

———. 2002a. A building like a tree, a campus like a forest: Sustainable design comes to New England higher education. *Connection: The Journal of New England Board of Higher Education* 13 (1): 16–18.

———. 2002b. *A new geography of hope: landscape, design, and the renewal of ecological intelligence.*

———. 2002c. *Cradle to cradle: Remaking the way we may things.* New York: North Point Press.

———. 2002d. *Designing for the triple top line: New tools for sustainable commerce.*

———. 2002e. Eco-intelligence: The anatomy of transformation: Herman Miller's journey to sustainability with MBDC. Green@work

———. 2002f. Eco-intelligence: The promise of nylon 6. Green@work

———. 2002g. The extravagant gesture: Nature, design, and the transformation of human industry. In *Sustainable planet: Solutions for the 21st century,* ed. J. B. Schor and B. Taylor. Boston: Beacon Press.

———. 2002h. *Transforming the textile industry: Victor innovatex, eco-intelligent polyester and the next industrial revolution.*

———. 2003a. *Intelligent materials pooling: Evolving a profitable metabolism through a supportive business community.*

———. 2003b. Regulation and re-design: Tapping innovation and creativity to preserve the commons. Green@work.

———. 2004. The guardian reborn: A new government role in environmental protection. In *Environmentalism and the technologies of tomorrow: Shaping the next industrial revolution,* eds. R. Olson and D. Rejeski. Washington, DC: Island Press.

McDonough, W., M. Braungart, P. Anastas, and J. Zimmerman. 2003. Applying the principles of green engineering to cradle-to-cradle design. *Environmental science and technology* 37: 434–441.

Palfreman, J. (writer, producer, and director). 2000. *What's up with the weather?* (documentary). New York: NOVA/Frontline.

President's National Science and Technology Council. 1993. *Why hydrogen?* Washington, DC: President's National Science and Technology Council.

Sanders, E. 2005. Where others mined wealth, Congo villagers scrape living. *Los Angeles Times.*

Scripps Institute of Oceanography. 2005. *Climate science power: Charles David Keeling.* Institute of Oceanography

Steinbrager, S. 2004. *The pirates of Illiopolis: Why your kitchen floor may pose a threat to national security.* Orion.

Titanic and Other White Star Ships. 2005. *Technical facts about the Titanic.*

U.S. EPA (Environmental Protection Agency). 2005. *Municipal Solid Waste.* Washington, DC: EPA.

U.S. Department of Energy. 2001. *Nature's power: Increasing America's use of renewable and alternative energy.* Washington, DC: U.S. Department of Energy.

Waldman, P. 2005. Common industrial chemicals in tiny doses raise health issue. *The Wall Street Journal,* July 25, A1.

Zadorozhnaja, T. D., R. E. Little, R. K. Miller, N. A. Mendel, et al. 2000. Concentrations of arsenic, cadmium, copper, lead, mercury, and zinc in human placentas from two cities in Ukraine. *Journal of Toxicology and Environmental Health* 61: 255–263.

PART TWO

Indoor Environmental Quality

CHAPTER FIVE

Indoor Air Quality

Linda Nussbaumer, PhD

Introduction

Beginning in the 1940s, poor indoor air quality was causing an illness that doctors did not understand. It was known by names such as environmental illness, chemical hypersensitivity, and total allergy, among others. Because it was not well understood, it was sometimes thought to be more psychological than physiological. Today, this illness is most commonly known as *multiple chemical sensitivity* (MCS), and it is an illness in which the individual reports sensitivity to numerous chemicals and other irritants at very low levels of concentration. Exposure can affect one or more of the body's organ systems (EPA 2003). The major cause of MCS is poor *indoor air quality* (IAQ). Indoor air quality refers to the condition of the air inside buildings, including the extent of pollution caused by smoking, dust mites, mold spores, and radon and other gases, including chemicals off-gassed from construction materials, furnishings, finishes, and equipment (EPA 1995).

Sick Building Syndrome

Poor indoor air quality is also related to *sick building syndrome* (SBS), which is defined as a variety of symptoms (e.g., cough, runny nose, inflamed and/or itchy eyes, sore throat, headache, etc.) affecting some of a building's occupants while they are in the building. Although the symptoms cannot be traced to specific pollutants or sources within the building, nor can a specific illness be identified, they diminish or disappear when people with SBS leave the building (EPA 2007). One difference between MCS and SBS is that individuals with MCS will continue to experience symptoms after they have left a building.

OTHER IAQ-RELATED ILLNESSES

In addition to MCS and SBS, many people experience allergic reactions in particular interior environments. People with asthma may also find that they are more likely to have an episode in a particular interior environment. Both situations are related to poor IAQ. The exact chemical that is responsible for the reaction may never be identified. However, places where the allergy or asthma episode occurs can be identified. Careful notation of time, place, and activity for a sufficiently long period of time will help to identify any patterns and provide information that will permit the individual to identify and modify or avoid the interior environment that is related to the allergic or asthmatic episode. It must be noted that environments not associated with allergic or asthmatic episodes may still be problematic for people with MCS or SBS, as they may react at lower levels of the reagent.

CHEMICAL TRIGGERS

Chemicals may trigger symptoms of MCS or SBS. However, SBS is an acute illness, whereas MCS is a chronic condition. Therefore, exposure to chemicals may trigger symptoms of MCS and is of grave concern. Exposures may occur in one of two ways. The individual may be exposed to high doses of a chemical in a short time period and then become ill, or exposure may take place in two phases. First, the individual may be exposed to low doses of a chemical over a long period of time; later, the individual may be exposed to a different chemical that triggers the symptoms of MCS or SBS. Although MCS is not well understood, some researchers think that exposure to a particular chemical may cause a synergistic reaction. One chemical mixing with another chemical creates a volatile reaction with the body (Bower 2000). It is similar to the reaction that occurs when two potent chemicals are inadvertently mixed (e.g., alcohol and barbiturates or ammonia and chlorine bleach).

Chemicals that trigger symptoms of MCS or SBS include volatile organic compounds (VOCs) and petrochemical fuels. Volatile organic compounds become a gas or vaporize at room temperature (EPA 2003). These compounds are either natural or synthetic organic compounds (Godish 2001). Petrochemical fuels include diesel, gasoline, and kerosene (EPA 1994). See Table 5.1 for a list of such chemicals.

Almost any product that contains chemicals can trigger symptoms of MCS or SBS. Common products include a variety of household products, such as latex, tobacco smoke, personal care products, or chemical dyes. Many materials used in construction, as well as finishes and furnishings, contain chemicals that can cause illness. Table 5.2 includes a partial list of such products.

Products that are ingested can also cause MCS or SBS symptoms. Table 5.3 identifies products that can trigger MCS or SBS when ingested.

Exposure to chemicals may take place in a variety of areas. For example, exposure can take place in communities with high air or water pollution or in airtight buildings with poor IAQ. The cleaning products used by custodians can be the culprit. Exposure can also take place in unique situations, such as when pesticides are sprayed at the individual's work site or home, or when the lawn or any adjacent farm fields are fertilized, treated for insects or fungus control, or sprayed to kill weeds.

Table 5.1 Chemicals That Can Trigger MCS or SBS

Category	Chemical
Naturally occurring gases	Chlorine
	Fluorine
Landfill emissions	
Animal waste emissions	
Petrochemical fuels	Diesel
	Gasoline
	Kerosene
	Oil
Petroleum-based products	
Volatile organic compounds (VOCs)	Formaldehyde
	Pesticides
	Solvents
	Cleaning agents

Source: EPA (2003).

Table 5.2 Products and Materials That Contain Chemicals That Can Trigger Multiple Chemical Sensitivity (MCS) or Sick Building Syndrome (SBS)

Building Materials and Furnishings

Plywood	Paint	Pressed wood furniture
Fiberboard	Finishes	Solvents
Particleboard	Carpet and other adhesives	Veneered wood (e.g., paneling)

Graphics and Craft Materials

Adhesives	Permanent markers
Glues	Photographic solutions

Household Products

Air fresheners	Fabric softeners	Potpourri
Detergents and soaps	Plastics	Scented candles
Cleaning products	Waxes	Food preservatives

Office and Paper Products

Carbonless paper	Correction fluid	Laser printer
Copy machine	Ink	Newsprint

(*Continued*)

Table 5.2   (*Continued*)

Personal Care Products

Aftershaves	Nail polishes and removers	Hair-styling products
Colognes	Perfumes	Shampoos
Deodorants	Scented body products	Soaps
Toothpastes	Hair sprays	Hair dyes and colorings

Textile-Related Products

Dry-cleaning solvents	Mattress ticking	Vinyl shower curtains
Latex	Mothballs	Synthetic textiles
Permanent press clothing	Carpet-cleaning products	Stain-repellant finishes

Vehicle-Related Materials and Products

Car exhausts	Plastic off-gassings	Interior textiles

Other

Chlorinated water	Fumes from road tar
Fumes from roof tar	Tobacco smoke

Source: EPA (1995).

Table 5.3   Ingested Products That Can Trigger Symptoms of MCS or SBS

Alcohol	Food preservatives
Artificial colorings	Synthetic food sweeteners
Caffeine	Medicines, including aspirin
Artificial flavorings	Synthetic vitamins
Food additives	Chocolate

Sources: Rea (1994), Rea et al. (1992), and WebMD (2007).

Appropriate Materials and Products

To improve conditions for individuals with chemical sensitivities, materials and products must be carefully researched prior to specification. Even after specifying the appropriate material, the appropriate installation and maintenance of the material and/or product is essential.

SOFT FLOOR COVERING: CARPET

One of the most common floor coverings, carpet is used in both residential and nonresidential applications. Carpet is made from natural or synthetic fibers. Natural fibers include wool, cotton, or jute, and commonly used synthetic fibers include nylon, polyester, olefin, or polypropylene.

Carpeting is a major source of triggering agents for individuals with MCS or SBS. Sometimes the fiber, carpet pad, or adhesive that contains the chemical, and often the finishes (e.g., chemicals used for color, stain resistance, or static control), trigger complaints from those with MCS or SBS. At other times, poor maintenance is responsible for complaints, because dust, dirt, mold, fungus, and/or mildew in carpeting or its backing can trigger symptoms. When designers specify carpet, they should begin by contacting the carpet manufacture for information on low-emitting carpet as well as recommendations for carpet pads and adhesives that have been shown to be safe in most instances. Additional information regarding carpet materials, IAQ, and "green-label" testing may be found at the Carpet and Rug Institute Web site: www.carpet-rug.com.

Figure 5-1
The lobby of the Kelley Engineering Center at Oregon State University, Corvallis, Oregon, by Yost Grube Hall Architecture, features area rugs, which define the lounge space, rather than wall-to-wall carpeting to reduce the emission of harmful chemicals. Photo by Pete Eckert, Eckert & Eckert.

To prevent the emission of chemicals during carpet installation, the method of installation is important. Prior to installation, the new carpet should be unrolled and allowed to off-gas in a clean, well-ventilated area. Once installation begins, individuals with MCS should neither enter the space during the installation nor immediately after the installation. This will allow time for any toxins that are released to be emitted from the space. During the installation, opening doors and windows will, in most instances, increase the quantity of fresh air; this will also reduce the exposure of installers and other occupants to chemicals that are off-gassed from newly installed carpet. After installation, window fans and room air conditioners can continue to increase the quantity of fresh air as well as exhaust the noxious gases to the outdoors. It is important to have ventilation systems in proper working order and in continuous operation during installation and for 48 to 72 hours after installation (EPA 1994). Once the carpet is installed, the designer should recommend chemical-free cleaning products and work with the client to create a maintenance schedule.

SOFT FLOOR COVERING: AREA RUGS

Area rugs are popular and can be used over hard or resilient surfaces. In areas where carpeting will receive heavy traffic, an easily cleaned area rug (e.g., one made of olefin) is the best choice. Where there is less traffic, the area-rug fiber choices should be researched in a method similar to that used for broadloom carpet research.

HARD SURFACE FLOOR COVERING: WOOD

Wood flooring must be specified with care. Processed wood often contains formaldehyde, which should be avoided; the Environmental Protection Agency (EPA) has recently recognized formaldehyde as carcinogenic. The best choice is solid wood flooring with a water-based, ultraviolet-cured finish that is applied in the factory (AIA 1997; Riggs 2003).

HARD SURFACE FLOOR COVERING: TILE, STONE, ETC.

A hard floor covering such as stone, ceramic, or porcelain tile is one of the best floor-covering choices for individuals with MCS. These coverings are solid and inert and, thus, durable, and safe for people with MCS, as they will not emit toxic gases into the interior (AIA 1997). However, care must be taken that the grouting is not artificially colored or treated to resist staining, because it may contain reagents.

RESILIENT FLOOR COVERING

Resilient floor coverings include vinyl tile, sheet vinyl, and linoleum. Vinyl tile and sheet vinyl contain polyvinyl chloride (PVC), which is a product that negatively affects (1) IAQ, through VOC emissions, and (2) the environment, because it is nonbiodegradable. On the other hand, linoleum is a natural, biodegradable product that does not off-gas VOCs. Consequently, linoleum is a better choice among

Figure 5-2
Austin City Hall, Austin, Texas, designed by Antoine Predock, a registered architect and licensed interior designer, features 1,576 tons of limestone and 66,000 square feet of copper (82 percent recycled material). The building, which competed in 2004, was awarded a LEED Gold certification. Photo by Dorothy Fowles.

resilient floor coverings (AIA 1997). Care must be taken to ensure that the adhesives are appropriate and that the client understands the maintenance required. Because linoleum does not require waxing, neither wax nor strippers are introduced into the interior space; therefore, maintaining linoleum has no effect on IAQ.

WALL COVERINGS

Wall coverings include paint as well as paper, fiber, and/or polyvinyl chloride. Many paints contain VOCs, which are used to improve durability, enhance the finish, and shorten the drying time (AIA 1997). Although there are paints that off-gas VOCs still on the market (Riggs 2003), there are now low-odor, low/no-VOC paints available with characteristics (e.g., coverage, cleanability) similar to traditional water-based latex paints (Hirshfields 2002; Diamond Vogel 2002). There are also paints with built-in ability to resist the growth of bacteria and mold (Hirshfields 2002). Although this protects IAQ for most people, care must be taken because this additive can be a trigger for some chemically sensitive people.

Wall coverings manufactured with paper, fiber, or polyvinyl chloride are commonly used in both residential and nonresidential environments. Wall coverings made from PVC-based (vinyl) materials are easy-care products; they resists stains and are durable for heavy-use applications. However, when manufactured, a toxic by-product is produced; when used, the vinyl emits VOCs. Biodegradable paper that contains recycled content—such as paper or fiber—is a safe, healthy product if the finishes are also inert. The type of adhesive used in the product is also a concern. Synthetic adhesives and self-stick wall coverings have a high VOC content; however, traditional wallpaper paste, which is organic, is safe and is the preferred product (AIA 1997; Riggs 2003).

CEILING TREATMENTS

Wallboard and acoustical ceiling tile are the two most common ceiling materials. Fly ash, a waste product of coal burning, can replace the gypsum in wallboard, which is not a replenishable material. When wallboard is installed, it requires paint or another type of finish that must be specified to ensure that there is no off-gassing of VOCs. On the other hand, acoustical ceiling tile does not require paint or another finish. Sometimes it is produced from recycled materials such as newspaper, mineral wool, perlite, or clay, and it is less expensive to install. However, some ceiling tile and sprayed-on ceilings contain hazardous materials such as formaldehyde, asbestos, or crystalline silica (AIA 1997; Riggs 2003). Therefore, the best choice is a mineral-fiber ceiling tile without a vinyl surface material (Armstrong 2005). Some acoustical ceiling tile is mold resistant, protecting the IAQ if the tile becomes wet; however, the chemicals used to create mold resistance may trigger symptoms of MCS or SBS.

Figure 5-3
Acoustic ceiling tiles with water damage. Courtesy of EPA. Photo by Terry Brennan.

Figure 5-4
Stains on wood left by water damage. Courtesy of EPA.

TEXTILES

Textiles are used for many applications and products in interior environments including window treatments, upholstery, cushions, wall coverings, bed coverings, and more. Synthetic fibers are produced from petroleum products and, therefore, by definition, contain chemicals. Fabrics made with these fibers can pose problems for individuals with MCS. It is often assumed that natural fibers and fabrics are safe. However, although cotton is a natural fiber, it is produced using multiple chemicals in large quantities (e.g., pesticides, bleaches, dyes, and finishes). The production of cotton requires more chemicals than any other material in the world (Allen Woodburn 1995). Conversely, there are textiles being produced that are totally organic and environmentally safe. Products such as EnviroTex (DesignTex 1998) and Climatex LifeguardFR (Carnegie n.d.) do not negatively affect IAQ and are manufactured using environmentally safe practices.

CASE GOODS

Case goods are made with pressed wood, plywood, or solid wood, with or without wood, metal, or plastic laminate veneers. If fabricated wood is not encapsulated with a veneer, VOCs will be emitted into the indoor air from the materials in the fabricated wood. Many commonly used adhesives off-gas formaldehyde, which has been shown to be carcinogenic, and formaldehyde-based products are slowly being phased out of production. Individuals with MCS should be especially careful to avoid these materials. The finishes used for these products can be petroleum based and, therefore, can negatively affect IAQ (Riggs 2003). Often, if an odor is present, VOCs are also present.

MAINTENANCE

Once materials, furnishings, finishes, and equipment are installed, maintenance must be carefully considered. To maintain good indoor air quality, cleaning products should not contain either VOC- or formaldehyde-related chemicals. An increasingly large number of resources are available on the Internet, providing useful information on these products. Table 5.4 contains product recommendations and associated Web-site resources.

Table 5.4   Recommendations for Materials and Associated Web Addresses

Material	Recommendations	Web Address
Floor Coverings		
Carpet	Low-emitting carpet, carpet pad, and adhesives	www.carpet-rug.com/index.cfm
	IAQ and green labeling	
	Installation process	
Hard	Stone and tile	
	Solid wood	
Resilient	Linoleum	www.greenguard.org
Wall Coverings		
Paint	Low odor, low VOCs	www.vogelpaint.com
	Microbial protection	www.greenseal.org
		www.hirshfields.com/hpm_microban.html
Paper	Recycled content and environmentally safe	
Paste	Wallpaper paste	
Ceilings		
Acoustical tile	Recycled newspaper, mineral, wood, perlite, or clay	www.armstrong.com
Textiles		
Upholstery	Natural, organically grown cotton	www.carnegiefabrics.com
		www.dtex.com
Various Materials and Products		
General	Select materials that promote good IAQ	www.greenguard.org
		www.greenseal.org
		www.usgbc.org

Housing Options: A Safe, Healthy Environment

People's homes should be a respite from their daily work routine; but for many individuals, the home has become potentially dangerous. It is clear that many products emit chemicals into the air within the built environment, but there are other concerns as well. One relates to the way in which energy-efficient, airtight houses prevent the gases emitted from products and activities of daily living to escape. Because people spend more time indoors in these airtight buildings than in the past, the length of exposure to these gases has been increasing. The chemicals in the interior environments cause the increase in chemical sensitivity that people with allergies, asthma, or MCS experience (EPA 1994, Pilatowicz 1995).

Individuals with chemical sensitivities need clean, safe, healthy interior environments. When symptoms of chemical sensitivity have been triggered, the individual who is ill may not be able to work outside the home. Therefore, appropriate housing must be a priority, and yet appropriate housing can be a challenge.

There are various housing types available in the marketplace: single-family homes, condominiums, townhomes, apartment buildings, mobile homes, institutional facilities (e.g., prisons or dormitories), and temporary housing (e.g. hotels, dormitories, or camping trailers). See Table 5.5 for advantages and disadvantages of different housing types.

Housing units that are thirty years old or more are usually the safest environments, unless changes have been made with new materials that are problematic. On the other hand, older housing types may harbor indoor air pollution from previous owners (e.g., odors from smoking, fragrances, cooking, etc.). When possible, building new, with chemical-free materials, is the best solution. Very few newer or remodeled homes can be considered chemical free. Although a few houses are being built with chemical-free products and materials, often specifically for

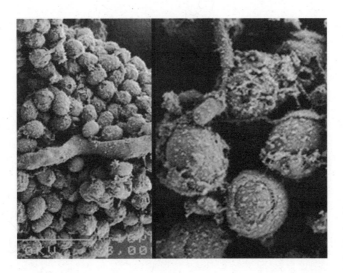

Figure 5-5
Mold spores, highly magnified.
Courtesy of EPA. Photo by John Martyny, PhD.

Table 5.5   Housing Types with Advantages and Disadvantages

Housing	Advantages	Disadvantages
Older housing	Older materials without toxins	Possible use of insecticides or termiticides
	Hardwood floors	Lingering odors of artificial fragrances
	Solid wood cabinetry	Possible use of asbestos or lead paint
	Not remodeled, a "fixer-upper"	Possible remodeling with toxic materials
	Remodeled with nontoxic materials	Mold from leaky roof or damp basement
	Furnace replaced with efficient system with electronic filters	Old furnace system
Lustron home: built in 1940–50s	Suitable for MCS	Not energy efficient
	Built of steel: inert material	
	Some located in cities with outdoor air pollution (e.g., Pittsburgh)	Some located in cities with outdoor air pollution (e.g., Pittsburgh)
	Magnets can be used	Difficult to hang pictures on walls of steel
Mobile home	Older (25–30 years) is healthier	Older units often have outdated electrical, HVAC, and plumbing
	Materials such as paneling and plywood have gassed out	Lingering odors of fragrances and/or cigarette smoke
	Older materials manufactured without toxins	Older units may have been remodeled with toxic materials
	Newer unit is safer during a fire	Poorly insulated
Apartment units	Older preferred	Newer apartments are often mass-produced
	Older materials without toxins, such as hardwood floors and plaster walls	Least-expensive materials often contain toxins
	Upper floors are a greater distance from basement and traffic fumes	Old or new: odors, smells, fumes from other units
	Steam heat	Forced hot-air heat

Temporary housing	Hotels and motels: similar to information under apartment units	Tents treated with waterproofing chemicals
	Dormitories: similar to information under apartment units	New campers constructed with synthetic products that may off-gas toxins
Remodeling or new houses	Require nontoxic materials with safe installation and application techniques	Must allow for release of toxic gases prior to move-in
	Choose longer lasting materials	May be initially more expensive
	Ability to hire a contractor familiar with nontoxic construction	Not all contractors are familiar with nontoxic construction

clients with chemical sensitivities, most people must choose their housing from the marketplace and then make it as safe as possible for their given situation. It is clear that materials, finishes, and equipment used in the constructing and furnishing of a home must be carefully researched in order to create a chemical-free built environment (Bower 1993).

AVOIDING HEALTH PROBLEMS RELATED TO INDOOR AIR QUALITY (IAQ)

There are several strategies that can be taken to avoid or to treat health problems related to IAQ:

1. Create a healthy place to live;
2. Create an oasis within the home;
3. Practice avoidance strategies;
4. Use natural materials and products;
5. Maintain clean environments; and
6. Take medication for chemical desensitization.

CREATE A HEALTHY PLACE TO LIVE

Often the individual with MCS has no choice but to stay in the present residence (home, apartment, etc.). Therefore, creating a safe environment for the client, one that is relatively free of chemicals, is essential. To create this type of environment in an existing space requires that several steps be taken. First, if smoking has been allowed in the past, it must now be forbidden within the home. Second, the carpet should be removed and replaced with a hard (e.g., tile, stone, or wood) or resilient surface (e.g., linoleum). If the carpet cannot be removed, chemical odors must be removed from the existing carpet. To minimize chemical and other odors, scatter soda on the carpet, allow to set from two to six hours, and then vacuum thoroughly. Third, new products that contain chemicals need to be removed, or "out-gassed" by placing out-of-doors, with protection from the elements, for an extended period. Fourth, if there is a wood-burning stove, remove or seal it tightly. Fifth, some accessories may need to be removed to limit the number of items that collect dust particles and are difficult to keep clean.

If it is possible to build or purchase a new home, the home should be built using materials and products that are free of chemicals. All interior finishes and furnishings (floor and wall coverings, furniture, cabinetry, bedding, etc.) specified for the home must also be free of chemicals. Once the home is occupied, a continuously clean environment must be maintained. This should begin by creating a space that is easy to clean. For example, the designer should select a washable floor covering such as porcelain tile and use large area rugs that can be easily cleaned for aesthetics and comfort. Accessories should be chosen that are easy to clean.

STRATEGIES TO CREATE A SAFE, HEALTHY ENVIRONMENT

- Build or remodel with materials and products that are free of chemicals.
- In existing areas, remove carpet or treat with baking soda to remove odors.
- In existing areas, remove any newer, noxious, or toxic materials.
- Remove or seal wood-burning stove or fireplace.
- Choose furnishings and accessories that are easy to clean.
- Prohibit cigarette or cigar smoking.
- Maintain a continuously clean environment.

CREATE AN OASIS WITHIN THE HOME

For individuals with MCS, an environment, or a space within that environment, must be totally free of chemicals; it must be an "oasis," defined in relation to indoor air quality as a place in which all products and materials are free of chemicals, a space that serves as a safe haven for a person with chemical sensitivities.

Frequently the oasis is a bedroom, an ideal place because it can easily be isolated from other areas of the home and a large portion of the day is spent there. What follows are a few suggestions for materials and products an environmentally responsible interior designer should consider for the oasis:

- A hard-surface material (e.g., porcelain tile) for floor covering is preferred.
- To add warmth and increase aesthetics, area rugs made from organic, natural fibers should be used. Organic natural fibers do not contain chemicals that are often added or applied to most fibers in the production or manufacturing process.

- A wall covering, such as low/no-VOC paint or untreated paper, should be selected.

- To eliminate dust particles in the air, seal the heat ducts with foil or an air-tight material that contains no chemicals.

- The best choice in window treatment is a hard treatment such as metal blinds. To soften the look, a simple valance made from organic cotton is an excellent choice. Organic cotton must also be used for the mattress and all bedding. Both window treatments and the bedding must be completely washable and must not be treated with chemicals.

- If bedroom accessories are used, there should be a limited number, as these products will easily collect particles of dust. The addition of an air machine to this room will continuously filter the air.

Figure 5-6
American Clay earth plaster—which is made of natural clays, recycled and reclaimed aggregates, and natural pigments—is nondusting, mold and fade resistant, repairable, and moisture controlling (absorbing and then releasing moisture to control condensation). Courtesy of American Clay.

STRATEGIES FOR CREATING AN OASIS

- Expose or install hard flooring.
- Use nontoxic installation techniques if new flooring is installed.
- Use area rugs made with organic, natural, and untreated fibers.
- Install a HEPA (high-efficiency particulate air) filter in the furnace, or seal ductwork in room.
- Use a room air exchanger.
- Remove all synthetic textiles.
- Remove any natural textiles treated with dyes, bleaches, or finishes.
- Use only organic, natural fibers, free of chemicals.
- Remove all furniture that is not constructed of solid wood, glass, or metal.
- Paint walls and ceiling using no/VOC-, low-odor paint.
- Use prefinished wood molding in its natural color, finished with water-based urethane that is ultraviolet cured.
- Avoid nonfunctional accessories that are difficult to keep clean.

AVOIDANCE

Another strategy is avoidance. Avoiding any interior environment that is newly built, remodeled, or decorated is important for anyone with chemical sensitivities. Chemical emissions are stronger in the first year as products are out-gassing. The designer must recognize that the client may not be able to accompany her to specific stores that carry merchandise that can trigger an episode. Stores should be avoided during the seasonal change of merchandise, when new materials emit the greatest concentration of gases. Many people with chemical sensitivities avoid stores with leather products, live plants and flowers, pet shops, cleaning products, scented candles, potpourri, or similar products with strong odors. Fabrics that require dry cleaning should be avoided, because the cleaning solution used for dry cleaning contains chemical solvents. The designer should assist the client so that there is no need to sit or stand near someone who is wearing perfume or other strong scents. During the spring, summer, or fall, be alert to the pollens in the air and "ozone days." Wet areas where mold is present should also be avoided.

STRATEGIES FOR AVOIDING CHEMICAL REAGENTS

- Avoid spaces with newly installed materials and new products.
- Avoid stores during seasonal changes of merchandise and any stores that sell live plants and flowers, cleaning products, scented candles, leather products, and similar products with strong odors.
- Avoid fabrics that are labeled "dry clean only."
- Avoid people wearing perfume.

- Avoid moist or damp spaces where mold might grow.
- Avoid being outdoors when pollen counts are high.

NATURAL PRODUCTS

Natural products should be substituted for all products containing chemicals. Most cleaning products for furniture, windows, floors, sinks, and bathroom fixtures contain chemicals; many contain some form of formaldehyde or phenol. Recommended cleaning products are water and nonperfumed, chemical-free soap. A damp cloth should be used for dusting (to collect the dust rather than sending it airborne as with a dry cloth or feather duster). For the tough jobs, only soap, water, untreated steel wool, and "elbow grease" should be used. The designer should consider appropriate cleaning methods and materials before recommending a maintenance program appropriate for the client.

Live plants may do more than create a positive aesthetic; some research has shown that with a sufficient number of plants, the level of noxious gases in the air can be reduced. However, in more recent studies, plants did not reduce the level of noxious gases (e.g., carbon monoxide, formaldehyde, carbon dioxide, etc.). Having plants in an interior can add contaminants (mold and/or mildew) if not properly handled. When plants are used, choose types that need less water to decrease the possibility of mold and to reduce insect infestation and plant disease. Plants that require a minimal amount of fertilizer should be selected.

Figure 5-7
An apartment building in Vancouver, British Columbia, uses green plantings on the interior and exterior to filter out airborne chemicals, absorb carbon dioxide, and release oxygen during photosynthesis. Photo by Dorothy Fowles.

Figure 5-8
At the British Columbia Law Court, designed by Arthur Erickson, indoor plantings improve indoor air quality. Photo by Dorothy Fowles.

MEDICATION

There are medications available that some people with chemical sensitivities find useful when they are in environments that are not safe places for them (e.g., churches, restaurants, grocery stores). This desensitization allows some people with chemical sensitivities to encounter chemicals that trigger their illness for a limited amount of time without becoming ill. This may be helpful in traveling between safe places.

CLEAN ENVIRONMENT

A clean environment is important to an individual whose chemical sensitivities include allergies to dust, mold, mildew, or mites. To reduce the dust level, designers should minimize surfaces that collect dust and recommend dusting several times a day with a damp cloth, if necessary to keep dust particles at a minimum. In warm climates, dehumidifiers can eliminate moisture and the subsequent development of mold and mildew.

FOOD ALLERGIES

The designer should be aware of food allergies that relate to microbial pollutants such as mold (yeast is a useful mold). The solution to food allergies is for people with chemical sensitivities to consume only natural products and not to consume products with yeast, wheat, sugar, vinegar, dairy products, and some herbs. By producing and/or purchasing homegrown, organic vegetables and herbs, many of these problems can be avoided. But other allergies are more challenging, such as the allergy to wheat, the main ingredient in breads, pastas, and many other products. The designer should determine if food allergies affect storage or work areas in the client's kitchen and plan accordingly. Food allergies are not the focus of this chapter, so no further discussion will be given to this topic.

Looking Toward the Future

Many individuals with MCS have learned to cope with their illness. Coping methods include (1) an oasis within a chemically free home; (2) avoidance; (3) organically grown and/or natural products; (4) medication; and (5) maintenance of a clean environment. With the use of medication and avoidance of allergens and intolerances, some chemicals are tolerated in the public, built environment. Over time, many individuals with MCS return to a more typical lifestyle. They are able to work and shop, but they continue to avoid new or remodeled stores and those that carry strongly scented products. It is, however, their home, and the oasis within their home, that is the most important part of their tolerance.

When the individual is able to tolerate environments outside of the home and able to return to the workplace, Americans with Disabilities Act Accessibility Guidelines (ADAAG) requires that the workplace be made safe for the person with chemical sensitivities. If this is impossible, the designer needs to focus on the area in which the individual works to make certain it is free of chemicals or that an oasis is provided.

Summary

The Foundation for Asthma and Allergies (n.d.) reports that more than 50 million Americans (1 in 20) have allergies, and 20 million have asthma. Every day 12 people in the United States die from asthma. Environments with good indoor air quality will not only be safe for individuals with MCS, SBS, asthma, and allergies but also for everyone who uses the space. Exposure to mold or mildew growth, tobacco smoke, and other indoor particulates can cause an allergic or asthmatic attack (Bower 2001; EPA 1994). Interior designers have a responsibility to design interior environments that protect the users' health, safety, and welfare.

References

AIA (American Institute of Architects Colorado). 1997. *Sustainable design resource guide*. Retrieved June 27, 2003, from http://www.aiacolorado.org/SDRG/div09/index.html.

Armstrong. 2005. *Ceiling systems*. Retrieved May 20, 2005, from http://www.armstrong.com/commceilingsna.

Allen Woodburn. (1995). Cotton: The Crop and its Agrochemicals Market. Allen Woodburn Associates, LTD. Managing Resources Ltd.

Bower, J. 1993. *The healthy house building.* New York: Healthy House Institute.

———. 2000. *The healthy house: How to buy one, how to build one, how to cure a sick one,* 4th ed. New York: Healthy House Institute.

Carnegie. n.d. *Climatex Lifecycle.* Retrieved June 27, 2003, from http://www.carnegiefabrics.com.

Carpet and Rug Institute (CRI). n.d. *CRI: The Carpet and Rug Institute.* Retrieved on May 20, 2005, from http://www.carpet-rug.org.

DesignTex. 1998. *About the company.* Retrieved June 27, 2003, from http://www.dtex.com/about/abt_cohist.htm.

Diamond Vogel. 2003. *Diamond Vogel paints: Architectural product name index.* Retrieved June 27, 2003, from http://www.vogelpaint.com/ProdNamIndx.html.

EPA (Environmental Protection Agency, U.S.) 1994. *Indoor air pollution: An introduction for health professionals.* Washington, DC: EPA.

———. 1995. *The inside story: A guide to indoor air quality.* Washington, DC: EPA.

———. 2003. *Indoor air quality: Glossary of terms.* Washington, DC: EPA.

———. 2007. *Indoor air facts no. 4 (revised): Sick Building Syndrome.* Washington, DC: EPA.

Godish, T. 2001. *Indoor environmental quality.* New York: Lewis Publishers.

Greenguard. n.d. *About Greenguard.* Retrieved on May 20, 2005, from http://www.greenguard.org.

Green Seal. 2005. *About green seal.* Retrieved on May 20, 2005, from http://greenseal.org/about.htm.

Hirshfields. 2002. *Microban anti-microbial protection.* Retrieved June 26, 2003, from http://www.hirshfields.com/hpm_microban.html.

Pilatowicz, G. 1995. *Eco-interiors: A guide to environmentally conscious design.* New York: John Wiley & Sons.

Rea, W. J. 1994. The environmental aspects of chemical sensitivity. *Japanese Journal of Clinical Ecology* 3 (1): 2–17.

Rea, W. J., A. R. Johnson, G. H. Ross, J. R. Butler, E. J. Fenyves, B. Griffiths, and J. Laseter. 1992. *Multiple Chemical Sensitivities: Addendum to Biologic Markers in Immunotoxicology.* Washington, DC: National Academies Press.

Riggs, J. R. 2003. *Materials and components of interior architecture,* 6th ed. Upper Saddle River, NJ: Prentice Hall.

U.S. Green Building Council (USGBC). 2005. *Leadership in energy and environmental design (LEED).* Washington, DC: USGBC. Retrieved on May 20, 2005, from http://www.usgbc.org.

WebMD. 2007. Allergies: Multiple chemical sensitivity. Retrieved August 18, 2007, from http://www.webmd.com/allergies/guide/multiple-chemical-sensitivity.

CHAPTER SIX

Environmentally Responsible Lighting Design

Dorothy L. Fowles, PhD, IESNA, FIDEC, FASID, FIIDA, LC

The built environment is designed not only to provide light, but also to be experienced in light. Whatever we are doing in our lives, light plays a part. . . . light is energy; light is magic. Light is life.
    —Made of Light: The Art of Light and Architecture

The Impact of Effective Lighting

Lighting has a substantial history of environmental abuse over the past 50 or so years. With the introduction of fluorescent (1939) and high-intensity discharge (i.e., metal halide, 1964) lamps, standards for "minimal" quantities of lighting increased substantially for several decades. The 1971 oil embargo created an energy crisis in the early 1970s. This provided a wake-up call of sorts that got the attention of the lighting industry and lighting researchers. Manufacturers refocused product development on lamps and luminaires that would produce more and better light with less energy. Researchers increased their efforts to understand the effect of lighting quantity and quality on productivity and user-comfort issues. These initiatives have resulted in opportunities for having more effective lighting.

Effective lighting has economic implications. Over a 30-year life for a commercial building, the initial construction cost, including lighting components, is estimated at only 2 percent. Operation and maintenance costs, including replacing burned-out lamps and paying electricity bills, consume about 6 percent. The other

92 percent of the cost relates to personnel expenses (Avant and Ogden 2005). Thus, improving productivity can have a large financial effect, while the initial cost of better lighting and control of the environment is relatively inexpensive in this life-cycle-cost view of a building. If quality environmentally responsible lighting improves productivity even a small percentage, it becomes cost-effective. Unfortunately, consumers still do not adequately appreciate this potential savings and the impact of quality lighting.

Issues of Sustainability

The goal of environmentally responsible lighting design (ERLD) focuses on the amount of energy used to produce a given quantity of light. Energy-efficient lighting considers factors that at first may seem tangential to sustainable lighting design.

Lighting is installed for specific purposes, including providing safety, enhancing visual performance or productivity, and eliciting emotional or motivational responses. These purposes appear to have little to do with energy consumption or other obvious sustainable design issues. That is, unless you understand that "the principles of sustainability integrate three closely intertwined elements—the environment, the economy, and the social system—into a system that can be maintained in a healthy state indefinitely" (Coleman and Robinson 2000, 2). Thus, environmentally responsible approaches to lighting design need to consider several components: energized systems, nonenergized systems, human-response systems, as well as the effect on the global environment (National Lighting Bureau n.d.).

The *energized systems* in lighting include lamps, luminaires, and related components such as ballast, control systems, and shielding/diffusing elements. The *nonenergized systems* include daylight and physical characteristics of the interior spaces. The *human-response systems* include visual perception, human behavior, and emotional components, as well as biological and physiological health-related responses to light (National Lighting Bureau n.d.). *Global concerns* include nighttime light pollution, manufacturing waste, toxicity, etc.

Lighting accounts for about 35 percent of electrical consumption in the United States (U.S. Department of Energy n.d. *a*). Additional cost for space cooling as a result of heat generated from lighting can account for another 10 to 15 percent of electrical use (Energy Information Administration 2003). Lighting accounts for about 9 percent of residential use of electricity (Energy Information Administration 2005). Because of this high energy use, lighting has been targeted by the Department of Energy (DOE) for development of energy-efficient technologies (U.S. Department of Energy n.d. *a*).

QUALITY OF LIGHT: VISUAL IMPACT

Good lighting relates to the quality of light as much or more than to the quantity of light. Quality of light issues relate to visual comfort and have been identified as central to the lighting design–programming process developed by the Illuminating

> The technical definition of a *luminaire* includes the lamp, fixture, ballast, transformer, and shielding/diffusing elements. For clarity in the discussion, these components are discussed separately.

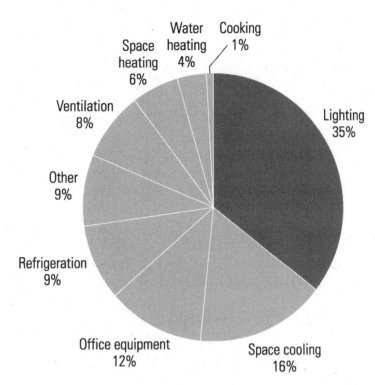

Figure 6-1
Lighting's share of all energy used.
Source: Reprinted by permission
of E source; data from Buildings
Energy Data Book (2005).

Engineering Society of North America (IESNA) (see Rea 2000, chapter 10). What constitutes "quality of light" will vary with the type of facility, geographic location, cultural expectations, and functional demands.

Good lighting becomes a matter of having the right amount of light in the right place. This involves light levels, distribution of the light, glare control, brightness perception, and the appearance of the space. Safety, security, and emergency needs are primary to any discussion of lighting quality. Good lighting will support visual performance, personal interactions, and a positive emotional response (Rea 2000).

Light conservation involves relating light levels to visual performance and functional tasks. Higher light levels are needed for difficult and sustained visual tasks. Evenly flooding a space with general overhead illumination will provide a work environment free of distracting shadows as well as flexibility for differing and changing uses, but this type of lighting is considered environmentally neutral and energy wasteful. A shadowless, evenly lit environment is often perceived as being bland or dull. Often, though inappropriate, overall light levels are raised in an attempt to counteract this monotonous effect. Rather, the addition of sparkle (i.e., small amounts of bright light) to an environment uniformly lighted with indirect luminaires has been perceived by occupants as being brighter, thus allowing the general light level to be reduced (Akashi 1999). Additionally, lighting placed close to the task and controlled by the user will facilitate reduction of the ambient or overall light level.

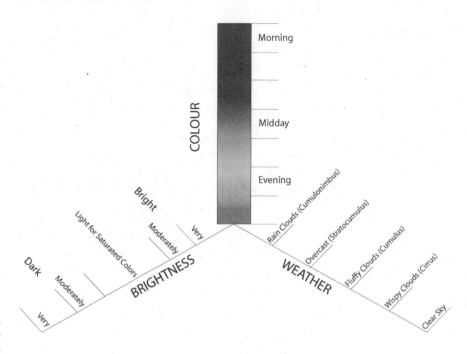

COLOUR

Morning

Midday

Evening

Bright

Moderately

Very

Light for Saturated Colors

Dark

Moderately

Very

BRIGHTNESS

Rain Clouds (Cumulonimbus)

Overcast (Stratocumulus)

Fluffy Clouds (Cumulus)

Wispy Clouds (Cirrus)

Clear Sky

WEATHER

Daylight Categories
LIGHT LOCI

Figure 6-2
Daylight categories in the three-part light loci to be considered when designing with daylight. Source: Adapted from Canzier (2002).

The effect of brightness and brightness contrast in a space is related to the lightness and darkness of surface finishes in the space. Dark surfaces absorb light hitting them and thus reflect less light back into the space. By providing light-valued surfaces for ceilings, walls, and floors, less light is needed to achieve the necessary minimum ambient light level in a space—and less energy is used for lighting.

Contrast in brightness levels provides information about an environment and creates a more visually stimulating environment. Well-placed light will help to model faces and objects. A play of light and shadow creates a psychologically interesting environment. But if viewed as a reflection in a computer screen, strong contrast effects can cause visual discomfort. Use of indirect, direct-indirect, or low-intensity direct lighting will minimize this problem.

Control of glare, both direct and reflected, is important to achieve good lighting and a positive indoor environmental quality. Surfaces with a specular or polished finish reflect light and frequently act as a concentrated or focused spot light that is uncomfortable for the viewer. Direct light in one's line of vision, whether from a luminaire or a window, can produce discomfort or disabling effects on the viewer and should be avoided. Veiling reflectance or indirect glare, while unfocused and uniform over a surface, also has a negative effect on the user.

QUALITY OF LIFE: HEALTH IMPACT

The impact of light on nonvisual health issues is now understood to be substantial. Research is identifying and verifying connections between light, darkness, and daylight with personal health and well-being. Preliminary information suggests that a portion of the visual neural fibers send signals to various areas of the body and brain that control hormone centers and the biological time clock. Cycles of light and dark exposure affect circadian rhythms, melatonin levels, sleep cycles, body temperature rhythms, and nighttime alertness (Benya 2005). *Seasonal affective disorder* (SAD) is related to limited access to light. Light is used to improve the weight gain in premature infants (Nagourney 2002) and to aid the synthesis of vitamin D.

An increasing number of researchers, including Peter Boyce, Gerrit van den Beld, George Brainard, and Gene Glickman, have focused on studies addressing aspects of photobiology (Lien 2004). Light-related hormone imbalances have been linked to sleep disturbance, carbohydrate craving, confusion and poor coordination, as well as susceptibility to infectious diseases. A central finding is that ganglion cells, rather than rods and cones, pick up short wavelength signals (460–480 nm). Exposure to this indigo blue light during waking hours is important to facilitate the biological effects (Raloff 2006). It is probably not coincidental that these wavelengths are richly available in daylight. Other evidence indicates that excessive blue light may have negative effects on the eye as well as altering sleep/alertness patterns (Cromie 2006).

Daylight

Daylight, part of the *nonenergized* system, is an important component of environmentally responsible lighting design. Architectural daylighting design decisions can help or hinder the potential for effective use of daylight and achieving visual comfort inside buildings. While a detailed development of daylighting design is beyond the scope of a discussion of environmentally responsible interior design (ERID), the integration of daylighting with electric lighting is important. "Daylighting," a section from the *Whole Building Design Guide*, provides a substantial discussion of all aspects of daylighting (Daylighting n.d.). An understanding of the issues, benefits, and guidelines related to daylighting is important to developing ERID.

Windows provide a psychologically important connection to the outdoors. Access to a view and interaction with daylight provide valuable environmental information: a dynamic measure of time passage, information about immediate weather conditions, and a sense of place. Having a view to the outside reduces eye strain, allowing the muscles contracted from extended near-focus to relax (Butler and Biner 1989; Heerwagen et al. 2004). Research evidence from education, corporate, retail, and health-care settings is confirming the positive health and performance impacts of daylighting (Heschong Mahone Group 199a, 2001, 2003a, 2003b, 2003c, 2003d; Kuller and Lindsten 1992; Wilson 2004; Heerwagen 2001).

Figure 6-3
Daylighting has been shown to improve retail sales. Photo by Vaughn Bradshaw.

A major benefit of daylighting is the reduction in both fossil fuel and electric energy use. Fossil fuel is used for heating and cooling, while electric energy is used for lighting. Daylighting can provide savings of 35 to 65 percent in electric use for lighting and 20 to 60 percent overall energy savings. Coupled with energy-efficient and effective electric lighting, the savings will be even greater. Energy budgets can be substantially reduced to well below American Society of Heating, Refrigerating and Air-Conditioning Engineers, Inc. (ASHRAE) Standard 90.1 requirements (Hakkarainen 2005).

Daylighting does have limitation and liabilities that must be addressed for its successful use in interior environments. Using daylight requires recognition of the variability of this light source due to geographic location, time of day, time of year, and weather conditions that affect the sky; this affects the color of the light as well as the brightness and distribution (Canzler 2002).

The problem is not so much daylight but, rather, sunlight. A direct beam of sunlight is an extremely high source of light as well as heat. Thus, direct sunlight as a light source needs to be minimized, while maximizing the use of diffused daylight. Excessive heat gain and ultraviolet damage to materials can be two negative results of daylighting that need to be balanced with the advantages gained from daylighting in a particular building. Glazing material can be selected to reduce both of these problems. Tinted glass though can block biologically important wave lengths and/or distort the color spectrum of daylight. Glazing should have high visible-light transmission (VLT) qualities and a low solar-heat gain coefficient (SHGC) for maximum daylighting benefits (Reis 2000).

Glare is the biggest daylighting problem; it reduces the ability to see details. A school study of daylighting effects (Heschong Mahone Group 1999a) reported

Figure 6-4
Even delicate environments, like this museum, can employ daylighting. Photo by Vaughn Bradshaw.

that glare from windows reduced test scores 15 to 25 percent. High contrast is created along with glare, either directly between the glazed surface and adjacent interior surface or indirectly where light falls on a surface. Daylight needs to be balance with light-colored interior surfaces to reduce the potential for these strong contrasts. Guidelines note that the window should not be more than 100 to 300 times as bright as the objects in the room (Miller and Maniccia 2005). Furthermore, direct sunlight on task areas or reflected glare on television and computer screens can be avoided through orientation and shading. "Daylight factor" is a calculation used to compute the amount of daylight outside compared to a point inside (Rea 2000).

One daylighting strategy involves "harvesting" light. The idea is to minimize direct sunlight penetration while maximizing daylight use. Integrating high ceilings

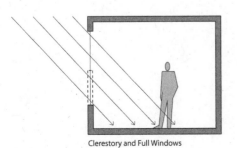

Clerestory and Full Windows

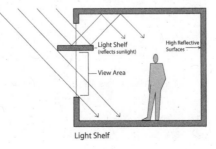

Light Shelf

Figure 6-5
Light shelves contribute to a more even distribution of daylight while also increasing daylight penerration into a room Drawing by Glenn Burmeister.

and bringing in daylight from two directions help to increase daylight utilization. Sidelighting uses vertical glazing. For daylighting use, the glazing is located high on the wall or overhead, while vision or view glazing is positioned within a seven-foot distance from the floor.

Light shelves are a frequent addition to high lights or clerestories to increase the penetration of daylight further into the interior space. Continuous horizontal windows are better than individual windows or vertical ones. A light shelf facilitates deeper daylight penetration into a space, but it contributes even more to a uniform distribution of the daylight. A light shelf can also be effective in blocking direct sun at certain times of the year and day.

Toplighting is any daylighting delivered from the ceiling plane. This location for daylighting provides the potential for even distribution of daylight throughout a larger space and integrates well with electric lighting. Wall washing is possible with toplighting. Care in the design and placement of skylights is needed to avoid the problems of glare, excessive heat gain, and harsh contrast from direct sunlight. If toplighting is designed using deep wells and/or diffuse materials, these problems will be reduced. Sawtooth ceilings, light monitors, and north-facing clerestory windows, which were all popular in industrial settings a century ago, are effective ways to harvest daylight.

Figure 6-6
The clerestory windows and ribbon skylights in the David L. Lawrence Convention Center, LEED Gold, Pittsburgh, Pennsylvania, can light the exhibition halls without the assistance of electric light. Photo by Dorothy Fowles.

The following are Strategies and principles for effective daylight in interior spaces:

- Collaborate early with design team members to maximize building features that support daylighting.
- Provide soft, uniform light throughout the space.
- Provide thermal barriers for the windows to reduce heat gain or loss during unoccupied times.
- Use HVAC (heating, ventilating, and air-conditioning) to compensate for the additional radiation during daylighting hours.
- Provide glare-control and heat-gain shading systems.
- Orient a worker's sight line away from windows, preferably with daylight coming from the side of a person. Rear lighting may produce shadows on the work material.
- Integrate automatic controls with a manual override for the shading system.
- Provide control mechanisms that adjust electric illumination when adequate daylighting is available. These include:

    on/off system,

    continuous dimming, and

    step switching or step dimming for individual ballasts and lamps.
- Use a closed-loop photosensor that reads electric light and daylight in preference to an open-loop sensor that reads only the daylight.
- Use an advanced lighting system with electronic ballasts to supplement daylight to maximize energy savings.

In developing an integrated daylight and electric light strategy, light levels from daylight need to be higher in a space than comparable light levels from electric light. The footcandle perception of the two is not equal. The IESNA suggests a rule of thumb: add 1 lumen of electric lighting for the loss of 2–3 lumens of daylight (Rea 2000). While maximizing daylight use is an environmentally responsible strategy, electric lighting is a necessary supplement. Understanding and integrating daylight with electric light is important for achieving energy-effective and efficient electric lighting.

Footcandle (fc) is a measure of the quantity of light hitting a particular spot.

Electric Lighting

A systems approach to electric lighting is needed to achieve maximum energy-effective and energy-efficient design. This is the *energized* system that includes luminaires and controls. Luminaire is the technical names for the complete lighting unit that consists of the housing, lamps, ballasts, and transformers as well as light-controlling elements such as reflectors, shielding devices, and diffusing media.

In making any lighting decision, illumination needs must be established and trade-offs between electric lighting options need to be assessed. The cost-value benefit analysis for each option includes energy cost, lighting-system costs,

Lumen (lm) is a measure of total light output.

operating costs, and lighting-quality issues. Lighting-quality issues cover a range, including employee productivity and absenteeism, security and safety, business image and environmental "mood," and accommodation of spatial changes.

EFFICIENCY RATINGS

Efficiency of the electric lighting system is dependent on characteristics of each individual component as well as how the components work together to produce electric illumination. There are different measures of efficiency related to different components of the system.

Watt (w) is a measure of the electric power used to operate the lamp.

- *Lamp efficacy* is the technical term to describe how efficient a lamp converts electricity of visible light. This is stated as *lumens per watt* (LPW).
- *Luminaire efficiency* is the ratio between the light output from the fixture and the light output generated by the lamps it houses. This is stated as a percentage.
- *Coefficient of utilization* (CU) is concerned with the amount of light that reaches the work surface relative to the amount of light produced by the lamp. This measure of efficiency is affected not only by the characteristics of the luminaire but also by the size and shape of the room, as well as the reflectance of the ceiling, walls, and floor. Standardized procedures are used by the manufacturer to establish a CU table of values for each luminaire.
- *Visual comfort probability* (VCP) is a value that indicates how much glare a luminaire is likely to produce. The room dimensions influence this rating. A VCP of 80 or higher is considered necessary for highly computerized offices. This number means that 80 percent of the users located in the least desirable spot in the space would not be bothered by direct glare from an even pattern of luminaires mounted on or in the ceiling.
- *Ballast factor* (BF) is the relative light output produced by a lamp and ballast system relative to the manufacturer's rated light output of the lamp itself. A high ballast factor means fewer lamps and ballasts are needed to achieve a specific level of illumination. A low BF ballast would permit lowering the light level in an overilluminated space without replacing or rearranging existing luminaires.

COLOR RATINGS

Effective lighting is dependent on perception of the appearance of the light as well as the general appearance of the space, especially related to color. Two additional ratings are used to identify the color appearance of the light source and its effect on surfaces in a space:

- *Color temperature* (CT) *or correlated color temperature* (CCT): CT is used for lamps with filaments, including standard incandescent and halogen

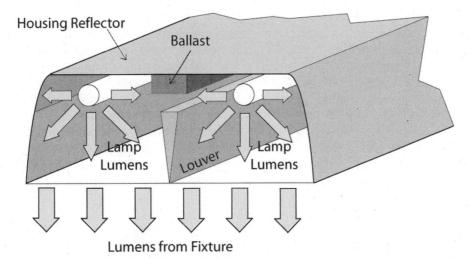

Housing Reflector

Ballast

Lamp Lumens

Louver

Lamp Lumens

Lumens from Fixture

Figure 6-7
Luminaire components. Source: adapted from Energy Star Building Upgrade Manual: Lighting *(Washington, DC: U.S. Environmental Protection Agency, 2004), 61.*

sources. CCT is used for nonfilament light sources, including fluorescent and metal-halide lamps. This measure, stated in degrees Kelvin (K), is based on the color change of a test wire as it is heated. The color of the wire goes from yellow to orange/red to white to blue as it increases in temperature. Sunny daylight at noon is about 5,500K, an overcast sky is about 7,000K, a 100-watt incandescent lamp is about 2,800K.

■ *Color rendering index* (CRI) provides an estimate of how "natural" or expected a standard set of colors appear when seen under a specific lamp relative to their color appearance under the standard test source with the same CCT. This latter appearance is rated as 100 CRI. Current energy codes define a rating of 70 CRI as the minimum value for lamps used in most interior environments.

These two color ratings are linked to energy efficiency in recent research findings. As CCT increases, the blue content of the light increases. A 5,000K light source has been found to provide more contrast and better resolution of details. With this bluer light, it is possible to design with lower foot-candle levels to achieve a perception of the same brightness in a space (Cargnel 2004).

Light sources with a higher CRI have been linked to energy efficiency. The *IESNA Lighting Handbook* reports that "lamps with color rendering indexes of 70, 85, and 100 require about 10%, 25%, and 40% lower illuminance levels than lamps with a CRI of 60, respectively, to achieve impressions of equivalent brightness" (Rea 2000). Thus, the higher the CRI number of the light source, the brighter a space should appear with the same energy use (Cargnel 2004).

LAMPS AND ENERGY-RELATED ISSUES

The lamp manufacturing industry has been one of the most responsive in addressing the need for environmentally responsible options in the past decades. As a result, the lamp selection process has become more complex due to a large range of available products that can reduce energy use, increase output per lamp, and/or reduce the hazardous waste in the lamps. Lamp-selection options for energy-efficient and energy-effective lighting should be based on end-use criteria: their efficacy (as described above), total amount of lumen output, light-distribution patterns, physical size, average rated life, ease of control, initial cost, and auxiliary components. General categories of lamps include: incandescent; halogen; compact fluorescent; fluorescent; high-intensity discharge (HID), including mercury vapor and metal halide; and low-pressure sodium. A detailed description of the various lamps in each category is beyond the scope of this discussion. Rather, an overview of those elements relevant to ERLD is presented below.

Figure 6-8
The Kelley Engineering Center at Oregon State University, Corvallis, Oregon, designed by Yost Grube Hall Architecture, shows the use of daylight sensors, light shelves, sun screening canopies, and indirect reflective luminaires.

Incandescent lamps as a group, and especially the standard A19 lamp, are the least energy-efficient light sources available. Approximately 80 to 90 percent of their energy is converted to heat with only 10 to 20 percent of the energy producing visible light. By modifying the filament and using Krypton gas improvements in efficacy (i.e., light efficiency) and lamp life are being made to many incandescent lamps. Silver reflectors in ER (ellipsoidal reflector) and BR (bulged reflector) lamps reduce the amount of heat and light trapped in a fixture. Nevertheless, these lamps remain quite energy inefficient.

Halogen lamps come as either line voltage (120 volts) or low voltage (12 volts), both requiring a transformer. These lamps are incandescent lamps filled with halogen gas that improves all aspects of performance compared to the traditional incandescent lamps. The rated life of halogen lamps is generally twice that of their incandescent counterparts and the lumen output is 25 to 30 percent greater. These lamps, especially the infrared (IR) versions, increase the light output, "burn" very hot, and produce brilliant and efficient white light in a small size lamp. Low-voltage versions provide high-efficacy, high-intensity light with a controlled beam spread. Energy efficiency is increased with the use of electronic ballasts. Thus, these lamps are especially efficient when a high light level is needed in a relatively confined area for displays and accents.

Fluorescent lamps are the most significant lamp category for ERLD. These lamps vary in length, tube diameter, tube shape, and CCT. They must be matched to the appropriate ballast: preheat, rapid start, instant start, or programmed. The use of rare earth (RE) triphosphor coatings on the inside of the tubes has increased the efficacy and the color rendering qualities of these lamps. Used as a system with electronic ballasts, even greater energy savings are possible.

Compact fluorescent (CFL) with *integral electronic ballasts* and a *standard screw-in base* should be considered only as an energy-efficient replacement for incandescent lamps. (Roberts and Flood 2003). This lamp family is 3 to 4 times more efficient and has a rated lamp life that is 5 or 6 times longer than that of incandescent lamps. Standard CFL lamps replicate incandescent color temperature, although several other color temperatures are available. The color rendering properties of CFL are good, but light focus or control in the fixtures is limited. While these lamps save considerable energy compared to the incandescent lamps that they replace, the ballast must be prematurely discarded with the spent lamp. A major sustainability problem is that these lamps can be replaced with incandescent lamps at any time, negating the energy reduction. Because of this, the wattage savings from use of screw-in base lamps does not count in power budgeting.

Dedicated CFL with *nonintegral ballasts* are available up to 80 watts, with the length of the CFL generally increasing proportionally. Two-pin base lamps that operate with an electromagnetic ballast are considerably less energy efficient than the four-pin base lamps that use an electronic ballast. The small diameter tube, high lumen output, and electronic ballast results in an energy-efficient system for a soft-edge light source. Amalgams added to these lamps improve their performance at lower and higher ambient temperatures, increasing the viability of the lamps

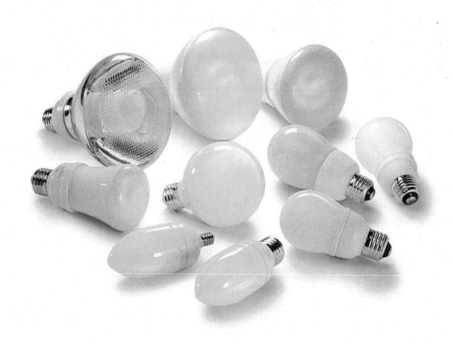

Figure 6-9
Compact fluorescent lamps with an integral ballast can replace incandescent lamps to conserve energy without degradation of color perception. Photo courtesy of Philips Lighting.

for outdoor use. (The amalgam lamps are slower to reach full lumen output when turned on: expect dim light at the start.) Compact fluorescent lamp developments continue to evolve rapidly with increased delivery systems and improved efficacy to support a full range of applications.

Linear fluorescent lamps account for over two-thirds of all electric illumination in the United States (National Lighting Bureau n.d.). In the past 25 years, these lamps have improved significantly, with more compact tubes, better color, greater efficacy, increased lumen maintenance, and improved lamp-life options with the T8 and T5 lamps. These smaller tubes use better and less phosphors than the T12 (which is 1½ in diameter) resulting in economic and environmental savings. The smaller tubes emulate a smaller line of light, allowing for more efficient luminaire designs and fewer luminaires in a space.

The T8 (1" diameter) is the dominant tube used today. It comes in RE-70 (70–79 CRI) or RE-80 (80–89 CRI) with standard color temperatures of 3,000K (warm), 3,500K (neutral), or 4,100K (cool). These lamps are being used to replace metal-halide HID lamps for large space illumination (e.g., big-box stores, warehouses), achieving energy savings of 25 to 55 percent, better uniformity, better control, and more flexibility (Cargnel 2004).

The newer, smaller T5 (~5/8" diameter) is a metric lamp that only operates with an electronic ballast. Because the T5 tube surface is 40 percent less than the T8, it has improved environmental qualities including the use of less mercury, glass, and rare earth phosphors. It also has the highest efficacy along with a higher CRI

(80–89) than other fluorescent lamps. Because of its extreme brightness, it works well in indirect luminaires.

Variations in fluorescent lamps include lamps with increased output, energy-saving or reduced wattage, and extended life. HO (high output) and VHO (very high output) versions are available for T8, T5, and T12. A HO version of the T5 lamp produces considerably more lumens, but it has a somewhat lower efficacy (i.e., ratio of watts to lumen output) than a standard T5. T12 HO and VHO lamps produce more light, but draw considerably more current and have shorter life—not

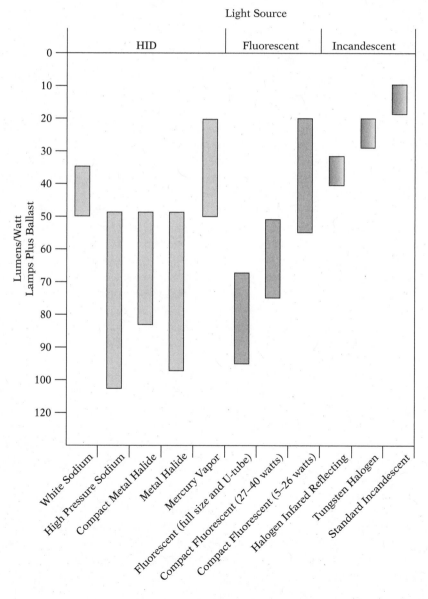

Figure 6-10
Light source efficacies. Source: adapted from Rea (2000), Chapter 26.

an ERLD lamp of choice. "Energy-saving" lamps provide reduced wattage as well as reduced lumen output, which works efficiently in retrofitting spaces with too much light. But these lamps are more temperature sensitive at lower temperatures.

High-intensity discharge (HID) lamps, in general, are not as energy efficient as the better triphosphor fluorescent lamps discussed above. Approximating a point source, HID lamps, coupled with the use of optical controls, become a very efficient source for high-wattage outdoor lighting and lower wattage concentrated-light accent applications. HID lamps are using electronic ballasts and becoming smaller, but dimming these lamps is still only marginally successful.

Generally, HID lamps have poor color temperature and rendering properties, medium to high efficacy, and limited dimming capabilities. Additional properties include long life, high wattages, and limited temperature sensitivity. Within the family of HID lamps—i.e., mercury vapor (H), high-pressure sodium (HPS), and metal halide (MH)—only metal halide is considered suitable for interior use. Mercury vapor and metal halide lamps experience high lumen depreciation over the life of the lamps that must be accounted for in lighting design.

The *low-pressure sodium* (LPS) lamp, while not an HID source, is usually discussed with HIDs due to some performance similarities. While it is an extremely energy-efficient source, the use of the LPS lamp lacks energy effectiveness due to its extremely low CRI. Colors are seen as shades of gray or brown, reducing the environmental visual information available to users.

The *ceramic metal halide* (CMH) lamp has seen improvements in all properties: CRI, CT, color consistency between lamps and over lamp life, lamp life, lumen depreciation, and efficacy. Decreased lamp size and availability in lower wattages have made this lamp an energy-effective and energy-efficient substitution for incandescent and halogen lamps, especially in retail environments. A 60 W CMH is equivalent to a 90 W halogen or 150 W incandescent PAR (parabolic aluminized reflector) lamp. The "White" HPS lamp also has improved color qualities, but this is at the expense of lumen output and lamp life.

The light-emitting diode (LED) is a relatively new semiconductor light source. Since LEDs do not have a filament, they do not get hot—an energy savings. Since LEDs do not contain mercury, they hold much future promise as an environmentally responsible source of illumination. A current problem with this lamp is the relatively large size of the heat sink that is required to accompany each. This is a rapidly emerging technology that will soon be viable for wide use as interior lighting. Its long life, small size, and limited electrical use already make it an effective and efficient choice for emergency exit signs. This "solid-state" lighting is considered to be the light source of the future.

In selecting lamps, a general rule of thumb for increased energy efficiency is to use a large wattage lamp rather than two smaller lamps of the same type and totaling the same wattage (e.g. one 48-T8, 2,800 lumens versus two 24-T8, 1,300 lumens each). But, as noted above, energy-efficient and effective lighting is achieved through a systems approach that includes the auxiliary equipment: ballasts and transformers that are integrated with the lamp source.

AUXILIARY EQUIPMENT

Ballasts control the current flow or voltage for fluorescent and high-intensity (HID) discharge lamps. Ballasts provide an initial voltage surge and then control the current for a stable operation. Two types of ballasts are available: electromagnetic and solid-state electronic. All *electromagnetic ballasts* are heavy, hum, and cause lamps to flicker. The so-called high efficiency, energy-saving electromagnetic ballast uses less energy and last twice as long as standard electromagnetic ones (National Lighting Bureau n.d. 27) and when used as part of an improved T12 fluorescent-lamp system can result in savings of 10 to 20 percent. Using 60 Hz frequency, even improved electromagnetic ballasts cannot match the systems saving achieved with high-frequency electronic ballasts. Electromagnetic ballasts are being phased out, with the year 2010 set by the industry and Department of Energy (see Energy Policy Act of 2005) as the target date for their almost complete elimination.

Electronic ballasts used in a fluorescent lighting system help achieve a system energy efficiency of 30 to 40 percent (15 percent for the ballast) and longer lamp life compared to a classic electromagnetic ballast-T12 lamp system, making it the preferred ERLD ballast for fluorescent lamps. Positive characteristics of the high-frequency electronic ballast as part of a fluorescent lighting system include lighter weight, smaller size, no hum, no visible lamp flicker, and accommodation of a range of lighting loads with a single ballast. Lamps run at the high frequency achieved with electronic ballasts gain 10 percent efficacy. Electronic ballasts allow added features, such as lamp dimming, expanded controls, and extended lamp life, that all contribute to the energy effectiveness of a lighting system.

Until recently, ballasts had not been interchangeable, but rather needed to be considered as a system with the lamp type and its characteristics. Some newer electronic ballasts can now operate multiple fluorescent lamps (1–4 lamps) or 2 two-lamp luminaires from a single external ballast. Variations can operate lamps in series or parallel modes. Other advances include circuits that can sense different input voltages and ballasts that can operate different lamp wattages.

Only select HID lamps can use electronic ballasts, and these operate at 60 Hz frequency. When used, the HID electronic ballast experiences lower energy loss and produces enhanced system performance. A hybrid electronic/electromagnetic ballasts is also being used to optimize performance over the life of HID lamps. While dimming does not work effectively with HID lamps, a two-level or step ballast is effective for reducing light levels (and energy use) when full light output is not needed.

For maximum efficient operation of a lighting system, a number of specific characteristics of the ballast need to be specified (Steffy 2001). These include the following:

- A starting sequence (important in maximizing lamp life)
- End-of-life protection
- Electromagnetic interference protection
- Current crest factor

- Total harmonic distortion
- Power factor (PF)
- Ballast factor (BF)

Ballast factor (BF) represents the percentage of rated lamp lumens produced by a ballast relative to those produced by a reference ballast.

There are other issues that should be considered when selecting a ballast. One of these is the *ballast factor*. Low-output ballasts have a low ballast factor and require proportionally lower power. Retrofitting luminaires in an over illuminated area with low-ballast-factor ballasts (less than 75%) results in reductions in both light level and energy use. In new installations, the use of high-ballast-factor ballasts, especially with T5 lamps, will reduce the number of fixtures needed to maintain appropriate light levels.

The several types of electron ballasts each have advantages and limitations relevant to ERLD. The *instant-start* ballast uses less energy to start a lamp, but the wear and tear of this type of start reduces lamp life. The best use of an instant-start ballast is in an installation where lamps are only turned on and off a few times during the day. This ballast type is not recommended for used with occupancy sensors.

The *rapid-start* mode is used to operate occupancy sensors and dimming ballasts. The rapid-start ballast can be used with different size and wattage lamps, but it should only be used with one wattage type on a circuit for consistent light output between lamps. A *programmed-start* ballast uses a controlled- or soft-starting process that in the rapid-start mode extends cathode life in the lamp by 50 to 100 percent.

A *stepped or multilevel electronic* ballast should be considered as an alternative to switching off one or more lamps in a luminaire to control light levels. A low-cost two-level ballast switches between low- and high-output levels, typically between 50 and 100 percent. A high-end *dimming electron ballast* has a full dimmable range, while less expensive versions dim to only 5 to 20 percent at the low level. Due to industry variations in dimming protocol, it is best to secure the dimming ballast and control device from the same manufacturer.

Another auxiliary device is a *transformer,* which is used to step down residential or commercial voltage for low-voltage lamps (12 or 24 volts) or to convert to direct current for neon and LED lamps. The transformer may be either integral in the luminaire or remote from it. Like ballasts, transformers may be either magnetic or electron, with similar contrasts of size, weight, and noise. The maximum distance from the transformer to the lamp(s) is related to the lamp wattage and the wire size. The electricity used by a transformer must be included in the energy-use calculations for determining power-budget usage.

LUMINAIRES

In addition to the lamp, ballast or transformer, a luminaire includes the hardware—the housing, wiring components, and light-controlling elements such as reflectors, shielding devices, and diffusing media. The major function of the luminaire is light control; it is designed to direct light where needed, to control glare, and to eliminate or minimize light where it is not needed or desired. (For example, lighting the desk or work surface where reading occurs, keeping brightness off the computer screen,

Advantage T8 Systems vs. Standard T8 Systems

| Energy Savings: 2 Lamp vs. 2 Lamp System | | | | | | | | Energy Savings: 2 Lamp vs. 3 Lamp System | | | | | | | |
Electronic Ballast	Ballast Factor	No. of Lamps	Lamp Watts	Standard T8 Lumens	Advantage T8 Lumens	System Watts	Savings	Electronic Ballast	Ballast Factor	No. of Lamps	Lamp Watts	Standard T8 Lumens	Advantage T8 Lumens	System Watts	Savings
Standard T8	0.87	2	32	2850		58		Standard T8	0.87	3	32	2850		88	
Reduced Light Output T8	0.75	2	32		3100	51	$2.80/yr	Increased Light Output T8	1.20	2	32		3100	78	$4.00/yr

Combine Advantage T8 lamps with Reduced Light Output Electronic Ballasts, with these Results:
- Produce comparable light output
- Save 7 system watts vs. standard T8 system
- Save $2.80 per fixture per year
- Energy savings based on 4000 hrs/yr @ $.10 kw/hr

Combine Advantage T8 Lamps with Increased Light Output Ballasts. A 2 Lamp Advantage T8 System vs. a 3 Lamp Standard T8 System will:
- Produce comparable light output
- Save 10 system watts
- Save $4.00 per fixture per year
- Energy savings based on 4000 hrs/yr @ $.10 kw/hr
- Reduce lighting installation costs (lamps, ballasts, fixtures and labor)
- Philips Advantage T8 lamps operate on ballast with ballast factors up to 1.32 with warranty intact

Figure 6-11
Example of economic comparison of advanced lighting systems with standard lamp systems. Courtesy of Philips Lighting.

and reducing light levels in the corridors or circulation area.) Understanding lighting needs is the starting point in selecting lamps and luminaires for a space.

In considering ERLD, the luminaire's energy effectiveness must be weighed with its energy efficiency and lamp efficacy. Luminaires, being designed to control light, are less efficient than the lamp and ballast system presented as a bare utility fixture sending light in all directions. But the intensity of the spot of light from this type of light would cause direct glare to the viewer and indirect glare in the computer screen with adverse affects on users. This would be an efficient, but not an effective, lighting solution.

In principle, the luminaire housing should be built around the lamp to maximize delivering light to the right location. Luminaires are rated for their efficiency. This rating is part of the photometric report provided by the manufacturer.

In luminaire design, many of the elements that are used to control the light being emitted from a luminaire contribute to a reduction in its efficiency. But reflectors, lenses, baffles, and louvers can play an important and effective role in directing light only to where it is needed while eliminating light where it is not desired. The intensity distribution curve, part of the manufacturer's photometric report, is useful in understanding the light distribution pattern of a luminaire.

With this understanding, the light distribution pattern is a primary criterion in the luminaire selection process. For example, what choice would you make if you wanted to accent a piece of crystal and had a choice of two luminaires and/or lamps with the same overall lumen output but with different light-distribution patterns? The optics of a small halogen source focuses the lumen output into a concentrated beam pattern as compared to the softer, broader light distribution of a compact fluorescent source with the same lumen output, making the former source the more effective and efficient choice in this example.

When making a selection from luminaires with similar distribution patterns, the choice should be the luminaire with the greater efficiency. The National Electric Manufacturing Association (NEMA) has published a set of Luminaire efficiency ratings (LER) for generic luminaire types. It is suggested that a selected luminaire should be in the upper 25 percent of efficiencies for that type of luminaire (Roberts and Floods 2003) But a note of caution: Do not use efficiency without addressing

Luminaire efficiency is the lumens emitted from the luminaire compared to lumens available from the lamp/ballast system.

Luminaire efficiency rating (LER) is calculated by dividing the total lamp lumens by the luminaire input watts and adjusted for the luminaire efficiency and ballast factors.

the light-distribution patterns for the luminaires appropriate for the lighting situation (e.g., potential glare in video display terminal for computer users in an office).

Several conditions that contribute to a decrease in luminaire efficiency are not taken into account in the luminaire photometric report. These include ballast factor, thermal factor, lamp-lumen depreciation, luminaire-dirt depreciation, and room-surface depreciation. These factors should be used to more accurately account for the field performance of a luminaire. Lighting-calculation details can be found in *The IESNA Lighting Handbook* (Rea 2000).

CONTROLS

Lighting controls provide one of the easiest ways to increase the energy efficiency of the lighting system. Conservation of energy through the use of controls occurs by integrating daylighting with electric lighting, turning off unneeded lights, and reducing peak-demand electricity usage. Additional energy savings occur when light levels are controlled as part of lamp-lumen adjustment and adaptation compensation. Control strategies need to integrate with the building design, HVAC system, and building-use patterns for full effectiveness.

Three major objectives for using light control are to: (1) reduce light energy use and cost, (2) improve the function and aesthetics of the space for the occupants, and (3) aid in code compliance (Rea 2000). Achieving these objectives is easier with advances in lighting-system controls technology that provide options for flexibility and function.

Figure 6-12
The indirect lighting in this office is controlled by a daylight sensor suspended from the ceiling. Photo by Dorothy Fowles.

Controls can range from simple switches and dimmers to more advanced sensors and timers and even more complex building-automation systems. Integration of controls in new construction is assumed, but retrofitting is a viable energy-saving option for existing spaces. The energy savings from lighting controls is estimated to be up to 50 percent in existing buildings and 35 percent in new buildings (Roberts and Floods 2003). Savings of this magnitude are dependent on the control system being used. Thus, a thorough analysis of the use of the space and the expectations of the occupants is an important component of the control-design process. To be effective, the system must accommodate the occupants' use patterns, their commitment to energy savings, and their ability to cope with the control system. The Lighting Controls Association (n.d.) Web site has considerable information available on selecting and using controls, including a room-by-room analysis.

A distinction is made between lighting-control strategies and lighting-control devices in *Lighting Controls: Patterns for Design* (Rundquist et al. 1996). The planned approach to the control of light is a strategy, while a device is the equipment used to achieve the desired control. Different devices may be used to achieve a lighting-control strategy. Lighting strategies include seven approaches:

1. *Occupancy response* is appropriate where lights are turned on when needed and turned off when occupancy or a task does not need the light. Control devices for this strategy include:

   o *Manual off/on switch:* The simplest lighting control device, requiring user control, has limited adaptability.

   o *Occupancy sensor:* Detects motion in a space and turns lights off when the space is unoccupied. This automatic control device is useful where the occupancy pattern is unpredictable. There are several variations including:

      1. *Passive infrared (PIR):* Requires a direct "line of sight" with a 15 to 20 foot effective distance and 40 foot maximum.

      2. *Active ultrasonic (ULT):* Good in irregular spaces but can pick up false signals.

      3. *PIR/ULT dual technology:* Useful in large spaces. Options include a manual on/off override that provides maximum savings when used with PIR or ULT. Systems with only auto-on/auto-off are most appropriate in common-use spaces, such as restrooms and corridors. Use of sensors with HID lamps should be restricted to a high-low option due to the long restrike time if these lamps are turned completely off.

2. *Prescheduled or timed response* has lights turned on and off on a predetermined, regular schedule or automatically turns lights off after a preestablished time period. Exact light levels are set for time periods that may be varied within a day, week, month, and/or seasonal cycle. Control devices include:

○ *Timer:* Inexpensive and easiest control device to install; useful in short-occupancy spaces.

○ *Time clock:* Range from a simple mechanical to complex, programmable electronic units covering 356 days. Variations include:

1. 24-hour or 7-day time clocks

2. Astronomical time clock that adjusts on/off times to sunrise/sunset times

   While rapid-start fluorescent lamp life may be decreased with frequent switching, the calendar replacement time for lamps may not be affected since the lamps are off more time. The energy saved by turning off lamps for periods of time far offsets (by more than three times) the cost of relamping, that is, replacing the lamps (Rundquist et al. 1996).

3. *Tuning* involves adjusting the light level to match users' needs or desires, which may vary with daylight availability, personal preferences, and energy awareness. Two variations of this strategy are *task tuning,* which involves individualized light control in a work space, and *manual dimming,* which involves light-level control of a large space. Since light levels that are turned down 25 percent are not noticed by occupants, the potential for a direct energy savings is obvious. Avoid systems that have abrupt changes in light levels, as this annoys occupants. Two approaches to tuning are:

○ *Continuous dimming:* Reduces both light output and energy consumption. Automatic dimming integral with photoelectric sensors should be used in daylighting control systems.

1. Linear fluorescent and some compact fluorescent lamps can be dimmed, typically down to 1 to 5 percent of the lamp output, if matched with dimming ballasts. Using electronic ballasts and dimming controls, the energy saved and light-level reduction are almost proportional (Wilson 2004). Lamp life may be decreased with extensive dimming. Some dimming ballasts can be "addressed": their dimming level is preset and achieved automatically by the push of a button on the control.

2. Incandescent lamp dimming saves energy and extends the lamp life, while warming the color of the light. A 20 percent reduction in energy results in about a 50 percent reduction in light output, so the savings from dimming is less than with fluorescent lamps. Low-voltage lamps need the dimmer matched to the transformer. Low-voltage lamps using a dimmer need to be burned at full power periodically to activate the halogen cycle.

3. HID dimming is more problematic, requiring both a special ballast and a dimming device. An abrupt change in light level results in a color shift for metal halide lamps. Due to advances in fluorescent

Figure 6-13
Lack of sufficient sun control through architectural design or internal shading creates excessive glare in this work station, especially on the computer screen. Photo by Dorothy Fowles.

Figure 6-14
The offices of the Chesapeake Bay Foundation's Phillip Merrill Environmental Center, Annapolis, Maryland, designed by the Smith Group, feature manually operated screening to control daylighting. Photo by Brunson Russum.

light technology and controllability, dimmable HID lighting is not recommended for indoor applications (Wilson 2003).

○ *Stepped or multilevel switching:* Turning off a portion of the lamps in a multilamp luminaire or banks of lights in a space, based on activity needs or daylight availability. This is a cost-effective means of reducing the light in increments. This reduction is accomplished by switching individual ballasts and lamps or by reducing the power load to the ballast. Multilevel ballasts can be used with HID to change the light output in steps. Stepped switching can be a low-cost method of providing some adjustment in light levels in a space.

4. *Daylighting* requires a response that adjusts the use of electric light to the amount of daylight available in interior spaces. As noted earlier, daylight will vary due to weather conditions, time of day, and season. Control is gained by the detection of daylight illuminance at a sensor that is integrated with the switching and dimming systems described above. Photoelectric control systems include:

    o *Photo switch (or photocell):* Generally unacceptable in interior spaces due to the abrupt change in light level with on/off switching. In locations with uniform daylight conditions and in spaces where daylight levels are well above the target levels, these devices may be acceptable and can save more energy than using photosensors. In these situations, they can be used most successfully with stepped switching (see above) to turn off some lights in a multilamp fixture, if adequate daylight is present.

    o *Photosensor:* Uses continuous sensing of available light to control fluorescent electronic-dimming ballasts and adjusts the electric-light levels, based on a predetermined light level. The system needs to be custom designed, is complex, requires detailed commissioning, and is difficult to maintain, but it is effective in saving energy. Most photosensors have important adjustments for time delay, response speed, and response sensitivity. Small individual sensors are being integrated into individual luminaires, promising even more refined control in the future. Two types of photosensor systems are used:

        1. *Interior closed loop:* The sensor looks into the space it controls, registering the sum of daylight and electric light in its sensing range. Using direct feedback, a single sensor can control only a small number of luminaires in a relatively small space. In addition to use in daylighting-control strategies, this sensor is used for tuning, lumen maintenance, and adaptation-compensation strategies.

        2. *Interior open loop:* The sensor looks out the window or skylight from a location remote from the space being illuminated. With remote sensing, a single sensor can control multiple luminaires in large areas.

Special considerations and cautions related to photosensor applications include:

o Sensors respond to reflectance changes, including a person wearing white clothing.

o Some sensors respond to spectral cues and should be matched to the visual-response curve (which peaks around 550 nanometers).

o Closed-loop sensors need to be placed so that they read the task surfaces, rather than open areas.

o Both sensors and photocells need to be shielded from direct light of the fixtures they are controlling as well as direct sunlight and bright skies.

6. *Adaptation compensation* responds to the human visual system and the adjustment of the eye to changes in light levels. Lower interior light levels at night are more comfortable and safer, since the eye does not have to adapt as much, especially when going from light to dark. This strategy is useful for saving energy at night, but it should only be used in areas that operate outside of daylight hours and where no critical visual tasks occur during these hours. Devices appropriate for this strategy include stepped switching and continuous dimming with photocells (see above.)

7. *Demand limiting or load shedding* is an economic response to energy availability and unit cost. During electrical emergency–alert periods, the automatic dimming of light levels and turning off unnecessary lights can help avoid brownouts. With advance recording systems, the total electricity demands of a building can be monitored and reduced when kilowatt costs temporarily rise during peak demand periods of a day.

8. *Lumen maintenance* aims to maintain an even light level over the life of a group of lamps. A reduced-light (or dimmed) level is used when lumen output of new lamps is higher than needed. As the lamps age and their lumen output decreases, the power is gradually increased to full range. With advances in lamp technology, there is currently minimal light depreciation for most lamp sources. Thus, the use of this strategy is generally not economically viable.

Lighting-control systems link together devices that determine the need for light (sensors) and the supply of power to the luminaires. Logical devices that integrate information signals from various devices may be part of the system. The simplest system combines devices in a local area or single space. Combining these local systems with a central computer and master control station expands the control to a whole building system. Combining the light-control strategies discussed above into an integrated system results in the maximum energy savings.

Other electric systems may also be controlled by this integrated building-automation approach. So-called smart buildings integrate other electrical systems (e.g., motorized shades, fans, air-conditioning and heating, and possibly security and alarm) with the lighting system. These total building systems are called energy-management systems (EMS) or building-automation systems (BAS). They have the ability to sense environmental conditions: time, amount of light, temperature, and air quality. Additionally, they can sense human intervention: occupancy or motion. These systems involve central or building protocol with a computer network–control system to communicate information between components in the system, which provides the potential of substantial energy savings (Center for Building Performance and Diagnostics n.d).

The central system information carrier can be a *low-voltage* or *relay system* (operates a relay inserted in a luminaire power circuit), which uses small wire and consumes little electricity. One such system that communicates through low-voltage wire is DALI (digital addressable lighting interface); it communicates to luminaires and individual-control devices, and from lamps or ballasts. This international standard for ballast control is reducing the problem of incompatibility between controls and ballasts.

Another information-carrier system option is a *power-line* or *carrier-current system,* which uses the building wire system to send high-frequency signals, thus offering a low-cost system with great flexibility. But this option is subject to interference and malfunction without the installation of special additional electrical components. The third and newest system uses *radio frequency* for communication. Wireless Mesh (ZigBee) and WiFi are two such systems.

Location options for the processors needed for the controls are: (1) local, next to device controlled; (2) central, utilizing a computer network–control system; and (3) distributed, decisions locally programmed but run centrally (unit failure affects only unit, not whole system).

The decision process for selecting a control system is based on occupant's needs, type of space use and functional needs, energy rates, and an electricity-use profile. Daylighting potential is also a factor. For straightforward projects, a decision model is available (Rundquist et al. 1996). For more complex situations, an economic-payback analysis is appropriate.

Commissioning is another key step in achieving the energy efficiency and effectiveness of an advanced control system. This is the process of tuning, calibrating, and adjusting the devices to be sure they work appropriately for the installation requirements and at peak performance levels. The time and expense of this critical task is being managed by computerized monitoring components. Commissioning is required in a project seeking LEED certification.

Computer programs are available to assist designers in developing daylight/electric-light layouts, including quantifying relative energy savings, modeling annual daylighting characteristics in a particular location, and sensor placement. One recent tool, Sensor Placement + Optimization Tool, or SPOT, was developed as part of California's Public Interest Energy Research (PIER) Program Lighting Research Project (LRP). While initially developed for classroom daylighting, it is useful for other types of spaces (Architectural Energy Corporation 2006).

A more comprehensive discussion of the increasingly complex array of control devices and systems is beyond the scope this discussion. Detailed information can be found in four sources: *Lighting Controls: Patterns for Design* (Rundquist et al. 1996); *IESNA Lighting Handbook* (Rea 2000); *Advanced Lighting Guidelines* (Roberts and Flood 2003); and the Lighting Controls Association Web site (www.aboutlightingcontrols.org). In making a decision about using any lighting-control strategy, an analysis of the life-cycle cost of the controls (unit, installation, electricity, and maintenance) needs to be weighed against the energy savings from using the system. Within the context of ERLD, these decisions will affect both the energy efficiency and effectiveness of interior lighting.

Environmental Impact Issues

While effective and efficient use of energy is a major concern in environmentally responsible lighting, there are other concerns related to lighting that are important in the larger context of ERID. These include issues of outdoor light trespassing and light pollution. There are also issues related to the sustainable loop for lighting products that includes the manufacturing of the lamps, luminaires, ballasts, as well as the disposal of lamps and ballasts at the end of their useful life.

NIGHT LIGHT—DARK SKIES

Outdoor night lighting is an essential consideration for environmentally sustainable lighting design. The use of outdoor lighting for both functional and design purposes increased in the last half century at an alarming rate. Concerns raised by astronomers, beginning in the 1970s, resulted in the excessive use of low-pressure sodium light, a poor quality light source by most measures.

The current excess in outdoor lighting has produced a number of problems, including light pollution, light trespassing, and energy waste. *Lighting pollution* is excessive outdoor night light, usually uncontrolled and frequently aimed upward. *Light trespassing* is light that extends over a property line and/or causes glare for individuals outside the local area. It is estimated that 30 percent of outdoor lighting is wasted. Indoor lighting escaping through facade or roof openings or through glazing can contribute to both light pollution and light trespassing. Part of the rationale for the increased use of outdoor lighting has been issues of visibility, safety, and outdoor comfort. But this excess in outdoor lighting fails to accommodate the circadian rhythm (bright day-to-dark nigh cycle) of all living things (Crawford and Davis 2006; Akashi 2005).

The International Dark-Sky Association (IDA) is teaming with IESNA to develop a model lighting ordinance and to design guidelines that provide a lighting-zone system to establish light levels, shielding, maximum lamp wattages, and curfew times (Lien 2004; IDA 2006). The recommendations for ERLD presented earlier apply to outdoor lighting as well: Use good light sources (energy efficient and with good color rendering), place the light where it is needed (downward), use controls to turn off or to reduce unneeded light, and install light-colored surface material where possible. Lack of awareness of the issues and appropriate solutions is a major hindrance to progress in reducing light pollution.

SUSTAINABLE LIFE CYCLE FOR LIGHTING PRODUCTS

Environmental responsibility extends beyond the selection and use of the lighting products discussed earlier. The product life-cycle impact analysis discussed for other interior materials applies to lighting products as well. The manufacturing of lighting systems uses natural resources, the operation of the system consumes energy resources, and the disposal of the components of the system at the end of their useful life can cause pollution.

In manufacturing lamps, glass, the major waste by-product, is starting to be recycled. Fluorescent lamps use mercury and rare earth phosphors. With smaller lamps (T8 and T5) less of these materials are used per lamp. Longer-life lamps further reduce the use of natural resources and energy in the manufacturing process.

Lamp manufacturers are continuing to develop technologies that further reduce the amount of mercury needed in a lamp.

The manufacturing process for luminaires also frequently uses materials and processes that are not environmentally friendly. Anodized aluminum is energy intensive to manufacture, while chrome plating involves using toxic solutions. Some wet-paint processes use toxic solvents and generate substantial paint residue, while the powder-coating process has a minimum of both of these problems. Lead solder is another toxic concern in the luminaire- and lamp-manufacturing processes.

Considerable packing material is used to protect lamps and luminaires in transit to the job site. An increasing number of manufacturers are concerned with the environmental waste generated by this packing material. Solutions include the use of environmentally responsible materials, reusable materials, or shipping options that minimize job-site waste disposal.

A major ERID concern is the disposition of products at the end of their useful life. For lighting products there are three concerns: (1) lamps with toxic elements (i.e., mercury and lead), (2) ballasts, and (3) recovery of luminaire materials. While some of the materials in luminaires have recycle value, the ability to handle these is currently limited. Toxic leakage into the soil and toxic air pollution as a result of bulb breakage are primary concerns.

Ballasts manufactured through 1979 contained polychlorinated biphenyls (PCBs) in their capacitors. (Ballasts manufactured after 1979 are labeled "no PCBs.") Green Lights, an Environmental Protection Agency (EPA) program, recommends that non-leaking PCB ballasts be handled as hazardous waste. This means that they should be disposed of through high-temperature incineration, recycling, or at a chemical- or hazardous-waste landfill. Leaking ballasts need to be destroyed through high-temperature incineration (EPA 1998).

Some lead may be found in incandescent and high-intensity discharge (HID) lamps. Fluorescent, neon, and HID lamps contain small quantities of mercury. Both substances, lead and mercury, have negative environmental and human impact and are considered hazardous-waste materials. The amount of mercury used in many fluorescent lamps today is less than 10 percent of the quantity used per lamp 40 years ago (as little as 3.5 mg per lamp) (Fong 2003). But the amount of mercury in fluorescent lamps varies widely. Lamps passing the Environmental Protection Agency toxicity characteristic leaching procedure (TCLP) are labeled "TCLP compliant" and are identified by green end caps. But by the addition of devices and chemical additives that reduce mercury-leaching rates during the testing procedure (though not necessarily later in the landfill site), some lamps having larger amounts of mercury may pass the test and will not be labeled as requiring hazardous waste handling (Lory 2004).

In the 1999 Resource Conservation and Recovery Act (RCRA), lamps containing mercury were reclassified as universal waste to facilitate increased recycling. Regulations affect the handling, storage, transport, and disposal of hazardous materials but not universal waste. The EPA's goal has been to raise the national recycling rate for mercury lamps from a 20-percent recycling rate in 2002 to 80 percent by 2009 (EPA n.d.c). Non-TCLP-compliant lamps must be handled as hazardous waste and disposed of in hazardous-waste landfill sites. In the Universal

Waste Rule, an exemption is made for "small quantity generators." While lamps used in residential and small-business settings, or "TCLP-compliant" lamps, do not have to be disposed of as hazardous waste, sound ERID practices would suggest that they be recycled to avoid mercury leaching. Lamps should be handled to avoid breaking the glass, which releases the mercury into the environment.

An increasing number of firms are available to handle recycling of luminaire components. Recycling firms separate the glass, metal, and mercury for reuse. Phosphor powder containing mercury is processed to reclaim the mercury. HID glass contains lead and, if not recycled, is sent to hazardous-waste landfills (EPA n.d. *a*; Lamprecycting.org n.d.; Fong 2003).

Regulations, Codes, and Standards for Lighting Efficiency

A number of regulations, codes, and standards impact ERLD. Since lighting is a major energy consumer in buildings, lighting-efficiency policies, codes, and standards are designed to minimize the energy used by the lighting system without compromising the quality of the lighting design. It should be remembered that energy savings can accumulate not only from a reduction in the amount of power used by the lighting system but also from a reduction in the time the system is operated. Energy savings, measured in kilowatt hours, does not ensure good lighting. As noted at the beginning of this chapter, the goal should be energy-effective lighting design rather than just energy-efficient lighting design.

Application standards use a performance-specification approach by requiring reduced energy consumption for lighting, while the equipment regulations define the minimum efficiency for lighting components. Standards and model codes for lighting have been developed by government agencies and private-sector initiatives. Government regulations address issues of energy conservation related to lighting equipment. These regulations, standards, and model codes are converted to building energy codes and laws at all levels of government in North America. Additionally, there are a number of nonregulatory government programs that support energy efficiency in lighting.

APPLICATION REGULATIONS

Application standards set limits on the amount of power used for lighting. The lighting industry benchmark model energy code, ANSI/ASHRAE/IESNA Standard 90.1, uses an application-standards approach. This consensus standard has been developed by the American Society of Heating, Refrigeration, and Air-Conditioning Engineers (ASHRAE) and the Illuminating Engineering Society of North America (IESNA) and has been updated regularly. Some version of this standard is used as the basis of regulations enacted by many states and provinces in North America. (See U.S. Department of Energy n.d. *b*)

The last version—ANSI/ASHREA/IESNA Standard 90.1: 2004 Energy Standard for Buildings except Low-Rise Residential Buildings—sets increased requirements for energy-efficient design in new buildings. Section 9 of this standard defines the energy-use limits for lighting in the form of power allowances of interior, exterior, and building-grounds lighting. The interior-lighting power allowance (watts per square foot) can be determined by the prescriptive requirements of either a building-area method or a space-by-space method. An alternate method involves an energy-cost budget approach that allows trade-offs between the lighting system and other energy systems in the building. The ASHRAE Standard 100 provides application standards for existing buildings (ASHRAE 2004). Another model energy code, the International Energy Conservation Code (IECC) references the ASHRAE/IESNA Standard 90.1 and allows a simpler compliance means for equivalent energy efficiency (diLouie 2004). Both codes are updated on a three year cycle.

The International Dark-Sky Association and IESNA are developing another application regulation in the form of a model lighting ordinance for outdoor lighting. This type of model ordinance can then be adopted by local governmental units to support environmentally responsible exterior lighting (IDA 2006).

REGULATION OF LIGHTING COMPONENTS

One of the most influential regulations affecting lighting has been the U.S. Energy Policy Act of 1992 (EPAct 1992). This act established energy-efficiency standards for the most commonly used lamps in the United States. As part of this act, the Federal Trade Commission (FTC) designed and implemented in 1995 energy-efficient labeling for lamps that includes lumen output, lamp wattage, rated lamp life, and design voltage. The Energy Policy Act of 2005 established improved standards, including the elimination of magnetic ballast by 2010 (DiLouie 2005a).

The Model Energy Code (MEC), containing a codified version of ASHREA/IESNA Standard 90.1, has been adapted or adopted by many states to meet the EPA requirement for a lighting code that meets or exceeds that standard. Recent versions of the code are also known as the International Energy Conservation Code (IECC). Currently, states are updating to recent standards that integrate more current lighting technology and energy-efficiency expectations (DiLouie 2004).

The National Appliance Energy Conservation Amendments (NAECA) of 1988 regulates minimum-efficiency levels of ballasts. This is based on a minimum ballast-efficacy-factor (BEF) value, which is a method for comparing the efficacy of the lamp and ballast system. The EPA has also established the handling and disposal regulations for lamps as discussed earlier, stemming from the 1976 Resource Conservation and Recovery Act legislation (EPA n.d. *a*).

Ballast efficacy factor (BEF) is defined as ballast factor (BF) in percent, divided by the total ballast input power in watts or BEF = BF × 100/ ballast input watts (diLouie 2005a).

NONREGULATORY GOVERNMENT LIGHTING PROGRAMS

The federal government has taken initiatives to promote energy efficiency and energy conservation with programs for the general public and the industry, as well as within the government. Much of these efforts have lighting and lighting products as integral components of the initiatives.

The best-known program is the Energy Star program, which is administered by the EPA in partnership with the U.S. Department of Energy. It is a voluntary labeling program with a marketing focus on identifying and promoting energy-efficient products and, more recently, energy-efficient buildings. To earn the Energy Star label, products must also meet minimum performance standards (*About Energy Star* n.d).

Another voluntary program administered by the EPA is the Green Lights program. In this program, companies and institutions commit to surveying the lighting in their facilities and retrofitting 90 percent of their lighting systems within five years with energy-efficient modifications (EPA 1998). The Building Technologies Program, listed on the DOE (Building Technologies Program 2005) Web site, provides links to Energy Star, Green Lights, and other voluntary initiatives.

The government has also made a commitment to promoting energy efficiency within the federal government. The Federal Energy Management Program (FEMP) under the DOE notes on its Web site: "As the world's largest volume-buyer of energy-related products, the federal government can reduce energy consumption and achieve enormous cost savings by purchasing energy-efficient products. Federal buyers are now required by the Energy Policy Act of 2005 to purchase products that are Energy Star-qualified or FEMP-designated. (These products are in the upper 25% of energy efficiency in their class)" (FEMP 2006).

PRIVATE-SECTOR INITIATIVES

As discussed in Chapter 9, LEED-rating systems use a consensus criteria for establishing the minimum standard of measure. Thus, the system gives credit or points for avoiding real problems, rather than providing guidelines for achieving good lighting (Benya 2005). In LEED-NC, 2.2, 8 to 22 points come from lighting-related issues. Light pollution and light trespass issues are part of "Credit 1, Sustainable Sites." Meeting or exceeding ASHRAE/IESNA 90.1–2004 requirements provides 2 to 10 points. Lighting decisions can contribute to achieving points in other categories: reuse of lighting, construction-waste management, recycled content, local- and regional-material use, energy and atmosphere, indoor environmental quality, daylight views, and potentially in the innovation and design process credit. Controllability and access to outside views provides a lighting opportunity for points, (e.q., operable windows and individual lighting control) (DiLouie 2005a; Fong 2003).

Another approach to high-performance building decision making is a proprietary Web-based tool called BIDS (Building Investment Decision Support). This case-based decision-making tool is being developed by the Advanced Building Systems Integration Consortium (ABSIC). It is a life-cycle tool focused on quality differences in seven (7) components and subsystems, including lighting control and access to the natural environment and environmentally appropriate finishes (BetterBricks 2002).

ECONOMICS

Economic considerations play a role in any environmentally responsible lighting design decision. Adoption usually requires documentation of a positive financial impact for the project, that is, when the savings on electricity will equal the additional energy-savings costs. The most direct model is to calculate a simple payback (first cost/annual savings) to determine the break-even date. Simple tools are available from lamp and luminaire manufacturers. A more detailed approach uses a life-cycle cost (LCC) analysis. Several LCC models and tools to handle this analysis are available (Livingston 2006).

It should be recognized that the use of advanced lighting sources, design strategies, and controls results in savings of 25 to 50 percent. Cooper Lighting (Cargnel 2004, 25) illustrates that replacement of a traditional 400-watt metal-halide fixture as a hi-bay warehouse source with fluorescent fixtures results in 25 to 55 percent energy savings before the use of controls or other energy-saving methods. Additionally, the use of fluorescent lamps allows for controls that are impractical with HID lamps, resulting in additional energy savings. If daylighting is added to the equation, energy use may be cut in half again (Rea 2000). The less financially tangible positive health benefits should also be added to the equation. In the larger energy-savings analyses, there is an HVAC reduction that adds an additional 10 to 35 percent savings. This savings not only has a direct owner benefit but also results in a savings of generated electricity and a related potential for reduced pollution.

Trade-offs occur with automatic lamp controls (increased switching on and off affects lamp life). Calendar life of a lamp increases due to running fewer hours each day, but absolute operating lamp life may be reduced due to shorter running time per cycle (e.g. 20,000 to 15,000 hour life). The reduced energy costs usually exceed relamping costs resulting from reduced lamp life (see Electric Power Research Institute 1994).

DESIGN STRATEGIES

Several approaches to energy-effective and energy-efficient lighting have been proposed by noted lighting experts. Nancy Clanton (2004) suggests six aspects of lighting to focus on to achieve a low-power density (i.e., watts used per square foot):

1. Quality daylight
2. Ambient, task, and accent lighting
3. Light-colored surfaces
4. Energy-efficient lighting equipment
5. Combination of automatic and manual lighting controls
6. Light surfaces, not volumes

The Advanced Building Systems Integration Consortium, Center for Building Performance and Diagnostics (ABSIC/CBPD), provides seven guidelines for high performance lighting (Center for Building Performance and Diagnostics n.d.):

1. Daylight-dominant lighting
2. Task lighting and ambient lighting
3. Indirect-direct lighting
4. High-performance luminaires
5. Plug-and-play fixtures
6. Dynamic zoning and advanced controls
7. System integration

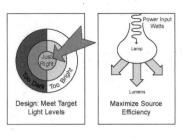 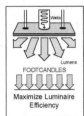  

Design: Meet Target Light Levels	Maximize Source Efficiency	Maximize Luminaire Efficiency	Automatically Control Lighting	Optimize Operations/Maintenance

Figure 6-15
Comprehensive lighting upgrade strategies. Drawn by Glenn Burmeister. Source: adapted from Energy Star Building Upgrade Manual: Lighting (Washington, DC: U.S. Environmental Protection Agency, 2004), 53.

The ABSCIC/CBPD also has twelve major decisions for other interior systems (Guidelines 2002).

A set of strategies to achieve energy-efficient lighting has been presented by Minnesota Department of Public Service in *Commercial Building Lighting Standards: Educational Project* (1993). The focus is on six aspects of lighting (needs, hardware, daylighting, control, maintenance, and operations scheduling) and defines action items for each:

1. Lighting needs (tasks and illumination requirements)
   o Identify visual tasks and locations.
   o Group task with same illuminance requirements.
   o Properly locate luminaires to provide light to tasks.
   o Consider light colors for walls, floors, ceilings, and furniture.
2. Lighting hardware (lamps and luminaires)
   o Install lamps with higher efficacy.
   o Investigate the use of reduced wattage lamps in existing luminaires when illuminance levels are greater than recommended.
   o Consider reduced-wattage fluorescent lamps in existing luminaires.
   o Consider replacing existing low-wattage incandescent lamps with fewer high-wattage incandescent lamps or compact fluorescent lamps.
   o Assess luminaire effectiveness for lighting [distribution and efficiency].
   o Consider energy-efficient, electronic ballasts.
   o Consider using heat-removal luminaires.
3. Daylighting
   o Use daylighting when it is appropriate.
   o Coordinate the plan organization to maximize the use of daylighting.
   o Assess which daylighting tasks are critical and noncritical (indirect, reflected, or filtered daylight vs. direct sunlight).
   o Maximize the effectiveness of fenestration and shading controls.
   o Consider the use of light colors (see above).
   o Increase the distribution of light deep into the space by using light shelves and light-colored room surfaces.
   o Integrate electric lighting with daylighting design.

4. Light controls
   o Install switching to adjust illumination levels to activity requirements.
   o Consider occupancy sensors to turn lights on and off as room occupancy varies.
   o Consider the use of dimming systems to adjust illumination levels.
   o Consider the use of time clocks to adjust lighting with occupancy schedule.

5. Lighting maintenance
   o Evaluate the present lighting-maintenance program.
   o Clean luminaires and replace lamps on regular maintenance schedule.
   o Replace outdated or damaged luminaires.

6. Operating schedules
   o Analyze lighting use during working and building-cleaning periods.
   o Light building for occupied periods only and as security requires.
   o Try to schedule routine building cleaning during occupied hours.
   o Restrict night parking to specific lots.

Environmentally responsible lighting design that is both energy effective and energy efficient becomes easier and more achievable with better products and processes. The contribution of ERLD to environmentally responsible interior design can be substantial.

References

About Energy Star. n.d. Washington, DC: U.S. Environmental Protection Agency (EPA) and the U.S. Department of Energy (DOE). Retrieved from EPA Web site: http://www.energystar.gov/index.cfm?c=about.ab_index.

Akashi, Y. 1999. Sparkle elements—A bright idea. *Architectural Lighting* (November): 38–41.

———. 2005. Toward migratory-bird-friendly lighting (Research Matters). *Lighting Design + Application* 35 (July 7): 12–13.

American Society of Heating, Refrigeration, and Air-Conditioning Engineers (ASHRAE). 2004. *Energy standard for buildings, except low-rise residential buildings: ANSI/ASHRAE/IESNA standard 90.1.* Atlanta, GA: ASHRAE.

Architectural Energy Corporation (AEC). 2006. *About SPOT: Sensor Placement + Optimization Tool.* Boulder, CO: Architectural Energy Corporation. Retrieved from AEC Web site: http://www.archenergy.com/SPOT/.

Avant, J., and J. Ogen. 2005. The myth of sustainable cost. *eco-structure* 3 (2): 51–54.

Benya, J. 2005. Lighting in a sustainable interior (The Century Series). *Lighting Design + Application* 35 (7): 70–73.

BetterBricks. 2002. Making the case for high performance buildings—part 1 (An interview with Vivian Loftness). *BetterBricks.com* (November). http://www.betterbricks.com/default.aspx?pid=article&articleid=297&typeid=10&topicname=increasedvalue&indextype=topic.

Building Energy Codes Program. 2007. *Energy Code (MEC & IECC) FAQs.* Washington, DC: U.S. Department of Energy, Office of Energy Efficiency and Renewable Energy, Building Energy Codes Program. Retrieved from DOE Web site: http://www.energycodes.gov/support/codes_faq.stm.

Building Technologies Program. 2005. *Program areas.* Washington, DC: U.S. Department of Energy, Office of Energy Efficiency and Renewable Energy, Building Technologies Programs. Retrieved January 22, 2008, from Building Technologies Program Web site: http://www.eere .energy.gov/buildings/program_areas

Butler, D. L., and P. M. Biner. 1989. Effects of setting on window preferences and factors associated with those preferences. *Environment and Behavior* 21: 17–31.

Canzler, G. 2002. Daylight categories, series (5). *Professional Lighting Design* 26 (July/August): 51–52.

Cargnel, J. 2004. Can you afford not to use fluorescent? *in-lighten* 1: 25–26. (Available from cooper Lighting, peachtree city, GA.)

Center for Building Performance and Diagnostics. n.d. Lighting: Lifecycle of 2 lighting strategies. Pittsburgh, PA: Center for Building Performance and Diagnostics, Carnegie Mellon University Advanced Building Systems Integration Consortium. Retrieved January 22, 2008, from CBPD Web site: http://cbpd.arc.cmu.edu/ebids/pages/group.aspx?group=3

Clanton, N. 2004. Light and human health. PowerPoint seminar presented at Green Build Conference (November 2004), Portland, OR.

Coleman, C., and D. Robinson, eds. 2000. *Design Ecology—The project: Assessing the future of green design.* White paper. Chicago: International Interior Design Association. Retrieved January 22, 2008, from Design Matters Web site: http://www.designmatters.net/whitepaper/design_ ecology.pdf.

Crawford, D., and S. Davis. 2004. Light pollution—The problem and the solutions. *in-lighten* 1: 12–14. (Available from Cooper Lighting, Peachtree City, GA.)

Cromie, W. J. 2006. When the blues keep you awake. *Harvard University Gazette.* February 01, 1.

Daylighting. n.d. *Whole building design guide.* BetterBricks.com. Retrieved from Betterbricks Web site: http://betterbricks.com/default.aspx?pid= article&articleid=470&typeid=8&topicname=daylighting&indextype=/.

DiLouie, C. 2004. *Energy code update* (December). Rosslyn, VA: Lighting Controls Association. http://www.aboutlightingcontrols.org/education/ papers/energycodeupdate.shtml.

———. 2005a. Energy Policy Act of 2005 sets new ballast efficiency standards (November). Rosslyn, VA: Lighting Controls Association. http:// www.aboutlightingcontrols.org/education/papers/ballast_law.shtml.

———. 2005b. Lighting and LEED (August). Rosslyn, VA: Lighting Controls Association. http://www.aboutlightingcontrols.org/education/papers/ greendesign.shtml.

Egan, M. D., and V. W. Olgyay. 2002. *Architectural Lighting,* 2nd ed. New York: McGraw-Hill.

———. 1994. *It pays to turn off the lights* (MI-103646). Pleasant Hills, CA: EPRI.

Electric Power Research Institute (EPRI). 1998. *Lighting retrofit manual* (TR-107130-R1). Pleasant Hills, CA: EPRI.

Energy Information Administration (EIA). 2003. *Preliminary End-Use Consumption Estimates.* Washington, DC: U.S. Department of Energy. http://www.eia.doe.gov/emeu/cbecs/enduse_consumption/intro.html.

———. 2005. *End-use consumption of electricity 2001.* Washington, DC: U.S. Department of Energy. http://www.eia.doe.gov/emeu/recs/recs2001/enduse2001/enduse2001.html.

EPA (Environmental Protection Agency, U.S.). n.d. *a. Universal waste: Lamp recycling effort.* Washington, DC: EPA.

———. n.d. *b. Mercury.* Washington, DC: EPA. http://www.epa.gov/epa-oswer/haswaste/id/univwast/lamps/putreacj.htm/http://www.epa.gov/epaoswer/hazwaste/mercury/live.htm

———. 1998. Green Lights Program. Lighting waste disposal. *Lighting upgrade manual.* EPA 430-B-95-004. Washington, DC: EPA, Green Lights Program.

Federal Energy Management Program. 2006. Energy-efficient products. Washington, DC: U.S. Department of Energy, Office of Energy Efficiency and Renewable Energy, Federal Energy Management Program (FEMP). http://www.eere.energy.gov/femp/procurement.

Fong, D. 2003. What can be done today to prepare for tomorrow: The principles of sustainability. PowerPoint seminar presented at Lightfair 2003 (May), New York, NY.

Frankel, M., and B. Erwine. 2005. Lighting elements of the LEED Green Building rating system. PowerPoint presented at Lightfair 2005 (April), New York, NY.

Gordon, G. 2003. *Interior lighting for designers,* 4th ed. Hoboken, NJ: John Wiley & Sons.

Guidelines for high performance buildings. 2002. *BAPP: Building as power plant.* Interior Systems Workshop, Carnegie Mellon University, Pittsburgh, PA. http://www.arc.cmu.edu/bapp/Workshops/w3_handout.pdf.

Hakkarainen, P. 2005. Balancing daylight. *Specified Lighting Design* (December): 6–8.

Heerwagen, J. 2000. Do green buildings enhance the well being of workers? Yes. *Environmental Design + Construction* 1 (July/August): 24–29. http://www.edcmag.com/CDA/Archives/fb077b7338697010VgnVCM100000f932a8c0.

———. 2001. Building biophilia: Connecting people to nature in building design. *Environmental Design + Construction* 2 (March/April): 30–34. http://www.edcmag.com/CDA/Archives/18f9f635d8697010VgnVCM100000f932a8c0.

Heerwagen, J., K. Kampschroer, K. Powell, and V. Loftness. 2004. Collaborative knowledge work environments. *Building Research & Information* 32 (6): 510–528.

Heschong Mahone Group. 1999a. *Daylighting in schools: An investigation into the relationship between daylight and human performance* (detailed report). Fair Oaks, CA.: Heschong Mahone Group.

———. 1999b. *Skylighting and retail sales: An investigation into the relationship between daylight and human performance* (detailed report). Fair Oaks, CA.: Heschong Mahone Group.

———. 2001. *Re-analysis report: Daylighting and schools, additional analysis* (research report). Fair Oaks, CA: New Buildings Institute

———. 2003a. *Daylight and retail sales.* Technical report: P500-03-082-A-5. Fair Oaks, CA: California Energy Commission.

———. 2003b. *Daylighting in schools: Reanalysis report.* Technical report: P500-03-082-A-3. Fair Oaks, CA: California Energy Commission.

———. 2003c. *Windows and classrooms: A study of student performance and the indoor environment.* Technical report: P500-03-082-A-7. Fair Oaks, CA: California Energy Commission.

———. 2003d. *Windows and offices: A study of office worker performance, indoor environment.* Fair Oaks, CA: California Energy Commission.

International Dark-Sky Association (IDA). 2006. Groundbreaking Model Lighting Ordinance Near Completion (press release). Tucson, AZ: International Dark-Sky Association. Retrieved from IDA Web site: http://www.darksky.org/news/press-2006-10-16.php.

International Building Code Council. 2003. *International energy conservation code.* Country Club Hills, IL: International Building Code Council.

Kuller, R., and C. Lindsten. 1992. Health and behavior of children in classrooms with and without windows. *Journal of Environmental Psychology* 12: 305–317.

Lamprecycle.org. n.d. http://lamprecycle.org.

Lien, M. 2004. Ch Ch Cha changes. *in-lighten* 1 (1): 17–19. (Availabel from cooper Lighting, Peachtree city, GA)

Light pollution. 2007. http://encyclopedia.thefreedictionary.com/light%20pollution.

Lighting Controls Association. n.d. *LCA applications guide.* Rosslyn, VA: Lighting Controls Association. http://www.aboutlightingcontrols.org/education/index.shtml.

Livingston, L. 2006. State-of-the-art design tools and practices: Lighting technologies. PowerPoint seminar presented at Lightfair 2006 (May), Las Vegas, NV.

Lory, C. S. 2004. *Shedding light on mercury in fluorescents: A workbook for design professionals.* New York: INFORM, Inc.

Miller, N., and D. Maniccia. 2005. Daylighting and electric lighting integration. PowerPoint seminar presented at Lightfair 2005 (April), New York, NY.

Minnesota Department of Public Service. 1993. *Commercial building lighting standards educational project: Workshop manual,* 3rd ed. St. Paul, MN: Minnesota Department of Public Service.

Nagourney, E. 2002. Vital signs patterns; light may help premature infants grow. *The New York Times,* February 26.

National Lighting Bureau (NLB). n.d. *The NLB guide to energy-efficient lighting systems.* Washington, DC: NLB.

Pierson, J. 1995. If the sun shines in, workers work better, buyers buy more. *The Wall Street Journal,* November 20, B1.

Raloff, J. 2006. Light impacts: Hue and timing determine whether rays are beneficial or detrimental (May 26). *Science News Online* 169 (21): 330. http://www.sciencenews.org/articles/20060527/bob9.asp

Rea, M. S., ed. 2000. *IESNA lighting handbook: Reference and application,* 9th ed. (CD) New York: Illuminating Engineering Society of North America.

Reis, M. 2000. Un-glaringly good advice on daylighting. *Environmental Design + Construction* 1 (July/August): 33–39.

Roberts, J., and R. Floods, eds. 2003. *Advanced lighting guidelines.* White Salmon, WA: New Buildings Institute. http://www.newbuildings.org/lighting.htm

Rundquist, R. A., T. G. McDougall, and J. R. Benya. 1996. *Lighting controls: Patterns for design.* TR 107230. Pleasant Hills, CA: Electric Power Research Institute.

Steffy, G. R. 2001. *Architectural lighting design,* 2nd ed. New York: John Wiley & Sons.

U.S. Department of Energy (DOE). n.d. *a. Lighting research and development.* Washington, DC: U.S. Department of Energy. Retrieved from DOE Web site: http://www.eere.energy.gov/buildings/tech/lighting.

————. n.d. *b. Status of state energy codes.* Washington, DC: U.S. Department of Energy. Retrieved from DOE Web site: http://www.energycodes.gov/implement/state_codes/index.stm.

————. n.d. *c.* Lighting recycle effort. Washington, DC: U.S. Department of Energy. Retrieved from DOE Web site: http:www.eere.energy.gov/buildings/tech/lighting.

————. 1996. *Energy Information Administration (EIA): Annual energy review for 1995.* Washington, DC: U.S. Department of Energy.

Veitch, J. A. 2000. Choosing the right light: The benefits of full-spectrum lighting continue to be researched and debated. *Business in Vancouver Construction Directory* 575A (December 1): 11 (National Research Institute in Construction [NRCC-44747]). http://irc.nrc-cnrc.gc.ca/pubs/fulltext/prac/nrcc44747/.

————. 2003. Lighting controls: Beyond the toggle switch. *Environmental Building News* 12, 6 (June): 1, 9–13.

Wilson, A. 2004. Productivity and green buildings. *Environmental Building News* 13, 10 (October): 1, 10–15.

Winchip, S. M. 2005. *Designing a quality lighting environment.* New York: Fairchild Publications.

CHAPTER SEVEN

Energy, HVAC, and Water

Jeffrey S. Tiller, PE, LEED AP
Jeanne Mercer-Ballard, MA, LEED AP, LC, IESNA, IDEC

What is the use of a house if you haven't got a tolerable planet to put it on?
—Henry David Thoreau

Critical Resources

The most important resources in our economy over the past century have been energy and water. Energy from petroleum, natural gas, coal, and uranium has driven the world's economies. Water also provides energy in the form of hydro-power, but it is much more important for human consumption, agriculture, and industrial processes. Unfortunately, these resources are limited. We are currently at a critical point in determining how to transform our societies in ways that provide the comforts we expect without completely depleting supplies of energy and water.

Figure 7-1 shows the enormous gap between the United States, other industrialized countries, and underdeveloped countries in terms of energy use per person. While the United States' dominance in energy use is alarming, of equal concern is the rapid growth of per capita energy use in India and China. Between 1980 and 2003, per capita energy use in these countries doubled. Total energy use grew 237 percent in India and 163 percent in China (Energy Information Administration 2004). Clearly, our scarce energy resources will be severely strained in coming decades. The United States needs to demonstrate its leadership in using available technologies to reduce its energy use per person.

Buildings consume about 40 percent of our nation's energy resources. In 1999, commercial building owners and operators paid over $98 billion in energy bills,

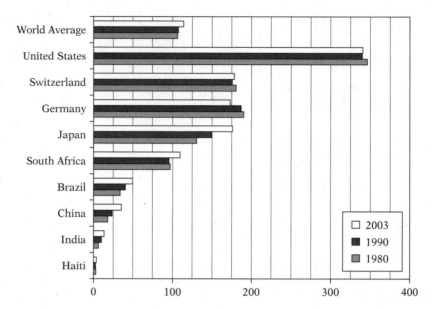

Figure 7-1
Energy use per capita for selected countries. Note the difference in energy use between the United States and underdeveloped countries, as well as the enormous growth in energy use in China and India.
Source: Energy Information Administration (2004).

while residential homeowners and renters paid $137 billion. Electricity (including the losses for generation) provided 68 percent of total energy use in residential and commercial buildings, followed by 24 percent for natural gas and 6 percent for petroleum (Wilson and Yost 2001).

Unfortunately, our energy use has contributed to substantial reductions in air quality. The main culprit in the case of buildings is high consumption of electricity that uses coal as its primary source. Burning coal without modern air-pollution controls spews millions of pounds of sulfur oxides and nitrogen oxides into the atmosphere. Petroleum and natural gas contribute substantial nitrogen oxides as well. All three fuels produce carbon dioxide when burned, which is the main concern of those trying to reduce the threat of climate change and global warming.

As with energy, the United States is by far the leading user of water per capita (Center for Economic and Social Rights n.d.), as shown in Figure 7-2. The United States' water resources have become critically short in many cities in recent years. Water shortages are due to a combination of lower levels of rainfall and increased consumption—primarily for buildings and agriculture. In response, many localities have adopted short-term rationing requirements.

Wastewater poses its own set of problems. Building designers plan for storm water from large rooftops and paved areas to flow into storm-sewer systems. This water picks up contaminants along the way. During heavy rains, storm sewers become deluged and overflow, causing flooding conditions in our cities and towns. Wastewater from buildings must travel to sewage-treatment plants, which are over capacity in many of our urban areas and can increase pollution levels in our rivers and streams.

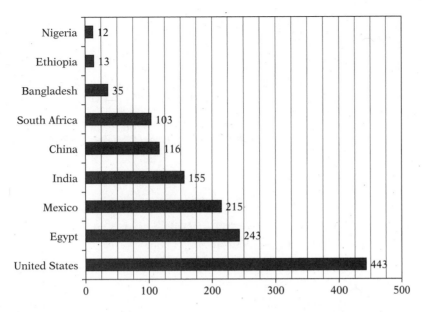

Figure 7-2
Water use per capita for selected countries. The United States has been and is the leading user of water per capita. Note the extreme differences in water use in the United States, China, Bangladesh, and Nigeria.
Source: The Center for Economic and Social Rights (n.d.).

The energy required to pump potable water to buildings and to receive and treat wastewater is significant. Green buildings include measures that reduce water consumption, which in turn also save energy for our economy.

The Role of Green Buildings

There is no single solution to the critical supplies of energy and water and the environmental threats created by their overuse. Therefore, it is necessary to pursue a wide variety of options to reduce use of traditional sources of energy and water.

Buildings are one of the most attractive targets for implementing alternative approaches. Investments in reducing energy and water use quickly pay off by lowering utility bills. In most cases, the savings will return the initial costs (i.e., achieve payback) in a few years.

Even though they can provide building owners with significant savings, the design team has traditionally had a hard time selling increased first-cost investments, because capital building budgets and operating budgets are typically managed and accounted for separately. Building owners and the environment can benefit when management takes a holistic approach and views the two budgets as a single pool of money. First cost, life-cycle cost, maintenance costs, as well as the payback period, should all be an initial part of designing, constructing, and operating a building.

There are other advantages to well-designed buildings that save energy and water (Tiller and Creech 1999), for example:

■ Increased comfort
■ Improved durability

- Less space occupied by ductwork and piping
- Reduced fading of textiles in front of window areas
- Better indoor air quality
- Reduced square footage, yielding fewer resources used, reduced construction waste, and reduced resources associated with building operation

In many cases, more efficient buildings, particularly those that use natural daylighting, provide benefits that far exceed the energy savings (Wilson 1999a), including:

- Improved productivity
- Reduced absenteeism
- Higher employee morale
- Improved test scores in daylighted schools
- Increased product sales in retail applications

A report on thirty-three green buildings in California estimated their financial costs and benefits. The estimated additional cost for the buildings was about 2 percent of construction costs—around $4 per square foot. The projected savings per square foot included $5.50 in energy savings, $0.50 in water savings, and $8 in reduced cost for operations and maintenance. The analysis estimated an additional savings of $35 per square foot for enhanced productivity and improved health. Overall, the savings far outweighed the additional costs (Kats 2003).

The net result of a successful design process for a green building is a structure that initially costs little, if any, more than a comparable traditional building and that provides its occupants tangible improvements in their living and working environments. Since the building uses less energy and water, it will have substantially less negative environmental impact and will serve as a model for future buildings. The end product is a building that is easier to market and, therefore, perceived favorably by the client. Smart businesses recognize the added benefits and are more willing to pay extra for their monthly leases (Kats 2003).

The Role of the Interior Design Professional

Interior designers serve in a unique role in the design process. They combine art and science by using knowledge of technology and psychology to support their expertise in aesthetics, space planning, traffic flow, lighting design, and materials and to respond to client preferences. Interior designers who place a high priority on green building design have an opportunity to change every building on which they work. The more members of the design team committed to green building features and willing to collaborate in a team approach to design, the more likely the initial environmentally responsible concepts will continue through to building occupancy.

Unfortunately, many design projects that begin as green buildings lose key features during the multiple phases (e.g., design development, bidding, value engineering, construction, final occupancy, operations, and maintenance) of the design process. This is due to budget cuts; lack of information, knowledge, and understanding, as well as contractors who are reluctant to try something different than the well-trod approach.

Interior designers should consider the building as a system and use integrated design approaches to optimize performance and economics. The design team must realize that in the design and construction phases, through the use of integrated systems, all of the disciplines are interrelated. In some cases, eliminating just one design feature in an integrated design may sacrifice key elements of a high-performance building, such as thermal comfort, control of moisture, provision of quality indoor air, energy and water savings, or minimal environmental impact.

The design team often looks to the interior designers to make the building as appealing as possible to the client and end users. When the client wants a green building, the interior designers should consider part of their role to be preserving and honoring the green building features. By remaining firm on the initial design, interior designers can often make a difference not only in one building but in the future string of buildings constructed by the client and design team.

Key Components of Green Buildings Related to Energy and Water

It is critical that green buildings demonstrate the positive economics that successful design will generate. The savings from some features can pay back the initial investment in two years or less. Other features and technologies may be excellent choices, but they take longer to return their initial cost.

ENERGY AND WATER EFFICIENCY

Designs and products that reduce consumption serve as the most important first step to reducing energy and water use. Efficiency measures can be grouped in the following key components:

- *Building envelope:* The outer "skin" of the building, usually consisting of the ground floor, exterior walls, windows and doors, and the roof system.
- *HVAC systems:* The heating, ventilation, and air-conditioning (HVAC) systems that should provide comfort, fresh air, and improved indoor air quality.
- *Lighting systems:* Integration of electrical and daylight systems that result in client satisfaction, increased productivity, and reduced energy use. Chapter 6 addresses green building approaches to lighting design.
- *Appliances and equipment:* The choice of these devices, ranging from water heaters to refrigerators, has a major impact on energy and water consumption.

- *Fixtures:* Plumbing fixtures vary dramatically in their demand for water; more efficient fixtures reduce not only water use but also the energy required to provide hot water and the systems necessary to process the wastewater.

SOLAR DESIGN FEATURES

All aboveground buildings are solar buildings, that is, at least one facade receives heat and light from the sun. Unfortunately, many buildings receive too much solar energy in the summer, resulting in exorbitant cooling bills. Others have windows that could make use of solar energy to provide heating in the winter, but they are oriented in such a way that the windows lose more energy than they contribute. The general priority of solar-design features, in terms of economic payback, is as follows:

- *Passive solar heating and cooling features:* Proper window orientation and appropriate use of shading devices can substantially reduce energy bills.
- *Daylighting:* Properly designed windows located on walls or fenestration on rooftops can illuminate interior spaces with minimal supplemental electrical lighting during the daylight hours. Chapter 6 discusses the integration of daylighting systems.
- *Solar water heating:* Solar collectors—glass-covered panels with interior piping to circulate water—provide thermal energy to heat water for bathrooms, shower rooms, laundries, kitchens, swimming pools, and a multitude of other uses.
- *Solar space heating:* Solar collectors that provide space heating and, in most cases, hot water.

WATER-CONSERVING DESIGN FEATURES

In addition to plumbing fixtures themselves, a variety of approaches exist to decrease water consumption, preserve local underground water resources, and reduce impact on wastewater-treatment facilities. Traditional potable water disposal via sewage- and rainwater-control systems through storm-sewer systems are outdated and being replaced by environmentally responsible alternatives.

- *Rainwater capture:* Designs that capture rainwater and store it in catchment systems for use in nonpotable applications.
- *Storm-water reduction:* Techniques such as porous pavement for parking and driveway areas that allow rainwater to return to the soil.
- *Gray-water recycling:* Systems that collect and filter water from activities such as bathing, laundry, and dishwashing for nonpotable applications like toilet flushing and landscape irrigation.
- *On-site wastewater treatment:* Facilities that treat wastewater before returning it to the ground or to the building for use as gray water.

Figure 7-3
One of four cisterns that collect rainwater used for irrigation at the Chicago Center for Green Technology. Photo by Dorothy Fowles.

Figure 7-4
The David L. Lawrence Convention Center (2003), built in Pittsburgh, Pennsylvania, was awarded LEED-NC Gold certification. It has an on-site water-purification facility and gray-water system that recycles water from basins for use in toilets and urinals. Photo by Dorothy Fowles.

LIVING MACHINES TO PROCESS WASTEWATER

Even though low gallons-per-flush (gpf) toilets send far less water per flush to wastewater treatment facilities, the total amount of water sent for processing is enormous. Conventional water treatment systems use high quantities of energy to process wastewater. An alternative to conventional wastewater-treatment systems is a living machine. Living machines use natural wetlands in combination with conventional processes to treat and purify wastewater. Living machines are designed and constructed on-site, either in the landscape as a series of natural wetlands or in the building as a series of pools designed to filtrate, process, and purify the water. The interior system is new technology based on exterior systems that successfully use natural processes. An interior living system is a closed-loop system that returns gray water to toilets and urinals for reuse. The system design can be aesthetically pleasing, often creating interior landscapes. Contrary to preconceptions, if they are designed and operated properly, they do not create offensive odors. Currently, installed systems have high energy use and increased heating and cooling loads. While this technology is not currently in mainstream use, advances should decrease energy requirements and increase benefits, making it a viable option for future buildings (Hoffman and Allan n.d.).

RENEWABLE ELECTRICITY TECHNOLOGIES

Gaining in popularity, renewable electricity can become part of an integrated design for a facility that may actually produce more energy than it consumes. Zero-energy homes and buildings seek to minimize the use of traditional energy resources through the use of high-efficiency insulation, windows, HVAC systems, appliances, and lighting systems. The small amount of traditional energy

Figure 7-5
This Habitat for Humanity home is a zero-energy home due to the contributions of solar power and energy-conservation measures.
Photo by Jeffrey Tiller.

required can be matched by a renewable energy system, using technologies such as the following:

- *Photovoltaic (PV) electricity system:* Specially manufactured modules that generate electricity when bombarded by the sun's rays. Photovoltaic systems can be installed on rooftops, nearby land areas, or, in some cases on vertical walls.
- *Wind energy:* New generations of wind turbines have become competitive with traditional sources of electricity in some geographic regions.
- *Small-scale hydropower:* Uses rapidly flowing water from streams in relatively steep areas to generate electricity with small turbines.
- *Fuel cells:* Devices that are able to generate electricity directly from hydrogen. One of the key issues with fuel cells is how best to provide the hydrogen. Options for sources of hydrogen include coal, natural gas, biomass, and other renewable electricity options.

As opposed to conventional energy production, renewable energy systems are typically installed in, and connected to, the building where the electricity is consumed. This proximity drastically reduces transmission and distribution losses, thereby providing an additional savings over traditional energy-delivery systems.

ENERGY AND WATER EFFICIENCY

Energy- and water-efficiency measures serve as the starting point for green building design. One major advantage is the savings on utility bills that they provide after payback of any additional construction costs.

Integrated design is a key concept. Integrated designs do not focus on one aspect of the building at a time but consider how all of the elements interact. For example, a building with windows that provide improved shading may cost more, but they will reduce the required size of the cooling system. If the cooling capacity decreases by using smaller equipment, the ductwork will be smaller, which will save additional energy. Reduced duct sizes will also lower the size of spaces through which ducts must pass, which could increase the amount of space in the building for occupants, or decrease the total cubic footage or the total height of the building, thus saving additional resources and energy.

THE BUILDING ENVELOPE

The building envelope is composed of the outer surfaces of the building, including the roof and ceiling; walls, windows, doors; and floor system. The outer envelope of the building is the most critical point at which moisture problems begin and energy losses occur. The key components that reduce energy losses include insulation, window design, and air sealing.

Key Steps for Controlling Bulk Moisture

- Drain rain away from the building via high-quality guttering with guards over the downspouts to prevent clogging.
- Use quality flashing details around windows, doors, and other penetrations in the exterior walls.
- Both residential and commercial buildings typically have penetrations through the roof. These are common points of bulk-water entry, so they should be flashed and sealed carefully with materials that will last for several years.
- Use a foundation-drainage system that includes a foundation drain next to the building footing and a drainage mat against underground foundation walls typical of basements in residences and below-grade areas of commercial buildings.

MOISTURE CONTROL

The design team must provide proper details to prevent water—e.g., rain, melting snow, condensation, or groundwater—from entering the building envelope. In addition, the team must address control of water vapor in the interior air.

Another way that water moves through buildings is through *capillary action*, also known as wicking. The same process is evident if you dip a small portion of a paper towel in a cup of water—the entire towel becomes saturated. Common building materials such as wood, concrete, and brick are porous. If they are exposed to liquid water, such as underneath a concrete slab, they will wick moisture into the building.

Bulk moisture and capillary action allow liquid water to flow into the building. Water vapor contained in air is also a concern. The key strategy for controlling the movement of water vapor is to *seal air leaks* in the building envelope. Central and northern climates (zones 5 and above in the climate map shown in Figure 7-6) require vapor retarders on back of the inside surface (usually drywall) on exterior walls. Vapor retarders have permeabilities, as measured by the perm rating system, of 1 or less. Table 7.1 lists perm ratings for common building materials.

The initial concern for moisture control is *bulk moisture*, which enters the building due to weather or as ground water. Climates with substantial wind-driven rain may make buildings particularly susceptible to bulk-moisture intrusion.

Because the perm rating of polyethylene is so low, it can make the building unforgiving if moisture does accumulate inside the walls. In general, polyethylene is not recommended as a vapor retarder material for walls except

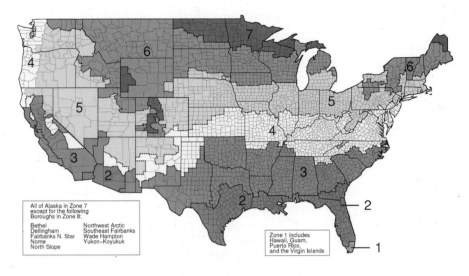

All of Alaska in Zone 7
except for the following
Boroughs in Zone 8:

Bethel   Northwest Arctic
Dellingham   Southeast Fairbanks
Fairbanks N. Star   Wade Hampton
Nome   Yukon–Koyukuk
North Slope

Zone 1 includes
Hawaii, Guam,
Puerto Rico,
and the Virgin Islands

Figure 7-6
The 2006 International Energy Conservation Code (IECC) divides the United States into eight climatic zones and specifies minimum insulation requirements for both residential and commercial structures in each zone.

Table 7.1 Typical Perm Ratings of Building Materials

Material	Perm Rating
Asphalt-coated paper backing on insulation	0.40
Polyethylene plastic (6 mil)	0.06
Plywood with exterior glue	0.70
Plastic-coated insulated-foam sheathing	0.30
Aluminum foil (.35 mil)	0.05
Vapor-barrier paint or primer	0.45
Drywall (unpainted)	50.0

Source: Tiller and Creech 1999, 25.

in climates with very cold winters. Install insulation with asphalt-impregnated paper backing instead or paint the inside surface of the wall with a vapor-barrier primer.

Another moisture issue is *condensation*. The moisture forming on a glass of ice water was previously water vapor in the air around the glass. The outside surface of the glass is cold and below the *dew point,* the temperature of the air in the room. When the air next to the glass cools, its relative humidity rises to 100 percent. The air can no longer hold the moisture, so it allows the water vapor to condense on the walls of the glass. In buildings, the primary surfaces on which condensation can occur are windows, ductwork, water piping, and uninsulated building components. To minimize problems with condensation:

- Make sure the entire building envelope is insulated properly and all air leaks are sealed.
- Use high-quality windows with improved insulating values, such as low-emissivity windows.
- Provide adequate and continuous insulation for supply ductwork, i.e., the ductwork that transports air from the main HVAC units to the rooms of the building.
- Insulate cold-water piping in areas with high relative humidity or hot temperatures, such as in attics above insulation.

It is important that the interior designer recognizes moisture concerns within a building interior. It is critical for the designer to search for the visual cues to a moisture problem before specifying an interior finish material. If the problem is not identified, the finish will fail soon after it is installed, and it will need to be replaced after the moisture problem is addressed. Unidentified moisture problems provide the ideal situation for growth of mold and mildew. If not quickly brought under control, this growth could lead to the need to gut or even demolish the building to protect the health and welfare of the people using the building. (See Chapter 5 for information on indoor air quality.)

Strategies for designing walls and interior treatments that will create minimal opportunities for a moisture problems include:

- In relatively humid climates with warm summers, avoid the use of vinyl wall coverings on the inside surface of exterior walls. Humidity will not be able to penetrate the wall covering, and condensation may occur. Major mold outbreaks have occurred on the underside of vinyl wall coverings.
- Because metal is an excellent conductor of heat, walls built with steel studs can quickly transfer heat from inside to outside in the winter and outside to inside in the summer. In some situations, the cold surface of the metal provides an opportunity for condensation to form. As a consequence, the exterior or interior finish shows vertical and horizontal striping where the studs are located. The designer should insist that steel-stud walls have foam insulated sheathing applied to the exterior.
- In most areas of the country, plastic vapor barriers are not required for wall systems. As Figure 7-6 illustrates, only the northernmost climate zones require vapor barriers, according to the latest revision of the International Energy Conservation Code. Further south, no wall vapor barrier is required or recommended. In fact, during summer months, the cooling system will tend to dry out the interior of the walls if no vapor barriers are installed.

- Mold is an excellent indicator of moisture problems and a major contributor to poor indoor air quality. Mold grows best when four conditions are met:
  - ○ Relative humidity is high or construction materials are wet.
  - ○ Cellulosic materials, such as paper, wood, or fibers, are available for mold to ingest.
  - ○ Temperatures are relatively warm (above 40°F).
  - ○ The area is relatively dark.

Mold should never be covered with a finish material without first solving the moisture problem. Unfortunately, painting a primer coat containing mildewcide is not the solution to ridding an interior space of mold. A contractor who specializes in mold remediation should identify the cause for the mold outbreak and correct it. Only then can the interior finish be safely installed.

INSULATION

Quality insulation serves a variety of purposes in buildings, including: reduced energy use, increased comfort, reduced potential for condensation to occur, decreased HVAC unit(s) size(s), and minimization of noise transmission.

R-value and *U-factor* are measures of the insulating values of building components. The R-value, where R stands for resistance to heat flow, is most well-known. The inverse of the R-value, the U-factor, measures the conductivity of a material or building component. Thus, a wall with an R-value of R-20 would have a U-factor of 1/20, or 0.05. In general, higher R-values and lower U-factors are more desirable.

> *Example:* A window has a U-factor of 0.33. What is its equivalent R-value?
>
> *Answer:* The R-value is the inverse of the U-factor, so R-value of the window would equal 1/0.33 or about R-3.

The most common types of insulation include the following (Tiller and Creech 1999):

- *Fiberglass* and *mineral-wool* products come in batt, roll, and loose-fill forms, as well as a high-density board material. Many manufacturers use recycled glass in the production process. Fiberglass is used for insulating virtually every building component—from foundation walls, to attics, to ductwork.
- *Cellulose* insulation, made from recycled newsprint, comes primarily in loose-fill form. Loose-fill cellulose is used for insulating attics and can be used for walls and floors when installed with a binder or netting. Because of its high density, cellulose has the advantage of helping stop air leaks in addition to providing insulation value.

- *Rock wool* insulation is typically available as a loose-fill product. It is fire-proof, and many manufacturers use recycled materials in the production process.

- *Molded expanded polystyrene* (MEPS), often known as bead board (not to be confused with the wood interior finish material), is a foam product made from molded beads of plastic. It has the lowest R-value per inch and is also the least expensive. It is used in many alternative building products, including insulated concrete forms (ICFs) and structural insulated panels (SIPs).

- *Extruded polystyrene* (XPS), also a foam product, is a homogenous polystyrene produced primarily by three manufacturers with characteristic colors of blue, pink, and green.

- *Polyisocyanurate* and *polyurethane* are insulating foams with some of the highest available R-values per inch. They are not designed for use below grade, unlike the polystyrene foam insulation products.

- *Open-cell polyurethane foam* is used primarily to seal air leaks and provide an insulating layer.

- *Icynene foam,* used primarily to seal air leaks and provide an insulating layer, is made with carbon dioxide rather than more polluting gases, such as pentane or hydrochlorofluorocarbons, used in other foams.

- *Aerated concrete,* including lightweight, autoclaved (processed at high temperature) concrete, can provide a combination of moderate R-values, thermal mass for floors, walls, and ceilings, and structural building components.

- Insulation made from *recycled denim* has been available on the market.

A successful insulation design meets or exceeds local energy codes, requires continuous coverage, and specifies that an insulation inspection will occur. Too often, buildings that look great on paper fail in reality due to cost cutting just before construction or to poor installation. A construction inspection process will help deter poor quality work.

The 2006 International Energy Conservation Code (IECC) divides the United States into eight climatic zones, as shown in Figure 7-6. The IECC contains minimum insulation requirements for both residential and commercial structures, which are summarized in Tables 7.2 and 7.3.

> *Example:* What insulation levels would be required in a home in Columbus, Ohio, for ceilings, walls, and floors over unheated crawl spaces? What is the required U-factor for windows?
>
> *Answer:* Columbus is in Zone 5, which requires R-38 ceilings and R-19 walls or R-13 walls with R-5 exterior sheathing. The windows should have a maximum U-factor of 0.35.

Table 7.2   Residential Building Insulation Values from 2006 IECC

Climate Zone	Window U-Factor	Window SHGC*	Ceiling R-value	Wall R-value	Floor R-value	Basement Wall R-value**	Slab R-value and Depth***	Crawl Space Wall R-value†
1	1.2	0.4	30	13	13	0	0	0
2	0.75	0.4	30	13	13	0	0	0
3	0.65	0.4	30	13	19	0	0	5/13
4 except Marine	0.4	any	38	13	19	10/13	10, 2 ft	10/13
5 and Marine 4	0.35	any	38	19 or 13 + 5††	30	10/13	10, 2 ft	10/13
6	0.35	any	49	19 or 13 + 5	30	10/13	10, 4 ft	10/13
7 and 8	0.35	any	49	21	30	10/13	10, 4 ft	10/13

Source: International Conservation Code (2006).

*SHGC is the window solar heat-gain coefficient, basically the fraction of sunlight that penetrates the window.

**The first R-value is for continuous insulation, such as exterior foam; the second is that required for a framed wall.

***The slab R-value is for slab floors near grade, not slab floors deeply underground. The depth is how deep the insulation goes below grade.

†The first crawl-space wall R-value is for continuous insulation, such as exterior foam insulation; the second R-value is that required in a framed wall.

††The R-13 + 5 means the framed walls need at least R-13, and the exterior sheathing should have a minimum of R-5.

Table 7.3 Commercial Building Insulation Values

Climate Zone	Window U-Factor	Window SHGC** (minimal overhang)	Window SHGC** (modest overhang)	Window SHGC** (large overhang)	Roof/Attic R-value***	Wood/Metal-Framed Wall R-value[†]	Concrete Wall R-value[††]
1	1.2	0.25	0.33	0.4	15/30	13/13	none
2	0.75	0.25	0.33	0.4	15/30	13/13	none
3	0.65	0.25	0.33	0.4	15/30	13/13	5.7
4 except Marine	0.4	0.4	any	any	15/30	13/13	5.7
5 and Marine 4	0.35	0.4	any	any	20/30	13/13 + 3.8	7–6
6	0.35	0.4	any	any	20/30	13/13 + 3.8	9.5
7	0.35	any	any	any	25/38	13/13 + 7 – 5	11.4
8	0.35	any	any	any	25/38	13 + 7 – 5/13 + 7 – 5	13.3

Source: International Conservation Code (2006).

*The 2006 IECC requires slab insulation only in Zone 8.

**SHGC is the window solar heat–gain coefficient, basically the fraction of sunlight that penetrates the window. For a window that is 8 feet tall, a modest overhang would extend 2 to 4 feet horizontally out from above the window. A large overhang would be longer than 4 feet.

***The first value is the R-value for continuous foam insulation on the roof; the second value is the R-value for the floor of an attic.

[†]The first value is the R-value for a wood-framed wall, with the "+" sign indicating that exterior insulated sheathing is required; the second value is the required minimum R-value for a steel-framed wall. For example, in Zone 7, a metal-framed wall needs R-13 between the studs and R-7 – 5 on the exterior.

[††]Concrete walls have to weigh more than 35 pounds per square foot to qualify.

Example: You are designing a commercial retail building in Birmingham, Alabama. The building has slab-on-grade floor construction, metal-framed walls, and a built-up roof with foam insulation on top. The 8-foot-high windows have an average overhang of 3 feet projected horizontally above the glass. What specifications would meet the 2006 International Energy Conservation Code for the floor, roof, walls, and windows?

Answer: Birmingham is in Zone 3, where the IECC 2006 requires no insulation for the slab floor, R-15 foam insulation on roof decks, and R-13 insulation in metal-framed walls. The windows have a modest overhang and should have a U-factor of 0.65 or less and a solar heat–gain coefficient of 0.33 or less.

Table 7.4 shows typical flaws in insulation for commercial buildings. Clear communication during construction and a thorough insulation inspection will help avoid these pitfalls.

Table 7.4   Typical Flaws in Insulation Systems for Commercial Buildings

Insulation above dropped ceiling tiles	Air leaks around insulation between the tiles themselves; many gaps for lighting, ductwork, and where moved for maintenance or renovation work.
Wall insulation stops at ceiling tiles	If roof deck is insulated, portion of wall above ceiling tiles will be uninsulated; in this situation, the wall finish should extend to the roof, not just the top of the framed wall.
Upstairs slab floor perimeters uninsulated	Upstairs slab floors that extend to the perimeter of the building often are not insulated, presenting problems of excessive energy losses and discomfort, as well as the potential for moisture condensation and mold formation.
Uninsulated slab floor over unheated areas	Slab floors often extend over unheated space, such as above exterior entry areas. If uninsulated, they can be long-term sources of heat loss, discomfort, and potential moisture problems.
Steel framing without exterior insulation	Steel framing conducts heat readily to the outside and basically cuts the insulating value of the insulation inside the wall by half. Over time, many steel-framed walls without insulated sheathing experience "striping" (i.e., discoloration on the inside or outside of the walls) and other moisture-related problems.

INSULATION AND INDOOR AIR QUALITY

Green buildings have additional considerations besides the R-values of the insulating materials. Concerns about whether the insulation material also minimizes air leakage, what constitutes the raw material or recycled content of the insulation, and how the insulation affects indoor air quality may create preferences for products that have somewhat higher initial costs. Unfortunately, some issues, such as impact on indoor air quality, are often unresolved in the scientific community. For example, advocates of fiberglass insulation publicly emphasize potential negative issues concerning cellulose, and vice versa. In general, insulation installed within a sealed-wall cavity or above a sealed ceiling will have little impact on air quality

> *Example:* You are working on a building to be constructed with 2 × 4 steel framing. The architect has specified R-13 fiberglass insulation in the walls and exterior drywall as the exterior finish. What are two options that might improve the insulation system from a green building viewpoint?

> *Answer:* One problem with steel framing is its high conductivity. Some poor designs create light striping on the interior wall or exterior finish where moisture has formed on the metal surface of the studs. Also, insulation installers often leave gaps between the insulation and the wall framing, thus dramatically lowering the insulating value of the walls and increasing air leakage. Green building options: (1) Use ½ to 2 inches of extruded polystyrene insulation as part (or all) of the exterior sheathing of the building; (2) install blown fiberglass insulation in the walls to achieve full coverage; (3) substitute spray foam insulation for the fiberglass, preferably icynene due to its reduced off-gassing potential.

Air Leaks

Air leaks are often a critical problem in buildings, because they lead not only to higher energy bills but also to potential moisture problems. The key to success is creating a continuously sealed air barrier within the building envelope. The process

CREATING A CONTINUOUSLY SEALED AIR BARRIER
- Eliminate gaps through the building envelope, particularly around holes for ducts, plumbing, and electrical chases; stairwells; and interfaces between diverse building elements.
- Use the final exterior or interior finish, such as drywall, as the interior air barrier. Seal all seams and run the drywall continuously over insulated wall cavities.

- Seal all penetrations for ductwork, plumbing, electric wiring, and other elements, through the roof, floor, and wall systems into the building.
- For residences and smaller commercial buildings, test for air leakage using blower door equipment.
- In commercial buildings, seal air leaks between spaces above dropped ceilings and outside walls and roofs.
- Make sure to seal between the interior spaces of buildings and shafts such as stairwells and mechanical chases.

involves a diligent effort from the design stage to final construction. See "Creating a Continuously Sealed Air Barrier" below for critical elements in elimination of air leaks (Tiller and Creech 1999).

Too often, no one accepts responsibility for ensuring that air-sealing guidelines are followed properly. As a member of the design team, the interior designer can remind the building designer and general contractor of the importance of minimizing air leaks in order to reduce energy bills, improve comfort, and prevent moisture and other indoor air quality problems related to air leaks.

ENERGY-EFFICIENT WINDOWS

Windows and doors connect the interior of a building to the outdoors; they can provide ventilation and daylighting; and they are a key aesthetic element. Windows and doors are often the architectural focal point of a building design, yet they provide the lowest insulating value in the building envelope. Although the efficiency of windows has improved markedly, they still represent one of the major energy liabilities in new construction.

Well-designed buildings carefully consider window location and size. Radiant energy from the sun travels through the glazing. In passive-solar buildings, windows can provide a significant amount of heat in the winter. In summer, unshaded windows can double cooling costs. Year round, poorly designed windows can cause glare, fading of textiles and other interior materials, and reduced comfort.

Windows lose and gain heat in the following ways:

- Conduction though the glass and frame
- Convection across the air space in double- and triple-glazed units
- Air leakage around the sashes and the frame

Goals of Efficient Windows

Over the past several decades, the window industry has developed higher-efficiency windows. The most important development related to better glazing has been the *low-e* (low-emissivity) window, which contains an invisible layer of silver bonded to one of the panes of glass in a double- or triple-paned unit.

Window Construction

Low-e windows reduce the U-factor of the glass, which increases resistance to heat loss. They also block more sunlight, which helps reduce summer-cooling bills and decrease fading. Some designers of daylighted buildings prefer not to use low-e glass on windows intended to provide daylighting. However, other designers consider low-e windows a necessity for designs that feature daylighting (Collaborative for High Performance Schools [CHPS] 2006b). Designers should consider geographic location, proportion of glazing to solid wall, and location of the windows to determine if low-e glass is the preferred option in any given situation.

Key considerations in efficient window design are as follows (CHPS 2006b):

- *Low U-factors:* A maximum U-factor of 0.60, corresponding to a minimum of R-1.7, which requires double-glazed glass. Thermal breaks that create a separation between the interior and exterior frame are required for metal-framed windows. Low-e glazing is preferred.
- *Low air-leakage rates.*
  ○ Less than .25 cfm per linear foot of sash opening for double-hung windows.
  ○ Less than .10 cfm per linear foot for casement, awning, and fixed windows.
- Moderate to high transmission rates of visible light.
- *Low transmission rates of invisible radiation:* Ultraviolet and infrared light energy.

Few windows can meet all of these goals, but in the past several years, the window industry has unveiled an exciting array of higher-efficiency products. The most notable developments include the following (Tiller and Creech 1999):

- Low-emissivity coatings, which hinder radiant-heat flow
- Inert gas fills, such as argon and krypton, which help deaden the air space between layers of glazing and thus increase the insulating values of the windows
- Tighter weatherstripping systems to lower air-leakage rates
- Thermal breaks to reduce heat losses through highly conductive glazing systems and/or metal frames

NATIONAL FENESTRATION RATING COUNCIL TESTING PROGRAM

The National Fenestration Rating Council (NFRC) offers a voluntary testing program for window and door products. The NFRC reports average whole-window U-factors. Windows listed by the NFRC include a label that shows test data and other information. The council also has an approved procedure to determine air infiltration of other fenestration products. The NFRC labels now provide the following information (NFRC n.d.):

- *U-factors:* The conductivity of the window
  - 0.90 for single-paned windows (about an R-1.1)
  - 0.55 to 0.75 and up for most double-paned windows (R-1.33 to R-1.8)
  - 0.30 to 0.40 for most low-e windows (R-2.5 to 3.3)
- *Solar heat–gain coefficient* (SHGC): The fraction of sunlight transmitted through the window
  - 0.65 and up for single-paned windows
  - 0.5 and up for double-paned windows
  - Less than 0.40 for most low-e windows
- *Air leakage* (AL) rates
- *Visible transmission* (VT): The fraction of visible light that is transmitted

DESIGN CONSIDERATIONS

Interior designers have special concerns regarding windows; more specifically, they want the windows to ensure interior comfort, natural light, accurate color perception, lack of glare, and minimal textile or other material damage (e.g., color changes in wood flooring or furnishings located in direct sunlight). While the window itself determines responses to these concerns, window treatments greatly affect client satisfaction with the interior environment. What follows are some key considerations in selecting environmentally responsible windows:

- In new construction, always specify low-e windows as a minimum; the extra insulating value of the window unit will save energy in winter; and the low solar heat–gain coefficient will improve comfort, decrease glare, and reduce cooling bills in summer.
- The primary exception to a low-e requirement would be in climates with warm winters. Such climates typically have hot summers, so low SHGCs are needed. Low-e windows provide lower SHGC, but windows with tinting and reflective films can be more effective.

Window Treatments

A large percentage of an interior designer's work is within existing structures. Existing windows can be problematic for the interior environment—particularly large expanses of glass that have high U-factors (low R-values) and that transmit too much solar gain. When choosing window treatments, consider their ability to reduce heat loss or gain, the ultraviolet (UV) filtering qualities, light controlling qualities, and desired aesthetics.

WINDOW FILM

The least expensive option for controlling solar gain is to install a window film that attaches directly to the exterior or interior of the windows. Window films generally reduce transmission of sunlight and help create interiors with greater comfort, less glare, and lower cooling bills. They can also reduce fading of textiles and other materials located near the windows by screening out ultraviolet radiation.

Virtually any type of window film will affect the appearance of the building, so careful selection is necessary. While films are typically not visible to occupants, they can create a reflective appearance on the exterior of a building. Their visual appearance and quality varies by manufacturer; some low-price films may only last a few years before cracking or sagging.

In cooler climates, window films should also help provide additional insulating value. Low-e films have an invisible metal coating that allows light to enter but obstructs heat from leaving through the fenestration.

FABRIC SHADES

Another window treatment option is two-layered shades, such as honeycomb designs. If sized properly, these shades increase the thermal value of a window; when fabric is carefully chosen, they can reduce glare by diffusing natural light. Shades intended to reflect sunlight should have a light color or metallic finish facing the exterior. Otherwise, they will absorb sunlight and reradiate the heat into the room.

QUILTED SHADES

In cold winter climates, some designers specify movable insulation, a window treatment typically composed of a quilted fabric with an internal Mylar film to stop air leaks. This shade usually slides on a track or folds in the form of a Roman shade. A key design feature is an air seal around the shade that is formed by the sliding tracks or by Velcro (or weighted edges for Roman shades). Movable insulation should have a white or reflective finish toward the exterior.

DRAPERIES

In applications where glare is a concern, loose, open-weave textiles will diffuse incoming sunlight, but they have no thermal value. Draperies with a thermal liner can be specified to reduce transmission of heat into or out of the room. However, the liner also reduces light transmission. thereby darkening the room, which may or may not be desirable.

ALTERNATIVE SOLUTIONS

Interior designers should realize that the best solution to a problem may not always be a typical interior solution. Sometimes, a consultant with expertise in another field might help resolve the problem.

Problem: In a renovation project, a window with western exposure transmits an undesirable amount of direct sunlight; privacy is not an issue.

Solution 1: A landscape architect is retained by the interiors firm for this project. She recommends additional landscaping to alleviate the problem. The plantings will block direct sunlight in the summer to reduce heat gain and allow direct sunlight in the winter, for the heat gain. The need for a window treatment that would obstruct the view is eliminated. The outcome is a more desirable interior space: heat gain is controlled, glare is no longer a problem, and the view out of the window is improved, creating a positive connection between inside and outside.

Solution 2: Exterior shades, operated with an electronic timer, are used to eliminate transmission of sunlight for part of the day during the summer months, to reduce heat gain. The shades also provide storm protection, in addition to increased security.

Daylighting

A common feature of many green buildings is natural daylighting. The key components of good daylighting systems are properly oriented windows, design elements that diffuse incoming sunlight and prevent glare, lighting fixtures that can be dimmed electronically, and lighting controls that can be set to automatically respond to sunlight by increasing or decreasing the quantity of electrical light. Chapter 6 discusses daylighting and lighting controls, such as photosensors, in more depth.

LIGHT SHELVES FOR DAYLIGHTING

A light shelf is a common element of daylighting designs. Light shelves are planar elements placed perpendicular to the window on the interior or exterior, or extending from outside to inside. They can be custom designed or specified from a manufacturer. Their placement is related to the orientation of the window and its relationship to the sun and is calculated to intercept and reflect sunlight. On the exterior, the light shelf acts as an overhang, shading the window. On the interior, light shelves can reflect sunlight onto the ceiling, thus providing desirable indirect natural lighting deep into a space. Designers should be careful not to obstruct this natural light with opaque interior partitions. Indirect natural lighting also minimizes direct sunlight, thus eliminating glare and fading. A study by the Florida Solar Energy Center found a 46 percent energy savings in offices that incorporated light shelves (Boehland 2002).

Figure 7-7
Interior and exterior light shelves help diffuse and direct sunlight at the Kelley Engineering Center, Oregon State University, Corvallis. Designed by Yost Grube Hall Architecture. Photo by Pete Eckert, Eckert & Eckert.

Figure 7-8
The light shelf and dropped-ceiling panel reflect daylight deep into the office space to control glare and provide better light distribution. Photo by Pete Eckert, Eckert & Eckert.

PASSIVE SOLAR ENERGY

A passive solar structure is designed to allow direct sunlight into the building during the winter months, thus warming the space during the day. Passive solar design options include:

- *Direct gain:* Key design features are vertical glazing that faces within 30 degrees of due south and interior thermal mass. Heavy materials—such as concrete-slab floors, masonry walls, or even water-filled containers—are positioned in direct sunlight to absorb heat, which is then released slowly when there is no direct sunlight. The south-facing glass must be shaded in summer with overhangs or, at a minimum, interior shading devices to prevent undesirable heat gain.

■ *Sun spaces:* Rooms without heating and cooling systems designed to serve as buffer spaces are called sun spaces. They have large expanses of south-facing glass and thermal mass to reduce dramatic swings in temperature.

■ *Thermal-storage walls:* These walls have a vertical wall of south-facing glass with an air space (i.e., a plenum) between the glazing and a vertical wall built of concrete or other solid masonry material. The exterior of the masonry wall has a flat finish and is as dark as possible to enhance heat absorption. Vents at the top of the masonry wall allow heated air to flow into the building, and vents at the bottom allow cold air to return to the plenum so that it can be reheated, thereby creating a natural convection loop. Thermal-storage walls built of concrete are also known as Trombe walls, named for the man who developed this design approach. The walls are only recommended in areas that receive high levels of direct sunlight most of the winter.

■ *Air collectors:* Flat panels on the building exterior with double glazing facing the sun are air collectors. There are flat black metal sheets inside the panel, but they contain no thermal mass. Vents to the interior space allow warm air to flow into the house on sunny days. A small blower can improve performance.

Passive solar buildings have implications for the interior designer's selection of materials and finishes. Following are considerations for the specification of materials and finishes:

■ *Thermal mass:* Horizontal or vertical surfaces capture heat from solar gain and then release heat at night. Common materials include concrete, stone, and ceramic tile. Care must be taken that nothing in the room blocks the direct sunlight. Dark colors are typically used because they capture the most heat.

■ *UV damage:* Due to the large quantity of direct sunlight, especially in passive-solar buildings using direct-gain designs, the interior materials and finishes are at risk of sun damage. Durability of materials and finishes in direct sunlight, and handling UV light, are of utmost importance to the interior designer. Both paint and wood can change color in direct sunlight. Textiles, which are particularly vulnerable, must be carefully chosen for their fibers' inherent ability to prevent UV degradation. Low-e windows are recommended to reduce the risk of fading.

Heating, Ventilation, and Air-Conditioning Systems

Heating, ventilation, and air-conditioning (HVAC) systems are often called comfort-conditioning systems, because they are intended to provide cooling when buildings become uncomfortably warm and heating when buildings become uncomfortably cool. Ventilation, a code requirement in commercial buildings, supplies fresh air to the occupants of the building with the intent of preserving or improving indoor air quality.

OPTIONS FOR HEATING

Furnaces

The primary types of heating systems for buildings are furnaces, boilers, and heat pumps. *Furnaces* use a fuel such as natural gas, fuel oil, coal, or wood to heat air. In most cases, they contain fans or blowers to distribute the heated air throughout the building via ductwork. *Boilers* burn fuels to generate hot water or steam, which circulates in piping through the building as the heat source. *Heat pumps* work just like air conditioners in the summer months, but in winter, they run in reverse to provide space heating.

Green buildings always seek to avoid waste; thus heating and cooling systems should be sized properly by an engineer or mechanical designer to meet the needs of the building. Systems that are excessively large or undersized operate less efficiently, may create comfort problems, and can add unnecessary costs to the building construction and/or operating budget.

Annual Fuel Utilization Efficiency

Green buildings should use *high-efficiency heating systems*. The efficiency rating for furnaces is the *annual fuel utilization efficiency* (AFUE). If using natural gas, always select a furnace with an annual fuel utilization efficiency rate of greater than 90 percent (100 percent would be the maximum efficiency) except in climates with mild winters where the extra costs for the high-efficiency unit would not garner sufficient savings on heating bills to pay back the extra investment within ten or twelve years. Oil furnaces are not yet available with as high AFUE values as gas furnaces; instead, seek a unit with an AFUE over 80 percent. Because electric furnaces are less efficient than electric heat pumps, they are not recommended for buildings designed for sustainability.

Boilers

Boilers provide hot water or steam to one or more buildings via piping. The circulating system provides heat to the building in the following ways:

- *Radiant panels or fin-tube radiators* typically attached to the wall.
- *Tubing in concrete-slab floors or underneath wood floors in a radiant-floor system:* Appropriate finishes for concrete radiant-slab floors include natural stone, ceramic tile, linoleum, or stained concrete. Tubing under wood floors is not as efficient as inside concrete slabs and can create hot spots. Most manufacturers will provide tubing diagrams to guide installation and optimize the system in each situation.

■ *Fan-coil units* blow air across a coil into which the steam or hot water flows, in a system conceptually similar to an automotive radiator. After being heated by the coils, the air flows into the space that is being heated.

The AFUE rating applies to boilers as well as furnaces. Boilers that produce hot water have higher efficiencies than those that produce steam. Natural gas hot-water units are now available with efficiencies up to 98 percent, while high-efficiency steam boilers have AFUE ratings over 82 percent. High-efficiency fuel-oil boilers have AFUE ratings of 80 percent and up, to just over 90 percent for hot-water units (Energy Star 2006).

Backdrafts

When furnaces and boilers burn fuels, they have flues (i.e., exhaust ductwork) that transport the products of combustion to the exterior. Occasionally, a fuel-based heating system will backdraft, meaning the flue gases are pulled back into the building. Backdrafting can potentially create dangerous indoor air quality conditions, primarily due to the threat of carbon monoxide poisoning. The solution is to specify sealed combustion units, in which the flue gases and the combustion air (the air needed to supply oxygen to the fuel for burning) are completely separate from the air within the building.

Heat Pumps

Heat pumps are an efficient way to use electricity to provide heating, and they should always be selected if the only available energy source is electricity. They use electricity to compress fluids called refrigerants. In the fluid-compression cycle, pumps compress the refrigerant, creating heat that causes the fluid to become a vapor; refrigerant lines circulate the vapor from outside to inside. The vapor cools as its heat is transferred to the inside air, causing the vapor to become a liquid. This liquid refrigerant is circulated back outside to be compressed, restarting the cycle of changing the fluid to a vapor. Heat pumps operate in reverse to cool interior environments during the summer. Some heat pumps, typically in larger commercial buildings, heat water in piping, which in turn circulates the heated water inside the building to provide space heating.

There are two efficiency ratings for heat pumps. The *coefficient of performance* (COP) indicates how much space heating is provided per unit of electricity consumed. Heat pumps usually have rated COP values at 47°F and 17°F outside temperature. Typical values for an efficient unit would be 3.5 at 47°F and 1.6 at 17°F. A COP of 3.5 means that for every unit of electricity the heat pump consumes, it provides 3.5 units of heat; in effect, it is operating at an efficiency of 350 percent (Tiller and Creech 1999).

The other heat-pump efficiency rating is the *heating season–performance factor* (HSPF). The HSPF estimates the average efficiency of residential-scale heat pumps during the entire heating season. Efficient units tend to have HSPFs of

8 or above. The rating is a little complicated. It measures how many Btu (British thermal units) of space heating 1 watt-hour of electricity provides (1 kilowatt hour of electricity is the same as 1,000 watt-hours). Thus, an HSPF of 8 would provide 8 Btu of space heating for every watt-hour of electricity consumed. There are 3.412 Btu in 1 watt-hour. Since 8 Btu would be 2.34 watt-hours (8 Btu/3.412 Btu/watt-hour = 2.34 watt-hours), the HSPF of 8 is equivalent to an approximate efficiency of 2.34—about 234 percent efficient (Washington State University n.d.).

Question: What is the average COP of a heat pump with an HSPF of 8.4?

Answer: The HSPF of 8.4 means the heat pump provides 8.4 Btu of heating for every watt-hour of electricity consumed. Dividing 8.4 Btu by 3.412 Btu per watt-hour, the average COP is 2.46, or about 246 percent average efficiency.

Geothermal or ground-source heat pumps work differently than standard air-to-air heat pumps. While standard heat pumps compress heat out of cool outside air, geothermal units obtain heat from underground or from ponds. They use long lengths of piping to transfer as much heat as possible from the source to the material in the piping. The primary cost of geothermal units is the exterior piping system. Most building sites do not have a readily available pond of sufficient size for a geothermal system, so the HVAC contractor installs piping in long, horizontal trenches or in wells drilled several hundred feet underground.

Geothermal heat pumps can provide hot water for building use in addition to heating and cooling. They also avoid the cost, noise, and aesthetic disadvantages of outside units that heat pumps and standard air conditioners require.

COMPARING THE COST OF SPACE-HEATING OPTIONS

Many consumers are concerned about the type of space-heating system to purchase. Typically, they have to choose between a natural gas–fired furnace, an air-to-air heat pump, and a geothermal heat pump. The following steps show how to compare "apples to apples" when judging the cost of heating from different equipment.

Step 1: Find out the cost per million Btu for the energy source.

- Natural gas is usually sold in dollars ($) per 1,000 cubic feet; since 1,000 cubic feet is about one million Btu, the price in $ per 1,000 cubic feet is approximately the price per million Btu. If the price is in $ per therm, multiply by 10 to get $ per million Btu. Thus, $0.85 per therm is the same as $8.50 per million Btu.
- Electricity is usually sold in $ per kilowatt hour (kWh). To get $ per million Btu, divide $ per kWh by 0.003412 (the number of million Btu per kWh). Thus, $0.85 per kWh is the same as $24.91 per million Btu.

Step 2: Find out the average annual efficiency of the heating system.

- For natural gas furnaces, the efficiency is the AFUE. An efficient gas furnace would have an AFUE of around 92 percent.
- For electric heat pumps, you begin with the HSPF. Divide it by 3.412 (the number of Btu in a watt-hour), to get the average efficiency. Thus, an electric heat pump with a HSPF of 7.8 would have an average efficiency of 7.8/3.412 = 2.29.

Step 3: To find out the average cost of space heating, divide the energy cost in $/million Btu (from *Step 1*) by the average annual efficiency (from *Step 2*).

EXAMPLE 1

A natural gas furnace with an AFUE of 92 percent and a fuel cost of $0.82 per therm.

- *Step 1:* $/million Btu = 10 * $0.82/therm = $8.20/million Btu
- *Step 2:* Average annual efficiency = AFUE = 0.92
- *Step 3:* $/million Btu of space heating = $8.20/million Btu/0.92 = $8.91/ million Btu of space heating

EXAMPLE 2

A standard heat pump with a HSPF of 8.2 and an electricity cost of $0.073 per kWh.

- *Step 1:* $/million Btu = $0.073/kWh/0.003412 million Btu/kWh = $21.38/ million Btu
- *Step 2:* Average annual efficiency = HSPF 8.2/3.412 = 2.40
- *Step 3:* $/million Btu of space heating = $21.38/million Btu/2.40 = $8.91/ million Btu of space heating

Air-Conditioning Systems

Virtually all commercial buildings and most residences in the United States have air-conditioning systems that provide cooling, dehumidification, and some air filtration. The proper design of air-conditioning systems is critical to ensure high levels of comfort, reduced relative humidity, and good indoor air quality.

Virtually all air-conditioning systems involve duct systems to distribute cooled air. (A section on ductwork guidelines follows.) The sources of cooled air include:

- *Standard, split-system air conditioners,* which include two primary components: an outside unit containing the compressor and an interior system connected to the ductwork. Both indoor and outdoor units have blowers and coils to transfer heat. The efficiency rating for these units, depending on their size, is the *energy-efficiency ratio* (EER), which is the efficiency at certain conditions; for smaller units, the *seasonal energy-efficiency ratio* (SEER) estimates the average annual efficiency of the units. The minimum SEER recently increased from 10 to 13. Like the HSPF for heat pumps, the SEER measures how many Btu of cooling are provided by 1 watt-hour of electricity. To convert to an approximate efficiency, divide by 3.412 Btu per watt-hour (Washington State University n.d.). Thus, a SEER 13 air conditioner operates at an efficiency of about 3.81, or 381 percent (13/3.412 = 3.81).

- *Packaged units,* often located on rooftops in commercial buildings, which combine the interior and exterior units' components into one box. Packaged units include *packaged terminal air conditioners* (PTAC) and *packaged terminal heat pumps* (PTHP). As a gauge of minimum efficiency levels, the city of Rochester, New York, provides rebates for equipment that meets the following efficiency ratings (RPU n.d.):
  - Equipment with less than 65,000 Btu per hour—at least SEER 14
  - 65,000 to 135,000 Btu per hour—at least EER 10.3
  - 135,000 to 240,000 Btu per hour—at least EER 9.7

- *Chillers* provide cooling for larger commercial buildings or, in some cases, complexes of buildings. *Centrifugal chillers* are usually more efficient than *reciprocating chillers.* Both types of chillers cool a refrigerant, which cools air in the building. As the refrigerant cools the building, it becomes warmer and evaporates. Cooling systems that use chillers also have a condensation cycle that requires the use of exterior air cooling fans or cooling towers. They are often the most visible portion of a large building's air-conditioning system. The chiller and condenser are usually hidden in a mechanical room inside the building. Systems with cooling towers are typically more efficient than those with air-cooling fans. In green buildings, there are a wide variety of energy-efficient options for chiller-based cooling systems that provide cost-effective savings.

DUCTWORK AND AIR-DISTRIBUTION SYSTEMS

One of the major sources of energy loss in many buildings is the ductwork system. Ductwork materials options include round metal, rectangular metal, plastic flex duct, fiberglass ductboard, rigid plastic, or fabric. Most experts recommend ducts without insulation material facing the moving airstream, to maintain indoor air

Figures 7-9 & 7-10
*To create natural cross-
ventilation, the David L. Lawrence
Convention Center, Pittsburgh,
Pennsylvania, takes advantage of
both the chimney effect, created by
the sweeping roof, and convection
currents from the Allegheny River
flowing next to the building.
The Convention Center, built in
2003, was awarded LEED-NC
Gold certification. Photos by
Dorothy Fowles.*

Figure 7-11
In the David L. Lawrence Convention Center, air distribution is handled through a fabric system by DuctSox. Photo by Dorothy Fowles.

quality (Modera 1999). For example, both ductboard and lined metal ducts have insulation on the interior that could be carried by the moving airstream and then mixed with the room air, decreasing the indoor air quality.

Most commercial buildings have relatively simple ductwork systems that resemble those in residential construction. Supply ducts move air that has been heated or cooled by the HVAC unit to the rooms in the building as required. Return ducts transfer air from the building back to the HVAC unit.

In larger buildings, *variable air volume* (VAV) distribution networks usually provide the most control over comfort at the highest efficiency. The VAV systems have small air handlers located throughout the building to provide heating and cooling to individual zones, which can be as small as a single office (Modera 1999). These air handlers contain a blower, a source of heating and cooling (such as a heating and cooling coil), and electronic controls that operate the air handler properly.

Duct leakage is a major source of air leakage in buildings. Both residences and commercial buildings have substantial amounts of ductwork located outside of the building envelope—in attics, unheated crawl spaces and basements, on the exterior of the building, and in other similar locations. Mark Modera of Lawrence Berkeley National Laboratory estimates that sealing duct leaks in existing commercial buildings would save an average of 0.5 to 1.3 kWh per square foot of floor area in buildings less than 10,000 square feet and 1 to 2 kWh per square foot in larger buildings (Modera 1999).

Thus, more efficient duct systems are one of the highest priority energy-saving measures in both new and existing buildings. In new construction, the following specifications are important:

- Locate as much of the duct system as possible within the building envelope so that any leakage stays inside the building.
- Use durable sealants, such as duct-sealing mastic with mesh tape, to seal duct leaks.
- Insulate ductwork to meet or exceed the International Energy Conservation Code, 2004 Supplement, which requires minimum R-5 insulation for ductwork in unconditioned spaces (such as unheated basements or attics) and R-8 insulation when located outside the building (International Conservation Code 2006).
- Test ductwork for airtightness.

When renovating commercial buildings, ductwork should be a primary target for improvement. There are a variety of approaches for sealing existing ductwork. The most common approach is for heating and cooling contractors to remove duct insulation around leaks, seal the leaks with duct-sealing mastic, and reapply the insulation. This manual approach is labor intensive, but can be very cost effective. A system developed at Lawrence Berkeley National Laboratory, known as aerosol duct sealing, is designed specifically for existing duct systems and sprays gel-like particles through the duct system. The particles coagulate at leaks and provide a long-term seal, much like platelets in the bloodstream repair a wound (Modera 1999).

DUCTS AND INTERIOR DESIGNERS

Ductwork can become the nemesis of the interior designer for a variety of reasons:

- There can be inadequate space to run ductwork under floors, in walls, in chases, or above ceilings. The design team must coordinate with the HVAC designer to provide vertical chases and adequate room above dropped ceilings for ductwork, including duct insulation. If there is insufficient space, construction costs will increase and completion will be delayed.
- Diffusers are the visible portion of the duct system, so their location and aesthetics are very important. Diffusers are usually located in the floors of residences and in the ceilings, walls, and sometimes in the floors of commercial buildings. Interior designers should coordinate duct locations and diffuser types with the engineer to maintain design integrity and to avoid conflict with ceiling features, lighting systems, fire-protection and emergency systems, and wall elements.

- Conflict with lighting systems is a common problem. The reflected ceiling plan will often reveal potential conflicts between diffusers and lighting systems but not conflicts with the hidden ductwork. The interior designer should review the engineer's documents for potential conflicts with light fixtures, such as recessed lighting, particularly in shallow ceiling spaces where there may not be enough room for the ductwork and the fixture.
- Duct location is an important design consideration, as some diffusers, or the surface areas around the diffusers, become locations for mold growth as well as excessive deposits of dust. The HVAC designer must be aware of the potential for mold problems, which often results when humid air in the building comes in contact with the cool surfaces of the diffusers.
- Many buildings feature exposed ductwork. Noninsulated ducts can suffer substantial condensation when the outer surfaces of the ducts are cool during the summer months and the building interior is humid. Interior designers should work with the HVAC designers to alleviate this potential problem. One solution is to keep the cooled air in exposed ductwork a few degrees warmer than usual to reduce the likelihood of condensation.

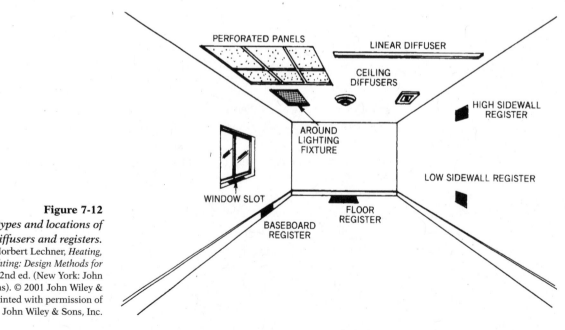

Figure 7-12
Common types and locations of air diffusers and registers.
Source: Norbert Lechner, *Heating, Cooling, Lighting: Design Methods for Architects,* 2nd ed. (New York: John Wiley & Sons). © 2001 John Wiley & Sons. Reprinted with permission of John Wiley & Sons, Inc.

Thermostats and Energy-Management Systems

The HVAC systems in many buildings are under the control of single thermostats, with no provision to set back the thermostat setting during unoccupied times. Puget Sound Energy estimates that businesses can save 8 to 9 percent on heating bills by setting nighttime temperatures down to 60°F, 16 to 19 percent at setback temperatures of 55°F, and 24 to 28 percent with setback temperatures of 50°F (Puget Sound Energy n.d.). Therefore, an important green building feature for virtually any building is a programmable thermostat.

Buildings with more complex HVAC systems often require an energy-management system—a computerized comfort-control system with temperature sensors located throughout the building. Energy management systems can not only control temperatures throughout the structure but also monitor energy consumption. Unfortunately, the energy-management systems in some buildings are too complex for the building maintenance staff and, therefore, are not used properly. The extra cost for these systems, which can be substantial, is wasted unless they are used as intended.

WATER HEATING

Water heating is the second largest energy user in residences and the fourth largest in commercial buildings (Wilson 2002b). Obviously, installing an energy-efficient water-heating system can result in substantial energy and economic savings. Additionally, "a standard residential electric water heater is responsible for nearly half of the carbon dioxide emissions of an average passenger car," according to A. Wilson (2002). Key considerations for water-heating systems in green buildings include:

- *Water-heater energy source:* Generally natural gas or propane is preferable to electricity from an environmental viewpoint, except in areas with substantial renewable electricity generation from hydropower or other sources. However, with recent fuel price increases, gas-fired water heaters may no longer have the cost advantage they once had over electric water heaters. Solar water heaters are an environmentally responsible option used in buildings throughout the country.

- *Water-heater efficiency:* Only Energy Star models should be specified. The American Council for an Energy-Efficient Economy (ACEEE) lists a wide variety of efficient models in their annual guide, *The Most Energy-Efficient Appliances 2006* (ACEEE 2006). Water heaters are rated by the energy factor. Gas-fired water heaters should have an energy factor of at least 0.62, and electric water heaters should have a factor over 0.90. There has been a resurgence of interest in heat-pump water heaters, which operate at about twice the efficiency of electric water heaters.

- *Stand-by losses:* Standard water heaters have tanks holding 40 gallons or more of hot water. According to the American Council for an Energy-Efficient

Economy, 10 to 20 percent of energy used for water heating is for stand-by losses—i.e., simply keeping the water in the tank hot (ACEEE 2006). At a minimum, green buildings should use insulation jackets over water heaters to reduce stand-by losses. On-demand water heaters are an option that eliminates stand-by losses. These units not only save energy but also water. How many times have you turned on the water and let it run in order to get hot? One manufacturer claims "that a typical American household wastes an average of 9,000 gallons of water annually waiting for hot water" (Wilson 2003). In an on-demand unit, hot water is heated where it is used, as it is needed.

The size and number of demand water heaters is based on the maximum amount of hot water required to meet peak hot water demand. Using the following assumptions on water flow for various appliances, the appropriate size of the on-demand unit can be estimated (U.S. Department of Energy 2005).

- *Kitchen faucets:* 1.5 to 2.5 gallons per minute
- *Lavatory faucets:* 0.75 to 1.5 gallons per minute (should be less than 1 gallon per minute with water-efficient fixtures)
- *Low-flow shower heads:* 1.2 to 2 gallons per minute (should be less than 1.6 gallons per minute with water-efficient fixtures)

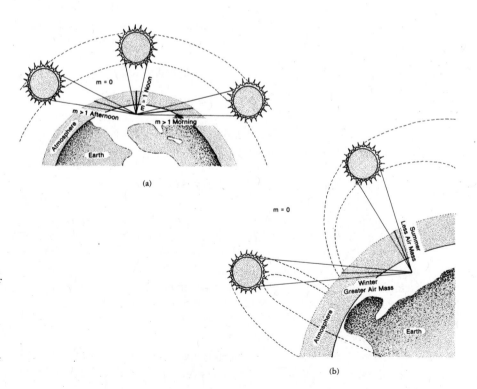

(a)

(b)

Figure 7-13

Air mass affects the intensity of sunlight and varies throughout the day and from season to season.
Source: Vaughn Bradshaw, *The Building Environment: Active and Passive Control Systems* (Hoboken, NJ: John Wiley & Sons, 2006). Courtesy of John Wiley & Sons, Inc.

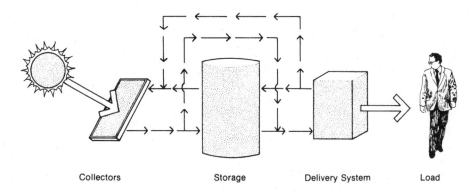

Figure 7-14
A solar energy system is a continuous loop made up of these four components: collectors, storage, delivery system, and load.
Source: Vaughn Bradshaw, *The Building Environment: Active and Passive Control Systems* (Hoboken, NJ: John Wiley & Sons, 2006). Courtesy of John Wiley & Sons, Inc.

Collectors   Storage   Delivery System   Load

EXAMPLE: A NEW SMALL OFFICE HAS 1 KITCHEN FAUCET, 3 LAVATORY FAUCETS, AND 1 SHOWER. WHAT CAPACITY ON-DEMAND WATER HEATER WOULD IT NEED?

According to the given estimates for water flow, the office would need 2.5 gallons per minute for the kitchen faucet, 4.5 gallons per minute for 3 lavatory faucets, and 2 gallons per minute for the shower, for a total of 9 gallons per minute of peak hot water use. The designer should determine incoming cold water temperatures, as well as desired hot water temperatures, to ensure that the on-demand water heater will deliver all of the water-heating needs. Oversizing an on-demand water heater should be considered to avoid problems if more hot water is needed than originally estimated.

- *Older, standard shower heads:* 2.5 to 3.5 gallons per minute
- *Clothes washers and dishwashers:* 1 to 2 gallons per minute (efficient units may use less than 1 gallon per minute)

Renewable Energy for Heating, Cooling, and Hot Water

If possible, some portion of the heating, cooling, and hot water needs should come from renewable sources, such as solar energy, wood, other forms of biomass, or electricity derived from renewables. Examples of renewable technologies that have been used extensively in the United States include:

- *Passive solar design:* Integrates south-facing glass with interior mass from concrete floors and walls to provide a portion of the space heating requirement. Passive-solar design features must control sunlight entering the building in the summer months to reduce cooling bills.
- *Daylighting:* While not specifically a solar technology for heating and cooling, properly designed daylighting systems provide heat during the winter, reduce

the cost of cooling the building in the summer, and reduce the required size of the cooling system.

■ *Solar water-heating systems:* Solar water heaters have a long history of providing hot water for residences and commercial buildings. Because hot water is required during both summer and winter, solar systems provide savings in energy costs 365 days a year.

■ *Solar-heated ventilation air:* A number of buildings use solar collection areas on south-facing walls or rooftops to heat ventilation air in the winter. Almost all commercial buildings must provide ventilation air to enhance indoor air quality. In climates with cool or cold winters, heating the ventilation air can increase the total heating cost more than 30 percent. Solar preheat systems can provide cost-effective savings.

■ *Solar space-heating and cooling systems:* Collectors, typically located on rooftops, can provide a portion of the space heating required during the winter. With additional hardware, the system can provide space cooling during the summer months.

■ *Solar photovoltaic electricity systems:* All around the country, buildings have integrated photovoltaics, special modules that generate electricity when exposed to direct sunlight. The modules contain several dozen solar cells composed of specially treated semiconductor materials. While photovoltaics are currently one of the more expensive solar options, they have a promising future.

Figure 7-15
This hotel uses roof-mounted, solar photovoltaic collectors to heat water.
Source: Vaughn Bradshaw, *The Building Environment* (Hoboken, NJ: John Wiley & Sons, 2006). Courtesy of John Wiley & Sons, Inc.

- *Solar thermal electricity systems:* Solar energy can be focused to heat fluids to high temperatures in order to drive various types of generators that produce electricity. Waste heat from these systems can be used to heat water or provide space heating for the building itself. The U.S. Department of Energy's Energy Information Administration (2003) reports that the cost of electricity from solar thermal systems is currently lower than that from photovoltaic systems.

- *Green-power programs:* All across the United States, electric utility companies are providing green-power programs as an option for their customers. Building operators can opt to buy a given amount of green power each month. They will then know that at least a portion of their electricity comes from renewable sources.

Water

Water shortages are of such urgency in some regions of the United States that governmental regulations related to the construction of new structures have been passed to help alleviate the problem. In 2001, California passed a law requiring developers of large subdivisions (500 or more homes) to prove that the water supply for the new development is adequate for at least twenty years (Newsbriefs 2001).

Figure 7-16
The David L. Lawrence Convention Center taps Pittsburgh's "fourth river," the aquifer that runs beneath the downtown area, providing make-up water for the center's refrigeration-system cooling towers, thereby reducing the demand for water from the city water system. Photo by Dorothy Fowles.

Eleven percent of total water consumption in the United States is for public supply. Unlike irrigation and power-plant cooling, which constitute 72 percent of withdrawals from water sources, public-supply water must be returned to sewage-treatment plants before reentering the environment. Competition for water sources, long a factor in the western United States, has become a major political issue in eastern states as well, such as between Virginia and Maryland; Virginia and North Carolina; and Georgia, Alabama, and northern Florida (Hoffman and Allen n.d.).

Considering the "reduce, reuse, recycle" mantra, reduction is the most important part of the equation. To reduce decreases the need to reuse and/or recycle.

Demand-side reduction strategies can greatly impact water demand, which can result in substantial energy, economic, and environmental savings. The interior designer can reduce water demand by specifying the following types of fixtures and appliances:

- Low-flow showerheads
- Water-efficient faucet aerators
- Sensor-activated faucets
- Low gallons per flush (gpf) or composting toilets
- Nonwater-use urinals
- Efficient clothes washers
- Efficient dishwashers
- Foot or knee controls for faucets, such as kitchen-sink faucets, can also reduce hot water demand

These specifications reduce both water demand and the energy associated with both the generation of the water supply and the production of hot water.

A study of 26 buildings in the Tampa, Florida, area revealed that office buildings used an average of 14,695 gallons per day of water. The primary use was for cooling systems, (consumed in cooling towers), but 24 percent of the water use was for domestic purposes—primarily in restrooms and showers. Kitchens used 6 percent of water, irrigation only 1 percent, and other uses 33 percent (Southwest Florida Water Management District 1997).

A similar study in Massachusetts found 14 percent of water use in kitchens, 47 percent for domestic purposes, 34 percent for cooling, and 5 percent for other uses. The Massachusetts Water Resources Authority, which sponsored the study (Hutson et al. 2000), reports on two examples of water conservation measures:

One building undergoing renovation replaced 126 existing 3.5 gallon per flush toilets with 1.6 gallon per flush models. The new toilets should reduce total water use by about 15 percent. The cost of the new models is $32,000. With the expected savings from decreased water bills equaling $22,800 per year, the replacement will pay back the cost in 1.4 years.

Another commercial building installed 30 faucet aerators, which reduced water use 190,000 gallons per year. With an installed cost of only $300 and an annual savings of $1,250, the measure paid back the cost in 2 months!

ENERGY AND WATER SAVINGS IMPLEMENTATION

Interior designers are often in the position of specifying fixtures and appliances. While their main priority may be aesthetics and function, energy use should also be considered. Understanding programs, such as Energy Star, can provide the designer with the knowledge and resources to make intelligent selections for their specifications.

Most power plants consume water to make electricity. Wastewater treatment plants consume electricity. Therefore, a fixture can be directly water efficient; by being water efficient, the associated electricity to deliver the water and treat the wastewater is reduced. While the following information highlights a product's energy-saving features, do not forget the impact of the associated water savings in the production of the power or vice versa.

Appliances and Equipment

The U.S. Environmental Protection Agency's Energy Star program provides a valuable service to interior designers by identifying and labeling appliances and equipment that have relatively high energy efficiencies.

In residential applications, Energy Star specifications can reduce energy costs by about one-third. Energy Star ratings can be found on appliances, equipment, and architectural elements such as windows, doors, and skylights. The Energy

Figure 7-17

Energy Star is a government-sponsored program that helps individuals and businesses protect the environment through superior energy efficiency. The program uses U.S. Department of Energy (DOE) and U.S. Environmental Protection Agency (EPA) guidelines to help reduce energy consumption and pollution, promote cleaner air, and prevent global warming by reducing greenhouse gas emissions.

In 1991, the Green Lights program was introduced by the U.S. EPA. This program encouraged organizations to retrofit their existing lighting systems to more energy-efficient systems and controls. This program became a segment of the Energy Star program in 1998.

Star program also qualifies new homes by independently verifying that they are at least 30 percent more energy efficient than homes built to the 1993 National Model Energy Code or 15 percent more efficient than state energy codes, whichever is more stringent. The Energy Star web site states that in 2004, Energy Star practices "saved enough energy to power 24 million homes and avoid greenhouse gas emissions equivalent to those from 20 million cars, all while saving $10 billion". In business applications, such as commercial and institutional buildings, Energy Star recommends management strategies that measure energy performance, set goals, track savings, and reward improvements.

Following are guidelines for selecting fixtures, appliances, and equipment for various areas of buildings.

FOOD PREPARATION AREAS

Sink faucets that include water-efficient aerators should be specified. They are an inexpensive way to save water, thus reducing water and water-heating costs. A low-flow aerator mixes air into water to maintain pressure while reducing the amount of flowing water. A flow of 2.75 gallons of water or less per minute is required for the faucet to be considered low flow. A 1.5 gallons per minute (gpm) faucet is typically adequate for a kitchen (*Low flow aerators and showerheads* n.d.).

Refrigerators and freezers are more efficient today than models available in the past. According to the American Council for an Energy-Efficient Economy's 2005 report on the most energy-efficient refrigerators, a typical new unit with automatic defrost and a top-mounted freezer uses less than 500 kWh per year versus a similar 1973 model that used over 1,800 kWh. To qualify as Energy Star units, refrigerators must exceed the federal efficiency standard by 15 percent or more; Energy Star freezers must exceed the federal efficiency standard by 10 percent or more. Energy Star compact refrigerators and freezers have to surpass the federal efficiency standard by 20 percent or more. Since refrigerators are the single largest energy consumer in most homes, energy savings can be significant without sacrificing features or performance. The American Council for an Energy-Efficient Economy (ACEEE) publishes an annual guide to energy-efficient appliances. Annual electricity costs for refrigerators with more than 21 cubic feet of capacity can be as low as $45 (ACEEE 2006b).

Interior designers should also be aware of the importance of the location of the refrigerator. In order to maximize efficiency, refrigerators should not be positioned near a heat source, such as an oven, a dishwasher, or direct sunlight. The designer should also provide space between the condenser coils and the wall or cabinets to allow air to circulate.

Commercial solid-door refrigerators and freezers that qualify as Energy Star approved are designed with components to increase energy efficiency. These units can result in energy savings of up to 46 percent and payback in as little as 1.3 years (*Commercial solid door refrigerators and freezers* 2005).

Dishwashers use energy in three ways: the motors that operates the dishwasher itself, the energy required to heat water for dishwashing, and the energy used to provide heat for dish drying. New developments in today's energy-efficient models include: booster heaters so that the hot water temperature can be lowered to 120°F at the tank; reduced requirements for hot water, often one-half that of earlier models; and soil sensors that, depending on how dirty the dishes are, automatically adjust water use. According to the ACEEE report on the most energy-efficient dishwashers, recent studies have shown that new models provide excellent cleaning without prerinsing the dishes prior to loading the dishwasher, saving time, water, and energy (ACEEE 2006a). Energy Star dishwashers use 25 percent less energy than the federal standard. The ACEEE annual survey of 2005 lists dishwashers with annual-energy use in the $17 to $30 range.

LAUNDRY AREAS

Clothes washers have also become more efficient in recent years. A new standard for efficiency became effective in 2007. In addition, many new clothes washers also spin faster than conventional models, thus reducing the moisture content in the clothes and lowering the energy used by clothes dryers.

New federal efficiency guidelines have two ratings for clothes washers. The modified energy factor (MEF), which considers both tub capacity and energy use, and the water factor, which is the number of gallons required per cubic foot. To meet Energy Star guidelines, clothes washers may have to have a water factor of less than 9.5 (Energy Star n.d.). Energy-efficient models use as little as 115 kWh of year, including electric water heating. Energy Star–qualified washers use 50 percent less energy than conventional washers (ACEEE 2005a). Additionally, these washers use 18 to 25 gallons of water per load, in comparison to the 40 gallons used by a conventional machine.

Several new products combine clothes washer and clothes dryer into a single unit. Thor Industries manufactures a unit that has no dryer vent and uses only

$6 per year to operate in buildings with natural gas water heating and $19 per year in buildings with electric water heating.

Commercial clothes washers for hotels, commercial laundries, and other uses also have energy-efficient options. For example, Staber Industries manufactures a unit that uses 66 percent less water, 75 percent less detergent, and 50 percent less energy than conventional models (Staber Industries 2005). If five loads are washed per day, there would be a savings of 49,000 gallons of water each year, 3,500 kWh of electricity, and 43 gallons of detergent, as well as associated reductions in air-pollutant emissions due to lower electricity use.

Currently, there are no Energy Star–qualified clothes dryers, because they all use similar amounts of energy. Clothes dryers consume large quantities of energy; therefore, air drying provides significant savings. To encourage air drying, an interior designer should design a ventilated area with features that facilitate hanging wet clothes.

RESTROOM AREAS

Proper ventilation in restrooms is critical to indoor air quality (IAQ). Interior designers should specify fans that are Energy Star labeled. They should have low sone ratings (be quiet to operate) and high efficiency (deliver the required air flow with minimal energy use). Ventilation fans exhaust poor-quality indoor air and/or humid air from the building, thus helping prevent mold, mildew, and other IAQ problems.

Lavatory faucets and showerheads should be specified to have low water usage, typically less than 1 gallon per minute. One way to achieve efficient use of water is with efficient aerators. As in the kitchen, a low-flow aerator is an inexpensive way to save water and money.

In addition, interior designers should specify sensor-activated faucets. These units, often used in nonresidential settings to meet requirements of the Americans with Disabilities Act, result in water savings by automatically turning off the water when no longer in demand. Designers must choose from a variety of automatic faucets in the marketplace. Many of these faucets use electricity for the sensor; therefore, they have to be hardwired unless they use batteries, which have to be replaced, creating toxic waste. Some automatic faucets contain new technology that uses a small hydropowered generator to charge the batteries. When the water flows, it spins a hydropower generator and recharges the battery. This technology has been popular in other countries for commercial buildings and is predicted to become an informed and popular choice in the United States (Wilson 2003a). Additionally, automatic faucets have health benefits, since the faucet can be used without being touched.

Only low-flow or ultra-low-flow showerheads should be installed. Much like faucet aerators, these showerheads force air into the water stream and create a high-velocity spray. The result is a shower with a full spray using much less water. To reduce the amount of water wasted while waiting for hot water, the water heater should be located close to the point where it is used or an on-demand water-heating system should be installed.

Designers should also consider wastewater heat-recovery devices. They circulate incoming cold water around the outgoing drain pipe, which preheats water before it reaches the faucet.

Commercial hand dryers provide another opportunity for green building design. Like many of the decisions an interior designer makes, there are pros and cons for each option. Paper towels are made from trees processed into paper, and they create waste when they are used. Electric hand dryers use electricity produced at power plants and produce hot air that can increase cooling costs. Which is the lesser of two evils?

A study commissioned by *Environmental Building News* (Malin 2002a) provided an answer for this question. Using life-cycle assessment (LCA), the study found that the new high-velocity hand dryers, with higher temperatures and automatic motion-sensor controls, use less energy than virgin or recycled paper towels. The article notes that "just on the basis of energy use, electric hand dryers are far better, without even considering the many other environmental impacts of the manufacture and disposal of paper, including resource depletion, water pollution, and solid waste" (Malin 2002a).

Specification of these hand dryers provides the end user with the most environmentally responsible option. Additionally, this choice has health benefits since the automatic dryer is not touched by the user.

Although toilets are one of the largest consumers of water in many commercial buildings, technology has dramatically decreased the amount of water used per flush. In the 1950s, toilets used 5 to 7 gallons per flush (gpf), which was reduced to 3.5 gpf in 1980. The Energy Policy Act (EPAct) of 1992 went into effect in 1994 and established a national standard of 1.6 gpf (Wilson 2004a). One person flushing a 1.6 gpf toilet an average of five times a day will consume approximately 3,000 gallons of water annually. The technology exists to further decrease the amount of water used per flush. Many other countries have already established limits of 0.8 to 1.2 gpf.

The interior designer often specifies plumbing fixtures, in part, to achieve a certain aesthetic. An environmentally responsible interior designer should specify a toilet or urinal that combines high-quality functions, minimal maintenance, and the desired aesthetic with the least water usage. Following are types of flush toilets available with 1.6 gpf or less (Wilson 2004a):

- *Conventional gravity-flush toilets* use gravity to allow water from a tank to flow into the rim holes to rinse the sides and into the siphon hole to initiate the siphon.
- *Better gravity-flush toilets* are gravity-flush toilets with higher pressure, advanced technology, better design of the bowl shape and trapway, and less condensation.
- *Flapperless gravity-flush toilets* use a bucket design instead of a flush valve in the tank.
- *Pressure-assist flushometer-tank toilets* use a pressurized, internal tank to force a strong flush with less water and no condensation.

- *Flushometer-valve toilets* use a tankless toilet that delivers a strong flush using line pressure from the water supply.
- *Vacuum-assist toilets* incorporate a vacuum works in conjunction with the gravity push of the flush to pull the waste material from the bowl.
- *True vacuum toilets* are linked systems in which several toilets are connected to a waste-collection tank and the system operates under negative pressure.
- *Pump-assist toilets* contain a pump, which requires an electrical connection, in the low tank to force water into the bowl.
- *Air-pressure toilets* use a remote air compressor with a very low amount of water (1 to 2 quarts).
- *Dual-flush toilets* have two flush buttons or split flush handles so the user can select a high-volume flush for solid waste or a low-volume flush with less water for liquid waste. These toilets typically use gravity-flush technology and are popular in Europe and Australia.

When remodeling space, the interior designer should advise the client to replace older toilet and plumbing fixtures to significantly reduce water use. The payback on replacing water-wasteful toilets with units that conserve water is often in the 2- to 3-year range, depending on the cost of water, the quantity used per flush, and the total number of flushes.

In the United States, the water used to fill toilets is potable (i.e., drinkable); although it is not necessary to use, potable water for this purpose. Some buildings use nonpotable, gray-water systems that capture water from various sources (including rain and treated wastewater from sinks, showers, and washing machines) to flush toilets.

Composting toilets have been used for many years by those interested in environmental responsibility. This type of unit is often chosen in areas that are difficult to reach with public sewer systems. Composting toilets do not use water. They convert waste into compost that can be used to add beneficial nutrients into the soil. This type of system truly embodies the idea of "waste equals food": one living thing produces waste that is food for another living thing. This concept sustains ecosystems and could potentially sustain the environment.

Composting toilet systems are being employed in many mainstream, low-rise commercial buildings, such as the Chesapeake Bay Foundation's Philip Merrill Environmental Center, Annapolis, Maryland. Built in 2000, the Merrill Environmental Center achieved the first LEED Platinum rating, and it is considered an excellent example of environmentally responsible building practices. Visitors have been surprised during tours when they open the compost tanks and find no offensive odors. The composting toilets, with other water-saving features, allow the Merrill Environmental Center to use 90 percent less water than a conventional office building (*Nonpoint Source News-Notes* 2002).

Water-saving and waterless urinals are an option often selected in green buildings. While conventional thinking is often resistant to the idea of water-free

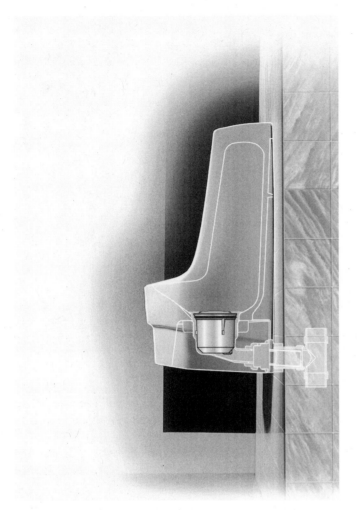

Urine

Sealant Liquid

To the drain

Figure 7-19
A cross section of the canister in the waterless urinal illustrates the way in which the funnel shape of the nonporous material ensures that all urine flows directly into the cartridge. The urine then passes through a floating liquid sealant directly to the waste drain. The sealant floats on the liquid below it to provide an airtight barrier between the urine and the restroom to prevent odors from escaping the drain. Courtesy of Falcon Waterfree Technologies, LLC.

Figure 7-18
A cross section of the waterless urinal shows the placement of the replaceable cartridge, which is installed at the bottom of the urinal into a fitting connected to a drainpipe. The only maintenance required is routine cleaning of the fixture and an easy change of the cartridge three to four times per year. Courtesy of Falcon Waterfree Technologies, LLC.

urinals, many of those who have installed this technology rave about its performance. Waterless urinals cover the waste products with a protective fluid layer. Several manufacturers offer nonwater-using options, but there are differences in operation. All of the urinals use oils to provide a sanitary trap at the bottom of the fixture. Periodically, this oil has to be replaced. Some waterless units use a replaceable cartridge-type trap that contains the oil and requires replacement after 6,000

Figure 7-20
This bank of waterless urinals, installed in a public restroom, illustrates the invisibility of the waterless functionality. Courtesy of Falcon Waterfree Technologies, LLC.

to 7,000 uses. With these toilets, the old cartridge is discarded as waste. Other options, which do not have a replaceable trap, require flushing, with approximately a quart of water and replacement of the oil to clear uric-acid deposits monthly or after approximately 5,000 uses. The interior designer must make certain that the maintenance staff has a full understanding and acceptance of the technology involved before specifying waterless urinals.

HOME ENTERTAINMENT

Audio and visual systems for home entertainment are also Energy Star labeled. Televisions, VCRs, DVD players, home audio products, and other electronic equipment have energy-saving models that require only a few watts of electricity as standby power. The designer should specify a power-off option, for use when the equipment will not be in service for an extended period of time, to eliminate the energy used for standby operation.

OFFICE EQUIPMENT

Home office equipment, such as computers, monitors, printers, fax machines, copiers, scanners, and multifunction devices, should be selected with an Energy Star label. Home PCs should have power-management capabilities to reduce standby power consumption.

OTHER COMMERCIAL BUILDING EQUIPMENT

Energy Star–qualified water coolers use about half as much energy as conventional coolers. Qualified coolers are available for both residential and commercial installations.

Elevators are building elements that have changed dramatically in the past few years. Low-rise buildings have typically used hydraulic elevators. Hydraulic fluid requires constantly operated heaters, and the fluid commonly leaks into the ground, creating environmental problems in groundwater. Midrise elevators are geared traction machines and are more efficient than hydraulic elevators. New technology has further increased efficiency. The new elevators are typically gearless, permanent-magnet motors with variable-speed, variable-frequency drives that are "two to three times more efficient as hydraulics and 30–50% more efficient than standard geared elevators" (Wilson 2004b). The motor is typically mounted in the hoistway, reducing the need for square footage dedicated to a machine room or penthouse machinery space. Reduction of square footage saves resources and reduces the energy required to heat and cool the building, thus reducing the environmental impact and saving the client money. There are other technological advances currently in development that should enter the marketplace in the near future (Wilson 2004b).

Interior designers often allocate space for the elevator and its equipment, and they typically design and specify the elevator cab. Knowledge of the elevator system might put the designer in a position to recommend and/or specify a more energy-efficient elevator.

Building Elements

FENESTRATION

Fenestration, such as doors, windows, and skylights, should be selected for its appropriateness to the regional climate. Location, orientation, and type of windows can have a major impact on the building's energy use. When specified correctly, these elements can save energy and money, increase comfort, and filter damaging direct sun rays. Residential doors, windows, and skylights are available with the Energy Star label.

LIGHTING

Residential light fixtures are available with Energy Star certification. These fixtures use about 66 percent less energy, have a long life, and distribute light efficiently and evenly as compared to standard fixtures. Specifying energy-saving lamps, such as compact fluorescents, ensures energy savings. Compact fluorescent lamps and other gaseous discharge sources create more lumens per watt, and they do not create as much heat energy as an incandescent lamp; therefore, they do not contribute as much wasted heat energy to the interior environment. Replacing lamps in existing fixtures with more efficient sources is a simple way to reduce energy use in existing interiors.

Just as the natural world is interconnected—what happens in one segment of the natural world affects other segments—the built world is an interconnected system, too. A designer's decisions can directly impact one aspect and indirectly affect another. Although gaseous discharge fixtures, such as fluorescents, do not create as much heat, all light fixtures create increased heat loads, taxing HVAC systems. Using photosensors to control the electric lighting, based on contribution of daylight, minimizes the use of electric fixtures, thus reducing the heat load, resulting in more energy savings. Lighting and lighting controls, such as dimming, timing, occupancy, and daylighting controls, are discussed further in Chapter 6.

Related Considerations

EMBODIED ENERGY

Embodied energy is all of the energy associated with the raw material extraction, manufacturing, distribution, and life of a product. A product's embodied energy should be taken into consideration when choosing products for their environmental advantages. One product can contain environmentally responsible materials, but its production or transportation can make a significant contribution to the product's embodied energy.

LIFE STREAM

Designers should consider the life stream of a product or system, which is everything associated with the birth, life, and death of a product and its effect on other products or systems. A product that seems to be environmentally responsible may actually fare better or worse when its life stream is taken into consideration. A designer's decisions could have an even greater impact on the environment than what is related to the product's life stream. For instance, since both thermoelectric and hydroelectric power plants consume water to produce electricity, energy savings also result in water savings. Therefore, any energy-saving feature incorporated into a building will also save water that would otherwise have been used to produce electric power in the thermoelectric or hydroelectric power plants.

MAINTENANCE

Another consideration for the designer is maintenance requirements. For instance, if the designer specifies a fixture that saves water but requires additional energy or frequent maintenance, the savings on water bills may be offset by the energy or labor costs. For instance, manual blinds that require daily operation may lead to higher costs for service workers' time than the amount that is saved on energy bills. An environmentally responsible designer will consider the product's origin, installation, use, and useful life and will question manufacturers regarding environmentally responsible design in order to make informed decisions.

Online Resources

American Council for an Energy-Efficient Economy: http://aceee.org

Environmental Building News: www.buildinggreen.com

Flex Your Power: www.fypower.org

Southface Energy Institute: www.southface.org

U.S. Department of Energy: www.doe.gov

U.S. Environmental Protection Agency: www.epa.gov

U.S. Environmental Protection Agency, Energy Star Program: www. energystar.gov

U.S. Green Building Council: www.usgbc.org

References

American Council for an Energy-Efficient Economy (ACEEE). 2005a. *Most energy-efficient clothes washers*. Washington, DC: American Council for an Energy-Efficient Economy. Retrieved March 12, 2006, from the American Council for an Energy-Efficient Economy Web site: http://www.aceee.org/consumerguide/ref_21-25cubic_feet.pdf.

———. 2005b. *Most energy-efficient dishwashers.* Washington, DC: American Council for an Energy-Efficient Economy. Retrieved March 12, 2006, from the American Council for an Energy-Efficient Economy Web site: http://www.aceee.org/consumerguide/ref_21-25cubic_feet.pdf.

———. 2006a. *The most energy-efficient appliances.* Washington, DC: American Council for an Energy-Efficient Economy.

———. 2006b. *Most energy-efficient refrigerators 2005*. Washington, DC: American Council for an Energy-Efficient Economy. Retrieved March 12, 2006, from the American Council for an Energy-Efficient Economy Web site: http://www.aceee.org/consumerguide/ref_21-25cubic_feet.pdf

American Society of Heating, Refrigerating, and Air-Conditioning Engineers, Inc. (ASHRAE). 2005. *2005 Handbook Fundamentals.* Atlanta, GA: ASHRAE.

Boehland, J. 2002. C/S interior lightshelves (product review). *Environmental Building News* 11 (11): 7.

Center for Economic and Social Rights (CESR). n.d. *The right to water fact sheet #1: Global statistics*. Brooklyn, NY: CESR. Retrieved August 2, 2007, from CESR Web site: http://www.cesr.org.

Collaborative for High Performance Schools (CHPS). 2006a. *Best practices manual, Volume I: Planning.* San Francisco: CHPS. Retrieved August 2, 2007, from CHPS Web site: http://www.chps.net/manual/index.htm

———. 2006b. *Best practices manual, Volume II, Design.* San Francisco: CHPS. Retrieved August 2, 2007, from CHPS Web site: http://www.chps.net/manual/index.htm

Energy Information Administration. 2004. *International energy annual, 2004.* Washington, DC: U.S. Department of Energy. Retrieved July 31,

2006, from U.S. Department of Energy Web site: http://www.eia.doe.
gov/emeu/iea/contents.html

Energy Star. n.d. *a. Boilers product list.* Retrieved on December 10, 2006,
from Energy Star Web site: http://www.energystar.gov/ia/products/
prod_lists/boilers_prod_list.pdf.

———. 2004. *Market impact analysis of potential changes to the ENERGY
STAR criteria for clothes washers* (August 6). Retrieved September
7, 2007, from Energy Star Web site: http://www.energystar.gov/
ia/partners/prod_development/revisions/downloads/clotheswash/
2ESCWCriteriaAnalysisFinal.pdf.

Gas Appliance Manufacturers Association (GAMA). 2006. *Consumers'
directory of certified equipment ratings for heating and water heating equipment.* Arlington, VA: GAMA. Retrieved January 19, 2008,
from GAMA Web site: http://www.gamanet.org/gama/inforesources.
nsf/vAllDocs/Product+Directories?OpenDocument.

Hoffman, D., and R. Allan. n.d. *The connection: Water supply and energy
reserves.* Retrieved September 3, 2007, from U.S. Department of
Energy Web site: http://www.iags.org/n0813043.html.

Hutson, S. S., N. L. Barber, J. F. Kenny, K. S. Linsey, D. S. Lumia, and
M. A. Maupin. 2005. *Estimated use of water in the United States in
2000* (U.S. Geological Survey Circular 1268). Washington, DC: U.S.
Government Printing Office.

International Codes Council (ICC). 2006. *International energy conservation
code.* Falls Church, VA: ICC.

Kats, G. 2003. *The costs and financial benefits of green buildings. California's
Sustainable Building Task Force.* Retrieved September 2, 2007, from
California Integrated Waste Management Board Web site: http://www.
ciwmb.ca.gov/greenbuilding/Design/CostBenefit/Report.pdf.

Low-Flow aerators and showerheads. n.d. Retrieved July 31, 2005, from
The Energy Coalition Web site: http://www.energycoalition.org/energy_
tips/water.pdf.

Lstiburek, Joseph. 2002. Moisture control in buildings. *ASHRAE Journal*
(February): 36–41.

Malin, N. 1992. Assessing sheathing options. *Environmental Building
News* 1 (2): 1, 10–13.

———. 2002a. XLerator—The electric hand dryer reinvented (product
review). *Environmental Building News 11* (1): 6–7.

———. 2002b. Falcon waterfree urinals compete with waterless (product
review). *Environmental Building News 11* (2): 10–11.

———. 2004. The elevator revolution. *Environmental Building News
13* (8): 1, 12–15.

Modera, M. 1999. *Building's End-Use Energy Efficiency: Commercial Thermal
Distribution Systems.* Prepared for California Energy Commission. Retrieved

September, 2007, from http://www.energy.ca.gov/reports/2002-01-10_ 600-00-004.pdf.

Massachusetts Water Resources Authority (MWRA). *Water efficiency and management in commercial buildings.* Boston: MWRA. Retrieved September, 2007, from MWRA Web site: http://www.mwra.state. ma.us/04water/html/bullet4.htm.

National Fenestration Rating Council (NFRC). n.d. *The NFRC label.* Greenbelt, MD: NFRC. Retrieved September, 2007, from NFRC Web site: http://nfrc.thecornerstonepros.com/label.aspx.

Newsbriefs. 2001. *Environmental Building News* 10 (11): 4.

Nonpoint Source News-Notes. 2002. Chesapeake Bay Foundation builds environment-conscious home. *Nonpoint Source News-Notes* 67: 5–8. Retrieved August 2, 2007, from http://www.epa.gov/owow/info/ NewsNotes/issue67/67issue.pdf.

North Carolina Division of Pollution Prevention and Environmental Assistance. *Water efficiency water management options: Kitchen and food preparation.* Retrieved September, 2007, from http://www.p2pays.org/ ref/04/ 03103.pdf.

North Carolina State Energy Office. n.d. *Programs residential.* Retrieved December 10, 2006, from the Web site: http://www.energync.net/ programs/residential.html.

Pilatowicz, G. 1995. *Eco-Interiors.* New York: John Wiley and Sons.

Puget Sound Energy. *Energy Smart Library for your business: Programmable Thermostats.* Retrieved September, 2007, from http://www.energyguide .com/library/EnergyLibraryTopic.asp?bid=pse&prd=20&TID=12148& SubjectID=7552.

Riggs, J. R. 1999. *Materials and components of interior architecture*, 5th ed. Upper Saddle River, NJ: Prentice-Hall.

Rochester Public Utilities (RPU). *High-efficiency cooling equipment rebate application.* Retrieved September, 2007, from http://www.rpu.org/ pdfs/2007_ci_cooling_app3.pdf.

Southwest Florida Water Management District (SFWMD). n.d. *Water conservation @work.* Brooksville, FL: SWFWMD. Retrieved September 22, 2005, from SFWMD Web site: http://www.swfwmd.state.fl.us/conservation/waterwork/checkoffice.htm.

———. 1997. *ICI conservation in the tri-county area of the SWFWMD.* November. Brooksville, FL: SWFWMD.

Spiegel, R., and D. Meadows. 1999. *Green building materials: A guide to product selection and specification.* New York: John Wiley and Sons.

Staber Industries. 2005. *Staber washing machines.* Groveport, OH: Staber Industries. Retrieved September 22, 2005, from Staber Industries Web site: http://www.staber.com.

Thor model laundry machines. n.d. Retrieved September 22, 2005, from Thor Appliance Company Web site: http://www.thorappliances.com.

Tiller, J. S., and D. B. Creech. 1999. *Builder's guide to energy efficient homes in Georgia*. Retrieved September, 2007, from. Division of Energy Resources, Georgia Environmental Facilities Authority Web site: http://www.gefa.org/Modules/ShowDocument.aspx?documentid=42

Union of Concerned Scientists (UCS). 2007. *How solar energy works*. Cambridge, MA: UCS. Retrieved September 2, 2007, from UCS Web site: http://www.ucsusa.org/clean_energy/renewable_energy_basics/how-solar-energy-works.html.

U.S. Department of Energy (DOE), Energy Efficiency and Renewable Energy. n.d. *How to buy an energy-efficient commercial heat pump*. Washington, DC: U.S. Department of Energy. Retrieved September 3, 2007, from U.S. Department of Energy Web site: http://www1.eere.energy.gov/femp/procurement/eep_comm_heatpumps.html.

————, Energy Efficiency and Renewable Energy. 2005. *Demand (tankless or instantaneous) water heaters*. Washington, DC: DOE. Retrieved October 18, 2007, from DOE Energy Efficiency and Renewable Energy Web site: http://www.eere.energy.gov/consumer/your_home/water_heating/index.cfm/mytopic=12820.

U.S. Department of Energy, Energy Information Administration. 2003. *International energy annual, 2003*. Washington, DC: U.S. Department of Energy. Retrieved July 31, 2006, from U.S. Department of Energy Web site: http://www.eia.doe.gov/emeu/iea/contents.html.

Washington State University (WSU). n.d. *Using the energy cost calculator*. Retrieved December 10, 2006, from WSU Energy Program Web site: http://www.energyexperts.org/fuelcalc/Inst.stm.

Wilson, A. 1995. Insulation materials: Environmental comparisons. *Environmental Building News* 4 (1): 1, 11–17.

————. 1996. Windows: Looking through the options. *Environmental Building News* 5 (2): 1, 10–17.

————. 1997. Water: Conserving this precious resource. *Environmental Building News* 6 (8): 1, 8–14.

————. 1998. Energy Star programs: Uncle Sam's partnerships for energy efficiency. *Environmental Building News* 7 (6): 1, 10–15.

————. 1999a. Daylighting: Energy and productivity benefits. *Environmental Building News* 8 (9): 1, 10–14.

————. 1999b. Daylighting—Part 2: Bringing daylight deeper into buildings. *Environmental Building News* 8 (10): 1, 10–14.

————, and P. Yost. 2001. Buildings and the environment: The numbers. *Environmental Building News* 10 (5): 1, 10–14.

————. 2002a. Radiant floor heating: When it does—and doesn't—make sense. *Environmental Building News* 11 (1): 1, 9–14.

———. 2002b. Water heating: A look at the options. *Environmental Building News* 11 (10): 1, 8–15.

———. 2002c. Save energy to save water. *Environmental Building News* 11 (10): 3–4.

———. 2003a. EcoPower faucet relies on hydropower. *Environmental Building News* 12 (1): 6.

———. 2003b. A third non-water-using urinal: McDry from Duravit. *Environmental Building News* 12 (2): 5–6.

———. 2003c. New on-demand hot-water recirculation system from Taco. *Environmental Building News* 12 (5): 8–9.

———. 2003d. Lighting controls: Beyond the toggle switch. *Environmental Building News* 12 (6): 1, 9–15.

———. 2003e. Moisture control in buildings: Putting building science in green building. *Environmental Building News* 12 (7): 1, 11–18.

———. 2003f. Bricor Venturi-effect showerheads. *Environmental Building News* 12 (7): 9.

———. 2003g. Uridan non-water urinal. *Environmental Building News* 12 (11): 6–7.

———. 2004a. All about toilets. *Environmental Building News* 13 (1): 1, 7–15.

———. 2004b. The elevator revolution. *Environmental Building News* 13 (8): 1, 12–15.

PART THREE

Evaluation of Interior Finishes and Furnishings

CHAPTER EIGHT

Certification Programs and Evaluation Instruments

Certification Programs for Environmentally Responsible Product Evaluation

Amanda Gale, NCIDQ Certified, IDEC

An invasion of armies can be resisted. . .
But not an idea whose time has come. . . .
    —Victor Hugo

Dispelling Greenwashing

With the emerging field of environmentally responsible interior design (ERID) came several certification programs, assisting in the prevention of *greenwashing*, that is, the purposeful dispersion of false or exaggerated information aimed at presenting an environmentally responsible image to the public (Greenpeace 2003).

Environmentally responsible design is a vastly burgeoning area in the fields of architecture, interior design, and facility management; therefore, manufacturers and others whose success is dependent on their product image can easily exploit it. There are several organizations that have certification programs, which act as guides to design professionals by providing reliable reference information regarding specification of products that can make projects, and the field itself, more environmentally responsible. In addition, these organizations help to set industry standards while consistently "raising the bar" by achieving higher efficiency and effectiveness in their certification process. The certification programs reviewed in this chapter include: Green Seal, CRI Green Label, Greenguard, Energy Star, and Sustainable Forestry Practices (SFC).

Green Seal

Green Seal (2005) is an independent, nonprofit organization founded in 1989 as a product ecolabeling program. Stationed in Washington, DC, Green Seal's holistic approach to identifying products and services includes reduction of pollution and waste, conservation of resources and habitats, and the minimization of global warming and ozone depletion. This organization's mission is "to achieve a more sustainable world by promoting environmentally responsible production, purchasing, and product" (Green Seal 2005, par. 9). Green Seal (2005) works to achieve this mission by partnering with major institutional purchasers and federal agencies to make the most effective impact by greening operations and purchasing.

It has initiated several programs, such as Greening Your Government, Greening the Lodging Industry, and Product Standards and Certification. Green Seal provided an operating manual, recommendations for lessening environmental impact, and assistance in contract language for federal agencies in the Greening Your Government Program. It has worked with thirteen different government entities thus far. Through Greening the Lodging Industry, Green Seal developed a certification program specifically for lodging properties and authored a purchasing and operations guide applicable to the lodging industry. Green Seal has certified more

Figure 8-1

than forty lodging properties in ten states and Washington, DC. The Product Standards and Certification program was the beginning of ecolabeling for Grean Seal. The initial ecolabeling program was modeled after similar programs operating in Germany and Canada. Green Seal has evolved from certifying a few products to having certified more than 300 products from over 40 major product categories.

Green Seal's (2005) ecolabeling uses standards set by the International Organization for Standardization—specifically, ISO 14020 and 14024—and the U.S. Environmental Protection Agency (EPA). The total certification process has nine steps and includes a life-cycle approach using both quantitative and qualitative information, peer review, performance requirements, and environmental evaluations. The nine steps in the certification process are as follows:

1. Determine the product category and review the standards found on Green Seal's Web site.
2. Provide the company and product information to a Green Seal consultant to determine the evaluation fee.
3. Submit both the application for certification and the confidentiality agreement, along with the product-evaluation fee.
4. Explanation of process by consultant and further gathering of data.
5. Submit the requested data and product samples in duplication to Green Seal.
6. Schedule an audit of the manufacturing facility involved in production.
7. Permission granted to use the Green Seal on the product, its packaging, and promotion.
8. Incorporation of Green Seal Certification Mark and the accompanying text on product packaging with design staff.
9. Continuous annual retesting of product(s).

There are thirty-two environmental standards ranging from residential to industrial, lighting to packaging, and cleaners to paints (Green Seal 2005). Each of the thirty-two standards has the following sections with product specific information: scope, definitions, and performance and environmental requirements (Green Seal 2005). The evaluation fee varies depending on variables such as number of products and the size of company (Green Seal 2005).

Carpet and Rug Institute

The Carpet and Rug Institute (CRI) is the national trade association representing the carpet and rug industry. It represents 90 percent of the carpet manufacturers and the suppliers of raw materials used to produce carpeting (CRI n.d.). Its headquarters is located in Dalton, Georgia. The CRI has shown its concern with the environment by embarking upon such key issues as indoor air quality, incorporation of recycled content, and reduction of industrial wastes. In regard to indoor air quality, CRI introduced a labeling program in 1992 to classify

Figure 8-2

carpeting and rugs that have low VOC emissions. Since the inception of the program, the industry has made substantial reductions in the total level of VOCs, as well as reductions in 4-phenylcyclohexene (4-PC). The labeling program was designed to inform consumers of products with low emissions by displaying a label on the carpet samples. The program offers two labels, the Green Label and the Green Label Plus, to designate the low level of emissions the carpet or adhesive has achieved.

Air Quality Sciences (AQS), an independent laboratory based in Atlanta, tests each product (CRI n.d.). The AQS tests products to identify pollutant sources, using environmental chamber technology (CRI n.d.). In each case the manufacturer voluntarily participates in the program. If the product successfully passes the testing, it will be provided an individual number for the label (CRI n.d.). There are currently 44 different manufacturers with more than 120 products that meet the Green Label criteria (CRI n.d.). Each product is retested quarterly to assure continued compliance for total VOCs and annually for compliance with all individual compounds (CRI n.d.). To receive certification, carpet and adhesive products undergo a 14-day testing process; subsequent testing of certified products is based on a 24-hour dynamic-chamber testing for targeted chemicals and the total level of VOCs (CRI n.d.). The current criteria for the green-label program includes testing for the following chemicals: formaldehyde, 4-phenylcyclohexene, styrene, VOCs (CRI n.d.).

For carpet or adhesive to acquire the Green Label Plus, it must pass the Section 01350 guidelines, which measure emissions for a range of possible chemicals (CRI n.d.). Carpet products are tested for emission levels for 13 chemicals: acetaldehyde, benzene, caprolactam, 2-ethylhexanoic acid, formaldehyde,

1-methyl-2-pyrrolidinone, naphthalene, nonanal, octanal, 4-phenylcyclohexene, styrene, toluene, and vinyl acetate (CRI n.d.). According to CRI, the "test methodology was developed in cooperation with the U.S. EPA and has been adopted by the American Society for Testing and Materials (ASTM) as D5116, Guide for Small-Scale Environment Chamber Determinations of Organic Emissions from Indoor Materials/Products" (CRI n.d., par. 4). There are currently 37 different manufacturers with more than 140 different products that meet the Green Label Plus criteria (CRI n.d.). The product type includes broadloom and modular tiles. Adhesive products are tested for emission levels for 15 chemicals: acetaldehyde, benzothiazole, 2-ethyl-1-hexonal, formaldehyde, isooctylacrylate, methylbiphenyl, 2-methyl-pyrrolidinone, naphthalene, phenol, 4-phenylcyclohexene, styrene, toluene, vinyl acetate, vinyl cyclohexene, and xylenes (CRI n.d.). There are currently 16manufacturers with adhesive products that meet the Green Label Plus criteria (CRI n.d.).

Greenguard

The Greenguard Environmental Institute (GEI) is an independent nonprofit organization founded in 2001 to oversee the certification program for low-emitting products and materials. Greenguard is primarily concerned with the emission off-gassing of products that affect indoor air quality (GEI n.d.). It certifies products that hold off-gassing to low emission levels. However, the GEI is not only a resource for products with low emissions; it is also a resource for general information on indoor air quality, sustainable building practices, and healthy indoor environments. The GEI advisory board consists of nine members from varying universities and organizations. Each member volunteers without compensation to represent his or her colleagues who are equally concerned with indoor air quality.

The certification program evolved from the AQSpec List program developed in 1996 by Dr. Marilyn Black and Air Quality Sciences, an independent laboratory. Initially, the standards consisted of a one-time test of the products against

Figure 8-3

the general product emissions standards established by the State of Washington and the office furniture emissions standards established by the EPA. The products with low emissions were included in the AQSpec List registry. The original testing did not include a life-cycle perspective or performance standards. Currently, the Greenguard certification program tests products annually to ensure continued compliance to the low-emission guidelines and standards. The tests are conducted in dynamic environmental chambers following the guidelines of ASTM D 511-97 and D 6670-01. The chambers simulate the airflow of rooms and buildings, providing accurate results scalable to any room size. The products undergo a weeklong testing process. Results provide information on total emissions, emission rate, and predicted air concentration. Products are tested for formaldehyde, volatile organic compounds (VOCs), aldehydes, respirable particles, ozone, carbon monoxide, nitrogen oxide, and carbon dioxide emissions. The GEI has developed a quality management program (QMP) for its verification partners who participate in the procedures to assure quality through assessment, organization, and conditions (GEI 2005). In addition, the laboratories involved in the certification process comply with all of the requirements stated in ISO 9001 or ISO 17025 (GEI 2005).

The GEI (n.d.) certification process involves nine steps, and the amount of time it takes to complete the process varies. The nine steps are as follows:

1. Submit company and product information to Web site or over the phone to a consultant.
2. Provide proposal for estimation of costs, scope, and time frame.
3. Select product preliminary tests to determine emission levels.
4. Conduct initial product test on selected products.
5. Register product in the Greenguard product guide.
6. Conduct tests on entire product line, including such variations as fabric, padding, and sizes.
7. Provide a statement of the company's environmental practices, such as packaging, waste reduction, recycling, and health programs.
8. Use Greenguard label on product line and in promotional materials.
9. Retest products on a regular basis.

An application fee is required to initiate the certification process and cover the initial certification expenses (GEI n.d.). In addition, there is an administration fee based on the number of certification-testing categories (GEI n.d.). Lastly, there is also a licensing fee; it varies depending on the industry, company size, and number of certified products (GEI n.d.). The following product categories are available for certification: adhesives and sealants, appliances, architectural paints and coatings, ceiling systems, consumer products, general construction materials, hard-surface flooring, insulation, office equipment, office furniture, textiles, and wall coverings (GEI n.d.).

Energy Star

Energy Star is a government-backed program promoting energy efficiency through the identification of products that meet the guidelines set by the EPA and the U.S. Department of Energy. The Energy Star program was introduced in 1992 by the EPA to assist individuals and businesses in protecting the environment through the selection of energy-efficient products. The benefits of using energy-efficient products include minimization of greenhouse gas emissions, significant money savings, and reduction in energy reliance. The initial product categories to receive the Energy Star label were computers and their monitors. The program has since grown and now labels products in fifty different categories, including major appliances, office equipment, lighting, and home electronics (EPA 2003).

Energy Star continues to expand its program by identifying new practices and products for consumer use. In addition to labeling products, the Energy Star label is awarded to residential, commercial, and industrial buildings that are top energy performers. The program offers businesses guidelines for energy management as well as tools and resources to save energy. It also provides assessment, benchmarks, and the EPA's national energy-performance-rating system (EPA 2003).

New houses that are single family or multifamily, either one, two, or three stories, are eligible for the residential Energy Star label. An independent third-party verification of the home's energy efficiency will occur prior to its receiving the label. Energy Star–qualified homes are affordable, good for the environment, energy

Figure 8-4

efficient, and have increased resale value (EPA 2003). In addition to the Energy Star program, residential buildings are also eligible for the Energy Home Sealing and Home Performance program, which incorporates Energy Star windows with well-sealed openings to prevent air loss. Tightening a home's building shell will reduce heat loss to save money. Trained professionals conduct energy audits and make suggestions to increase the efficiency of the home in the Home Performance with Energy Star program (EPA 2003).

Forest Stewardship Council, Sustainable Forestry Practices

The Forest Stewardship Council (FSC) is a nonprofit international organization that was founded in 1993 by loggers, foresters, environmentalists, and sociologists to encourage "the responsible management of the world's forests" (FSC n.d., par. 1). FSC's goal "is to promote environmentally responsible, socially beneficial and economically viable management of the world's forests, by establishing a worldwide standard of recognized and respected principals of forest stewardship" (FSC 2005b, 2). The FSC, with a global network consisting of national offices in more than forty countries, has their international headquarters located in Bonn, Germany. Its governance structure has three levels of decision making—the general assembly, the board of directors, and the executive director.

The FSC accredits independent organizations to assess and certify forest-management operations according to preset standards and guidelines. These certification organizations are responsible for verifying that the operations comply with FSC principles and criteria for forest stewardship. There are currently fifteen accredited certification bodies from ten countries. Uncertified wood can contribute to the degradation or destruction of forests throughout the world. However, FSC-certified wood provides consumers with evidence the guidelines were followed. Their certification process and management prevents forest destruction and degradation while helping to secure forest resources.

There are two types of certification from accrediting bodies: the forest management (FM) certificate and the chain of custody (COC) certificate (FSC 2005b).

Figure 8-5

The FM certification entails inspection of the forest-management unit and evaluation against the FSC principals of responsible forest management (FSC 2005b). However, prior to selling their products as FSC certified, producers must also become COC certified (FSC 2005b). Chain of custody certification tracks the raw material harvested from the forest to the consumer, including all stages such as manufacturing, distribution, and printing. Once COC certification has been granted, the operations are entitled to label their products as FSC certified (FSC 2005b).

There are a total of 739 FSC-certified forests worldwide in 65 different countries, a total of 50 million hectares (FSC n.d.). In the United States alone, there are 25 states, with 15 of them having more than one certified forests within their borders (FSC 2005a). In total there are 98 certified forests with a total acreage of 13.5 million in the United States (FSC 2005a).

References

CRI (Carpet and Rug Institute). n.d. The science-based source for the facts on carpet and rugs. Retrieved October 12, 2005, from The Carpet and Rug Institute Web site: http://www.carpet-rug.org

Energy Star. n.d. Energy star qualified products. Retrieved October 13, 2005, from Energy Star Web page: http://www.energystar.gov

EPA (Environmental Protection Agency). 2003. *ENERGY STAR—The power to protect the environment through energy efficiency*. Retrieved October 13, 2005, from Energy Star Web page: http://www.energystar.gov/ia/partners/downloads/energy_star_report _aug_2003.pdf

FSC (Forest Stewardship Council). n.d. Because forests matter. Retrieved October 5, 2005, from FSC Web site: http://www.fscuc.org

———. 2005a. *FSC-certified forests in the U.S.* Retrieved October 5, 2005, from FSC Web site: http://www.fscus.org/images/documents/FSC_Certified_Forests_in_US.pdf

———. 2005b. *Principals and criteria for forest stewardship*. Retrieved October 5, 2005, from FSC Web site: http://www.fscus.org/images/documnets/FSC-Principals_Criteria.pdf

GEI (Greenguard Environmental Institute). n.d. The clear choice for clean indoor air. Retrieved October 5, 2005, from Greenguard Web site: http://www.greenguard.org

———. (2005). *Greenguard product certification program: Laboratory qualifications and proficiency requirements*. Retrieved October 5, 2005, from Greenguard Web site: http://www.greenguard.org/uploads/LabQualification.pdf

Greenpeace. 2003. *Green or greenwashing? A Greenpeace detection kit*. Retrieved October 21, 2005, from Greenpeace Web site: http://archive.greenpeace.org/comms/97/summit/greenwash.html

Green Seal. 2005. The mark of environmental responsibility. Retrieved October 7, 2005, from Grean Seal Web site: http://www.greenseal.org

Evaluation Systems for Environmentally Responsible Project Evaluation

Louise Jones, ArchD, LEED AP, IDEC, ASID, IIDA

Ensuring Optimal Performance

The design and construction of high-performance buildings is dynamic and evolving. It is commonly recognized that a whole-building, integrated-design approach is most effective when implementing environmentally responsible design criteria. This ensures the optimal performance for the desired design goals. It is critically important that valid evaluation systems are available to set parameters that can improve quality, decrease the life-cycle environmental impact, and optimize life-cycle costs of the buildings. These rating systems must provide the data required to support innovative principles and practices that protect people's health and well-being as well as planet Earth's health and well-being. Only then will this generation be able to meet their needs without negating the ability of future generations to meet their needs.

Five rating systems were referenced most frequently in the environmentally responsible design literature: BREEAM, CASBEE, GBTool, Green Globes, and LEED. The information in this chapter regarding each rating system is publicly available and relatively easy to locate, it was compiled using the Internet and conference proceedings, as well as trade and journal articles.

Rating Systems

BREEAM

The Building Research Establishment's Environmental Assessment Method (BREEAM) was developed in the United Kingdom in 1990, making it the oldest of the commonly used assessment methods. Offices, homes, schools, industrial and retail units,

Figure 8-6

are among the range of building types BREEAM explicitly addresses. In addition, other building types can be assessed using custom-made versions of BREEAM.

In a BREEAM assessment, points are awarded for meeting each criterion; the points are then added for a total score. The overall building performance is awarded a rating based on the score: pass, good, very good, or excellent. BREEAM evaluative categories for design and procurement include the following:

- *Management* (commissioning, monitoring, waste recycling, pollution minimization, materials minimization)
- *Health and well-being* (adequate ventilation, humidification, lighting, thermal comfort)
- *Energy* (submetering, efficiency, and CO_2 impact of systems)
- *Transport* (emissions, alternate transport facilities)
- *Water* (consumption reduction, metering, leak detection)
- *Materials* (asbestos mitigation, recycling facilities, reuse of structures, facade, or materials, use of crushed aggregate and sustainable timber)
- *Land* (previously used land, use of remediated contaminated land)
- *Ecology* (land with low ecological value or minimal change in value, maintaining major ecological systems on the land, minimization of biodiversity impacts)
- *Pollution* (leak-detection systems, on-site treatment, local or renewable energy sources, light-pollution design, nonuse of ozone-depleting and global-warming substances)

Codeveloped by the Building Research Establishment Ltd. (BRE) and ECD (now part of Faber Maunsell's Sustainable Development Group), BREEAM has a long track record in the United Kingdom, but it is rarely used in the United States. Therefore, it is somewhat difficult to obtain current information. The BREEAM program is updated annually; however, the current version is not publicly available for purchase and must be acquired through a licensed assessor organization. This organization determines the BREEAM rating for a given building based on quantifiable sustainable design achievements. Although most people involved in environmentally responsible design are aware of BREEAM and many rating systems have used it as a base for their developments, the rating system is neither used nor recognized in the United States by most design practitioners. Sample reporting and certification pages are available online for a BREEAM evaluation (see http://www.breeam.org).

CASBEE

The Comprehensive Assessment System for Building Environmental Efficiency (or CASBEE) was developed in Japan in 2001. The system assesses buildings in different stages of the life cycle: predesign, new construction, existing buildings, and renovation. The CASBEE system introduced a new concept for assessment that distinguishes environmental load from quality of building performance. In relating

Figure 8-7

these two factors, CASBEE results can be seen as a measure of ecoefficiency, or BEE (building environmental efficiency).

The outcome of the assessment is plotted on a graph, with environmental load on one axis and quality on the other. The best buildings will fall in the section of the graph representing lowest environmental load and highest quality. Each criterion is scored from 1 to 5, with 1 defined as meeting minimum requirements, 3 meeting typical technical and social levels at the time of the assessment, and 5 showing a high level of achievement. The CASBEE technical manual presents detailed explanations of each rating for each criterion and includes reference material and calculation tools when needed.

The CASBEE's major categories of criteria include the following:

- Building environmental quality and performance
- Indoor environment (noise and acoustics, thermal comfort, lighting and illumination, and air quality)
- Quality of services (functionality and usability, amenities, durability and reliability, flexibility and adaptability)
- Outdoor environment on-site (preservation and creation of biotope, townscape and landscape, and outdoor amenities)
- Building environmental loadings
- Energy (thermal load, use of natural energy, efficiency of systems, and efficient operations)
- Resources and materials (water conservation, recycled materials, sustainably harvested timber, materials with low health risks)
- Reuse and reusability and avoidance of chlorofluorocarbons (CFCs) and halons
- Off-site environment (air pollution, noise and vibration, odor, sunlight obstruction, light pollution, heat-island effect, and load on local infrastructure)

The CASBEE program is managed by the newly formed Japan Sustainable Building Consortium (a nongovernmental organization comprised of industry, the Japanese government, and academic members). Although CASBEE was developed for the Japanese market, it is available in English. It has not been tested in the United States; however, it is potentially applicable in the U.S. market and has the advantage of providing the unique "BEE approach" to representing performance data. The system requires documentation of quantifiable, sustainable design achievements that are evaluated by architects who have passed the CASBEE assessor examination. Although major modifications of the program are expected to be made annually, the process is not clear. Fewer than ten buildings have been evaluated using the system, and all of those are in Japan. An example of a CASBEE documentation evaluation is available online (http://www.ibec.or.jp/CASBEE/english/method2E.htm).

GBTOOL

The Green Building Assessment Tool (GBTool) was developed for the Green Building Challenge, which was an international project involving more than twenty-five countries that began in 1998. In response to the geographic differences of the countries involved, the GBTool is designed to be adapted to reflect regional conditions and context. It includes criteria in categories such as:

- Site selection
- Project planning and development
- Environmental loading
- Energy and resource consumption
- Indoor environmental quality
- Functionality
- Long-term performance
- Social and economic aspects

Categories are evaluated using scales that are based on local benchmarks of "typical" practice. Scores include: -1 to indicate below typical practice, and +1 to +5 to indicate good to very high performance. All categories must be scored to provide a complete assessment of the building. Benchmarks of typical practice and criteria weightings are established by the testing organization to represent national, regional, or local codes, practice, context, conditions, and priorities.

The GBTool has evolved over time as it was used by participating countries, and the results have been presented at a series of international conferences. Originally developed as an as-designed evaluation, versions are being developing to address predesign, design, as-built, and operations. The instrument is comprised of two spreadsheets, one for data entry (to be completed by the project team) and

Figure 8-8

one for establishing weights and benchmarks and for completing the assessment (to be completed by third-party assessors). The criteria for the GBTool's major categories include the following:

- *Energy consumption* is assessed through (1) use of nonrenewable energy (embodied and operational); (2) electrical-peak demand for operations; (3) use of renewable energy; and (4) commissioning.

- *Resource consumption* is assessed through (1) materials used (i.e., salvaged, recycled, bio-based and sustainably harvested); (2) materials produced locally; (3) designed for disassembly, reuse, or recycling; and (4) water use for irrigation, building systems, and occupant use.

- *Environmental factors* include (1) greenhouse gas emissions; (2) other atmospheric emissions; (3) solid wastes; (4) storm water; (5) wastewater; (6) site impacts; and (7) other local and regional impacts.

- *Indoor environmental quality* is assessed through (1) indoor air quality; (2) ventilation; (3) temperature and relative humidity; (4) daylight and illumination; and (5) noise and acoustics.

Criteria for the other categories include selection of appropriate site (in terms of land use, brownfields, access to transportation, and amenities), project planning, urban design (density, mixed uses, compatibility, native plantings, and wildlife corridors), building controls, flexibility and adaptability, maintenance of operating performance, and a few social and economic measures.

The GBTool was developed and revised by the International Framework Committee, which is composed of representatives of all participating countries (to date, approximately twenty-five), including the United States. The GBTool is an international system that has been used to evaluate U.S. buildings for the Green Building Challenge. A third-party team establishes the qualitative and quantitative measures used to evaluate environmentally responsible design achievements and expected building performance. Since its inception in 1998, the system has undergone four updates, based on evaluators' experiences in the field. Due to the flexibility inherent in the application of the GBTool, it tends to require greater technical expertise to implement than other rating systems, which has limited its use in the U.S. market. An example of the GBTool evaluation documentation is available online (http://greenbuilding.ca/gbc2k/gbtool/gbtool-main.htm).

GREEN GLOBES

Green Globes USA was adapted from the Green Globes Canada rating system in 2004. Green Globes Canada was developed as a Web-based component of the BREEAM/Green Leaf suite of of environmental assessment tools. The development of Green Globes USA was funded by the Green Building Initiative, a 501(c)3 nonprofit organization. It is an online evaluation process designed for use by architects and builders for commercial buildings.

Figure 8-9

The preliminary assessment occurs after the conceptual design, and the final assessment occurs after the construction-documentation stage. A Green Globes evaluation is based on the number of applicable points available in a given category, with the possibility of "not applicable" in a given category. Projects that have been third-party verified and achieved over 35 percent of the points available earn a rating of 1 to 4 Green Globes. Major categories of criteria include the following:

- *Project management* (integrated design, environmental purchasing, commissioning, emergency response plan)
- *Site* (site development area, reduction of ecological impacts, enhancement of watershed features, site ecology improvement)
- *Energy* (energy consumption; energy-demand minimization; "right-sized," energy-efficient systems; renewable sources of energy; energy-efficient transportation)
- *Water* (flow and flush fixtures, water-conserving features, reduction of off-site treatment of water)
- *Indoor environment* (effective ventilation systems, source control of indoor pollutants, lighting design and integration of lighting systems, thermal comfort, acoustic comfort)
- *Resources, building materials, and solid waste* (materials with low environmental impact; minimized consumption and depletion of material resources; reuse of existing structures; building durability, adaptability, and disassembly; and reduction, reuse, and recycling of waste)

The Green Building Initiative received accreditation as a standards developer by ANSI, and it is developing Green Globes USA as an official ANSI standard. Following the completion of the ANSI process, the Green Building Initiative expects the standards to be revised. Although Green Globes can be used for self-assessment, environmentally responsible design and construction information is submitted online for third-party verification, which is provided by a professional who is approved by the Green Building Initiative and trained to use Green Globes assessment software. Although there has been much publicity regarding Green Globes USA, only four buildings have received Green Globes ratings in the pilot program, with an additional sixty-three buildings registered, which means they may pursue verification. An example of Green Globes evaluation documentation, is available online (http://www.thegbi.org/assets/PDFs/Example_Reports.pdf).

LEED

Leadership in Energy and Environmental Design, or LEED, as it is commonly known, was developed and revised by the U.S. Green Building Council (USGBC) member committees. It was piloted in the United States in 1998, with government funding support, as a consensus-based rating system that is centered on the use of building technology that is currently available. The rating system addresses specific human and environmental health related criteria, using a "whole-building" environmental performance approach. In addition to LEED-NC (for new construction and major renovations), there are versions for existing buildings, commercial interiors, core and shell, homes, schools, retail, and neighborhood development. USGBC is also developing LEED for healthcare, and LEED for labs. Application guides can be used to increase the applicability and flexibility of LEED (e.g., multiple buildings, campuses, health care, laboratories, and lodging). To earn certification, a building project must meet certain prerequisites and performance benchmarks ("credits") within each category. Projects are awarded Certified, Silver, Gold, or Platinum certification depending on the number of credits they achieve. *The LEED Reference Guide* provides detailed information on how to achieve the credits within the major categories:

- *Sustainable sites* (construction-related pollution prevention, site-development impacts, transportation alternatives, storm-water management, heat-island effect, and light pollution)
- *Water efficiency* (landscaping water-use reduction, indoor water-use reduction, and wastewater strategies)
- *Energy and atmosphere* (commissioning, whole-building energy-performance optimization, refrigerant management, renewable-energy use, and measurement and verification)

Figure 8-10   **Build green. Everyone profits.**

- *Materials and resources* (collection locations for recyclables, building reuse, construction-waste management, and the purchase of regionally manufactured materials, materials with recycled content, rapidly renewable materials, salvaged materials, and sustainably forested wood products)
- *Indoor environmental quality* (environmental tobacco-smoke control, outdoor-air delivery monitoring, increased ventilation, construction indoor air quality, use of low-emission materials, source control, and controllability of thermal and lighting systems)
- *Innovation*
- *LEED-accredited professional*

LEED is currently the dominant evaluative system in the U.S. market, and it is being adapted to multiple markets worldwide. A *Product Development and Maintenance Manual,* which governs how changes are made to the LEED rating system, is publicly available. The steps followed for the development of USGBC rating system products included technical development by committee, pilot testing, public comment period, approval by council membership, and then release for public use. Minor updates can occur no more than once a year, while major updates are expected to occur on a three- to five-year cycle and follow a defined process that includes a public comment period. Documentation of the quantifiable and sustainable design measures are submitted to the U.S. Green Building Council, a 501(c)3 nonprofit organization and the developer of the LEED rating system, for third-party verification. The evaluators have been trained and must pass an examination. More than 1,400 U.S. buildings have received LEED ratings and more than 16,200 buildings are registered and may, therefore, seek certification. The LEED rating program is the U.S. market leader; this makes it easy to communicate a building's sustainable design achievements. An example of LEED Version 2.2 evaluation documentation is available online (https://www.usgbc .org/ShowFile.aspx?DocumentID=1095).

Conclusion

There are industry-accepted principles and practices for incorporating environmentally responsible design principles into a building's life cycle. Rating systems can be used to examine the performance, or expected performance, of a "whole building" and to translate the performance data to allow comparisons of the building to other buildings or to a performance standard. Many states, as well as the U.S. government, require that new construction meet the USGBC's LEED criteria. As resources are expended to implement environmentally responsible building practices, it is imperative that easy-to-use evaluation systems are available to document the degree of success and to suggest areas for improvement.

COMMONLY MARKETED ENVIRONMENTALLY RESPONSIBLE BUILDING RATING SYSTEMS

Literature reviews and Internet searches were used to identify the most well-known environmentally responsible building-rating systems. Although some evaluation instruments are original (i.e., not based on modification of another system), many were created by modifying a single system or integrating multiple systems. This information is noted at the end of each entry.

BREEAM (Building Research Establishment's Environmental Assessment Method): Original

Calabasas: Development based on LEED

CASBEE (Comprehensive Assessment System for Building Environmental Efficiency)

CEPAS (Comprehensive Environmental Performance Assessment Scheme): Development based on LEED, BREEAM, HK-BEAM, and IBI

Earth Advantage Commercial Buildings (Oregon): Development base not disclosed

EkoProfile (Norway): Development base not disclosed

ESCALE: Development base not disclosed

GBTool: Original

GEM (Global Environmental Method) for Existing Buildings: Development based on Green Globes

GOBAS (Green Olympic Building Assessment System): Development based on CASBEE and LEED

Green Building Rating System (Korea): Development based on BREEAM, LEED, and BEPAC

Green Globes Canada: Development based on BREEAM Green Leaf

Green Globes U.S.: Development based on Green Globes Canada

Green Leaf Eco-Rating Program: Original

Green Star Australia: Development based on BREEAM and LEED

HK BEAM (Hong Kong Building Environmental Assessment Method): Development based on BREEAM

HQE (High Environmental Quality): Development base not disclosed

iDP (Integrated Design Process): Original

Labs21: Original

LEED (Leadership in Energy and Environmental Design): Original

MSBG (State of Minnesota Sustainable Building Guidelines): Development based on LEED, Green Building Challenge '98, and BREEAM

NABERS (National Australian Built Environment Rating System): Development base not disclosed

Promise (Product Lifecycle Management and Information Tracking Using Smart Embedded Systems): Development base not disclosed

Protocol ITACA: Development based on GBTool

SBAT (Sustainable Buildings Assessment Tool): Original

Scottsdale's Green Building Program: Development base not disclosed

SPiRiT (Sustainable Project Rating Tool): Development based on LEED

TERI Green Rating for Integrated Habitat Assessment: Original

TQ Building Assessment System (Total Quality Building Assessment System): Original

SOURCE: FOWLER AND RAUCH 2006.

References

ATHENA Sustainable Materials Institute. 2002. *LEED Canada adaptation and BREEAM/Green Leaf harmonization studies: Part I, Project summary and overview observations.* Retrieved September 15, 2006, from Athena Web site: http://www.athenasmi.ca/projects/leed/docs/PartI_LEED_CanadaHarm.pdf

Building Research Establishment's Environmental Assessment Method (BREEAM). 2006. *Learn more about BREEAM.* Retrieved September 15, 2006, from BREEAM Web site: http://www.breeam.org/

Comprehensive Assessment System for Building Environmental Efficiency (CASBEE). 2004. *New Construction Technical Manual,* 4th ed. Retrieved September 15, 2006, from CASBEE Web Site: http://www.ibec.or.jp/CASBEE/english/

Center for Sustainable Building Research. 2004. *Minnesota Sustainable Building Guidelines, Version 1.1.* College of Architecture and Landscape Architecture, University of Minnesota. Retrieved September 15, 2006, from http://www.csbr.umn.edu:16080/B3/MSBG_v1_1.pdf.

Faber Maunsell. n.d. *Learn more about BREEAM.* Retrieved September 15, 2006, from: http://www.breeam.org

Fowler, K. M., and E. M. Rauch. 2006. *Sustainable building rating systems summary.* Completed by the Pacific Northwest National Laboratory for the General Services Administration under Contract DE-AC05-76RL061830. Retrieved September 15, 2006, from U.S. Green Building Council Web site: https://www.usgbc.org/ShowFile.aspx?DocumentID=1915

Green Building Initiative. 2006. *Green Globes USA, Green Globes Canada, GEM UK*. Retrieved September 15, 2006, from Green Building Initiative Web site: http://www.thegbi.org/commercial/about-green-globes/faq.asp

International Initiative for a Sustainable Built Environment . 2005. *GBTool Overview*. Retrieved September 15, 2006, from Green Building Canada Web site: http://greenbuilding.ca/gbc2k/gbtool/gbtool-main.htm

National Association of Home Builders (NAHB). 2006. *NAHB's Model Green HomeBuilding Guidelines*. Retrieved September 15, 2006, from NAHB Web site: http://www.nahb.org/fileUpload_details.aspx?contentTypeID=7&contentID=1994

U.S. Army Engineer Research and Development Center (ERDC). 2000. *Sustainable Project Rating Tool (SPiRiT)*. Retrieved September 15, 2006, from ERDC Web site: http://www.cecer.army.mil/earupdate/nlfiles/2000/sustainable2.cfm

US Green Building Council (USGBC). 2007. *Leadership in Energy and Environmental Design*. Retrieved October 10, 2007, from USGBC Web site: http://www.usgbc.org/DisplayPage.aspx?CategoryID

United States Green Building Council and LEED Certification

Louise Jones, ArchD, LEED AP, IDEC, ASID, IIDA

Never doubt that a small group of thoughtful committed citizens can change the world. Indeed it's the only thing that ever has.
—Margaret Mead

Synergism in the Building Industry

Since its inception 1993, the United States Green Building Council (USGBC) has provided a forum for leaders in the building industry to work together to develop industry standards, design guidelines, policy positions, educational tools, and events. Its mission statement expresses the foundation upon which they are building the understanding, adoption, and promotion of environmentally responsible design:

> The U.S. Green Building Council is the nation's foremost coalition of leaders from across the building industry working to promote buildings that are environmentally responsible, profitable, and healthy places to live and work. (USGBC 2003, 1)

The USGBC is the only national consensus organization that represents the entire building industry with regard to issues related to the interaction of the built and natural environment. The collective power created by the diversity of the

Figure 9-1   Build green. Everyone profits.

membership provides opportunities to initiate change in the way buildings are designed, built, operated, used, and maintained (USGBC 2003).

What Is Environmentally Responsible Design?

Definitions of environmentally responsible design range from a very broad concept of "meeting the needs of today without compromising the ability of future generations to meet their needs" (United Nations 1987) to very narrow concepts, focusing on one element, such as protecting tropical rain forests. The USGBC's definition addresses the risks to people and the environment:

> Design and construction practices that significantly reduce or eliminate the negative impact of buildings on the environment and occupants in five broad areas:
>
> ■ Sustainable site planning;
> ■ Safeguarding water and water efficiency;
> ■ Energy efficiency and renewable energy;
> ■ Conservation of materials and natural resources; and
> ■ Indoor environmental quality (USGBC, 2005a).

Why Build Green?

The built environment has a profound impact on the natural environment, public health, productivity, and the economy. In the United States, buildings account for (USGBC 2005a):

■ 36 percent of total energy used;
■ 65 percent of electricity consumption;
■ 30 percent of greenhouse gas emissions;
■ 30 percent of raw materials use;

- 30 percent of solid waste production;
- 136 million tons of construction waste annually (2.8 lbs per person per day); and
- 12 percent of potable water consumption.

As recently as 25 years ago, few people would have thought it possible to design, build, live, or work in buildings that enhance user's health and well-being, conserve natural resources, increase productivity, and contribute to the owner's financial success. However, breakthroughs in building science, technology, and material availability have made it possible for designers, builders, and owners to maximize both economic and environmental performance.

Environmentally responsible design is optimal for the environment, for people's health and well-being, and for corporations' bottom lines. With a minimal investment (up to 2 percent of construction costs) in environmentally responsible initiatives, the U.S. building industry could (Kats 2003):

- Reduce water use by 40 percent;
- Reduce energy costs and dangerous emissions from power generation by 30 percent;
- Divert 50 to 75 percent of construction and demolition waste from landfills;
- Save $58 billion per year in lost sick time due to poor indoor air quality; and
- Gain $180 billion per year in worker productivity with improved daylighting and thermal comfort.

The National Geographic Society Headquarters complex of commercial office buildings in Washington, DC, was the first project to be certified under the LEED for Existing Buildings Rating System (LEED-EB). According to the National Geographical Society chief financial officer, Chris Liedel: "The Society added millions of dollars in value from this LEED-EB Silver certification" (USGBC n.d. d). The National Geographic Society is one of the world's largest scientific and educational nonprofit organizations; its project demonstrated that LEED-EB was feasible for older buildings. The building operating practices were updated; the heating and cooling systems were upgraded, as were the lighting systems; these and other capital improvements in the four buildings increased the market value by $4 for every $1 spent. The business benefits that resulted in an increase in value of millions of dollars included (USGBC n.d. d):

- Documented lower operating costs;
- Lower waste-disposal expenses;
- Higher appraised value;
- Ability to receive higher tenant rents;
- Improved credit ratings; and
- Lower interest rates on debt instruments.

Figures 9-2 and 9-3
The Interface Showroom in Atlanta, Georgia, was the first LEED-CI (contract interior) Platinum-certified project. Extensive daylighting and efficient electrical lighting (including metal halide in the drum fixtures shown here), with occupancy sensors and photovoltaic cells to monitor daylighting and adjust the electrical lighting accordingly, reduce energy consumption in the showroom. Photo by Jeanne Mercer-Ballard.

WHAT DOES IT COST TO BE GREEN?

Even as the word LEED becomes synonymous with green building, discussion continues over whether it actually costs more to build to the U.S. Green Building Council's Leadership in Energy and Environmental Design (LEED) standards. Numerous studies have been conducted that suggest there's no added cost for building green. But other reports have found just the opposite.

"Cost depends on project specifics and the LEED level targeted," said Dennis Wilde, senior project manager at Gerding/Edlen Development Co. "Gold ratings can increase hard construction costs between 1 percent and 2 percent while attempts at platinum can be upward of 5 percent. But LEED certified or silver certified projects should see no increase, especially if the participants have experience. If you've been to this party before, and you know what you're doing, there should be no material cost increase," Wilde said. "Streamlining the process, and getting everyone from engineers to contractors involved in the LEED attempt from the outset, is key," said Terry Miller, green building specialist at the city of Portland's Office of Sustainable Development.

Alan Scott, principal at Green Building Services, a green building consulting firm, echoes the "it all depends" sentiment. "A LEED-certified building can cost less to build than a standard building. It's also true it can cost a little bit more." Scott puts the cost between 0 percent and 3 percent, especially for commercial buildings. "Developers tend to look at retail and other commercial projects on a 20-year timeline. Cost per square foot is typically lower, and potential long-term returns on LEED projects may not be as important financially as it is in public projects. An institutional client will typically build a higher-quality building because they know they'll have it for 50 to 100 years," Scott said.

Tax credits are an effective incentive, especially energy tax credits, which reduce the final cost of buildings certified as LEED Silver or higher. "That's the biggest carrot out there to go green. Really savvy developers have demonstrated that that's enough, sometimes, to offset the cost," Miller said. Local architects and designers are also starting to "get good at going green."

"The perception that building a LEED project is going to cost more still exists," Wilde said, "but it's a fairly uneducated reaction. It does take more time on the front end," he said, "and some aren't willing to put up with that." The idea that it actually costs more—and isn't worth it because it costs more—is something Mark Edlen, managing principal of Gerding/Edlen, said "has more to do with unfamiliarity with LEED than with reality."

"The benefits also aren't necessarily things that have a quantifiable value. That's especially true in geographic areas where passion for green building creates the desire for LEED certification just as much as passion for investment returns," Edlen said. Then there's what Wilde calls "the cool factor." "LEED-certified buildings have definite perceived benefits in the marketplace, especially on the residential side due to concern with indoor air quality. When we started doing this, we did it because we thought it was the right thing to do. That's still our primary motivation, but we're also finding that it's good for business," Wilde said.

There's also evidence that's fairly anecdotal at this point, but it indicates that siting an office in a green building leads to higher productivity, reduced absenteeism, better health, and an all-around happier workplace. "The smarter tenants realize that when you give people higher ceilings, operable windows, and environmental benefits, you have happier employees," Wilde said. Another bonus is better design. "We put a lot of effort into designing environmentally responsible buildings. A byproduct of that is better design. . . . Design has a tremendous amount to do with whether people enjoy an environment and go back again and again," he said.

Those familiar with LEED building standards maintain that practices related to certification efforts should be the rule rather than the exception. "A LEED building should just be standard," Miller said. "People should demand high-quality, well-performing buildings. That's not innovation, that's just what should be done."

SOURCE: RYAN 2005.

Figure 9-4
The National Geographic Society Headquarters in Washington, DC, was the first project to be certified under the LEED for Existing Buildings Rating System (LEED-EB). Photo by Mark Thiessen. ©2007 National Geographic.

Genesis of the USGBC

In the mid-1980s, David Gottfried, a contractor and real estate developer, and Michael Italiano, an environmental lawyer, were both working on William McDonough's Environmental Defense Fund Project in New York City.

> We saw the start of a new movement, and so many people . . . were excited about it, we saw a lot of energy. . . . We built an entrepreneurial kind of catalyst group, and we needed a new organization in which to seed that. . . . So we got the idea to start a new group called the U.S. Green Building Council. . . . We had the AIA host our first potential membership meeting in April of '93 with about a hundred folks attending. . . . We were successful at that opening April meeting and raised $125,000 by June of '93, which was exciting, and we launched the U.S. Green Building Council. (Gottfried 2001)

Since its inception, the USGBC has provided an opportunity for leaders in the building industry

> The United States Green Building Council's mission is to promote the design and construction of buildings that are environmentally responsible, profitable, and healthy places to live and work (USGBC 2006d).

to work together to develop industry standards, design guidelines, policy positions, and educational tools. It is the only national, non-profit, consensus based organization that represents the entire building industry regarding issues related to the interaction of the built and natural environments. This coalition of leaders from across the building industry is working together to promote buildings that are environmentally responsible, economically viable, healthy places to live and work. Their goal is to enable the building industry to understand, adopt, and promote environmentally responsible design and construction. To accomplish this, the USGBC objectives are:

- to educate both owners and practitioners;
- to integrate the many sectors involved in the design and construction of buildings; and
- to lead market transformation. (USGBC 2005a)

STRUCTURE AND ORGANIZATION

Environmentally responsible building design brings all of the stakeholders together—from the design team to the construction team, the operations and maintenance staff, and the building occupants. All have a role to play. The collective power created by the diversity of the USGBC membership provides opportunities to initiate change in the way buildings are designed, built, operated, used, maintained, reused, and demolished. Linking everything that the USGBC does is an unshakable commitment to the environment as a cornerstone of human health, prosperity, and well-being (Fedrizzi 2005).

The USGBC is membership based; more than 14,600 (2008) member organizations, businesses that design, construct, manage, finance, insure, and own buildings, as well as government and nonprofit agencies, are defining environmentally responsible design and construction (USGBC 2005a). By working together to promote environmentally responsible design, the membership can foster greater economic vitality, environmental health, and occupant well-being at lower life-cycle costs. Organizations, not individuals, form the USGBC membership, ensuring that members have both the will and the ability to make changes. The membership includes (USGBC n.d. a):

- Architectural and design firms;
- Building commissioning providers;
- Building-control service contractors and manufacturers;
- Building FF&E (furnishings, finishes, and equipment) manufacturers and dealerships;
- Building owners and facility managers;
- Construction materials manufacturers;
- Consulting firms
- Developers, contractors, builders, and construction managers;
- Engineering firms;
- Federal, state, and local governments;
- Financial and insurance firms;
- Nonprofit organizations and environmental organizations;
- Practitioner societies (e.g., AIA [American Institute of Architects], IDEC [Interior Design Educators Council], IIDA [International Interior Designers Association], IFMA [International Facility Management Association];
- Press;
- Professional firms: architects, engineers, interior designers, landscape architects, and urban planners;
- Real estate appraisers, brokers, developers, and property managers;
- Universities and institutes;
- Urban planners; and
- Utility companies.

In 1993, about 100 people attended the first USGBC meeting; more than 13,000 attended the USGBC Greenbuild meeting in 2006 in Denver. In September 2007, there were 16,278 buildings registered for LEED certification and 1433 certified buildings located in all 50 states and in 67 countries (USGBC 2007). The USGBC's unique perspective and collective power provide the 91,000 participants (2008) with an opportunity to affect change in the built environment by:

- Creating a national consensus for producing a new generation of high-performance buildings that protect the health, safety, and well-being of both the people using the buildings and the global ecosystems;

- Working together to develop LEED products and resources, the Greenbuild Annual International Conference and Expo, and policy positions, as well as educational and marketing tools that support the adoption of environmentally responsible building design principles; and

- Forging strategic alliances with key industry and research organizations, as well as federal, state and local government agencies, to transform the built environment (USGBC 2006d).

The USGBC works through a committee structure to gain consensus for market-based incentives to support environmentally responsible buildings. It employs consensus-based decision making from across its extremely diverse membership. USGBC policies require approval by two-thirds of the voters (USGBC 2006b). Members then influence change in all sectors of the building industry through their active participation in national conferences, regional chapters, and standing committees.

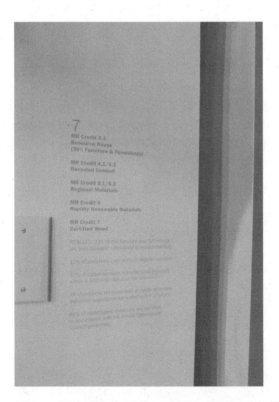

Figures 9-5 and 9-6 *Wall graphics in the Interface Showroom explain the credits earned for LEED-CI certification.*

USGBC COMMITTEE STRUCTURE

USGBC Chapter Steering Committee

USGBC Curriculum and Accreditation Committee

USGBC Education Committee

USGBC Emerging Green Builders Committee

USGBC Government Committee

USGBC Greening the Codes Committee

USGBC Professional Development Committee

USGBC Public Distribution List Committee

USGBC Research Committee

Greenbuild Conference Steering Committee

LEED Accreditation Advisory Committee

LEED Issues Committees (e.g., PVC and HCFC)

LEED Steering Committee

LEED Technical Science and Advisory Committee

SOURCE: USGBC 2006A.

EDUCATIONAL OPPORTUNITIES

USGBC offers programs on environmentally responsible design, construction, and operations for professionals from all sectors of the building industry. More than 58,200 developers, designers, builders, contractors, managers, and tradespeople have attended USGBC educational programs to gain practical knowledge, explore new business opportunities, and learn how to create healthier, more productive, and more efficient places to live and work (USGBC 2007). A range of educational programs are available:

- *Chapter-sponsored continuing education programming* enhances understanding of environmentally responsible design in more than sixty-three geographic areas.

- *Educational Partners Program* promotes training opportunities to serve the continuing educational needs of the rapidly evolving green building industry.

- *Expert Speaker Series* assists organizations planning programs about environmentally responsible design to identify presenters who are industry leaders, innovative practitioners, and/or researchers.

- *Emerging Green Builders Program* provides educational opportunities and resources to students and young practitioners with the goal of bringing tomorrow's leaders into the green building movement.

The USGBC technical advisory groups

(TAGs) provide support for design teams implementing **LEED-NC** in a range of building types (USGBC 2006a):

Sustainable Sites TAG

Energy and Atmosphere TAG

Indoor Environmental Quality TAG

Materials and Resources TAG

Water Efficiency TAG

The LEED program, developed by the USGBC, established rules for certification of all types of building construction and has become the accepted standard for green buildings. LEED educational programs qualify for continuing education credit (USGBC n.d. *b*) for AIA, ASID, BOMI, IFMA, and IIDA. LEED educational programs include:

- *100 series:* Introductory, half-day workshops offer an overview of the LEED rating system.
- *200 series:* Intensive, full-day workshops offer an in-depth discussion of a specific LEED rating system (e.g. LEED-NC).
- *300 series:* Tailored, half-day modules to explore topics specific to individual building types or areas of professional practice, as well as the economics of LEED certified projects.
- *Web-based learning course*: Covers the essentials of LEED professional accreditation for anyone seeking to become a LEED Accredited Professional (LEED AP). The interactive course builds upon a basic knowledge of the LEED-NC Rating System and covers the range of information required to manage the LEED certification process.

The Greenbuild International Conference and Expo is the nation's largest conference on high-performance building practices. Building industry professionals learn about new products, innovative projects, the latest building research,

Professional Practitioner Organizations

American Institute of Architects (AIA)

American Society of Interior Design (ASID)

Building Owners and Managers Institute International (BOMI)

International Facility Managers Association (IFMA)

International Interior Designers Association (IIDA)

U.S. Green Building Council (USGBC)

and much more. With workshops, hundreds of educational sessions, more than 700 exhibitors, internationally renowned speakers, green building tours, and the spirit and passion of the USGBC community, Greenbuild is the industry's premier event (USGBC n.d. *b*).

LEED Green Building Rating System

Soon after the USGBC was organized in 1993, the membership recognized that an evaluation system was necessary to define and measure environmentally responsible building design. A committee with a diverse membership, including an architect, building owner, lawyer, environmentalist, and industry representative, developed the Leadership in Energy and Environmental Design (LEED) Green Building Rating System. The LEED Version 1.0 Pilot Program was launched in 1998. Twelve projects completed the registration process and were certified. After extensive modifications, to address issues identified during the pilot program, LEED 2.0 was released in March 2000. Versions 2.1 and 2.2 clarified and simplified the certification process without changing any of the performance levels (Cassidy 2003). The workplan for LEED 3.0 was introduced at the 2005 Greenbuild Conference in Atlanta, Georgia. LEED was created to address multiple goals (USGBC 2005b):

- Define "green building" by establishing a common standard of measurement;
- Promote integrated, whole-building design practices;
- Recognize environmental leadership in the building industry;
- Stimulate green building competition;
- Raise consumer awareness of green building benefits; and
- Transform the building market.

The LEED Green Building Rating System is a voluntary, consensus-based, market-driven, building rating system that is based on accepted energy and environmental principles. The whole-building approach encourages and guides a collaborative, integrated design and construction process that optimizes environmental and economic factors. The intent is to strike a balance between established practices and emerging technological innovations. LEED evaluates environmental performance from a whole-building perspective, thereby providing a definitive standard for a green building (USGBC 2003).

LEED is a self-assessment, performance-oriented system; points are earned for satisfying the identified criteria. This first set of criteria is now identified as LEED for New Construction and Major Renovations (LEED-NC). There are multiple levels of certification, each depending upon the number of points earned. The total number of points differs for each LEED standard, the total for LEED-NC is 69 points (USGBC 2005a). The total points for each level of certification in LEED-NC are as follows:

- *Certified:* 26–32 points;
- *Silver:* 33–38 points;

- *Gold:* 39–51 points; and
- *Platinum:* 52 or more points.

LEED criteria are organized into five environmental categories. An additional category, Innovation and Design Process, recognizes environmentally responsible design measures not covered under the other five categories. A LEED-certified professional (LEED AP) who is involved in the project also earns a credit toward certification (USGBC n.d. *a*). The seven categories are:

- Sustainable sites (20%);
- Water efficiency (7%);
- Energy and atmosphere (25%);
- Materials and resources (19%);
- Indoor environmental quality (22%);
- Innovation and design process (6%); and
- LEED AP involved in the project (1%).

The percentage of points available for each of the individual categories differs for each LEED standard; the percentages for LEED-NC are shown in parentheses after the criteria (Cassidy 2003).

USGBC's members, representing every sector of the building industry, developed and continue to refine LEED. Any commercial building, as defined by standard building codes, is eligible for certification as a LEED building. "LEED certification validates a building as being environmentally responsible to occupants, the target market, and the community. It benchmarks the building's performance over time, thereby quantifying the return on investment of environmentally responsible design, construction, systems, and materials" (Cassidy 2003).

Although it focuses on office buildings, LEED-NC was designed for commercial and institutional buildings. It has been used to certify other building types, including government centers, schools and universities, health-care facilities, conference centers, sports arenas, and even a high-rise residential building. The rating system has been validated by the General Services Administration: "In a major boost to the U.S. Green Building Council's (USGBC) system for rating the environmental performance of buildings, the General Services Administration (GSA), which operates as the federal government's landlord, has issued a report that found the council's Leadership in Energy and Environmental Design (LEED) system to be the most credible among five systems evaluated" (USGBC 2006h).

The USGBC membership recognized a need for rating systems for other market segments and are developing LEED criteria for other domains (USGBC 2005a):

- *LEED-CI:* LEED for Commercial Interiors (launched 2004)
- *LEED-EB:* LEED for Existing Buildings (launched 2004)
- *LEED-CS:* LEED for Core and Shell (launched 2005)
- *LEED-H:* LEED for Homes (launched 2006)

- *LEED-ND:* LEED for Neighborhood Development (launched 2007)
- *LEED-S:* LEED for Schools (launched 2007)
- *LEED-R:* LEED for Retail (in pilot program)
- *LEED-MB:* LEED for Multiple Buildings (launches 2008)

LEED application guides, developed by and for practitioners, provide information regarding the application of LEED systems to target market segments. There are currently application guides for laboratories, retail, schools, health care, lodging (hotels or residential buildings of four habitable stories or less), and multiple buildings and on-campus building projects.

LEED FOR COMMERCIAL INTERIORS

The LEED for Commercial Interiors (LEED CI) rating system is an integrated design tool used to minimize the environmental impact of tenant spaces while maximizing occupant comfort and performance. Validation of the sustainability achievements of tenant improvement projects is documented with LEED-CI certification. As the building industry's benchmark for environmentally responsible design and construction of tenant spaces, it provides a recognized brand to promote interior environments that are healthy, productive, and efficient. The LEED-CI rating system informs tenants and design teams of the environmentally responsible decisions that can improve the indoor environment (USGBC 2005c). The benefits of LEED CI (USGBC n.d. *c*) include:

- Enhancement of occupant well-being and productivity;
- Improvement of employee retention and reduction in absenteeism;
- Reduction of liability associated with poor indoor air quality;
- Increased marketability;
- Decreased churn costs; and
- Lower operating and maintenance costs.

LEED ACCREDITED PROFESSIONAL

Professional accreditation distinguishes individuals with detailed knowledge of LEED–project certification requirements and processes. The LEED-AP (LEED Accredited Professional) designation is awarded to building industry practitioners who successfully demonstrate these proficiencies on a comprehensive exam. In September 2007, there were 40,471 green building practitioners who had successfully completed the LEED examination process (USGBC 2007). These LEED-APs understand green building practices and principles and are familiar with LEED requirements, resources, and processes. They have the knowledge and skills necessary to participate in the design process, to support and encourage integrated environmentally responsible design, and to streamline the application and certification process (USGBC 2006i).

Although there is only one credential—the LEED Accredited Professional, the candidate for certification is asked to select one of three content areas (i.e., tracks) in which to take the exam. The content areas will be offered as separate tracks that lead to achieving LEED professional accreditation. The new tracks recognize the specific knowledge and expertise of industry professionals involved in interior design, building operations, and maintenance. Currently, the three tracks are:

1. The *LEED for New Construction and Major Renovations Exam* (LEED-NC), which verifies that an individual possesses the knowledge and skills necessary to participate in the design process to support and encourage the design integration required by LEED and to streamline the process.

2. The *LEED for Existing Buildings Exam* (LEED-EB), which verifies that an individual possesses the knowledge and skills necessary to support and encourage the operation, upgrade, and project-team integration required for implementation of LEED on existing building projects. The exam will test an individual's understanding of the practices and principals of green building operations and upgrades as well as familiarity with LEED-EB requirements, resources, and processes.

3. The *LEED for Commercial Interiors Exam* (LEED-CI), which verifies that an individual understands green commercial interior-design practices and principals and tests an individual's familiarity with LEED-CI requirements, resources, and processes. The LEED accredited professionals who pass the LEED-CI exam track will help meet the growing demand from the private and public sectors for green commercial interiors.

Attaining LEED AP status distinguishes building industry professionals who have achieved a high level of knowledge of LEED requirements, resources, standards, processes, and who have a thorough understanding of green building practices and principles. Candidates who become accredited under the current version of the exam will not be required to retest once an updated version is released (USGBC 2006i).

The USGBC's LEED AP accreditation exam is focused on four objectives:

Section I: Knowledge of LEED credit intents, requirements, submittals, and technologies

Section II: Coordination of project-team members to achieve LEED certification

Section III: Implementation of LEED process and knowledge of project tools and resources

Section IV: Verification of LEED technical requirements and documentation

Conclusion

The value of environmentally responsible building construction starts, in the U.S., is expected to exceed $12 billion dollars in 2007 (USGBC 2007). Research has shown that the built environment has a profound impact on the natural environment, the global economy, and people's health and productivity. In 2006 the construction market accounted for 14.2 percent of the $10 trillion U.S. gross domestic product (USGBC 2007). The USGBC is leading the building industry in its journey to produce a new generation of high-performance buildings. The goal is to transform the building industry such that the design, construction, and use of the built environment enhances the health and welfare of the people who create and use the designed environment as well as the health and welfare of the planet that sustains them. Council members work together to develop industry standards, design practices and guidelines, policy positions, and educational tools that support the adoption of environmentally responsible design and building practices. Through consensus, the USGBC membership developed the Leadership in Energy and Environmental Design Green Building Rating System as the benchmark for the design, construction, and certification of environmentally responsible buildings. The widespread adoption of the LEED rating system criteria can be linked, at least in part, to the market-based incentives for environmentally responsible design and construction. Based on recognized scientific standards, LEED emphasizes leading-edge strategies for sustainable site development, water consumption, energy efficiency, materials selection, and indoor environmental quality. The USGBC provides a leadership forum and an integrating force for change in the building industry. Its members have an unparalleled opportunity to accelerate change and to help shape the green building industry (USGBC 2006g).

References

Cassidy, R., ed. 2003. White paper on sustainability: A report on the green building movement. (Supplement). *Building Design and Construction*. November. Retrieved January 22, 2006, from U.S. Green Building Council Web site: https://www.usgbc.org/Docs/Resources/BDCWhitePaperR2.pdf

Fedrizzi, R. 2005. Taking LEED to the next level. The LEED guide. *Environmental Design + Construction*. August. Retrieved September 25, 2007, from EDC Magazine Web site: http://www.edcmag.com/CDA/Archives/678b0104cd697010VgnVCM100000f932a8c0

Gottfried, D. 2001. *USGBC Past, present, and future.* 2001 Greenbuild Opening Plenary (transcription). Retrieved February 12, 2006, from U.S. Green Building Council Web site: https://www.usgbc.org/docs/Member_Resource_Docs/2001Summit-OpeningPlenary.doc

Katz, G. 2003. The costs and benefits of building green. In U.S. Green Building Council. n.d. *Build Green. Everyone profits.* (brochure). Washington, DC: USGBC.

Ryan, A. 2005. Experts disagree on whether green construction costs more. *Daily Journal of Commerce, October 11.*

UN World Commission on Environment and Development. (1987). *The Brundtland report: Our common future.* New York: Oxford University Press.

USGBC (U.S. Green Building Council). n.d. a. *Building a sustainable future.* (brochure). Washington, DC: USGBC.

———— n.d. b. *Educational programs.* (brochure). Washington, DC: USGBC.

———— n.d. c. *LEED for commercial buildings.* (fact sheet). Washington, DC: USGBC.

————n.d. d. *LEED for existing buildings.* (fact sheet). Washington, DC: USGBC.

———— 2005a, October. *Introduction to the US Green Building Council and the LEED Green Building Rating System.* (Powerpoint slide set). Retrieved January 22, 2006 from U.S. Green Building Council Web site: https://www.usgbc.org/FileHandling/show_general_file.asp?DocumentID=742

———— 2005b. *LEED.* Retrieved January 22, 2006, from U.S. Green Building Council Web site: http://www.usgbc.org/DisplayPage.aspx?CategoryID=19

———— 2006a. *Committees.* Retrieved March 1, 2006, from U.S. Green Building Council Web site: https://www.usgbc.org/aboutus/committees.asp?CMSPageID=132

———— 2006b. *Consensus.* Retrieved March 1, 2006, from U.S. Green Building Council Web site: https://www.usgbc.org/DisplayPage.aspx?CMSPageID=136

———— 2006c. *Education.* Retrieved March 1, 2006, from U.S. Green Building Council Web site: https://www.usgbc.org/DisplayPage.aspx?CategoryID=127

———— 2006d. *Meet the USGBC.* Retrieved March 1, 2006, from U.S. Green Building Council Web site: https://www.usgbc.org/DisplayPage.aspx?CategoryID=1

———— 2006e, February. *Newsletter.* Retrieved March 1, 2006, from U.S. Green Building Council Web site: http://www.usgbc.org/Docs/News/News2192.pdf

———— 2006f. *Professional Accreditation.* Retrieved March 1, 2006, from U.S. Green Building Council Web site: https://www.usgbc.org/DisplayPage.aspx?CMSPageID=69&#cred

———— 2006g. *Why build green?* Retrieved March 1, 2006, from U.S. Green Building Council Web site: https://www.usgbc.org/DisplayPage.aspx?CMSPageID=291&

———— 2006h. GSA Says LEED Most Credible Green Building Rating System. *Inside Green Business.* (September 27, 2006, press release). Retrieved October 1, 2006, from U.S. Green Building Council Web site: http://www.usgbc.org/News/USGBCInTheNewsDetails.aspx?ID=2628

———— 2006i. *About the LEED AP exam*. Retrieved September 15, 2007, from U.S. Green Building Council Web site: http://www.usgbc.org/DisplayPage.aspx?CMSPageID=1562&

———— 2007. *Green building by the numbers*. Retrieved September 15, 2007, from U.S. Green Building Council Web site: http://www.usgbc.org/DisplayPage.aspx?CMSPageID=1442

———— 2008. Green building facts. (April 2008, press release). Washington, DC: USGBC.

Yudelson, J. 2005. Is LEED broken? The LEED guide. *Environmental Design + Construction*. August. Retrieved September 15, 2007, from U.S. Green Building Council Web site: http://www.edcmag.com/CDA/Archives/d15f0104cd697010VgnVCM100000f932a8c0

CHAPTER TEN

Specification of Products for Environmentally Responsible Interior Design

Helena Moussatche, PhD, LEED AP, IDEC

The problems that exist in the world today cannot be solved by the same level of thought that created them.
> —Albert Einstein

The Material Selection Process

Environmentally responsible (ER) products are those that cause the least environmental impact on people (building occupants, workers, and the population of communities adjacent to factories) and on the sustainability of the global environment. ER material selection forces designers to be continuously well-informed so they can carefully evaluate, compare, and eventually rank products before specifying them. The examples of materials and products contained in this chapter were chosen to illustrate the variety of aspects that need to be considered in ER specifications.

Material selection criteria and rankings for indoor spaces depend, among other factors, on occupants' needs (e.g., floor resilience, noise protection, chemical sensitivities, allergies, etc.) and the specific conditions of the project (code requirements, ventilation rates, climate, ambient temperature and humidity, sun-ray exposure, etc.). Adding to this list, the global environmental impacts make an already complex task even more so. Dealing with this level of complexity requires a case-by-case evaluation and the establishment of a priority list of criteria for each project. For this reason, the material preferences indicated below are mentioned for educational purposes only.

The selection of ER materials and products for interior designs should start at the earliest stage of the design process. An early selection of materials directly influences the development of the project's concept. Contextual questions asked in this phase will guide product selection. Who are the users and what are their needs? How and where will products be used? Is recycling feasible (some areas do not have recycling facilities in close proximity)? Which performance characteristics are demanded of each particular application? In case of commercial projects, how often is the facility redesigned for image or functional purposes? With this information at hand, the interior designer can start searching for potential ER materials and products. The main issue, at this point, is to use one's own individual values about the environment to ask questions and search for more information.

The initial aesthetic and functional criteria must consider the possible impacts products might have on the occupants and the planet. Today's most innovative designs are the ones that create unusual and appealing visual effects through the careful use of materials that are appropriate to the facility's life cycle without compromising the health, safety, and welfare of the building occupants or the planet's ability to sustain human life. Another reason for early consideration of environmental issues is to avoid overspecification of performance criteria. Would it be wise to specify a very durable but not biodegradable material for a design that, due to marketing strategies, tends to be renovated every 3 to 5 years?

To respond to increasing demands for ER products, interior designers are now required to continually expand their technical knowledge of materials and also their ability to evaluate and compare products. Technical data, however, can be overwhelming at first, and time constraints might prevent a full investigation of products. Instead of being discouraged, one should establish priorities and focus on what can be handled at the time. With time and experience, ER material selection becomes almost second nature to ER designers, and evaluations more inclusive and sophisticated.

As a rule of thumb, interior design–ER products, most of all, are the ones that contribute to a safe and healthy indoor environment and that are also biodegradable or fully recyclable. Other ER attributes, such as recycled content or resource conservation, are equally important and should be part of the criteria but never compromise the interior designers' main responsibility: the health and safety of building occupants. Wilson (2006) categorizes products that help ensure a healthy indoor environment as:

1. Products that do not release significant pollutants into the building
2. Products that block the introduction, development, or spread of indoor contaminants

3. Products that remove indoor pollutants

4. Products that warn occupants of health hazards in the building

5. Products that improve light quality

6. Products that help control noise

Claims of environmental benefits are now very popular among manufacturers, but it is the designers' duty to distinguish ER products within the market's current "greenwashing," that is, the abundance of insufficiently documented environmental claims. Again, designers need to be careful and not rely on undocumented claims. This ongoing problem has generated many concerns.

Due to professional liability, every ER product selected for interiors must meet strict code standards and all the performance requirements for each particular application. A deep understanding of each material and product's characteristics and properties, as well as installation methods, can certainly prevent liability issues. This time-consuming practice is still absolutely necessary to ensure that designers and builders will not be held responsible for a material's failure to perform in all code-regulated aspects. However, a specification document of ER products must also contain and ask for detailed information on every product as it relates to indoor environmental issues. Spiegel and Meadows (1999) produced an excellent environmental impact questionnaire to be used as a guide for specifiers researching ER building materials.

The need for supporting documentation relates to another concern: the request that written documentation from manufacturers be included in the specification document. The material safety data sheet (MSDS) provided by the product's manufacturer, in most cases, contains information on contents and unique characteristics and properties of the product that should be carefully analyzed before approval. For example, the MSDS lists chemicals contained in the materials and results of tests conducted to ensure performance and impact on users. Nevertheless, MSDS information contains proprietary substances, the contents of which are not disclosed. In addition, most MSDSs do not provide all the information needed to evaluate environmental impacts. Therefore, it is the designer's responsibility to ask for additional information to be included in the evaluation.

Specifications are an integral part of the project's construction documents, and they are usually written under the building construction industry standard for master specification. The current standard uses *MasterFormat*, a publication of the Construction Specifications Institute (CSI). The CSI classifies materials in five-digit numbers and titles for specification sections that follow the order in which a building is put together. Several specification models have been created following the CSI divisions. For example, MASTERSPEC, a product of the American Institute of Architects (AIA), is currently the most commonly used by the building industry and it contains evaluations of materials for each CSI section. Although this is the industry's main source of information for product specification (Garrison 2002), ER products recently introduced in the market are not necessarily included. Furthermore, even though MASTERSPEC evaluations include environmental impact information, those might not necessarily follow the same protocol established by the designer and client for a particular project. To solve these problems, ER specifiers are now incorporating environmental issues into standard specifications. Spiegel and Meadows (1999), as well as Wilson, Malin, and Piepkorn (2006), for example, propose technical terminologies to be used in ER specification documents.

Another issue to consider is the substitution of specified ER products with "equivalent products" that do not exactly meet the criteria used for selection. Products are often substituted during the construction phase of a project for many reasons. For instance, the specified product might be momentarily unavailable or need more time to be delivered than the construction schedule allows, or unexpected expenses or changes in price might require more affordable products that fit within the accorded budget. The most common problems found in product substitution, however, are caused by insufficient information, in general or insufficient documentation requirements. To avoid inappropriate substitutions, ER specifications must include a clause stating that every substitution needs the designer's approval and submittals must be documented accordingly.

The information presented below has been collected and condensed from a large number of sources, such as governmental agencies, the U.S. Green Building Council, periodicals, books, and manufacturers. The materials and products listed are divided into three main categories: interior construction materials, interior finishes, and interior furnishings. Each of these general categories is subdivided into typical materials with some examples of specific ER products. Each material section describes a variety of characteristics and properties that might impact ERID.

One should always keep in mind that some recommended products might not meet strict code standards, and no single product is completely benign. Environmentally responsible materials and products always have positive and negative environmental impacts. For instance, every product contains natural resources, renewable or nonrenewable; some products can be biodegradable or recyclable, or both, and still be harmful to occupants; some products containing postconsumer recycled content may not necessarily be biodegradable or recyclable; and so forth. The following examples will illustrate this point by showing positive and negative aspects of the material or product to the extent they impact environmental responsible interior design (ERID).

Construction Materials

WOOD

Wood and wood products are construction materials with low embodied energy, much lower than plastics, concrete, and metals. Wood, in general, is a renewable natural resource, depending on how it is harvested and how the forests are managed. Overharvesting can damage natural habitats and biodiversity, oxygen generation, and carbon-dioxide absorption. In addition, overharvesting affects erosion and depletes resources. Although there are hundreds of tree species growing in the

Figure 10-1
The exterior wood structure and solar panels for the Chesapeake Bay Foundation's Phillip Merrill Environmental Center, Annapolis, Maryland, designed by the Smith Group. Photo by Brunson Russum.

Figure 10-2
The interior wood structure and ductwork are exposed in the offices of the Chesapeake Bay Foundation's Phillip Merrill Environmental Center. Photo by Brunson Russum.

world's forests, only a few species are commonly used in construction. This practice impacts the natural balance of the world's forests. Specifications for ERID tend to avoid old-growth trees of certain species, such as redwood and western red cedar, because they are becoming rare. Initial selections by ER designers for construction wood usually include less-known species, so that popular forests can recover. Poplar, for example, is a hardwood that is widely available in the United States, especially in the Eastern states. It is easy to work with, and it takes paint and stain very well. Poplar is versatile and can be used for light construction as well as for case goods and millwork.

Timber consumption is one of the major causes of deforestation. Timber and large cross-section lumber from old-growth sources should be avoided in building construction. New dimensional lumber of cross-sectional areas larger than 24 inches square—e.g., 4 × 6 and 2 × 12—is usually obtained from old-growth trees. By using salvaged wood, one preserves old-growth timber and conserves resources. These large-dimension timbers are a limited natural resource; reclaimed timber should be used sparingly and in its original dimensions whenever possible (Wilson, Malin and Piepkorn 2006).

To ensure the ER use of hardwood products, specifications for millwork and wood construction must require FSC (Forest Stewardship Council) product certification. FSC-certified wood and wood products come from socially and environmentally well-managed forests that help protect habitats and conserve resources. Some well-known woods—such as untreated, naturally rot-resistant redwood, western red cedar, bald cypress, elm, black locust, and American chestnut—should only be used when salvaged or FSC certified. For interior lumber construction, the specification should be for the lowest wood grade that meets performance requirements. Nevertheless, supplies of certified clear grades and large-dimension timbers are also limited.

Engineered-Wood Products

FSC-certified engineered-wood products used in interior construction must not contain formaldehyde binders to qualify as an acceptable alternative for dimensional lumber. These products are an efficient way to use resources. Their advantage over solid wood is the efficient use of fast-growing, small-diameter trees, and their use minimizes construction waste due to product uniformity.

Laminated lumber, for instance, can be used for beams, posts, studs, and joists. Laminated strand lumber (LSL), for example, is manufactured from fast-growing aspen and poplar trees that are shredded into strands. The strands are coated with a formaldehyde-free binder, pressed, and milled into dimensional lumber. The LSL lumber is very consistent and stable; it does not warp and twist like solid wood (Wilson and Malin 1999b). Lamination, then, allows for larger spans and/or spacing, which reduces material consumption.

Wood Treatments

The fact that wood and wood products are treated for decay and termite prevention, and that these treatments tend to use toxic preservatives, makes this selection an indoor air quality concern. Wood preservatives are usually of low emission, but they off-gas for long periods of time. Even though preservative-treated wood has increased durability, the choice of wood products with the least toxic treatment is recommended.

Wood preservatives used to make wood resistant to fungus growth and termite attacks contain toxins such as arsenic and chromium, which present health hazards when they become airborne. Though water-based preservatives, such as ammoniac-based products, are considered less toxic than oil-based preservatives, some can still be very toxic. Chromate copper arsenate (CCA), for example, was the most common waterborne wood-preservative treatment until 2004, even though the EPA had it listed as hazardous for many years before CCA was banned (Spiegel and Meadows 1999).

The ER alternative wood-treatment products available contain borate, a mixture of borax and boric acid. Borate products are considered less toxic than waterborne preservatives. Recently introduced lumber and plywood pressure-treated with sodium borate and sheathing products treated with integral zinc borate are considered safe when used in interior applications (as long as they are not exposed to weather or in contact with the ground).

Composite Wood Products

Composite wood products (fiberboards) have generated serious environmental concerns, especially for interior design. In terms of indoor air quality, common interior-grade plywood, particleboard, and medium-density fiberboard contain urea-formaldehyde binders instead of the less toxic phenol-formaldehyde resin used for exterior applications. Because formaldehyde is considered a carcinogen, wood products containing urea-formaldehyde have to be avoided in interior construction especially due to their long periods of off-gassing. Additionally, fiberboards containing formaldehyde-based binders are difficult to recycle, increasing the amount of solid waste sent to landfills.

The availability of ER composite wood products has improved significantly due to the research and development of new binders. Some medium-density fiberboards (MDF) and straw-based particleboards are now being manufactured with MDI (methyl diisocyanate), a binder that does not contain formaldehyde. Those are better alternatives then the conventional wood particleboard used for non-load-bearing interior wall partitions and millwork.

Straw particleboard, also called ag-fiber particleboard, is also an alternative to wood particleboard because it is 20 percent lighter (Wilson and Malin 1997). Recent environmental and safety regulations increasingly prohibit the burning of straw in the field, encouraging its use as a building material.

METALS

The mining practices used to obtain raw metals such as copper, aluminum, and the iron used to make steel produce habitat loss, significant soil erosion, and pollutant runoff to air, water, and soil. Besides, the supply of nickel, chromium, manganese, and other raw materials used in the alloying of steel is not abundant. Ore refinement processes produce heat and combustion emissions and consume great amounts of water; products containing metals, when thrown in landfills, often leak potentially harmful metals into underground water supplies. On the other hand, metals are durable materials, and most metals are recyclable. A few metals are naturally resistant to corrosion and can be reused.

However, although all metals are safe from the standpoint of indoor air quality (Leclair and Rousseau 1992), the use of metals in interiors is not as innocuous as one might think. On-site manipulation of metals can cause serious health impact to both workers and occupants. The term "trace metals" refer to metals that are present in very low concentrations, either in the environment or in the human body. Copper, iron, and zinc are examples of trace metals. Heavy metals, such as lead, mercury, and cadmium, are trace metals whose densities are at least five times greater than water. Many metals with high concentrations in the environment are now considered to be harmful to people. For instance, arsenic, beryllium, cadmium, chromium, and nickel dust (present in many building materials) can cause lung cancer in people with long-term exposure to them (Harte et al. 1991).

To avoid indoor contamination, building products containing heavy metals need to be brought to the site in their final format and dimensions. Factory-applied finishes emit fewer volatile organic compounds (VOCs) on-site, because the primary out-gassing occurs at the plant under controlled conditions. Powder-coated steel, for instance, is a preferable choice to solvent-based coating, because it uses a cleaner process. In addition, although still problematic, mechanical finishing processes (e.g., abrasive blasting, grinding, buffing, and polishing) generate less hazardous waste than chemical and electrical processes.

Alloyed metals are more difficult to recycle, because they must be separated by material type. Plated metals are not as difficult to recycle, but toxic metals can be released in the process. The EPA has identified many materials and technologies used for plating as environmental hazards (e.g. cadmium, chromium, cyanide-based electroplating, and copper- and formaldehyde-based solutions). Electroplated metals, for instance, should be avoided due to their toxicity and pollution. Replacement technologies available for plating include noncyanide copper plating, metal stripping, and zinc plating.

Steel

In construction, steel is the most energy-intensive framing material. Nevertheless, the use of steel in construction conserves natural resources and reduces solid waste. Steel is recyclable and can be magnetically separated from the waste stream easily. It is also possible to recover zinc from galvanized steel. The steel industry's recycling rate is over 65 percent and structural-steel framing members commonly have greater than 90 percent recycled content (Malin 2000). The manufacture of structural steel from recycled materials requires approximately 60 percent less energy than to process steel from raw materials (Spiegel and Meadows 1999). High-recycled-content steel reduces the environmental impact associated with mining waste and pollution.

Light-gauge steel framing, generally used for interior partitioning of commercial buildings, is specified more and more for residential construction, too. Steel studs are lightweight, dimensionally stable, resistant to insect damage, and of consistent quality, especially when compared to solid wood. Light-gauge steel typically

Figure 10-3
The stainless steel and glass structural elements in the lobby of the Hearst Building, New York City, hint at the unique diagrid structure. The Ice Falls, a three-story water feature, uses water from the rooftop water-collection system to cool and humidify the lobby. The use of minimal interior partition walls maximizes daylighting, while the low-e glass eliminates solar radiation, which can overheat interior spaces. Photo by Art Poskanzer.

Figure 10-4
Designed by Lord Norman Foster, the Hearst Building was the first high-rise office building in New York City to earn LEED-Gold certification. Its diagrid structure required 20 percent less steel than conventional construction. Photo by Herman Yung.

contains 20 to 25 percent recycled material (10–15 percent postconsumer content), though some manufacturers use more than 90 percent recycled content. Steel studs are also recyclable at the end of the building's useful life, diverting materials from the waste stream. Therefore, the specification of steel with high recycled content reduces pollution and conserves resources and energy.

Some precautions need to be taken, though, when specifying lightweight steel frame. Steel does not off-gas; however, the protective oil coat of some steel framing, if not removed prior to installation, can cause reactions in sensitive individuals. Powder coating reduces this risk. In addition, because steel is highly conductive, its use in interior construction can jeopardize a building's energy performance. Steel's high conductivity can cause thermal bridging in partitions separating rooms with significant temperature difference. Without thermal insulation, bridging wastes energy by causing condensation inside the wall, which may lead to mold growth (Malin 2000).

Some new steel framing systems, like the one offered by Tri-Chord Steel Systems, Inc., have been designed to minimize thermal bridging. These studs and trusses have triangular sections at each edge and open webs spanning the wall cavity instead of a solid, heat-conducting steel core. The product contains 66 to 68 percent postconsumer recycled content (Wilson, Malin, and Piepkorn 2006).

Stainless steel, which is alloyed with nickel, chromium, and other metals, has a higher environmental impact than other steel products. Its manufacturing process uses more energy, and emissions are higher due to the refinement of other metals.

Copper

The extraction of copper requires increasingly large mines due to declining concentrations in ore. To obtain new copper from ore, it is necessary to separate the copper from other minerals through smelting and then to refine the copper through fire or electrolytic processes. Copper smelting, for the production of copper and bronze, releases pollutants—such as acids and sulfur dioxide—into the environment.

Copper is resistant to corrosion and recyclable. Most copper construction components can be reused almost indefinitely. In the United States, approximately 50 percent of the copper used in construction comes from scrap, which is as usable as copper refined from ore (Spiegel and Meadows 1999). When possible, preference should be given to reclaimed copper to conserve resources.

Aluminum

Aluminum is fabricated from bauxite, a mineral found primarily in tropical areas. The desire to access bauxite mines has been a significant factor in the deforestation of tropical rain forests. Although it is less costly to recycle aluminum than to produce new aluminum, most aluminum building products contain virgin material. Aluminum manufacture is energy and water intensive, and it produces many wastewater contaminants such as petroleum tars, fluoride, nickel, cyanide, and antimony. Aluminum is subject to corrosion and must have a protective coating (an anodized finish).

MASONRY

Clay Masonry Units (Bricks)

Environmentally responsible specification of clay masonry units (or bricks) requires certificates provided by an independent testing agency assuring that the product is free from hazardous contaminants.

Fired clay bricks can easily be salvaged from building demolition, providing significant resource savings compared with new brick. One should keep in mind, though, that salvaged bricks need to be tested for structural properties and moisture resistance, which limits their construction use.

The production of new bricks, on the other hand, has significant environmental impacts. Brick firing produces fluorine and chlorine emissions, which contribute to air pollution. The use of contaminated soil in fired-clay brick mitigates hazardous materials, as it conserves resources, but it might be harmful to people living in the vicinity of factories. High-temperature firing, however, allows for waste materials—even toxic materials like oil-contaminated soil—to be safely incorporated into certain clay products.

Brick masonry is durable, water- and insect-resistant, and low maintenance. Its selection helps conserve resources. Due to brick's small unit sizes, its use in construction minimizes waste. Clay masonry units, in general, provide thermal mass, and their appropriate use may reduce energy consumption. Nevertheless, bricks are typically fired in large kilns at very high temperatures, which results in a significant embodied-energy rate. Low-fired or air-cured stabilized earth masonry, such as commercial adobe blocks, has significantly reduced embodied-energy rate.

Concrete Masonry Units

Concrete masonry units (CMUs) for concrete block construction is increasing in popularity among builders. Like most materials, this choice of masonry unit has positive and negative environmental impacts. Its small unit size, for example, minimizes construction waste, and manufacturing waste is typically recycled into new units. CMU is also water- and insect-resistant, which makes it durable and low maintenance. Salvaged units are available in many communities, helping with resource conservation. In addition, concrete masonry can reduce the use of energy in cold climates by providing thermal mass.

In contrast, the production of portland cement, which is one of the components of CMUs, emits a significant amount of carbon dioxide and dust into the atmosphere. It is also energy intensive, making the embodied energy of a CMU high. Some manufacturers are replacing a portion of portland cement with fly ash or ground, blast-furnace slag (a postindustrial recycled material). This type of CMU helps conserve energy at the same time that it uses waste material that otherwise would be sent to landfills. Likewise, the use of recycled or industrial waste aggregates, such as crushed stone or glass, reduces the amount of solid waste and minimizes the mining of gravel. Yet, CMUs can be used in environmentally responsible ways—for example, decorative concrete block sealed for dust prevention but without additional finish might save a large amount of resources.

Because CMUs act as thermal mass, their energy performance is an additional concern for most cooling systems. Concrete masonry units made of autoclaved, aerated concrete (AAC) has better insulation value (R-value of up to 1.25 per inch) with the additional benefit of making the blocks lighter, reducing its transportation impacts. Due to its reduced compressive strength, however, the use of AAC masonry units is somewhat restricted in comparison with regular CMU (Malin 2000).

Adobe Brick

Adobe is a natural material commonly used for construction in Latin American countries and in the U.S. Southwest. Nevertheless, adobe construction is suitable for a wide range of climates, including extremely cold and extremely wet climates. Its best performance is still in sunny climates, but it may vary with the type of soil used. Adobe masonry can be very durable if protected from erosion.

The primary ingredients of adobe brick are adobe soil and water. Adobe soil has sand and clay, and it is often acquired as a by-product of sand and gravel mining. Traditional adobe bricks are made on-site and are air-dried in the sun. Straw is sometimes added to the mixture to prevent cracking. Adobe units usually have low greenhouse gas emissions and low embodied energy rates. Demolished adobe masonry units disintegrate and return to the soil. Commercially available adobe blocks, however, might contain admixtures, such as asphalt emulsion, portland cement, and lime acting as stabilizers.

Gypsum Boards

Gypsum is a natural, abundant resource, and gypsum-based products are alternatives to more limited natural resources. However, any rock mining—gypsum included—contributes to dust, soil erosion, and destruction of habitats. Gypsum is also produced as a by-product of other industrial processes, and this kind is called synthetic or flue-gas gypsum. Obtained from pollution-control equipment for sulfur removal at coal-fired power plants, synthetic gypsum is slightly different from mined gypsum. It can contain impurities from the coal, including metals that can be health hazards (Leclair and Rousseau 1992).

Today, gypsum board manufacturers offer board products made with virgin, recycled, or synthetic gypsum, and most use recycled, unbleached paper facings bonded to the gypsum core. Recent advances in recycling technology allow paper to be separated from the gypsum core so that each may be recycled separately (Yost 2000). Recycled gypsum derives from manufacturing scrap and clean construction waste. Sheetrok brand gypsum panels (from USG Corporation) and G-P Gypsum Board (from G-P Gypsum Corporation) are examples of synthetic gypsum products.

In general, gypsum is a nontoxic material except for its dust, which is irritating and slightly hazardous if inhaled. Gypsum board's main health risk is related to installation, which produces large amounts of dust, and might involve toxic joint fillers and construction adhesives. Airborne dust from boards and joint compounds can seriously compromise indoor air quality, and premixed joint compounds tend to release a large amount of VOCs. To avoid contamination, dust should be minimized and low-VOC joint-compound products, like Murco M100, used. This type of product contains natural binders and no preservatives or slow-releasing compounds (Wilson, Malin, and Piepkorn 2006).

Gypsum boards are quick and easy to apply on-site, but ER specifications need to address other issues regarding installation methods. For example, 54-inch-wide gypsum board may be more efficient for wall coverage in rooms with 9-foot ceilings than the standard 48-inch-wide boards. In addition, the use of clips, such as No-Nail and Stud Claw, at corners and wall intersections results in a reduction in steel or wood studs, saving resources and reducing cost.

Paper and vinyl facings have become another indoor air quality concern. They provide a potential medium for mold growth, especially in high humidity and low air-circulation conditions. To eliminate the risk of mold growth, some drywall manufacturers are offering fiber-enhanced products without paper or vinyl facing. Fiber-reinforced panels tend to be stronger, stiffer, and denser than regular drywall; they increase thermal mass and reduce noise transmission. Those products, however, are difficult to recycle and contribute to landfill problems.

ER specifications for drywall give preference to products not vinyl faced and made with recycled content instead of synthetic gypsum. On the second tier are boards with cellulose or fiberglass fibers embedded in the gypsum core and without paper facing, when possible. The preferred manufacturers are those that use high percentages of recycled materials and take back construction scrap for recycling.

Interior Finishes

The list of interior finishes available today in the U.S. market is so extensive that it is not feasible to present them all in this chapter. The following materials and products are just a sample to illustrate specifications for ER interior finishes. They represent both conventional and new materials, as well as natural, converted, and synthetic products. The examples are categorized by the surfaces where they are most commonly applied. Adhesives and plastics, however, are presented separately due to their use in all kinds of interior surfaces.

ADHESIVES

The main issue regarding interior finishes is the use of adhesives, which can be a major source of indoor air quality problems, even more so than synthetic interior finishes. Adhesives are either solvent or water based. The problems associated with adhesives are often caused by solvent vapors. Solvents are used to dissolve substances, like epoxy or industrial glues, and they evaporate into the air during the drying or curing phase. Water-based adhesives use water as a predominant solvent, but they may also contain other solvents that emit VOCs. When drying, these adhesives release water, but there is little guarantee that they will not release other substances. Healthguard, Earthbond, or 3M Blue Glue are examples of water-based contact-cement products that still contain some synthetic additives. Most water-based adhesives have lower VOC emissions than solvent-based products. W. F. Taylor, Inc., has a line of flooring adhesives called ENVIROTEC, which was recently certified by Greenguard as the first line to pass the strict tests this agency uses to evaluate impacts on indoor air quality. Safe-Set and Henry Greenline Flooring Adhesives are examples of low- or zero-VOC, solvent-free adhesives (Wilson, Malin, and Piepkorn 2006).

Although water-based adhesives are adequate for ER selections, they can only be used when flooring manufacturers recommend them. Linoleum or cork manufacturers are the most restrictive about product use, requiring specific adhesives to ensure material performance. BioShield Cork Adhesive #16, for example, is a water-based, solvent-free adhesive specially designed for cork.

Factory-applied dry adhesives are also a viable alternative for some finishing products. Those usually have a solvent-free composition, are safe to handle, and emit little odor. The problem with this system is the generation of waste from the protective backing material.

Designers need to be cautious with some other alternative adhesives, like milk- or wheat-based glues. For example, casein glue is an adhesive found in many stores that sell natural products. It derives from milk, and it is water based. Casein glue is a type of adhesive frequently used by individuals who suffer from multiple chemical sensitivity, even though it might cause reactions in people who are allergic to milk. One needs to be very careful when specifying casein glue, because it is prone to mold growth and mildew where moisture is present.

When making product evaluations, ER specifiers must always contact the manufacturers for recommendations of the least emissive adhesives that ensure performance. In the case of alternative glues, such as milk- or wheat-based adhesives, designers should always get client approval before making the specification.

PLASTICS

Plastics are synthesized organic compounds derived from natural substances, such as wood, wheat, petroleum, and natural gas. There are a huge variety of plastics available with very different properties. Some are hard; other plastics are soft, clear, strong, or elastic. Plastics are typically divided into two groups: *thermoplastics* and *thermoset plastics*. Thermoplastic polymers can be repeatedly softened and reformed. Thermoset polymers cure permanently, and the resulting plastics tend to be durable and heat resistant. Heat-resistant plastics present lower risks for indoor air quality and people's health.

In general, thermoplastic polymers have a lower embodied energy impact than thermoset polymers. Interestingly, when compared with most plastics, PVC (polyvinyl chloride) has the lowest embodied energy impact, because it is mostly made of chlorine that requires little energy for extraction. Thermoplastics can be recycled;

thermoset plastics cannot. With thermoplastics, recycling is done by melting and reforming or re-extruding the plastics into the products being produced.

Although plastics (and especially PVC) tend to be blamed for several environmental problems, there are some very significant benefits to using plastics in construction. Most plastics are relatively durable. Maintenance requirements are often low (except for PVC flooring). Plastic's light weight reduces shipping energy and can help with energy efficiency. For instance, the highest R-value insulation materials available are made of foamed plastics. Polymer resins make engineered wood possible. And, in certain applications, plastics can replace old-growth timber or pressure-treated wood.

Unfortunately, some of the best performance attributes of plastics generate serious environmental impacts. The release of hazardous materials into the environment and the exposure of factory workers to harmful chemicals during manufacture are the primary negative health impacts related to plastics. Many plastics, like PVC, polystyrene, ABS, and certain resins, contain substances that could possibly be carcinogenic. When petroleum-based plastics are incinerated, carbon is released into the atmosphere, contributing to global warming. The disposal of certain plastics produce persistent organic pollutants that accumulate in living systems, resulting in a wide range of environmental and human-health problems. Halogenated plastics (those containing chlorine or bromine) may become sources of dioxins if they are burned under uncontrolled, high-temperature conditions, such as during accidental fires. Some dioxins are among the most toxic of synthetic compounds. PVC, which contains large amounts of chlorine, is the plastic of greatest concern relative to dioxin generation. Other plastics can also contain halogens, however. Some of the plastics promoted as environmentally attractive alternatives to PVC also contain toxic fire retardants.

Another consideration with plastics manufacture is the energy intensity of production. Interestingly, of the mainstream plastics on the market, PVC is the least dependent on fossil fuels, since 40 percent or so of its content is typically chlorine. Significant reductions in fossil-fuel consumption are now being achieved by using recycled-content plastics.

Today, PVC dominates all plastic-resin production for construction and building products, mostly because of its low cost; versatility; resistance to chemical, physical, and biological degradation; and inherent flame resistance. PVC is unique because of the relative ease with which it can integrate additives, particularly plasticizers that make PVC soft and flexible. Plasticizers used in PVC and some other flexible plastics are being investigated for both carcinogenic and hormone-disruption effects. Formaldehyde, for example, is a suspected human carcinogen.

In recent years, the plastics industry has invested in several technologies to clean up its manufacturing processes. The greatest environmental and health concerns of plastics manufacture now relates to manufacturing in developing countries, where regulations are usually far less stringent. For this reason, it is important for specifiers to consider not only the type of plastic resin used to make a product but also where that product was produced.

Because plastics do not break down easily, unless they are recycled or inciner-ated they can add significantly to long-term solid-waste disposal problems. Biological organisms use enzymes to assemble complex organic molecules, including natu-ral polymers. Chemical engineers, however, assemble polymers using catalysts. The resulting compounds are different, and natural organisms do not have the necessary enzymes to break down synthetic polymers. That is the main reason why plastics are so durable, but this resistance to organisms is also responsible for the persistence of these materials in landfills. Recycling is technically feasible for many polymers, but there are logistical problems associated with collection and separation of the product.

Ecoresin panels and the Varia line of products are produced by 3form. Ecoresin is made from an environmentally friendly and durable, specially formulated poly-ester resin. Ecoresin incorporates 40 percent postindustrial recycled content, while maintaining translucent qualities. Varia is the result of 3form's patented resin-encapsulation technology. Full Circle is a new Varia collection that consists of envi-ronmentally and socially conscious products that utilize rapidly renewable materials and serve as a positive force in the economies of developing countries.

Ultimately, a shift to bioplastics will avoid dependence on fossil fuels as the primary raw material for making plastics. As a recommendation, ER specifica-tions must consider alternatives to PVC and other halogenated plastics. Preference should be given to plastics that do not introduce significant environmental burdens of their own.

Two broad categories of plastic recently introduced in the market present environmental advantages: polyolefins and bio-based plastics (Wilson, Malin, and Piepkorn 2006). Polyolefins can now be viable replacements for PVC and other hazardous plastics. Bioplastics are made by living organisms rather than synthe-sized in chemical factories. These plastics derive from renewable resources and can be biodegradable. Fossil fuels are still used in processing these new products, but impacts from petroleum and natural gas extraction and processing are lower. In addition, there is less risk of harmful effluent or emissions from the manufactur-ing plant, and agriculturally produced bioplastics—when sustainable agriculture is practiced—can help protect ecosystems and support the farm economy.

Polylactide (PLA) is an example of bioplastic. It uses dextrose, derived from harvested corn, and converted into lactic acid, which is then polymerized into PLA, using bacteria. Applications for bio-based PLA include foam, emulsions, and fibers. A few years ago, Interface Flooring contracted with Cargill Dow to use PLA fibers for carpet manufacture (Wilson, Malin, and Piepkorn 2006).

Floor Materials and Coverings

The careful selection of floor materials is very important for both a healthy build-ing and a sustaining environment. Floors are systems with several components—for example, the underlay, adhesives, wood, carpet or resilient covering, and often a surface finish. The greater the number of layers or components in a system, the larger the amount of resources utilized. In addition, all these components are potential sources of emissions during installation, use, and especially when cleaning and waxing.

Floor materials cover large areas and require frequent maintenance. Emissions can be from solvents in adhesives; they can be organic vapors from engineered-wood or manufactured-wood products, VOCs from many synthetic floor coverings, and organic vapors from cleaning products. Fibrous floor coverings can act as *sinks* for trapping dust, dirt, and moisture or as *sponges* that absorb and re-emit VOCs released by other materials. These conditions might seem helpful initially, but they also create a breeding ground for dust mites, molds, and bacteria, which can be harmful to occupants.

The most healthy or inert floorings are hard floorings such as stone, ceramic tile, or terrazzo. Polished concrete and hardwood floorings require finishing, but they are good alternatives for indoor air quality. Emissions can come from many components of the floor system, not just the coverings. Emissions from the subfloor may be retarded by nonporous floor coverings and sealers. Frequent waxing, sanding, sealing, or replacement of floor coverings can produce emissions that adversely affect the growing number of sensitive individuals.

EXPOSED CONCRETE FINISHED FLOOR

Concrete flooring requires high embodied energy to produce, which is considered a negative environmental impact. However, this characteristic can be offset by concrete flooring's dual role as structure and finished floor, as well as by its durability, ease of maintenance, and possible service as thermal mass. Because global environmental impacts of concrete were described earlier (see concrete masonry units, page 297), it is not necessary to repeat them here.

As are other concrete building components, concrete floors are made of portland cement, water, fine and coarse aggregates, and sometimes admixtures to improve some of their specific qualities. Admixtures should be avoided when possible because they off-gas VOCs for long periods of time. Emissions, however, can vary depending on the types of chemicals added.

Because concrete is very porous and tends to absorb water, most structural concrete floors need to be treated with a finishing layer, which is made of a cement mix applied to the surface as a barrier. This surface coat is usually made of similar materials to concrete but mixed to a more liquid consistency, made stiff enough to adhere to the concrete subfloor. In most cases, admixtures are not necessary for the surface coat. This coat can be used both as a substrate for floor coverings or as a surface to be left exposed. The exposed surface may be smooth or have a decorative texture or pattern.

Colored cement flooring, for instance, requires very little additional materials. Coloring pigments made of recycled materials are often added to the materials for exposed concrete flooring. American Specialty Glass, for example, provides recycled-glass powder fines that can be used as coloring agents. The company also offers recycled-glass sand to create texture. The sources for recycled glass include postconsumer bottle-glass and postindustrial float-glass waste. Davis Colors is another company that produces color additives for concrete finished floors surfaces, but they are made of recycled or reclaimed steel and iron. Hoover Color Corp., in partnership with Iron Recovery, Inc., produces a wide range of pigments made from EnvironOxide, a natural iron-oxide product recovered from abandoned coal mines. These are premium quality pigments that are considered nontoxic, nonbleeding, and weather resistant (Wilson, Malin, and Piepkorn 2006).

However, concrete and cement applications generate dust continuously, and surfaces need to be sealed and resealed often. To avoid indoor air pollution, preferred sealants are bio-based and low-VOC products. Low-VOC product examples include: Safecoat Penetrating WaterStop, which is a zero-VOC sealer that is nonflammable and free of formaldehyde and hazardous ingredients; Intraseal, a low-VOC, water-based concrete sealer; and 9400 Impregnant, a water-repellent, UV-protective concrete coating that is formulated without solvents (Wilson, Malin, and Piepkorn 2006).

Natural Soy's Cure and Seal is an example of a bio-based product made from soy oil and other natural ingredients. A Cure and Seal concrete surface repels water, but it does not prevent heavier-oil penetration. Other examples of natural products are the sealers produced by Weather-Bos International, such as Masonry Bos: they are made from natural, nontoxic vegetable oils and resins, as well as other natural ingredients. These are low-odor, nonflammable products that are free of harmful fungicides; they can be used for waterproofing and protecting not just concrete but brick, adobe, and stones. Small amounts of pigment in some formulas provide UV protection (Wilson, Malin, and Piepkorn 2006).

WOOD AND WOOD PRODUCTS

Conventional wood flooring is biodegradable and can be reused and recycled. Environmentally responsible specification of wood floor products follow the same guidelines mentioned before for timber and lumber with a few additional recommendations. Salvaged flooring and reclaimed-wood flooring are the top ER choices, with FSC-certified wood next in the order of preference. In the case of reclaimed wood products, specification submittals must include documentation showing the origin of the product.

Underlayment also needs special consideration. Preferable products include natural cork, straw board, and recycled-paper-based fiberboard. Cork rolls and sheets used for underlayment add resilience to the floor system, with less thickness than fiberboard. When the manufacturer provides a foam underlayment, products with recycled content tend to be preferred. Substrates for wood flooring can be formaldehyde-free particleboard, MDF, or concrete with foam underlayment.

Engineered-wood-flooring products can be prefinished or finished on-site. Products that have a thick face veneer can be refinished, which adds to their durability and, consequently, reduces the need for new resources. Laminated, tongue-and-groove, prefinished flooring with $\frac{1}{8}$" face veneer, for example, may be refinished up to two times. The thicker the veneer the more refinishing is possible (Wilson, Malin, and Piepkorn 2006).

The level of maintenance required for each type of wood flooring product depends on the type of finish applied to the product. Wood flooring finishing products can be as toxic as many adhesives used for flooring installation. ER specifications require nontoxic, low-VOC, and water-based finishes. Some of the alternatives are natural vegetable and nut oil, bee wax, or water-based urethane.

Cork

Cork is the bark of the cork oak tree, and the fabrication of cork products does not require tree removal. The cork oak is the only tree that can regenerate itself after each harvest. About two-thirds of the tree's bark is stripped off the tree, which is found primarily in Spain, Portugal, and North Africa. Harvesters leave a thin layer of protective inner bark on the tree, and the outer bark rapidly regenerates itself.

Cork is biodegradable, and some cork products are made from postindustrial cork from bottle-cork manufacturing. Most cork products, however, are made from new cork. After it is stripped from trees, the cork is ground up, mixed with glue, and baked. Unlike the soft cork used for bulletin boards and bottle stoppers, the cork used for flooring is compressed to make it harder. Some cork flooring products are made with urea-formaldehyde binders and must be avoided.

Cork flooring is usually finished with up to five coats of acrylic and sometimes an additional layer of polyurethane. When impregnated with binders, cork becomes difficult to recycle as an ingredient for other products such as linoleum. Cork flooring is sold as square tiles, which helps reduce the amount of waste generated during installation. Cork-faced MDF tongue-and-groove planks are also available.

Following are two recommended cork-flooring products. KorQinc is a cork floor and wall tile pigmented in its natural binder and not the cork. The color permeates through the layer of granulated cork, and it is not susceptible to scratching

Figure 10-5
DuroDesign cork flooring is composed of 100 percent preconsumer recycled waste from the wine-stopper industry. This flooring can contribute to LEED credits for recycled content; rapidly renewable materials; low-emitting adhesives, sealants, and coatings; and innovation in design due to the unique resilient character that reduces sound transmission, increases thermal insulation, and augments acoustical control through sound dampening. Photo courtesy of DuroDesign.

off as with stained flooring. ProntoKorQ is a three-layer floating floor and wall tile. Its bottom layer is soft, insulating cork, and the top layer is a high-density granulated cork with a satin, water-based urethane sealer. Sandwiched in between is a layer of nonformaldehyde MDF that provides a tongue-and-groove assembly with no need for adhesives (Wilson, Malin, and Piepkorn 2006).

Bamboo

Bamboo is a durable and dimensionally stable building material that has been used in the Far East for centuries. Bamboo is a grass (not a tree), and there are over 1,000 species of bamboo growing worldwide. Most bamboo used for flooring comes from China, and bamboo flooring only recently has become available in the United States. The bamboo species used for flooring grows to harvesting sizes in five or six years, and they are not the kind pandas eat. The transportation of bamboo flooring from such long distance is a concern for ER specification, but the environmental benefits justify its use as a substitute for wood flooring.

As with all imported products, social issues must be considered during product selection. Although not verified yet, some concerns have been raised in relation to working conditions in Chinese bamboo flooring factories. Other negative environmental attributes relate to its laminating process, which typically uses urea-formaldehyde binders. Some products, like BamPlank, use a milk-protein based binder with only traces of formaldehyde. Other manufacturers, like MOSO products, claim that emissions of their product do not exceed stringent European standards, and Plyboo Bamboo Flooring products are laminated with a low- or no-VOC adhesive (Wilson, Malin, and Piepkorn 2006).

There are different types of bamboo flooring products available in the market. Laminated planks or strips come in a variety of thicknesses and colors, unfinished or prefinished. Because this is a fairly new product in the United States, its performance evaluation is still limited. Anecdotal information from homeowners suggests that bamboo flooring surface is easily scratched, permanently marked by puncturing objects, and changes color when exposed to sunlight; also, its durability is compromised by contact with moisture. These reports have possibly influenced the current claims made by the bamboo flooring industry. Bamboo Hardwoods, Inc., for example, claims that its engineered floor, which has a rubber tree–wood inner core, now uses a much harder bamboo laminated with benign treatments (melamine adhesives and a boric acid insecticide).

LINOLEUM

Linoleum is usually listed in ER specification manuals as a top-choice material for floor covering (Anink, Boontra, and Mak 2001). Linoleum is very durable, resilient, and slip resistant. Its ingredients are minimally processed and easy to obtain. Linoleum is made from natural substances (linseed oil, pine resin, sawdust, cork dust, limestone, natural pigments) applied over a jute backing. Unlike vinyl (PVC) flooring, linoleum contains insignificant amounts of petroleum-based products

Figure 10-6
Forbo linoleum is produced from renewable materials: linseed oil, resins, wood flour, jute, and ecologically responsible pigments. See the Web site for independent life-cycle analyses and environmental impact reports that show linoleum is preferred over vinyl, wool, or synthetic carpeting (www. forbo.com). Photo of Eccles Health Sciences Education Building, Salt Lake City, Utah, courtesy of Forbo Flooring. Photo by Matt Dalton.

and chlorinated chemicals, and it requires less maintenance to retain its appearance (Moussatche and Languell 2002). However, there are some concerns about linoleum's impact on indoor air quality, due to the continuous oxidation of linoleic acid contained in the material. This oxidation produces VOC emissions that, on one hand, give linoleum a bactericide characteristic but, on the other hand, make the material a health threat to sensitive occupants.

As far as format, some products—such as Artoleum from Forbo Linoleum, Inc., and Linosom, an Italian product distributed in the United States by Tarkett Commercial—are only available in sheets. Others, like the Armstrong World Industries's DLW Linoleum and Forbo's Marmoleum, are available in both tile and sheet formats. Armstrong's linoleum, Linodur, is also available in different thicknesses, including a 4-mm heavy-duty product. Linoleum-tile products are more economical, but this application has more seams, which might reduce the flooring's durability (Wilson, Malin, and Piepkorn 2006).

Installation of linoleum is not simple, and manufacturer-trained installers are recommended. As mentioned before, linoleum requires specific adhesives that are not always water-based and solvent-free products. A new linoleum hybrid product, called Prontolino, is made of natural linoleum tongue-and-groove planks laminated onto a thick cork backing. Although manufacturer's approval is recommended, Prontolino might perform well with BioShield Cork Adhesive #16, the new water-based and solvent-free adhesive designed specifically for cork. Nova Linoleum planks (manufactured in Switzerland) are another engineered product listed in the latest GreenSpec Directory (Wilson, Malin, and Piepkorn 2006). It consists of three layers: a linoleum wear layer; a high-density fiberboard core; and a core composition layer. This product is a floating floor system, and the planks snap together, requiring no on-site application of adhesives.

CERAMIC TILES

Although ceramic tiles have extremely high embodied energy and are made from less renewable resources than linoleum, they are often the second choice for interior floor coverings in ERID specifications. They might become the best choice in many applications where linoleum's durability is jeopardized or where sensitive clients react to linoleum's off-gassing. Ceramic tiles are made from clay, silica, and other raw materials that are readily available resources gained through low-impact mining. They offer the advantage of being less vulnerable to damage and with less impact on indoor air quality, particularly the nonporous tiles. Tiles are inherently low toxic and low maintenance, and are one of the most durable floor coverings available, particularly when a thick-set mortar is used. Ceramic tiles can also be reused and recycled as aggregates for concrete and terrazzo-type flooring. Ceramic tiles do not provide sound absorbance and area rugs are often required in large areas, adding to material consumption.

Installing ceramic tiles using a sand-and-cement mortar bed is less harmful to occupants than setting them with synthetic adhesives. Thick-set and thin-set mortars and adhesives might contain additives that off-gas during and after application. The same is true for grout materials and sealers; however, unsealed grout requires frequent cleaning to prevent mildew growth. Preferred grouting materials and sealants are water-based, low- or zero-VOC products, but water-based grout is more difficult to apply. When additives are required for mortar and grout products, acrylic additives are usually recommended because they are less harmful (CMHC 1997). Products containing acrylic do not off-gas after they are cured, but they need intensive ventilation during application. Larger tiles reduce the amount of grout needed and should be preferred when possible.

STONE TILES

Stone tiles provide a very durable, nontoxic, and low-maintenance floor surface. Stone floors can last the life span of a building. However, natural stone is a nonrenewable resource, and quarrying, transporting, and manufacturing stone require a significant amount of energy and water use. The process is slow and labor intensive, and extraction of vast quantities of stone can severely damage the landscape. Because stone flooring can be salvaged and reused as well as crushed and recycled, ERID prefers salvaged stone tiles, followed by natural stone. Cast-stone tile manufacturing is more polluting than solid, natural stone, due to the use of bonding agents. Synthetic stone is concrete mixed with high percentages of polyester, production of which pollutes significantly (Anik, Boonstra, and Mak 2001).

Figure 10-7
Nysan Shading System by Hunter Douglas features GreenScreen Eco, the first PVC-free fabric for solar-control systems. The prestretched polyester fabric imparts a woven, soft texture and maintains stability over large areas with no VOC off-gassing. It is dimensionally stable for large-scale use and will not sag or stretch, allowing shades to remain free of battens and seams. Custom colors and openness factors are available. Photo of Fluor Headquarters, Calgary, Alberta, Canada, courtesy of Hunter Douglas Contract. Used by permission.

Stone suitable for flooring is found all over the world, but it is not readily or uniformly available everywhere. Its greatest environmental cost is transportation, especially when application is far from where the stone is quarried. ER specifications of new stone usually prefer local or regional stones and manufacturers.

Another environmental issue related to stone products is possible radon contamination. Radon is a carcinogenic gas that naturally occurs in the underground of certain areas. Most contaminated stone products have insignificant levels of radon. However, to avoid using contaminated products, designers can ask for radon testing results, especially when specifying porous stones like sandstone and limestone.

Installing stone tiles using a sand-and-cement mortar bed is less harmful to occupants than setting them with synthetic adhesives. Preferred grouting materials and sealants are water-based, low-or zero-VOC products. When the use of these is not possible, the less harmful additive is acrylic, because it does not off-gas after it is cured. Every stone product needs to be sealed, particularly porous stones, to provide stain resistance and to prevent dirt and grit impregnation.

TERRAZZO

Terrazzo is a composite material in which crushed stone, glass, or tiles are mixed and bound in a base mix of white or gray portland cement and/or polyester resin. These materials are sometimes recycled from fabrication scraps or waste from demolition and construction sites that otherwise would be sent to landfills. Terrazzo is either poured on-site or precast and set in a mortar bed. Heritage Glass, Inc., and American Specialty Glass, Inc., both located in Utah, are examples of companies

Figure 10-8
GreenScreen Eco is available in five standard openness factors: blackout, 3 percent, 5 percent, 10 percent, and 25 percent, with an FR rating for North American and European standards (NFPA 701, M1, and B1). Optional metallized finish increases solar reflection by an average of 5 percent and reduces visible light transmission (glare) by 3 percent. Metallization reduces solar gain versus an unshaded window by up to 70 percent, thereby greatly lightening the HVAC load. Photo courtesy of Hunter Douglas Contract. Used by permission.

Figure 10-9
Fritztile Greentile is a flexible terrazzo floor tile that incorporates 70 percent recycled marble and granite into a matrix with low-maintenance characteristics, easy installation requirements, and exceptional wear warranties. Photos courtesy of Fritztile.

that offer recycled-glass aggregates for terrazzo applications in a variety of colors and sizes. QuartzStone is a terrazzo tile product from Quartzitec, a Canadian company, manufactured from quartz fragments bound with white portland cement instead of the more common but less desirable polyester resins. Polyester resins cause considerable pollution throughout the product's life cycle, from extraction to waste disposal. Wausau Tile, Inc., is one of the world's largest manufacturers of terrazzo; it produces a line of terrazzo-like tiles made with patented additives and recycled glass. The company claims that this product is stronger and more water resistant than traditional terrazzo (Wilson, Malin, and Piepkorn 2006).

Cast-in-place terrazzo requires expansion strips made of brass, zinc, or colored plastic, which adds to material consumption. Once cured, the terrazzo's surface is polished to create a smooth and even texture that exposes its colorful aggregates. Grinding during application produces large quantities of dust that need to be isolated. This risk to indoor air quality can be avoided by using precast terrazzo. Like exposed concrete floors, once polished, terrazzo floors need to be sealed to avoid constant production of dust. Sealed terrazzo also prevents the floors from absorbing and releasing VOCs and reduces the potential for mold growth. Well-sealed terrazzo floors can be specified for every activity area, including kitchens and bathrooms. However, resealing must be done often, which increases the maintenance for this otherwise low-maintenance flooring. The use of resins in the cement mix to improve water resistance tends to increase VOC emissions. Water-based, low- or zero-VOC emissions sealants as well as adhesives now used for setting terrazzo tiles help reduce potential health risks.

RUBBER

Recycled-rubber flooring products are made with discarded tires that, in the United States alone, amount to more than 200 million per year. This type of flooring is durable and resilient, providing a slip-resistant and anti fatigue walking surface, and it requires very low maintenance. Two recycling processes are used to transform ground rubber from tires into flooring products: vulcanization, which uses a sulfur additive and is energy intensive (vulcanization requires high heat), and agglomeration with synthetic binders (such as polyurethane). Although these products seem excellent in terms of recycling waste, both the rubber and its adhesives are significant sources of indoor pollutants, and they are only recommended for entrances or industrial applications with high ventilation rates. Nevertheless, Noraplan Commercial Flooring has been awarded Greenguard Indoor Air Quality Certification from the Greenguard Environmental Institute. This product is made from natural and synthetic rubber, mineral fillers, and color pigments, and it does not contain any PVC, plasticizers, or halogens (Wilson, Malin, and Piepkorn 2006).

CARPET

Carpet is one of the flooring materials that most directly relates to indoor air quality and other environmental impacts. Made from natural or synthetic fibers, carpets can be made from an absorbent interior design material that helps reduce ambient noise and creates a low-impact, comfortable floor surface. This same characteristic, however, allows it to hold moisture and harbor dirt, dust mites, mold, and bacteria as well as to absorb VOCs emitted from other sources. Additionally, these potential indoor air quality hazards reduce the carpet's service life, increasing waste production. To minimize potential indoor air quality problems and to increase

Figure 10-10
The gym at a YMCA features Replay and Triumph Johnsonite recycled-rubber flooring, which is resilient, slip resistant, and sound absorbing. The loose-lay, interlocking, multipurpose flooring tiles interlock and underlock so they can be repurposed. Photo courtesy of Johnsonite.

the carpet's durability, frequent maintenance—with significant use of energy and cleaning materials—is required (Drummond et al. 1999). When possible, area rugs are a good alternative to wall-to-wall carpet, because they can be removed and cleaned outdoors. The Carpet and Rug Institute (CRI) addresses issues of carpeting impacts on indoor air quality by sponsoring Green Label Plus, an indoor air quality testing program for carpets and adhesives. The Green Label Plus program establishes emission-level standards for total VOC emissions and for specific substances, such as styrene and formaldehyde.

Horizontally woven carpet uses far less material, has fewer emissions, and does not hold as much dirt as tufted carpet (because it is tightly woven). In addition, woven or felted carpets generally contain no chemical bonding agents. Tufted carpet is available with loop pile, cut pile, or cut and loop pile. Loop-pile carpets tend to be more durable and less absorbent than cut-pile carpet; but all tufted carpets require similar maintenance procedures. If the occupancy permits, area rugs may be an acceptable alternative to wall-to-wall carpet. They are easy to clean and can be found in a large variety of natural and synthetic fibers.

The natural fibers used for carpets and rugs are renewable, except for fibers obtained from endangered animal species, like the vicuña (a llama relative), that might be killed for this sole purpose (Bowers 2004). Many natural fibers used for carpet are harvested in developing countries, and their increased use in North America and Europe help strengthen their economy. Other positive attributes include low-impact disposal and recycling. When treated with natural substances, natural fibers are biodegradable, and some, like wool, are recyclable.

Wall-to-wall carpet and area rugs are available in many natural fibers—e.g., wool, silk, linen, cotton, sisal, sea grass, coir, reed, and jute. These materials, when untreated, tend to be nontoxic, but some, like wool, might cause allergies. Cotton, wool, and silk carpets are very soft and tend to age beautifully. Sisal rugs, on the other hand, are harsh to the touch, although they are more durable than jute rugs, which are softer. Neither sisal nor jute flooring products last long when used in grease-prone or wet areas because jute and sisal are very porous, as are many natural fibers. Sea grass and coir rugs are more moisture resistant than jute or sisal. Impregnated moisture, especially in natural fibers, becomes a breeding ground for mold and bacteria.

For broadloom carpets, wool is currently the preferred substitute for synthetic fiber. Wool carpets have a high sound-absorbance and low thermal conductivity, which reduces heat loss. They are high quality, long-lasting products that repel spills and resist soiling, thus making for easier maintenance. Due to high moisture and nitrogen content, wool fibers are naturally flame retardant and absorb chemical contaminants released in the interior of a building. Wool floor coverings, however, tend to be more costly and typically require more care than most synthetic-fiber products.

Earth Weave Carpet Mills, Inc., manufactures and promotes renewable resource floor-covering products for the twenty-first century. The company's commitment lies not in recycling petrochemical products but, rather, in taking advantage of renewable natural resources. Earth Weave manufactures innovative, high-quality floor coverings for both residential and light-commercial applications. EarthWeave BioFloor, for example, is a U.S.-made, totally nontoxic, chemical-free carpeting and rug system that uses natural, nondyed, untreated wool as the primary face, washed without harsh chemicals, and free of all mothproofing or fireproofing agents. The wool is backed by natural hemp, cotton, and jute, and secured with a natural rubber adhesive between the two backing materials. The result is a long-lasting, comfortable, and biodegradable product available as broadloom and as area rugs (Wilson, Malin, and Piepkorn 2006).

The majority of carpets specified today are made of nylon fibers and other petrochemicals, which are non renewable and non biodegradable substances. Some of these substances might off-gas, especially when adhesives are used. In the last decade, however, the carpet industry has made great progress in reducing the environmental impacts of its manufacturing methods and products. Some manufacturers are using closed-loop processes, and others are working hard toward reducing environmental impacts. Interface, Inc., Mohawk Industries, C & A Floorcoverings, J & J/Invision, and Shaw are examples of manufacturers that strongly invest in recycling technology and in the development of new ER carpet products. Some companies, like C & A, Interface, and J & J/Invision, have carpet reclamation programs that divert millions of yards of carpet from the waste stream. Interface and C & A accept old vinyl-backed carpets and recycle them into new floor coverings. J & J/Invision makes 60 percent of their carpet products eligible for the company's reclamation program. Interface even cleans the reclaimed carpets that are still in good condition and donates them to charity for reuse.

Along with reclamation programs, several carpet-manufacturing companies offer nylon products containing postconsumer and postindustrial recycled content. Lee Carpets (a division of Mohawk Industries) has a product called Visio that uses high recycled content of both constituents. Bentley Prince Street—part of Interface, Inc.—and J & J/Invision offer broadloom products with high percentages of postindustrial recycled nylon. Bentley Prince Street, which uses solar-generated power in its factory, has several standard broadloom products made with either postconsumer (e.g., Epic, Producer) or postindustrial (e.g., Bradbourne, Balance, Castlebay, Hyperion, and Moorfield) recycled content. J & J commercial carpet products use a variety of recycled nylon fibers. At the top of the list, however, is Mohawk Industries. In partnership with Honeywell (formerly BASF), Mohawk Industries offer residential and commercial carpets that not only contain nylon fibers with high recycled content but also can be continually renewed in a closed-loop process that preserves the carpet's original quality (Wilson, Malin, and Piepkorn 2006).

Mohawk Industries offers another residential carpet collection that uses polyester instead of nylon. This product has 100 percent recycled-content face fibers obtained from recovered soda-bottle polyethylene terephtalate (PET). Similar products are available in the market. This type of carpet is durable, easy to clean, and stain resistant.

Carpet tiles are now available for both commercial and residential applications. An alternative to broadloom carpet, tiles are environmentally preferred products because damaged tiles can be replaced individually, reducing the frequency of

Figure 10-11
Carpeting in a sitting area at the Interface Showroom, Atlanta, Georgia, was created with carpet tiles. Tiles are also shown stacked, ready for installation. InterfaceFLOR, the first modular floor covering for the residential market, is a new design option for consumers. Photo by Jeanne Mercer-Ballard.

entire floor covering replacement. FLOR, a residential tile product line from Interface Flooring Systems, Inc., is made with Cargill Dow's Ingeo fiber, which is a form of polyester derived from corn. Earth Squares, a Milliken Carpet program, offers commercial tiles created via a patented, closed-loop recovery process that cleans, retextures, and updates designs on used modular carpet. This program increases the carpet tiles' life cycle and provides substantial savings in cost in comparison to the cost of new carpet tiles. C & A Floorcoverings has a variety of modular carpet-tile collections that are 100-percent recyclable and have a minimum of 50 percent recycled content (25 percent postconsumer and 25 percent postindustrial content). In addition, the company offers a built-in tack-system (ER3 backing and cushion) that eliminates the use of wet adhesives, which can contribute to poor indoor air quality (Wilson, Malin, and Piepkorn 2006).

Walls

Interior walls and ceilings represent the larger surface areas in a building. Emissions from materials used to cover these surfaces can have a significant impact on indoor air quality. Wood paneling, wall coverings, paints, fillers, adhesives, and other finishes produce gases and particulates that affect the quality of the air.

When selecting wall finishes, ERID preferences are given to products and materials that produce the lowest possible emissions and odors. Again, the most inert materials are hard coverings, such as plaster, stone, or ceramic tiles. Even sensitive individuals tend to tolerate well a gypsum-board system (drywall) when finished with low-toxicity joint compounds and paints (CMHC 1997). Some natural woods may be an acceptable alternative. Wallpaper, however, is not always an acceptable choice for sensitive occupants.

As with all finishes, ease of maintenance is an important factor to consider when selecting materials and products for wall surfaces. Frequent cleaning or repainting, for example, can produce significant emissions.

PLASTER

Plaster provides a hard, durable, and smooth surface for walls (and ceilings) that can act as a substrate for paint, tiles, and many other interior finishing materials, like wallpaper or textiles. Plaster products with integral natural pigments can avoid the need for painting, but their traditional installation requires great skill to achieve a quality, durable finish. An alternative installation method, using veneer plaster, requires only one coat, simplifying the application. Traditional plaster applications, when left unfinished, tend to have minimal emissions and require very low maintenance, although mold growth is possible in high-humidity areas. However, some plaster products contain additives that might cause reaction in sensitive individuals. Lung and skin exposure to plaster dust during installation may also cause health problems. Curing takes a long time, but, once cured, plaster is usually well tolerated by most individuals.

There are different plaster compositions and application systems. Today, there are plaster products in the market made from lime, portland cement, gypsum, clay, sand, and cellulose in different combinations. Those are all abundant resources, making plaster a good alternative to materials that are obtained from limited resources. Plaster's durability also conserves resources. However, mining of some of these raw materials might result in dust, soil erosion, and destruction of habitats. Lime plasters have lower embodied energy than gypsum- or portland cement–based plasters, and they do not include petroleum-based ingredients, as acrylic plasters do (Wilson, Malin, and Piepkorn 2006). Reduced use of portland cement–based plaster and plaster containing chemical additives is recommended.

Traditional installation consists of three or more layers of plaster applied over a metal or gypsum lath. Cement-based plasters and stuccos are brittle and may crack, requiring additional coats. Veneer plaster is applied over blue board, a gypsum product developed as a veneer-plaster base. This type of application is tougher and more flexible than lime and gypsum plaster, and it is also less labor intensive than traditional plaster.

There are many natural plaster products in the market. Clay Plaster, offered by Clay Mine Adobe, Inc., is a product consisting of clay plaster, cement-stabilized or not. Clay Plaster is available in a variety of earth tones. American Earth Enterprises recently introduced a 100-percent natural earth-plaster veneer product made of clay and aggregates with 65 to 75 percent postindustrial recycled marble dust. American Clay also contains nontoxic mineral pigments and a boric acid mold inhibitor. This product can be applied to many substrates, including painted surfaces when primed, but it should not be used for surfaces in direct contact with water. American Clay is available in twelve colors, but custom colors can be ordered. When left unsealed, this water-based plaster product can be rewet and reworked indefinitely. The company states that this product is manufactured in New Mexico with materials exclusively sourced in the United States and without any water or heat.

Other products—like Terramed, Tierrafino Clay Plaster, and Aglaia Natural Plaster—are imported from Europe. Terramed, derived from Mediterranean clay, is an all-natural interior wall coating made out of clay, sand, and cellulose. It is available in twelve colors and shipped dry, to be mixed with water on site. Tierrafino Clay Plaster is another natural clay interior wall finish made from European sands and clays. It contains no pigments or chemical additives. The manufacturer claims the finish is suitable for areas of high humidity, except where it comes in contact with streams of water or excessively wet walls, like shower or cellar walls. Tierrafino is available in many colors, which can be changed after installation by working the surface with Tierrafino powder on a wet sponge. Aglaia Natural Plasters are biodegradable, plant- and mineral-based products imported from Germany. They are free of petrochemicals and artificial resins, but some products may have relatively high VOC levels from the plant-based ingredients, while others may not (Wilson, Malin, and Piepkorn, 2006).

GLASS

Glass is a recyclable material. Crushed glass is now used as an aggregate for concrete and for terrazzo flooring. Extensive use of glass, however, negatively impacts both resource and energy conservation.

The product's energy-intensive manufacturing process makes glass a material with very high embodied energy. Additionally, large extensions of glass can increase energy consumption. The use of glass in building construction significantly impacts indoor climate, creating significant variations in temperature. When glass is used for large windows or entire partition walls, unless it is modified to provide some insulation, equalized indoor temperature can only be maintained by extra heating in winter or extra cooling in summer. Modifications of glass to increase insulation always involve additional use of energy (e.g., tempered glass) or more natural resources (e.g., tinting), but energy savings obtained from the increased use of daylight and the decrease of heating and cooling consumption justify its inclusion in ERID specifications.

There are various ways in which glass can be modified or treated to prevent extreme variations of temperature. Tinting increases the amount of heat absorbed by the glass, so that less heat is transferred to another room. Reflective glass has similar effects. Glazing incorporates two or more glass panes separated by a spacer that is air-filled and sealed to increase insulation. Low-e (low-emissive) glass uses new technology coatings that allow maximum daylight into a room without heat transfer, acting as a form of thermal insulation (Wilhide 2001). Due to its hollow cavities, glass bocks can also reduce heat transfer without the loss of valuable daylight.

Recycled-Glass Tiles

As noted above, the glass manufacturing process is energy intensive, making glass tiles a material with very high embodied energy. However, because glass is a recyclable material, a number of specialty tiles and other products are now produced from recycled glass, and most are very attractive.

Several companies produce glass tiles from recycled glass. For example, Aurora Glass (Eugene, Oregon) makes Architectural Accents, a line of products that includes glass tiles made from 100 percent recycled glass. The profits obtained support homeless and low-income people through emergency services, housing, jobs, and other charitable programs. Oceanside Glasstile Co. produces different styles of glass tiles, hand-cast from 85-percent postconsumer recycled glass. They are semitransparent, have an iridescent surface, and are available in a large variety of colors and sizes. Sandhill Industries, a company from Boise, Idaho, manufactures wall and floor tiles from 100-percent postindustrial plate glass, with both glossy and matte finishes. Their tiles are available in a wide range of shapes, colors, and textures that can be combined in a variety of patterns. The company claims that its manufacturing process does not produce wastewater or air emissions (Wilson, Malin, and Piepkorn 2006).

Other companies, like Terra Green Ceramics, produce ceramic glass tiles with 58-percent recycled aviation glass. Terra Green tiles can be slip resistant or not, and they are available in many colors and sizes.

PAINT

Paint can help with resource and energy conservation. It protects and preserves materials like wood or metal and, when used to create light-reflective surfaces, can reduce the need for electric lighting. On the other hand, paint can be very toxic when made with chemicals that release high quantities of VOCs in the indoor air. Some pigments used in paint products also contain toxic heavy metals, such as lead, cadmium, and chromium. Recycled paint, in particular, needs to be carefully tested for lead content or other components that might have negative health impacts.

Latex or acrylic paints are water based. And, although they might not off-gas as much as petrochemical-based paints, some chemically sensitive people find them still difficult to tolerate. Some water-based products contain biocides, fungicides, or antifreeze additives that might contribute to indoor air quality problems or help them depending on the issue of concern. Other paint products are made from plant extracts and minimally processed minerals, such as chalk or iron oxide, but this does not mean they have low-VOC levels, nor are they necessarily better for indoor air quality (Wilson, Malin, and Piepkorn 2006).

ER interior design specifications give preference to very low-VOC or zero-VOC paint products as well as the least toxic alternative. Products to avoid are those containing formaldehyde, halogenated solvents, aromatic hydrocarbons, mercury or mercury compounds, and lead acetate or cobalt manganese drying agents. Total VOC levels in paint should preferably be less than 50 grams per liter (Wilson and Malin 1999a). Zero-VOC paint products contain less than 50 grams of VOCs per liter. Low-VOC, water-based paint products contain no more than 100 grams of VOCs per liter. Oil-based paints, when required, should have a maximum of 380 grams of VOCs per liter, no more than 10 percent of aromatic hydrocarbon content, and be free from petrochemicals. High-quality, soy-based oil paints can increase resistance to yellowing (Wilson, Malin, and Piepkorn 2006).

There are many safe paint products currently in the market. Even the large and more traditional paint manufacturers now offer zero-VOC interior latex paints. For instance, Sherwin-Williams' Harmony line contains zero VOCs and has replaced the company's low-VOC HealthSpec line. Benjamin Moore and Co. also offers zero-VOC acrylic latex interior paint products under the name of Pristine Eco Spec. Both of these product lines are available in primer, flat, eggshell, and semigloss and provide a durable low-odor, antimicrobial color coating.

Safe-coat paints, which have been used successfully by people with MCS for a long time, are another example of zero-VOC paint products. Manufactured by California-based American Formulating and Manufacturing (Wilson and Malin 1999a), Safecoat Zero-VOC Paints are also available in flat, eggshell, and semigloss, and they are tinted with zero-VOC colorants. The company claims that because this product does not contain formaldehyde, ammonia, crystalline silica, or ethylene glycol, it has little odor when wet and none when dry. Another product from the same manufacturer, Safecoat Enamels, are made with high-quality resins that do not contain heavy-metal drying agents, formaldehyde, or heavy-duty preservatives. The enamels provide a higher-quality paint film that can be used for sealing VOC-emitting materials and products.

Polymer science research has recently developed new technologies that are now being applied to new types of latex paint. For example, Southern Diversified Products is manufacturing a line of interior latex paints, called "American Pride," that have zero-VOC content and virtually no smell. The paint is certified by Green Seal as performing well when compared with other high-end interior latex paints. Their flat white paint has a scrub rating of 2,500 strokes, and the eggshell white withstood 3,100 strokes. American Pride High Performance, Zero-VOC paint is available through dealers located in Mississippi or by special order (Wilson, Malin, and Piepkorn 2006).

Some alternative natural paint products are also available: Sinan Co. manufactures natural paint products that include primers, satin professional wall paint, and milk paint in powder form, all of which are made from all-natural, primarily plant-based materials. They are manufactured in white, but they can be tinted with a concentrate available in eight earth-tone colors (Wilson and Malin 1999a). Healthy Milk Paint, for example, is manufactured by Walker Paint Co. (Dallas, Texas). This product contains 85 to 98 percent food-grade ingredients and fungicides and no VOCs. It is offered in a variety of colors, and custom mixing is possible too. Milk Paint, manufactured by the Old Fashioned Milk Paint Co. (Groton, MA), is a paint product made from casein (milk protein) mixed with lime, clay, and earth pigments, to which water is added. The product contains a natural mildewcide, and it is marketed primarily for wood substrates. In damp areas, however, the use of a sealer over the paint is recommended.

Recycled paints can be found in two types: (1) paints that are blended from unused or leftover paint collected under municipal waste programs and (2) paints that are collected and remanufactured to achieve higher quality and consistency. The first type does not undergo sophisticated testing and quality control; typically, it is sold as primers, because the colors are inconsistent. The second type is checked for quality, sorted, and reblended with virgin materials. A product with, at least, 50-percent postconsumer, secondary recycled content is VRI Remanufactured Latex Paint, produced by Visions Recycling, Inc. The company claims that this product is comparable in quality to major brands of virgin latex paints. Some recycled paint companies have announced that low-VOC products are being developed, but none are available at this time.

WALL COVERINGS

Textile, paper, and vinyl wall coverings are commonly used in residential and commercial applications for sound control and durability. Traditionally used as a wall covering, cork is a material naturally resistant to moisture, rot, mold, and fire. Cork wall tiles or sheets are available in various thicknesses; they create a durable, tackable, and sound-absorbent wall surface. Other natural materials commonly used for making wall coverings include linen, flax, and grass fibers.

Vinyl (PVC) wall-covering products are not recommended for various reasons: interior finishes containing PVC can be a significant source of VOCs; phthalate plasticizers used in most vinyl products have the ability to mimic natural hormones, causing major health concerns; combustion of PVC during building fires produces both dioxin and hydrochloric acid, which are extremely hazardous for firefighters and building occupants trying to escape; most vinyl wall coverings are nonbreathable, allowing mold to grow when moisture is trapped behind them; at the end of the wall coverings' service life, vinyl products do not biodegrade and cannot be recycled; finally, toxins may be released during disposal if the material is improperly incinerated (Wilson, Malin, and Piepkorn 2006). Polyester and cellulose blends, as well as polyethylene, are some of the substances now used as an alternative to vinyl wall coverings.

Innovations in Wallcoverings, Inc. (New York, NY), for example, offers the Innvironments Collection, comprised of Class A fire-rated, breathable products made of natural materials, such as cellulose, sisal, and cork, using water-soluble inks that contain no heavy metals. Their Allegory Series, for instance, is a Type II permeable wall covering made of 50 percent wood fiber and 50 percent spun-woven polyester. Xorel, from Carnegie Fabrics (Rockville Center, NY), is a woven polyethylene fabric inherently stain resistant, flame-retardant, colorfast, and water repellent. This fabric has extremely low VOC emissions, thereby avoiding indoor air quality concerns as well as fire-related problems associated with PVC products. Moment is another synthetic product designed specifically to substitute for vinyl wall coverings. It is a Type I, nonwoven and breathable wall covering with a Class A fire rating. Available in 40 colors, Moment is made of cellulose, polyester, and acrylic polymers, and it is fully recyclable.

Glass-fiber textiles are another type of wall-covering products. Some examples are DuraWeave and Textureglass, which are woven glass textiles designed to be painted. Available in a wide variety of textures and patterns, these products are nontoxic, nonflammable, and reparable. They are particularly recommended for high-moisture areas, because glass-woven textiles allow the wall to breathe, and they are resistant to mold and mildew. Once painted, the surface is washable and does not loose its texture even with several coats of paint. (Wilson, Malin, and Piepkorn 2006)

Wood Paneling

American hardwood forests provide more than twenty species suitable for millwork. Menominee Tribal Enterprises, for instance, offers a line of millwork products made of sixteen wood species harvested from the Menominee forest lands. These were the first forest lands certified to FSC (Forest Stewardship Council) standards. Designers and specifiers need to expand their repertoire of wood species and also use nontoxic, biocomposite materials and rapidly renewable materials, such as straw, bamboo, etc. Nevertheless, ER interior designers need to always keep in mind that aromatic woods may also off-gas and cause problems for individuals with chemical sensitivities.

Today, there are a large number of suppliers of reclaimed wood for millwork as well as millwork manufacturers that use FSC-certified wood and veneers. However, because those manufacturers use both certified and noncertified wood and veneers, specifications must always require FSC-certification. Materials for paneling include FSC-certified plywood and formaldehyde-free MDF, as well as alternative materials such as bamboo and straw panels. Phoenix Biocomposites offers different biocomposite panels—some made of straw, others made of sunflower-seed hulls, and also a paneling product called Environ, composed of recycled newsprint, soy flour, pigment, and a water-based catalyst that converts soy flour into a resin (Wilson, Malin, and Piepkorn 2006).

Veneered panels can also have a formaldehyde-free MDF core or substrate or be made from particleboard that is manufactured from straw and polymeric diphenylmethane diisocyanate (PMDI) binders. Prefinished panels are available now with recycled content, nontoxic binders, agricultural-waste fiber (straw), and FSC-certified wood. The Hamasote Company, for example, offers different Class A fire-rated paneling products with a substrate made of 100-percent recycled newspaper fiber and a paraffin binder. Another company, New England Classic, produces a wide range of wainscoting and wall-paneling systems in many styles (traditional and modern) made from formaldehyde-free wheatstraw. Panels are available with a variety of wood veneers.

One alternative to hardwood paneling is bamboo. Bamboo flooring suppliers, like MOSO, Smith and Fong, and Terragren, also offer bamboo panels and veneers. Some laminated products, however, use urea-formaldehyde binders.

Ceilings

ACOUSTICAL CEILINGS

The materials used in the manufacturing of acoustical panels and tiles vary, depending on its specific performance characteristics, such as sound absorption, light reflectance, fire resistance, durability, and so forth. The main substances used for making ceiling tiles or panels are mineral fibers, paper, and straw- or wood-based fibers. Many of these materials can be recycled from industrial waste or postconsumer fiber products. Some products contain formaldehyde-based binders, and fiberglass panels typically use lower percentages of phenol-formaldehyde binder than mineral-fiber products (Wilson, Malin, and Piepkorn 2005). Tiles designed to meet high sanitary standards (e.g., heath-care facilities or school cafeterias) usually have a PVC coating or a paint finish designed to reduce porosity and to allow scrubbing.

Most acoustical tiles and panels are made by wet-pressing mineral fibers mixed with waste paper, cornstarch, and some additives such as perlite (a natural ingredient) or phenol-formaldehyde binders. Armstrong World Industries, for example, offers a wide variety of products that contain 82-percent recycled content, including both postindustrial and postconsumer waste. Some of Armstrong's ceiling products are made of recycled newspaper, as well as mineral wool, perlite, and cornstarch (all abundant resources). Armstrong Ceiling Systems even offers a reclamation program that diverts used ceilings from landfill disposal to their factories, where tiles are recycled into new ceilings in a closed-loop process. Another ceiling systems company, USG Interiors, also offers a wide range of recycled-content ceiling tiles made of mineral fibers from slag (a waste product from steel manufacturing) mixed with waste paper, synthetic gypsum, and cornstarch. Their X-Technology line has 85 percent recycled content.

Some alternative acoustical ceiling systems are now available. For instance, the tiles from InStar Acoustical Ceiling System are made of compressed straw bound by a natural substance that is released when the straw is processed with high heat and extremely high pressure. Once bound, the panels are covered with hydro-Kraft paper, using water-based PVA glue. InStar tiles are offered in a wide variety of finish coatings and supported by a powder-coated, recycled-steel support system (Wilson 2001). Eurostone is another alternative acoustical tile, but it is made from volcanic perlite, clay, and an inorganic binder. These lightweight tiles are fired in kilns, increasing energy use, but the resulting material is impervious to water and does not support the growth of bacteria or mold. In addition, Eurostone is flame resistant and 100 percent recyclable (Wilson and Malin 1997). Tectum panels are high-impact acoustical wall and ceiling products made from strands of aspen-wood fibers blended with an inorganic mix. The product is noncombustible, lightweight, formaldehyde free, and it can be painted. Panels are available in different sizes and various noise-reduction coefficients.

METAL CEILINGS

Metal ceiling tiles or panels are usually made from aluminum, which is a low-weight, recyclable metal. Some products may include recycled content, but all of them can be recycled. For instance, Hunter Douglas Aluminum Ceiling Systems are made with close to 80 percent recycled content, and Gage ceiling and wall products contain 50 percent recycled aluminum. The durability and minimal indoor air quality impact of metal ceilings, in addition to its ability to be recycled, compensate for the negative environmental impacts of mining and processing metals. Aluminum ceiling panels are available painted or unpainted, and some products include a fiberglass backing to improve acoustical performance.

WOOD CEILINGS

As with all millwork products, ER preferences are for systems that use reclaimed, remilled, or FSC-certified wood. Wood Ceilings, located in Oregon, offers a suspended ceiling-panel system of FSC-certified woods, including black cherry, western hemlock, red oak, maple, mahogany, and teak.

Trim

ER interior design options for base, casing, trim, railings, wall caps, and miscellaneous millwork are salvaged, remilled lumber, FSC-certified wood, or laminated bamboo. There are suppliers of reclaimed-wood moldings in almost every state in the union, as well as millwork companies that offer FSC-certified wood moldings now. As an alternative, SierraPine Ltd., Medite Division, manufactures MDF moldings that are made with a formaldehyde-free MDI binder and factory-primed with a water-based latex product. SierraPine uses 100 percent recovered and recycled MDF.

Wall-protection products (e.g., handrailings, crash railings, corner guards) used for commercial, institutional, hospitality, and health-care facilities have a positive impact on sustainability, because they reduce wall damage and maintenance, especially in high-traffic and abuse-prone areas. Those products are usually made of wood or PVC. Due to environmental concerns with PVC, a few industries have invested in research of more environmentally responsible synthetic materials for their products.

One example is Construction Specialties, Inc., the manufacturer of Acrovyn, a PVC line of wall-protection products. Recently developed by C/S is a new PVC-free formulation called Acrovyn 3000 that does not contain toxic substances, that is, dioxin formers, phthalates, or halogenated fire retardants. According to the company, the testing of this new formulation stands up to the same impact and abuse as original Acrovyn, and it is UL (Underwriters' Laboratories) classified with a Class 1 fire rating. In addition, the Acrovyn Wood product line is now comprised of products made of FSC-certified wood, bamboo, and wood and metal combinations. These products are coated with water-based, low-VOC stains and finishes. The metals used are aluminum and steal that contain high percentages of recycled content; the aluminum components contain 80 percent recycled content (30 percent postconsumer content), and the stainless steel used contains 86 percent recycled content (56 percent postconsumer content).

InPro Corporation also offers a wide variety of ER products for wall protection and expansion-joint coverings. The company offers products made with FSC-certified wood and 100-percent postindustrial recycled high-density polyethylene (HDPE) instead of PVC. Bamboo moldings are also available as a substitute for wood products. In addition, InPro Corporation has a recycling program for PVC that offers 10 to 25 percent discounts on new orders when old products are returned.

Interior Furnishings

CASE GOODS

Although salvaged casework is the best way to conserve resources, these items are not always available in large quantities, or they may not be appropriate to a specific situation. When specifying custom or manufactured wood casework, as with all construction-wood components, designers need to make sure the "FSC-certified" is stated in the documents, because most casework manufacturers that use FSC-certified wood also sell noncertified wood case goods.

Preferences for casework should be "knotty" and "character-grade" woods, whenever possible, to avoid unnecessary impact on forest resources. Engineered-wood products are always an option, as long as they do not contain urea-formaldehyde binders. Products containing materials that tend to off-gas must be avoided or completely sealed.

Casework carcasses and substrates, when not salvaged, are specified with the same materials recommended for paneling. Those include FSC-certified veneered plywood and formaldehyde-free MDF, as well as alternative materials such as bamboo and straw panels. Wood veneers also need to be FSC-certified. For face frames, doors, and drawers, FSC-certified woods are preferred. CitiLog custom manufactures cabinets and millwork made of formaldehyde-free wheatboard cores veneered in FSC-certified North American hardwoods as well as South American tropical woods (Wilson, Malin, and Piepkorn, 2006).

Besides the increase in resource consumption, the use of plastic surfacing materials tends to contribute to indoor air pollution due to the adhesives required. Their use should be restricted to surfacing casework made of composite materials that contain urea-formaldehyde binders. In this case, all surfaces need to be covered to contain toxic emissions. Greenline (a division of Forefront Designs) also builds cabinets with wheatboard cores. The company uses high-pressure laminates as well as FSC-certified veneers and other certified materials. Their casework is formaldehyde-free and suitable for schools, laboratories, hospitals, and nursing homes.

COUNTERTOPS

Countertops need to have a nonporous surface that is, preferably, not easy to scratch or stain. To avoid the use of adhesives, countertops can be mechanically attached to the cabinet framing. Some solid materials available are wood, bamboo, stone, or solid surfaces like Corian, terrazzo, or concrete. Other materials can be applied to a wood or concrete base. Examples of the latter include stainless steel, ceramic tiles, linoleum, or plastic laminates. These materials would have the same environmental impacts described previously for flooring or wall surfacing. Most countertops can be salvaged and reused, which is always preferred over using new or recycled products.

Although solid plastic counter materials (e.g., Corian) are considered relatively safe in comparison to plastic laminated countertops, they are not the best ER choice due to their petrochemical base. Nevertheless, countertops made of recycled plastics (e.g., Avonite) are viable choices, as long as they do not off-gas toxic substances with temperature changes. Recycled plastic counter materials should have a minimum of 60 percent postindustrial recycled waste.

Stone countertops, despite their durability and ease of maintenance, produce significant environmental damage due to quarrying practices and the energy used

Figure 10-12
Fir beams reclaimed from industrial buildings constructed using huge old-growth trees from the once abundant Pacific Northwest forests. TerraMai reclaims wood that would otherwise be chipped, burned, or wasted from structures slated for demolition. SmartWood Certification Systems estimates that reclaiming one million board feet of lumber preserves one thousand acres of old growth forest. Photo courtesy of TerraMai.

Figure 10-13
Timbron premium interior moldings are durable, waterproof, mold and mildew resistant, termite proof, zero-VOC off-gassing, and ecofriendly with 90 percent recycled plastic (75% postconsumer and 15% preconsumer content). Photo by Mike Kaskel.

for transportation. Stone slabs, when used, should be quarried locally or regionally to reduce energy consumption. Specifying stone countertops also requires considering the practicalities involved. Granite is the most durable stone for countertops, especially with a honed finish. Polished granite requires frequent maintenance, and repairing the polish is difficult due to the substance's hardness. Marble tops should not be used in kitchens, as the surfaces are easily etched by mild acids, such as fruit juice and soft drinks. A highly polished marble countertop makes scratches evident, while a honed finish can be repaired easily and requires fewer maintenance products that are likely to off-gas.

Wood countertop manufacturers, like Endura Wood Products, make butcher-block countertops using FSC-certified wood or bamboo. Those are durable and strong materials for countertops that are made from renewable and biodegradable resources.

New materials in the market are recycled-glass terrazzo-like lightweight concrete, recycled-glass ceramic tiles, and others. Recycled-glass concrete, for example, is a precast or cast-in-place terrazzo-looking concrete made from portland cement, sand, and recycled-glass aggregates. Recycled glass for concrete can be acquired from American Specialty Glass, Inc.. in a wide range of sizes and colors. Vetrazzo and IceStone countertops are examples of terrazzo-like products made with recycled glass and available in many colors. Although these manufacturers add proprietary substances to the mixture, they claim that they are not epoxy based.

Another countertop product is Syndecrete, a cement-based composite containing fly-ash and postindustrial recycled polypropylene fiber waste from carpet manufacturing. Syndecrete has twice the strength of standard concrete with half the weight. It is more resistant to chipping and cracking than conventional concrete, tile, or stone, and it can be worked almost like wood (Wilson, Malin, and Piepkorn 2006).

Finally, All Paper Recycling, Inc., manufactures countertops and tabletops using 100-percent recycled paper processed into a product called Shetkastone. This product can be recycled over and over again, through the same patented process, using no binders or adhesives, just paper. Shetkastone has a Class A fire rating without the addition of chemicals.

UPHOLSTERED GOODS

One of the main environmental concerns related to upholstery goods is the cushioning foams used in furniture manufacturing. Until 1990, most high-performance upholstery foams were manufactured with ozone-depleting chlorofluorocarbons (CFCs) or with toxic chemicals. These "blowing agents" were used to expand the foam's closed cells to create structure and resilience. Since 1995, all CFCs used for this purpose were banned, and more environmentally friendly agents, such as carbon dioxide (CO_2) and nitrogen, were introduced (Leclair and Rousseau 1992). Specifications should require manufacturers' labeling stating that products are ozone safe. Many office-furniture manufacturers are now using polyurethane foam cushioning that does not require blowing agents of any kind. Others, like Steelcase, use water-blown cushioning foams. Furnature, a supplier of furnishings for the environmentally sensitive, offers upholstery goods made from chemical-free organic cotton fibers. This company provides chemically sensitive customers with a samples kit of all materials used in the furniture for individual testing.

Figure 10-14a
ECOsurfaces recycled rubber floor-ing in custom colors at the Oak Park Library in Illinois. Architects: Perkins + Will | Eva Maddox Branded Environments and Nagle Architects, Ltd. Photo courtesy of ECOsurfaces Commercial Flooring.

Figure 10-14b
This technicolor map of New York City, its boroughs and neigh-borhoods proudly labeled, was installed at City Hall Academy at the Tweed Courthouse, New York City, using ECOsurfaces recy-cled rubber. It was awarded the grand prize in the annual StarNet Commercial Flooring Cooperative Design Awards, which recognize those who are setting new stand-ards of creativity in commercial interior design through the innova-tive use of floor covering. Loffredo Brooks Architects. Photo courtesy of ECOsurfaces Commercial Flooring.

Fabric preferences lean toward the ones made of natural fibers with minimal chemical treatment. Wool, ramie, organically grown cotton and linen, silk, jute, sisal, and hemp are some examples of natural fibers. Natural fibers, as opposed to synthetic fabrics, require little energy to process and are biodegradable, but they might have other environmental impacts. Cotton is usually grown with chemical fertilizers and pesticides, though our preference is for organically grown cotton. Silk and wool are usually imported from overseas, and both are prone to moth attacks and microbial growth. To prevent infestation, chemicals are used for treatment. Hemp and jute are also obtained from overseas sources but are relatively resistant to pests. These fabrics can be manufactured with natural or synthetic dyes, which tend to achieve greater color retention. Chemical treatment should be made with nontoxic compounds, free of mutagens and carcinogens, and preferably biodegradable.

Cotton Plus, Inc., is a company that makes fabrics from 100 percent organically grown cotton fiber and offers them in a natural cotton color or dyed with low-impact materials. Designtex and Carnegie offer Climatex Lifecycle, an award-winning line of natural-fiber textiles developed by William McDonough and Michael Braungart. Made from wool and organically grown ramie, these textiles are designed to be composted and turned back into soil at the end of their useful life. Chemicals used are nontoxic through a full-cycle manufacturing process. The water flowing out of the company's manufacturing plants is safe to drink, and the fiber waste trimmings are pressed into felt and sold to farmers to be used as mulch. Climatex Lifecycle is available through Designtex and through Carnegie. Climatex Lifecycle by Carnegie is made specifically for upholstery. Carnegie has a Designtex license to develop its own patterns, colors, and styles (Wilson, Malin, and Piepkorn 2005).

On the synthetic side, polyester products are now made with 100 percent postconsumer recycled PET bottles. These fabrics are an ER alternative for commercial applications because of their inherent fire resistance. Deepa Textiles produces a line of fabrics called Please Be Seated that includes Pour It On, a solution-dyed upholstery fabric made from 100-percent postindustrial recycled polyester. Unika Vaev's Venture Collection is a line of upholstery fabrics also made from 100-percent recycled polyester. The fabrics have a soft texture and feel; they are recyclable and contain no UV or flame inhibitors.

Eco Intelligent polyester, also offered by Designtex, is a contract fabric for commercial interiors made with antimony-free polyester. The fabric does not require chemical backing during application, which would make recycling more difficult. All chemicals and dyes used have been screened for toxicity and ecological impact, according to a protocol established by McDonough Braungart Design Chemistry (MBDC) to ensure it is a "technical nutrient" that can be recycled indefinitely.

WINDOW TREATMENTS

Window treatments, such as interior shades, blinds, or curtains are interior design devices used functionally to control daylight, to prevent glare, and to reduce heat loss or heat gain through windows. Although in many situations high-performance windows may be more efficient than energy-conserving blinds or shades, window coverings have a significant role in most interior design projects. However, the use of PVC-based products as well as textiles that contain toxic substances should be avoided. Today, there are several companies that offer less impacting products for window treatments, such as natural-fiber shades and PVC-free interior shade and screen products. However, many of these new products are still under evaluation in terms of health impacts.

DesignTex and Maharam, Inc., are two of several textile companies that now offer environmentally responsible textiles designed specifically for window covering. Nysan Shading Systems, Ltd., produces GreenScreen, a PVC-free shading product made of polyester yarn impregnated with an acrylic-based material. Nysan Shading also offers a fully automated system called Matrix, which can be programmed to track the sun and automatically adjust shades during the day. Recently approved by MBDC is a new product from MechoShade Systems, Inc., called EcoVeil. This PVC-free interior shade screen was designed as a "technical nutrient" that can be recycled indefinitely. Its health impacts, however, are still being tested. According to recent evaluations, the only problem with EcoVeil is its reliance on a toxic brominated flame retardant. Otherwise, EcoVeil is washable, antimicrobial, resistant to ultraviolet rays, strong, and dimensionally stable.

Earthshade's window-covering products are made from natural, minimally processed and rapidly renewed grasses and reeds. The company claims that these natural materials are grown without the use of fertilizers of pesticides, hand harvested, sun-dried, and handwoven in Central and South America. According to BuildingGreen.com, the only treatment used is hydrogen peroxide, which is required to meet import regulations. The products are assembled in Texas, using water-based glues, finishes, and flame retardants.

SOFT FURNISHINGS

When selecting soft furnishings, such as bed and bath linens or mattresses, the ideal products are those made from organically grown plant fibers that are pest resistant. Such products are not always available, because fabrics are typically treated with chemicals to resist microbial attack. Many of these chemicals tend to affect indoor air quality and cause strong reactions in chemically sensitive people. In addition, some natural plant fibers, like cotton, are grown with heavy use of pesticides and chemical fertilizers.

The conventional manufacturing process of fabrics involves heavy metals and other toxins. To avoid them, nondyed fabrics or those treated with natural dyes are preferred, because they are less harmful to sensitive occupants than products that use synthetic dyes. When possible, products treated with chlorine bleaches and other hazardous chemicals should be avoided, especially in linens and beddings. There are some companies that offer ER products; for example, A Happy Planet and Furnature are two companies that offer bedding and linen products made of organic, natural, and renewable fibers in place of conventional and synthetic fibers. Coyuchi, Inc., offers a full line of organic-cotton bed linens in percale, satin, and damask fabrics. The company's linens include white products bleached with hydrogen peroxide instead of chlorine. Other companies, like Rising Star Stellar Home Furnishings (Bend, OR) are making futon mattresses with 100-percent recycled PET-fiber batt cased in 100-percent organic cotton fabrics or 50/50 cotton/polyester blend.

References

Anink, D., C. Boonstra, and J. Mak. 2001. *Handbook of sustainable building: An environmental preference method for selection of materials for use in construction and refurbishment.* London: James and James.

Bowers, H. 2004. *Interior materials and surfaces: The complete guide.* Buffalo, NY: Firefly Books.

CMHC (Canada Mortgage and Housing Corporation). 1995. *Building materials for the environmentally hypersensitive.* Ottawa, Ontario: CMHC

Drummond, W. et al. 1999. *Life cycle costing guidelines for materials and building systems for Florida's public educational facilities.* 2 vols. Tallahassee, FL: Florida Department of Education.

Garrison, E. M. S., ed. 2002. *The graphic standards guide to architectural finishes: Using MASTERPEC to evaluate, select, and specify materials.* Hoboken, NJ: John Wiley & Sons.

Harte, J. et al. 1991. *Toxics A to Z: A guide to everyday pollution hazards.* Berkeley, CA: University of California Press.

Leclair, K., and D. Rousseau. 1992. *Environmental by design: A sourcebook of environmental conscientious choices for homeowners, builders and designers.* Vol. I, *Interiors.* Vancouver, BC: Hartley and Marks, Inc.

Malin, N. 2000. Structure as finish: The pros and cons of leaving off layers. *Environmental Building News* 9 (3): 1, 9–13.

Moussatche, H., and J. Languell. 2002. Life cycle costing of interior materials for Florida's schools. *Journal of Interior Design* 8 (2): 37–49.

Spiegel, R., and D. Meadows. 1999. *Green building materials: A guide to product selection and specification.* New York: John Wiley & Sons.

Wilhide, E. 2001. *Materials: A directory for home design.* Gloucester, MA: Rockport Publishers.

Wilson, A. 2001. Compressed-straw wall and ceiling panels from affordable building systems. *Environmental Building News* 10 (4):7.

——— 2006. *Building materials: What makes a product green?* In: Alex Wilson, Nadav Malin, and Mark Piepkorn, eds. 2006. *GreenSpec directory: Product listings & guideline specifications.* Brattelboro, VT: Building Green, Inc.

Wilson, A., and N. Malin. 1997. Wood products certification: A progress report. *Environmental Building News* 6 (10): 1, 10–14.

———. 1999a. Paint the room green. *Environmental Building News*. 8 (2): 1, 11–19.

———. 1999b. Structural engineered wood: Is it green? *Environmental Building News* 8 (*11*): 1, 12–17.

Wilson, A., N. Malin, and M. Piepkorn, eds. 2006. *GreenSpec directory: Product listings and guideline specifications*. Brattelboro, VT: Building Green, Inc.

Yost, P. 2000. Interior finish system: Judging a building by its inside cover. *Environmental Building News* 9 (11): 1, 9–13.

PART FOUR

Case Studies

CHAPTER ELEVEN

Case Study: The Immaculate Heart of Mary Motherhouse, Monroe, Michigan

SMP Architects, Philadelphia, PA, architect

Lynn Rogien, project director, Christman Corporation, Lansing, Michigan, general contractor

Susan Maxman, Philadelphia, PA, interior designer

Louise Jones, ArchD, LEED AP, IDEC, ASID, IIDA

All things in this creation exist within you, and all things in you exist in creation: there is no border between you and the closest things, and there is no distance between you and the farthest things, and all things, from the lowest to the loftiest, from the smallest to the greatest, are within you as equal things.
    —Khalil Gibran

Education as Transformation

In 1845 the Order of the Sisters, Servants of the Immaculate Heart of Mary (IHM Sisters), was founded along the River Raisin in Monroe, Michigan, to provide educational opportunities for girls. Today the nuns are teaching the world, through words and deeds, the philosophy of environmentally responsible design. The IHM sisters built their motherhouse in 1932, after a fire destroyed their all-girls' boarding school (Rivera 2006). By the year 2000, a decision needed to be made: should they renovate the motherhouse or build a new structure?

> The IHM community's traditional ministry has been education. We have always valued education as a transformational process. In light of the need of the Earth community, we understand that we can use our educational skills to help transform our society from a consumerist culture to a sustainable culture.

> Our common call is rooted in common ground. We embrace the belief that for the future we must create livable and sustainable communities, we must curtail urban sprawl, preserve open space, make our communities more energy efficient, support energy conversion, promote the use of innovative technologies that use renewable energy resources, preserve natural habitats, and maintain biodiversity to sustain natural systems.

> We can educate for planetary citizenship. We began that education last April 22nd [2003]. Between Earth Day 2003 and January 1, 2004, more than 4,300 visitors came through our doors to take one of our two-hour educational tours of the sustainable features and practices we implemented in the Motherhouse and on our property. Sixty-seven percent of those visitors told us they would change some aspect of how they live as a result of what they learned from their visit (Pfau 2004).

Renovation of the Motherhouse

The IHM Sisters' vision is to transform the 280-acre campus in Monroe, Michigan, into a twenty-first-century center for sustainable living and learning—an eco-village. Sister Virginia Pfau, former IHM president, expressed the conception of their moral mandate for the twenty-first century: "We came to realize humans live in an interdependent relationship with each other and with all life on the planet. . . we hope to be a restorative presence on Earth rather than a destructive one" (IHM Sisters n.d. *b*). For the sisters, living sustainably is multidimensional, even though it is a simple concept. When they talk about living sustainably, they mean:

- Changing the way they think about life on Earth.
- Using resources wisely so as to avoid depleting them.
- Moving from disruptive behaviors to healing relationships and harmonious coexistence with the whole Earth community.
- Thinking beyond today and immediate gratification so that future generations will have adequate resources.
- Recycling materials and choosing products made in both "people friendly" and "Earth friendly" ways.
- Treating nature as a model and mentor. (IHM Sisters n.d. *c*, 9–10)

Figure 11-1
The 376,000-square-foot mother-house, built in 1932 in the classic art deco style, on the 280-acre campus in Monroe, Michigan, was renovated as a home and health center for retired Sisters, Servants of the Immaculate Heart of Mary. One of the largest residential sustainable renovation projects in the United States, it is registered with the U.S. Green Building Council and was awarded the AIA Committee on the Environment Top Ten Green Building Award.

Figure 11-2
View of the renovated sanctuary. The nuns consider sustainability and eco-justice to be their "spiritual and moral mandate for the twenty-first century."

In 2000 the IHM Sisters made another decision about their home: they decided to recycle the motherhouse on the urban campus, at a cost of $56 million, rather than demolish it and erect a new structure, which would have been less expensive. The majority of the renovated motherhouse is a home and health-care center for retired nuns. Built in 1932, in the art deco style, with 18-inch-thick concrete and brick walls, it was structurally sound enough to last well into the twenty-third century, but it was showing signs of age, and its building systems were antiquated. The historical and spiritual significance of the building, as well as the environmental impact of demolition and rebuilding, were important considerations in discerning the future of the beautifully detailed, 376,000-square-foot structure (IHM Sisters n.d. *e*).

Danielle Conroyd, who has been the IHM project director for the long-range master plan since 1998, spoke of the goal to renovate the motherhouse and to

Figure 11-3
Stained glass throughout the building was repaired and reused. In deciding whether to renovate or raze the existing building, the sisters came to realize that the "state of our home forced us to make a decision about the way we live. We came to realize that humans live in interdependent relationships with each other and with all life on the planet. . .we hope to be a restorative presence on Earth rather than a destructive one."

Figure 11-4
The main lobby at the entry to the sanctuary. The renovation was planned for adaptive reuse of the facility by the local community when it is no longer fully occupied by the sisters, whose numbers are declining. Each unit has a sleeping area with at least two windows, Internet connections, and a private bathroom with a shower.

Figure 11-5
Detail of restored ceilings in the main lobby area. Architectural details, doors, and woodwork, as well as the parquet, marble, cork, and tile flooring, were restored and reused during the renovation. The sisters chose to use new construction materials, furnishings, and finishes "that reduce our footprint and impact on the environment."

restore the campus so as to be one sustainable and cohesive system that would showcase wise and appropriate use of resources: "Our vision for this project was rooted in our deepening awareness that all of life is intricately connected, and choices made by individuals, corporations and nations can have profound global influence. . . . Transforming the Monroe campus into an 'Eco Village' is our spiritual and moral mandate for the 21st century. . . .the building is a metaphor for the way we need to live in relation to each other and to the planet" (Rackley 2003).

In the renovation of the IHM motherhouse, the rooms were reconfigured as living space for 240 sisters, whose median age was 84. Outdated and overburdened plumbing and electrical systems were replaced, and site improvements were made. Measures were taken to preserve the historic building and to enhance the comfort of residents. The design not only met the immediate needs of the sisters, three-fourths of whom needed assisted living or nursing home care, but will, in the future, be adaptable to the needs of others in the community beyond the IHM convent, when the sisters no longer need exclusive use of the motherhouse and campus (Aue 2001).

The renovation design replaced the antiquated building infrastructure with environmentally friendly and energy-efficient electrical, plumbing, and heating and cooling systems. The integration of technologies achieved synergies not possible in a piecemeal approach. The new systems were carefully integrated into the existing, historically significant structure, so as to be as unobtrusive as possible (IHM Sisters n.d. *a*). The motherhouse renovations included the following features:

- Daylighting is maximized by using energy-efficient, insulated glazing that balances light transmission with the windows' insulating and shading performance.

- A programmable control system integrates high-efficiency and high-performance compact fluorescent lighting, occupancy sensors, and daylighting.

- Water conservation features lower fresh-water consumption through the use of low-flow and water-conserving fixtures and fittings.

Motherhouse of the Sisters, Servants of the Immaculate Heart of Mary Construction Awards

- Leadership in Sustainability: Michigan American Association of Architects
- Clean Air Excellence Award: Environmental Protection Agency
- USGBC Certified LEED Version 2. Project number: 0009. August 2006.
- Building Award: Michigan Historic Preservation Network
- 2003 EPA Clean Air Excellence Award: Community Projects Category
- 2003 Build Michigan Award: Over $5 million category
- 2004 Pyramid Award: Best Project Team
- 2005 Design Honor Award, *Faith and Form* magazine and Interfaith Forum on Religion, Art, and Architecture
- 2006 AIA Committee on the Environment Top Ten Green Building Award

Figure 11-6
Cloister with interior windows to bring daylight into the sisters' living quarters. All period electrical light fixtures were retrofitted for compact fluorescent lamps; this change, plus programmable lighting and occupancy sensors, resulted in 30 to 40 percent savings in energy costs for lighting.

Figure 11-7
Efficiency bedroom and bathroom unit showing cedar lockers reused as built-in storage units and corner windows that were reglazed for energy efficiency. Marble toilet room stall partitions were saved and then cut for countertops and window sills during the renovation. Water-efficient plumbing fixtures—in coordination with the diversion 1 million gallons of water per year from the municipal system and a constructed wetlands and gray-water system to cleanse and recycle sink and shower water for flushing toilets—reduced freshwater consumption to 55 percent of the former usage, a savings of more than 5,500 gallons per day, even though 305 new bathrooms were added to the motherhouse.

- A gray-water flushing system reuses water from sinks and showers.
- Residents' rooms are heated and cooled with individual terminal units so each can choose the room temperature she prefers.
- A geothermal heating and cooling system as well as a heat-recovery system reduce energy consumption.

Gray water: A gray-water system uses dedicated pipes to transport water from sinks and showers to a constructed wetland for natural cleansing. It is then transported in dedicated pipes back into the building for the sole purpose of flushing toilets.

The Sisters of IHM dramatically reduced the consumption of fresh water and efficiently managed storm water through the utilization of water-conservation and water-management technologies, including *swales,* to channel rainwater. They reduced water consumption by 6,200 gallons with the installation of a *gray-water* system for flushing toilets. A separate piping system collects used water—i.e., gray water—from sinks and showers in the motherhouse and transfers the gray water to a constructed wetland on the campus. The three-acre wetlands, mimicking nature's purification system, cleanses the gray water and recycles it for use in the motherhouse for flushing toilets. This is only one of the water-conservation technologies incorporated into the project. In spite of adding 305 new bathrooms, the gray-water flushing system and high-velocity, low-flow, fixtures and fittings reduced overall freshwater consumption by 50 percent. In addition, the use of vegetated swales and wet meadows diverts almost 1 million gallons of water per year from the municipal storm-sewer system (Aue 2001).

Swale: A shallow troughlike depression that carries water mainly during rainstorms or snow melts.

The heating and cooling system is the largest privately-funded geothermal field in the United States. *Geothermal* systems use the Earth's temperature for heating and cooling. The closed-loop system with 232 bore-holes, each 450 feet deep, takes advantage of the Earth's steady 55°F underground temperature. Water, which is constantly circulated through the 47 miles of piping in the geothermal field, is warmed or cooled by the Earth. By starting with the warmer than ambient air heat source in the winter and the cooler than ambient air heat sink in the summer, a geothermal system provides significant energy savings as compared to conventional heating and cooling systems. In the summer, the 55°F water is circulated through the 5.87 miles of duct work in the motherhouse and returned to the geothermal field at a higher temperature, where it is again cooled to 55°F. A chiller provides supplemental cooling for the building. In winter, the process works in reverse: the 55°F water is circulated through a heat pump, where heat is extracted from the water. The cooled water is then recirculated to the geothermal field to be warmed again. An auxiliary boiler system provides supplementary heat on especially cold days. This geothermal system provides efficient and renewable heating and cooling, with the end result being lower heating and cooling costs (Rackley 2003).

Geothermal: Literally, heat from the earth; energy obtained from the hot areas under the surface of the earth.

The building renovation was planned so as to be the most cost-effective reuse of the existing structure. The renovation illustrated a holistic approach to environmentally responsible design. Geothermal mechanical systems were designed in conjunction with window-replacement criteria. Interrelated energy conservation measures included the use of: daylighting, high-intensity-discharge lighting, compact fluorescent lighting, and programmed integrative-lighting systems to reduce the demand for electricity. Over 30 percent of the construction debris and

Figure 11-8
Kitchen with exposed ductwork for the geothermal heating and cooling system that reduced energy costs for the 376,000-square-foot motherhouse by 50 percent, in concert with the computerized energy-management system.

50 percent of all construction materials were given to local nonprofits and recycling facilities. Moreover, the decision to reuse existing materials and furnishings was more than an environmentally responsible, cost-effective design decision. It helped to preserve the historical fabric of the building (IHM Sisters n.d. *c*, 11, 16).

The motherhouse project is registered with the U.S. Green Building Council, an organization composed of the nation's foremost leaders from across the building industry who are transforming the marketplace by educating owners and practitioners on environmentally responsible building practices. They define sustainable design as construction practices that reduce or eliminate the negative impact of buildings on the environment and on the people who live, work, and play there (USGBC 2006). Five broad areas identified by USGBC influenced the IHM motherhouse renovation (IHM Sisters n.d. *c*, 12–21).

SUSTAINABLE SITE PLANNING

- Reduced the impact on the environment by renovating an existing building rather than building a new structure.
- Restored the site with native species. The campus includes native trees that are more than 100 years old and an endangered oak-savanna ecosystem.

THE 3 Rs OF ENVIRONMENTALLY RESPONSIBLE DESIGN: REDUCE, REUSE, AND RECYCLE

The motherhouse renovation *reduced*

- The impact of construction on the natural environment by not building new
- The footprint on Earth by using sustainable products
- Material costs by implementing conservation practices that included reusing building components, such as existing doors and trim, woodwork, and light fixtures
- Furnishing costs by retaining, refinishing, and reusing original pieces whenever possible
- The environmental impact of new products and materials by reviewing the potential impact before specification for the project

The motherhouse renovation project *reused*

- 800 wooden windows, reglazed with double-pane, low-e glass
- 500 cherry wood doors
- Cedar storage cabinets
- Wood trim, wood wainscoting, and parquet wood floors
- Marble partitions from toilet stalls for windowsills and cabinet countertops
- More than 100 period light fixtures, retrofitting them to make them more energy efficient
- Topsoil, removed during construction, used in landscaping work

The motherhouse renovation *recycled*

- 45,260 square feet of carpet
- Sinks and toilets
- Wiring
- Ductwork
- Wooden cabinets
- Fire extinguishers
- Radiators
- Plaster (for road bed)
- Asphalt (for road bed)

SOURCE: IHM SISTERS N.D. *C*, 10–11.

The conversion of 5 acres of lawn to meadow and prairie improved the biodiversity of the site and protected existing natural habitat.

■ Preserved a green space in the urban area. The campus includes a landscape of meadows, courtyards, woodlands, constructed wetlands, walking paths, gardens, a cemetery, green space, and a pond.

SAFEGUARDING WATER AND WATER EFFICIENCY

- Reduced consumption of fresh water by more than 50 percent. Lavatory faucets used aerated outlets, rated at 1.5 gpm (gallons per minute); shower-heads have maximum flow of 1.8 gpm.
- Diverted almost 1 million gallons of water per year from the municipal water-treatment system by incorporating swales and wet meadows.
- Collected water from sinks and showers. The gray-water system collects the used water, cycles it through constructed wetlands that mimic nature's purification system, and recycles it to the motherhouse to flush toilets, thereby saving 6,200 gallons of water per day.

ENERGY EFFICIENCY AND RENEWABLE ENERGY

- Reduced dependence on nonrenewable energy sources by incorporating a geothermal heating and cooling system.
- Reduced demand for electricity with the use of daylighting, high-performance electric lighting, and programmable lighting controls.
- Employed strategies to ensure energy-efficient heating and cooling. For example, the HVAC (heating, ventilation, and air-conditioning) system's efficiency was maximized by implementing heat-recovery systems and sizing the units appropriately.
- Monitored energy-saving strategies with the use of a computerized energy-management system, thereby saving almost $200,000 for utilities in the first full year of operation.
- Maximized daylighting by balancing light transmission with the windows' insulating and shading performance.

Environmental footprint: A measure of the Earth's resources required to meet individual unit's needs. Small footprints are better than large ones.

CONSERVATION OF MATERIALS AND RESOURCES

- Reused building materials (e.g., windows, doors, cabinets) or recycled them (e.g., plaster, concrete, carpet).
- Specified new furnishings and finishes only after it was documented that they complied with sustainability criteria to reduce the *environmental footprint.*
- Specified new furnishings, finishes, and building materials that met environmentally responsible standards to reduce the environmental footprint:
  - Products manufactured using recycled postconsumer content. Trek, which is made from recycled wood and plastic, was used as flooring on the decks.
  - Products manufactured using recycled postindustrial content. For example, the mineral wool insulation is made from iron-ore slag.
  - Products manufactured using wood and wood products certified as being in compliance with forest management practices. For example, new parquet flooring is FSC certified.

■ Products manufactured using rapidly renewable raw materials. For example, linoleum is made from flax, wood flour, and linseed oil.

■ Products manufactured from natural materials with little or no processing. For example, cork, used in the interior cloister, can be repeatedly harvested without damaging the cork tree. The cork is factory finished with water-based polyurethane and cured with ultraviolet (UV) light. Original cork on stairs in the motherhouse was still in excellent condition after 70 years of use. Unfortunately, those stairwells had to be demolished and rebuilt next to new elevators to meet code requirements.

OPTIMAL INDOOR AIR QUALITY

Air-exchange rate: The rate at which outside air replaces indoor air in a given space.

Air changes per hour (ACH): Number of times per hour a volume of air, equivalent to the volume of space, enters that space.

■ Protected HVAC systems during construction to control contaminants.

■ Specified appropriate *air-exchange rates* to introduce fresh air.

■ Used low-emitting materials and products (e.g., low-VOC paints).

■ Specified operable windows to provide daylight, views, and fresh air.

■ Integrated occupant-controlled building systems (e.g., temperature, lighting).

QUALITY OF LIFE

■ Designed each resident room with at least two windows and a private bath with shower.

■ Built the second-floor veranda to overlook the community room and open into two courtyards.

■ Provided pedestrian pathways to landscapes that linked nature and the human spirit.

■ Designed each wing as a neighborhood with a living room, dining area, kitchen, laundry, and assisted bathing room.

■ Ensured that the motherhouse is fully accessible to people with physical disabilities.

■ Installed new fire-protection system to increase resident safety.

■ Landscaped courtyards to provide protected outdoor space for residents, who would otherwise have limited access to a natural environment.

SENSE OF COMMUNITY

■ Designed the renovation to respect the fabric of the structure. The extensive interior renovations minimally impacted the exterior appearance and historical character of the motherhouse.

■ Planned the motherhouse renovation according to concepts that support adaptive reuse. The sisters envision a time when the motherhouse will

Figure 11-9
The interior courtyard, as viewed from the second-floor veranda, illustrates the connections of inside and outside spaces. The garden, which creates contemplative spaces for enjoying the natural environment, is used by all of the sisters, but it is particularly important to the residents who would otherwise have very limited access to the outdoors.

Figure 11-10.
The courtyard fountain, which is surrounded by tiles honoring donors. Many people gave $150, the cost for renovation of 1 square foot. Seating is made of teak from managed forests, for durability with little maintenance.

transcend their needs, enabling them to open the home to others who may use the interior spaces in a different manner.

- Planned the interior to accommodate many uses and meet different needs with minimal disruption to ensure continued use of the facilities (e.g., resident rooms can be combined to form one- or two-bedroom apartments).
- Supported sustainable urban agriculture with an organic, community garden.

Conclusion

The sisters' vision for this project was rooted in a deepening awareness that all of life is intricately connected and that choices made by individuals, corporations, and nations can have profound global influence: "We believe in an ecological consciousness that fosters an interdependence of all nature, nurturing relationships that will enhance the well-being of the Earth and all persons" (IHM Sisters n.d. e). This understanding led them to define and model a sustainable community that nourishes life and fosters its capacity to flourish. It was their goal as educators to make use of this "living laboratory" to develop, refine, and demonstrate Earth-restoring practices and systems. Their commitment to use environmentally responsible design practices to reconceptualize their campus as an eco-village has become a model of development for the twenty-first century.

References

Aue, S. 2001. IHM motherhouse renovation. *The Guardian, A Heritage Newspaper,* June 21, 2001. Monroe, MI: Sisters, Servants of the Immaculate Heart of Mary Convent.

IHM Sisters (Servants of the Immaculate Heart of Mary). n.d. *a. Mission for the millennium: Facts.* Retrieved October, 12, 2007, from IHM Web site: http://www.IHMsisters.org/www/Sustainable_Community/Sustainable_Renovation/renconcepts.asp

———. n.d. *b. Mission for the millennium: IHM Green Team consultation services.* Retrieved October, 12, 2007, from IHM Web site: http://www.IHMsisters.org/www/Sustainable_Community/speakers.asp

———. n.d. *c. Mission for the millennium: The sustainable renovation of the motherhouse of the Sisters, Servants of the Immaculate Heart of Mary.* Monroe, MI: IHM Sisters, Servants of the Immaculate Heart of Mary Convent.

———. n.d. *d. Mission for the millennium: Frequently asked questions.* Monroe, MI: IHM Sisters, Servants of the Immaculate Heart of Mary Convent.

———. n.d. *e. IHM belief statement: A moral mandate.* Retrieved October, 12, 2007, from IHM Web site: http://www.IHMsisters.org/www/Sustainable_Community/sustaincommunity.asp

Pfau, V. M. 2004. *IHM Earth Day.* Monroe, MI: Sisters Servants of the Immaculate Heart of Mary Convent.

Rackley, J. 2003. Geothermal system helps sisters fulfill spiritual, moral mandate. *Geo Outlook Online* 1 (1): 1–7. Retrieved November 22, 2005, from The International Ground Source Heat Pump Association Web site: http://www.igshpa.okstate.edu

Rivera, G. 2006. How one bioneer's faith-based community of sisters is greening their world. Bioneers 2006 Conference (Oct. 20–22, 2006), San Rafael, CA.

U.S. Green Building Council. LEED Certification: Renovation of the Motherhouse. Project 0009. Retrieved February 14, 2006, from USGBC Web site: http://www.usgbc.org/LEED/Project/CertifiedProjectList

CHAPTER TWELVE

Case Study: The Everett L. Marshall Building at Eastern Michigan University

Kent Johnson, TMP Associates, Bloomfield Hills, Michigan, architect

John Herrygers, project director, Christman Corporation, Lansing, Michigan, general contractor

Louise Jones, LEED AP, EMU, Ypsilanti, Michigan, interior designer

Kay Sekerek, EMU, Ypsilanti, Michigan, project designer

Robert Black, AIA, Ann Arbor, Michigan, sustainable architecture consultant

Keith Fineberg, AIA, KSF Architects, Saline, Michigan, design consultant

Archie Lytle, Barton Mallow Inc., Southfield, Michigan, Technology consultant

Louise Jones, ArchD, LEED AP, IDEC, ASID, IIDA

We shape our buildings and our buildings shape us.
   —Winston Churchill

Early ERID Exemplar

The Everett L. Marshall Building at Eastern Michigan University (EMU), Ypsilanti, Michigan, was one of the first nonresidential interior design projects to exemplify environmentally responsible interior design (ERID). Although the building shell was not built to meet either green or sustainable criteria, all of the finishes, furnishings, and equipment (FF&E) were selected based on their green (to protect human health and well-being) and sustainable (to protect Earth's health and well-being) characteristics.

Dr. Louise Jones, director of the Interior Design Program at EMU, served as interim associate dean of the College of Health and Human Services for four years (1998–2002) in order to work with Dean Elizabeth King, PhD, to design a new building for the college that reflected environmental responsibility. They believed that people teaching and learning health and human services should be able to work and learn in a safe environment, one that did not cause stress for people with allergies, asthma, or multiple chemical sensitivity (MCS). The college adopted an American Indian adage as the touchstone for its decisions regarding the new building: "We do not inherit the earth from our ancestors, we borrow it from our children."

Figure 12-1
The central atrium is open to administrative and faculty offices on the third floor and the student commons on the second floor. Daylighting is supplemented with HID and fluorescent lighting on photosensors so that the electrical lighting is dimmed when there is sufficient daylighting. Furnishings and finishes include Benjamin Moore Eco-Spec paint, Zolotone multicolor water-based coating system, Forbo linoleum flooring, Falcon tables, Haworth seating, and DesignTex Climatex upholstery fabric. Photo by Logan Photography.

Building Statistics

The 75,000-square-foot Marshall Building was home to the schools of Nursing, Social Work, and Allied Health Professions. The $14 million ($187 per sq. ft.) design-build project was completed in August 2000. Although $2.7 million had been designated by the state legislature for the building's FF&E, the actual expenditure was $2,098,760, with $1,151,660 of that amount allocated to the technology infrastructure and equipment (e.g., 1,000 network and electrical connections, including one for every student in each of the 8 classrooms and 5 labs). An additional $100,000 in development funding supported the green and sustainable mandate when the environmentally responsible FF&E option's up-front costs were more than the typical university specification. Dr. King commends John Herrygers, project manager for Christman Corporation, for supporting the environmentally responsible goal by double bidding the FF&E to identify any cost differences between the university's typical specification and ERID products. In addition to the $100,000 in development funding, some manufacturers made gifts in-kind, recognizing that this would be the first environmentally responsible demonstration project in the northeast part of the American Midwest. In the final analysis, the project came in at $28 per square foot for FF&E and technology.

Figure 12-2
The podium for the smart classrooms was custom designed using recycled steel and plastic laminate on an agri-board substrate, as there were none in the marketplace, to house the instructional technology equipment and to accommodate users, whether seated or standing. Furnishings and finishes in the classrooms include Benjamin Moore Eco-Spec paint, Falcon tables, Vecta Kart seating, and Forbo linoleum flooring. Photo by Logan Photography.

Figure 12-3
The touch panel on the podium, which controls all of the instructional-technology equipment, conserves energy by only powering the equipment that is in use at any given time. The Lutron system controls the fluorescent lighting so that it is dimmed to a level appropriate for the imminent teaching and learning activity (e.g., lecture, discussion, video or slide presentations). Photo by Logan Photography.

ERID Process

In 1998, at the beginning of the research to identify appropriate FF&E, very few manufacturers' representatives knew about their companies' green and sustainable products or company policies. A few reported that their product was available in several shades of green (e.g., sage and spruce); others indicated they needed to check with management. To their surprise, most learned that their company had at least one environmental engineer! Although some of their product line was manufactured using environmentally responsible protocols, management did not use this information to market the product to the A&D (architecture and design) community. The perception was that architects and designers would reject the product due to negative preconceptions. When the project started in 1998, most of the A&D community still equated being environmentally responsible with the "hippie" lifestyle of the late 1960s and early 1970s. Most of the A&D community thought ERID products cost extra, had extended delivery times, were not durable, and stifled their creativity due to the limited availability of colors and styles (Ross 2003).

After an extensive search of the literature resulted in very little current information (most of what was found had been written in the 1970s in response to the energy crisis), Dr. Jones realized they would have to develop their own evaluation criteria. In 1987, the United Nations had defined sustainable development as the ability of the current generation to meet their needs without jeopardizing the ability of future generations to meet their needs (UN World Commission on Environment and Development 1987). The mandate for the project became the specification of only FF&E that were not detrimental to the health and well-being of the people who would use the Marshall Building or the health and well-being of global ecosystems.

The project criteria for determining vendors included the following:

- Company's environmental policies were sound and were being implemented
- Recycled or rapidly renewable raw materials were being used
- Production process respected global ecosystems and the employees' health and well-being (e.g., Climatex fabric manufacturing protocol)
- No measurable toxic product off-gassing (during production, installation, or use)
  - No volatile organic compounds (VOCs)
  - No chlorofluorocarbons (CFCs)
  - No formaldehyde
- Reusable shipping materials (e.g., blanket wrap)
- Installation and maintenance procedures were environmentally responsible
- Components were recyclable at the end of useful life—creating a closed loop

Environmentally Responsible Furnishings and Finishes

A variety of environmentally responsible products were used throughout the Marshall Building to illustrate the durability and beauty of green and sustainable products. In keeping with the Marshall Building's designation as a demonstration site, a wide range of flooring materials were specified. None of the flooring used in the Marshall building needs to be waxed; therefore, there is no off-gassing from waxes or strippers. Routine maintenance involves vacuuming and spot cleaning soiled areas with a solution of water mixed with an environmentally safe cleaning product (such as Unikleen by Ipax Cleanogel)—this solution in a scrubber or buffer is the preferred cleaning method for bamboo, cork, Madera, and linoleum.

- Cork flooring used in one conference room provides excellent sound-dampening properties and should last for more than 50 years without showing significant wear. The Chicago Library and the law library at the University of Michigan, Ann Arbor, have cork floors that have been in use since the turn of the nineteenth century! Cork is responsibly harvested from live trees and can be reharvested every 10 years for more than 200 years. The surface of the cork flooring was sealed at the factory using a water-based, UV-cured urethane.
- Bamboo flooring was used in the executive conference room to make an aesthetic statement about environmentally responsible design. Bamboo is

Figure 12-4
Meeting rooms can be scheduled as needed by faculty in all of the programs housed in the Marshall Building to avoid duplication of support spaces. Furnishings and finishes in this room include: Benjamin Moore Eco-Spec paint, Haworth seating with Carnegie upholstery fabric, Falcon tables, and Expanko cork flooring. Photo by Logan Photography.

harder than red oak (the industry standard for wood flooring), and it is easy to maintain. Unlike oak trees, bamboo is a rapidly renewable grass that grows to 8 inches in diameter and 40 feet in height in just four years.

■ Linoleum was used in the high-traffic areas and classrooms, where durability was a primary concern. Linoleum is made from rapidly renewable materials: (1) pine rosin and wood flour from sustainably managed forests and (2) linseed oil from flax. The color is consistent through the material, it does not need to be waxed (buffing between cleanings will maintain a low luster), and the life span is forty plus years.

Figure 12-5
The classrooms can be easily rearranged to facilitate lectures, collaborative activities, role play, or large group meetings. They can accommodate a wide range of teaching and learning styles and minimize the number of required specialized spaces. Daylighting is augmented with dimmable fluorescent lighting with parabolic louvers to eliminate glare on students' notebook computer screens. Furnishings and finishes include: Benjamin Moore Eco-Spec paint, Forbo linoleum flooring, Levolor blinds, Falcon tables, and Vecta Kart seating. Photo by Logan Photography.

- Madera, which was also used in a conference room, is a composite material that is manufactured to resemble stone tiles—from urban harvested wood (e.g., recycled wood furniture)—but without the weight or cold feeling associated with stone. The wood flour is mixed with lignasil, a natural wood resin, and then molded into 12-inch tiles that, when baked, are harder than red-oak flooring, moisture proof, and warranted for durability. Madera is installed with a thin-set mortar, just as stone or porcelain tiles are, but they can be cut with a wood saw instead of a wet stone saw. And, unlike stone, the tiles are not brittle; they have a lifetime warranty against cracking. The individual tiles meet code for commercial kitchens and restrooms and can be soaked in water for three days without decomposing, ensuring easy maintenance.

- Crossville Eco-Cycle porcelain tiles, made from factory-recovered waste clay, were used in the restrooms. The Eco-Cycle tile is fired with the first-run porcelain tile, but it is marketed at a reduced cost because the raw material is considered production waste; using it keeps it out of the landfill. The tile is offered with a smooth or raised grid surface to reduce slipping on wet tile. The grid-surface tiles were used in Marshall, but this was probably not the best choice. Maintenance found that the grid trapped dirt, and they experienced some difficulty in keeping it clean.

- Solenium by Interface was used in the office areas where a flooring that could help abate noise was required. The carpet tiles were the first flooring

Figure 12-6
For maximum flexibility, this meeting room can comfortably seat from ten to twenty-two people, depending upon the table arrangement. Abundant daylighting is controlled with metal horizontal blinds to control glare. Furnishings and finishes include: Benjamin Moore Eco-Spec paint, Madera wood tiles, Haworth seating with Guilford of Maine upholstery fabric, and Falcon tables. Photo by Logan Photography.

textile that could be totally recycled into more of the same product, creating a closed loop (i.e., a continuous source of raw materials). The tile is constructed using a flat rather than a tufted weave, resulting in a surface that can be swept, vacuumed, or mopped to clean up spills. An impermeable layer between the surface and the backing prevents moisture from getting under the tile, where it might support the growth of mold. Solenium is cleaned with hot-water extraction, further reducing the chance for mold growth.

■ EcoSurface recycled rubber flooring was used in the stairwells and for the central stairway. The rubber for the central stairs was from recycled rubber tires; it provided a resilient, nonslip surface that reduced the noise in the student commons located at the top and bottom of the stairway. The fire-stair flooring was made from recycled rubber roofing membrane (to meet fire code). The original specification was to seal the concrete in the fire stairs and use vinyl on the central stairs. The cost was such that the rubber could be used in all three stairways, eliminating the vinyl (PVC) off-gassing that the EPA has determined to be carcinogenic.

■ The Knoll open-office system incorporated recycled and recyclable materials. An agri-board substrate was used for the work surfaces; powder-coated, recycled steel for structure; and gypsum board with fly ash for the panel core. The panels were upholstered with a product from DesignTex, using a polyester fiber made from recycled soda bottles.

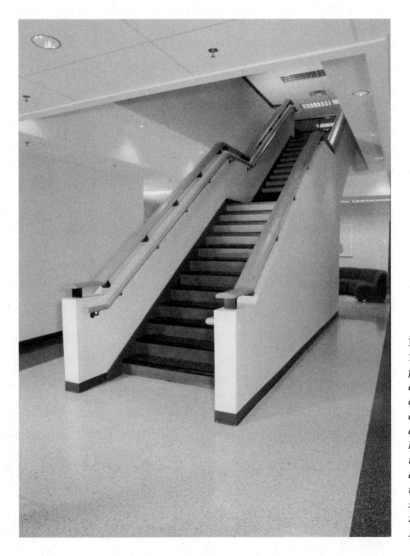

Figure 12-7
The central stair connects the first- and second-floor student commons and provides access to classrooms on both floors. The elevator is behind the stairs so as to be accessible when needed but to encourage use of the stairs to conserve energy. Furnishings and finishes include Zolotone multicolor water-based coating system, Fritztile flooring, and Eco-Surfaces recycled-rubber flooring. Photo by Logan Photography.

- Benjamin Moore EcoSpec paint and water-based Zolotone were used to finish the walls. The Eco-Spec is a water-based, latex paint that is almost odorless, with no VOC off-gassing. Zolotone is a water-based, multicolor-, three-dimensional coating system with a pigmented resin in an aqueous solution. It does not support fungus or bacteria growth, and it is abrasion and stain resistant to enhance durability.

William McDonough, an architect who is perhaps the most recognized spokesperson for environmental responsibility, designed a fabric using only 38 of the 8,000 chemicals that were tested to determine if they were safe for people and the environment. He has licensed this protocol to three fabric manufacturers, so that there is now a reasonable range of pattern and color available at a cost that is roughly equivalent to other commercial-grade upholstery fabrics. This wool and ramie blend was used as the upholstery fabric on almost all of the seating in Marshall. A range of seating from multiple manufacturers was used throughout the building; three of particular note were:

- Knoll's SoHo office chair, with a PETRA frame manufactured from recycled soda bottles;
- Steelcase's Prodigy chair, which set the industry standard for environmentally responsible, ergonomic office seating; and
- Herman Miller's Aeron chair, the first high-end office chair to be made primarily from recycled materials, using single-material construction so that it is 98 percent recyclable at the end of its useful life.

Figure 12-8
The teaming room was designed for faculty who had offices in other buildings but needed to collaborate on research projects. The flexible space allows them to work independently at the workstations or pull the tables and mobile carts together for collaborative work. Furnishings and finishes include: Benjamin Moore Eco-Spec paint, Knoll SoHo seating from recycled PET plastic with DesignTex Climatex upholstery fabric, Interface Solenium flooring (the first closed-loop textile-flooring product), Knoll office panels with DesignTex upholstery using recycled polyester (ten two-liter soda bottles make one yard of panel fabric), Haworth Next tables, Smed mobile carts, and Levolor metal blinds. Photo by Logan Photography.

Indoor air quality was an important part of the green mandate. Eliminating VOCs, CFCs, and formaldehyde off-gassing resulted in a new building without a new building odor. The voluntary "no-fragrance" policy further improved indoor air quality. People seemed to be surprised that their eyes, noses, and throats were not irritated after attending class, studying, or working in the Marshall Building. The Occupational Safety and Health Administration (OSHA) testing, three months after occupancy, found no measurable quantities of volatile organic compounds (VOCs), chlorofluorocarbons (CFCs), formaldehyde, fungus, or mold. The air inside the Marshall Building was cleaner than the air outside of the building—not a common outcome given today's sealed buildings and product off-gassing.

Conclusion

Finding environmentally responsible materials in 1998 was challenging because no one was familiar with them; whereas today the challenge comes from the tendency of companies to "greenwash" their products (i.e., provide misinformation about the green and/or sustainable characteristics of their products), leaving the designer with the responsibility of researching and documenting environmentally responsible FF&E for their projects. As demonstrated by the Everett L. Marshall Building, environmental responsibility can be incorporated into a tightly budgeted project without sacrificing aesthetic qualities. "Green materials don't cost more to use," said Lynn Rogien, of the Christman Corporation, "if you are smart about their use and take the time to get educated. If the project team takes a system-wide, integrated approach to green materials and considers life-cycle costs, LEED silver [certification] can be attained at little to no cost increase" (Guerin, Jones, and Ginthner 2004). The Marshall Building project was an early exemplar of using ERID to protect people's health and well-being as well as planet Earth's health and well-being.

References

Guerin, D., L. Jones, and D. Ginthner. 2004. Environmentally responsible interior design: A case study. *eJournal of Interior Design*, 30(3).

Ross, E. 2003. Barriers to specifying green/sustainable products. Master's thesis, Eastern Michigan University, Ypsilanti, MI.

UN World Commission on Environment and Development. 1987. *The Brundtland report: Our common future*. New York: Oxford University Press.

Glossary

Definitions are drawn from the following sources:

INVISTA, Wichita, Kansas

DuPont Flooring Systems, Kennesaw, Georgia

U.S. Environmental Protection Agency Glossary of Climate Change Terms, http://www.epa.gov/climatechange/glossary.html#O

Green Design Education Initiative, www.IDEC.org

National Resources Defense Council, New York

A

Absorption Process by which a substance is drawn into the structure of another.

Acid rain Precipitation of dilute solutions of strong mineral acids, formed by the mixing in the atmosphere of various industrial pollutants (primarily sulfur dioxide and nitrogen oxides) with naturally occurring oxygen and water vapor.

Act Bill passed by both houses of Congress; a law.

Acute exposure Single exposure to a toxic substance that may result in severe biological harm or death; usually characterized as lasting no longer than a day, as compared to longer, continuous exposure over a period of time.

Acute toxicity (1) Ability of a substance to cause severe biological harm or death soon after a single exposure or dose; (2) any poisonous effect that results from a single short-term exposure to a toxic substance.

Adaptive reuse Process that renovates buildings or sites for new uses while retaining historic features.

Adobe Sun-dried clay bricks common to buildings in the American Southwest and Mexico.

Adsorbent Material that is capable of collecting and binding substances or particles on its surface without chemically altering them.

Aerobic treatment Process by which microbes decompose complex organic compounds in the presence of oxygen, then use the liberated energy for reproduction and growth.

Aerosol Suspended droplets of liquid or liquid dispersions in air.

Air changes per hour (ACH) Number of times per hour a volume of air, equivalent to the volume of space, enters that space. See *Air exchange rate*.

Air exchange rate The rate at which outside air replaces indoor air in a given space. See *Air changes per hour*.

Air-handling unit Climate-control equipment that includes a fan or blower, heating and/or cooling coils, regulator controls, condensate drain pans, and air filters.

Air plenum Any space used to convey air in a building, furnace, or structure; the space above a suspended ceiling is often used as an air plenum.

Air pollution Harmful amounts of airborne contaminants or pollutants that can be harmful to the environment or human health pollutants are often grouped in categories: volatile organic compounds (VOCs); solids; particulate matter; nitrogen, oxygen, halogen compounds; radioactive compounds; and odors.

Air toxics Any air pollutant for which a National Ambient Air Quality Standard (NAAQS) does not exist that may reasonably be anticipated to cause serious or irreversible chronic or acute health effects in humans.

Airborne particulate Suspended particulate matter found in the atmosphere as solid particles or liquid droplets; sources include dust; plant pollens, emissions from industrial processes; combustion products from the burning of wood and coal; combustion products associated with gasoline, kerosene, or diesel engine exhausts, and reactions to gases in the atmosphere. See *Particulate*.

Alternative energy Energy from a source other than conventional fossil fuels (e.g., oil, natural gas, and coal). Also referred to as "alternative fuel" (e.g., sun, wind, running water). See *Alternative fuel*

Alternative fiber Fiber produced from nonwood sources for production of fabric or paper.

Alternative fuel Transportation fuel other than gasoline or diesel; includes natural gas, methanol, and electricity.

Alternative transportation Modes of travel other than private cars, e.g., walking, bicycling, rollerblading, carpooling, and mass transit.

Ambient air Surrounding air.

American Plastics Council (APC) Major trade association for the U.S. plastics industry, whose goal is to ensure that plastics are recognized as a preferred material by actively demonstrating they are a responsible choice in a more environmentally conscious world. www.plastics.org

American Society for Testing and Materials (ASTM) Not-for-profit organization that provides a forum for the development and publication of voluntary consensus standards for materials, products, systems, and services; two standards have been released in regard to sustainability. www.astm.org

Ancient forest Forest that is typically more than 200 years old with large trees, dense canopies, and an abundance of diverse wildlife.

Aquaculture Controlled rearing of fish or shellfish by people or corporations who then own the harvestable product; often involves capture of the eggs or young of a species from wild sources, followed by rearing more intensively than possible in nature.

Aquifer Underground source of water.

Ash Incombustible residue left over after incineration or other thermal processes.

ASHRAE (American Society of Heating, Refrigeration, and Air-Conditioning Engineers) International organization whose mission is to serve humanity and promote a sustainable world through research, standards writing, publishing, and continuing education. www.ashrae.org

Asthma Medical condition marked by labored breathing, constriction of the chest, coughing, and gasping for air; attack is often initiated by allergies.

Atmosphere 500-kilometer-thick layer of air surrounding the Earth that supports the existence of all flora and fauna.

Atomic energy Energy released in nuclear reactions. When a neutron splits an atom's nucleus into smaller pieces it is called fission; when two nuclei are joined together under millions of degrees of heat, it is called fusion.

B

BACT See *Best available control technology*

Bake-out Process by which a building is heated to accelerate VOC emissions from furniture and materials. See, *Volatile organic compound*.

Beach closure Prohibition of swimming, usually because of pollution.

BEES See *Building for Environmental and Economic Sustainability*.

Benefit/cost analysis Economic comparison of positive outcomes versus costs, e.g., assessing the benefits and costs of achieving alternative health–based standards at given levels of health protection.

Best available control technology (BACT) Emission limitation based on the maximum degree of emission reduction (considering energy, environmental, and economic impacts) achievable through production processes and currently available methods, systems, and techniques.

Bioaccumulant Substance that increases in concentration in living organisms as they take in contaminated air, water, or food because these substances are metabolized or excreted very slowly.

Biocide Product capable of killing microorganisms.

Biodegradable Waste that is composed of materials that occur naturally, are able to be decomposed by biological agents, and are absorbed into the ecosystem; e.g., wood is biodegradable, while plastic is not.

Biodiversity Large number and wide range of species of animals, plants, fungi, and microorganisms.

Biological contamination Contamination of a building environment caused by bacteria, molds and their spores, pollen, viruses, or other biological materials; often linked to poorly designed and maintained heating, ventilating, and air-conditioning (HVAC) systems. People exposed to biologically contaminated environments may display allergic-type responses or physical symptoms such as coughing, muscle aches, and respiratory congestion.

Biological oxygen demand (BOD) Amount of oxygen consumed in the biological processes that break down organic matter in water; used as an indirect measure of the concentration of biologically degradable material present in organic wastes. BOD can also be used as an indicator of pollutant level, whereas the greater the BOD, the greater the degree of pollution. Also referred to as "biochemical oxygen demand."

Biomass (1) Amount of living matter in an area, including plants, large animals, and insects; (2) plant materials and animal waste used as fuel.

Biomimicry Learning from nature to solve problems in design, business, and life.

Biosphere (1) Part of the Earth and its atmosphere in which living organisms exist or that is capable of supporting life; (2) the ecosystem composed of the Earth and the living organisms inhabiting it.

Biosphere reserve United Nations Educational, Scientific, and Cultural Organization (UNESCO) designation of an area that is a vital center of biodiversity, where research and monitoring activities are conducted to protect and preserve healthy natural systems threatened by development.

Birth defects Medical problems in newborns, often caused by the mother's exposure to environmental hazards or by the intake of drugs or alcohol during pregnancy.

Blood lead levels Amount of lead in the blood; high levels can cause brain damage or death, children are especially susceptible.

Brownfields U.S. Environmental Protection Agency's designation for existing facilities or sites that have been abandoned, idled, or underused and where expansion or redevelopment is complicated because of real or perceived environmental contamination.

Building envelope Elements of a building (e.g., roof, walls, and foundation) that enclose conditioned spaces. Also referred to as the "building shell."

Building for Environmental and Economic Sustainability (BEES) Software program developed by NIST (National Institute of Standards and Technology) to measure the environmental performance of building products using an environmental life-cycle assessment approach as specified in ISO 14000 standards; currently addresses categories of product choices and is therefore not specific to a type of product. The BEES software is being refined and expanded under sponsorship of the EPA's Environmentally Preferable Purchasing Program.

Building-integrated photovoltaics (BIPV) Solar panels that have been integrated into the design of a building, replacing conventional building materials, e.g., solar shingles replacing conventional asphalt shingles, providing roof protection while producing electricity.

Building-related illness Diagnosable disease or health problem whose cause and symptoms can be directly attributed to a specific pollutant source within a building (e.g., Legionnaire's disease). See *Sick building syndrome*.

By-product Material, other than the principal product, generated as a consequence of production.

C

Cairo Protocol Recommendations for stabilizing world population agreed upon at the UN International Conference on Population and Development, held in Cairo, Egypt, in September 1994; plan called for improved health-care and family-planning services throughout the world, and emphasized the importance of education for girls as a factor in the shift to smaller families.

Cancer Unregulated growth of changed cells to produce a tumor.

Captured rainwater Use of appropriate roofing materials and gutter systems to harvest and store rainwater for future nonpotable use, such as showers and hand washing.

Carbon dioxide (CO_2) (1) Naturally occurring greenhouse gas composed of oxygen and carbon, concentration's of which have increased as a result of burning coal, oil, natural gas, and organic matter; (2) odorless gas produced during respiration that is widely used as a measure of the ventilation adequacy of a space.

Carbon monoxide (CO) A colorless, odorless, and highly toxic gas created during combustion.

Carbon tax A charge on fossil fuels (coal, oil, natural gas) based on their carbon content. When burned, the carbon in these fuels becomes carbon dioxide in the atmosphere, a significant greenhouse gas.

Carpet America Recovery Effort (CARE) A voluntary initiative of the carpet industry and U.S. government to increase recycling and reuse of postconsumer carpet to prevent it from burdening landfills. www.carpetrecovery.org

Carrying capacity (1) In recreation management, the amount of use a recreation area can sustain without loss of quality; (2) in wildlife management, the maximum number of animals an area can support during a given period.

Certified wood Wood-based materials that are supplied from sustainably managed forests with documented chains of custody.

CFC See *Chlorofluorocarbon*.

CFM See *Cubic foot per minute*.

Chain of custody Documentation of the process of harvesting a raw material from a certified source through the entire manufacturing process until the final product is ready for sale.

Chemical oxygen demand (COD) Measure of the oxygen required to oxidize all compounds, both organic and inorganic, in water.

Chlorination by-products Cancer-causing chemicals created when chlorine, used for water disinfection, combines with dirt and organic matter in water.

Chlorine Highly irritating, poisonous, greenish-yellow gaseous halogen that is capable of combining with nearly all other elements; used widely to purify water, as a disinfectant and bleaching agent, and in the manufacture of many important compounds, including chloroform and carbon tetrachloride.

Chlorofluorocarbon (CFC) Artificially created chemical compound containing carbon, chlorine, fluorine, and sometimes hydrogen (i.e., HCFC) that depletes the stratospheric ozone layer, which protects Earth and its inhabitants from excessive ultraviolet radiation; CFC phaseout governed by 1987 Montreal Protocol.

CITES See *Convention on International Trade in Endangered Species of Wild Fauna and Flora*.

Clean fuel Fuel that has lower emissions than conventional gasoline and diesel fuel; refers to alternative fuels as well as to reformulated gasoline and diesel.

Clear-cutting Logging technique in which all trees are removed from an area, typically 20 acres or larger, without regard for long-term forest health.

Climate change Regional change in temperature and weather patterns; current science indicates a discernible link between human activity and climate change over the last century, specifically the burning of fossil fuels. See *Global warming*.

Closed-loop recycling Recycling system in which (1) a particular material is remanufactured into the same product (e.g., glass bottles remanufactured into glass bottles); (2) a used product or manufacturing waste is recycled into a similar product.

Coalition for Environmentally Responsible Economics (CERES) Leading U.S. coalition of environmental, investor, and advocacy groups that have committed to continuous environmental improvement by endorsing the CERES Principles, a ten-point code of environmental conduct. www.ceres.org

Cogeneration Simultaneous production of electrical or mechanical energy (power) and useful thermal energy from the same fuel/energy source such as oil, coal, gas, biomass, or solar.

Commissioning Process by which the operating systems of a building are tested and adjusted prior to occupancy.

Community right to know Public accessibility to information about toxic pollution.

Comparative risk analysis Environmental decision-making tool used to systematically measure, compare, and rank environmental problems or issues; process typically focuses on the risks a problem poses to human health, the natural environment, and quality of life, and results in a list of concerns ranked in terms of relative risk.

Compost Process whereby organic wastes, including food, paper, and yard wastes, decompose naturally, resulting in a product rich in minerals and ideal for gardening and farming as a soil conditioner, mulch, resurfacing material, or landfill cover.

Conservation Use, protection, and improvement of natural resources according to principles that will ensure their highest economic or social benefits.

Construction waste management plan (CWMP) Diversion of construction debris from landfills through conscientious plans to recycle, salvage, and reuse materials.

Construction waste recycling Separation and recycling of recoverable waste materials generated during demolition, construction, and renovation; packaging, new material scraps, appliances, masonry materials, doors and windows, and debris all constitute potentially recoverable materials.

Contaminant Physical, chemical, biological, or radiological substance that has an adverse effect on air, water, or soil.

Contamination Introduction into water, air, and soil of microorganisms, chemicals, toxic substances, wastes, or wastewater in a concentration that makes the medium unfit for its next intended use; presence of extraneous material that renders a substance or preparation impure or harmful.

Convention on International Trade in Endangered Species of Wild Fauna and Flora (CITES) International agreement between governments to ensure that international trade in specimens of wild animals and plants does not threaten their survival; resolution adopted in 1963 at a meeting of the IUCN (World Conservation Union), but didn't come into effect until 1975 after ratification by 80 countries.

Coproducts Materials that are intentionally, or incidentally, produced when making another product.

Cost/benefit analysis Economic strategy for assessing the costs and benefits of any given action. See *Benefit/cost analysis.*

Cradle-to-cradle Term used in life-cycle analysis to describe a material or product that is recycled into a new product at the end of its defined life in a closed-loop process; this concept of "no waste," modeled after nature, was introduced by architect William McDonough.

Cradle-to-grave Term used in life-cycle analysis to describe the entire life of a material or product from creation through disposal (often before the end of its defined life) with no consideration of environmental responsibility.

Critical mass Amount necessary or sufficient to have a significant effect or to achieve a result

Cubic feet per minute (CFM) Cubic feet per minute, a common measure of airflow.

D

Daylighting Method of introducing natural light into interior spaces; can reduce levels of electric lighting but requires control mechanisms to minimize glare and optimize lighting quality.

Decay rate Math calculation that reflects the declining emissions of a product over time.

Deconstruction Process to carefully dismantle or remove usable materials from structures as an alternative to demolition; options include: reusing the entire building by remodeling, moving the structure to a new location, or taking the building apart to reuse lumber, windows, doors, and other materials.

Deep-well injection Deposition of hazardous waste by pumping it into deep wells, where it is contained in the pores of permeable subsurface rock.

Deforestation Cutting and clearing away trees or forests.

Demand-side management (DSM) Attempt to reduce demand by encouraging efficiency.

Demand-side waste management Process whereby consumers use purchasing decisions to communicate to manufacturers their preferences for environmentally responsible products.

Diesel Petroleum-based fuel that is ignited by compression rather than by a spark; commonly used for heavy-duty engines, including buses and trucks.

Dioxin Chemical by-product formed during the manufacturing, molding, or burning of organic chemicals and plastics that contain chlorine; with toxicity second only to radioactive waste, it is a potent carcinogen and the cause of severe weight loss, liver and kidney problems, birth defects, and death.

Disposal Final placement or destruction of toxic, radioactive, or other wastes; surplus or banned pesticides or other chemicals; polluted soils; and drums containing hazardous materials from removal actions or accidental releases; accomplished through approval of secure landfills, surface impoundment, land farming, deep-well injection, ocean dumping, or incineration.

Dose-response Relationship between exposure levels and adverse effects.

Down-cycling Recycling a material for use in the production of a different product that will not be recyclable (i.e., extends the period of useful life, thereby delaying relegation to a landfill or incineration).

Dump site Waste-disposal area.

Dynamic environmental chamber Controlled system (including temperature, relative humidity, and air quality/purity) that utilizes realistic airflows for the assessment of chemical emissions from products and materials.

E

Eco-efficiency Concept of creating more goods and services while using fewer resources and creating less waste and pollution; coined by the World Business Council for Sustainable Development (WBCSD) in its 1992 publication *Changing Course*.

Ecologist Scientist concerned with the interrelationship of organisms and their environment.

Ecology Branch of science concerned with the interrelationship of organisms and their environment.

Ecosystem Interconnected and symbiotic grouping of animals, plants, fungi, and microorganisms that function as an interdependent unit to sustain life through biological, geological, and chemical activity.

Efficiency Accomplishment or ability to accomplish with a minimum expenditure of time and effort.

Electric vehicle Vehicle that uses electricity (usually derived from batteries recharged from electrical outlets) as their power source.

Electromagnetic field (EMF) Area of electromagnetic radiation ranging from extremely low (ELF) frequencies at 60 Hz (produced by the alternating current used by electric appliances) to radio frequency (RF) fields at 300 GHz; some research has linked high frequency EMFs to miscarriages and other disorders, including tension, irritability, and depression.

Embodied energy Energy initially required to extract, manufacture, transport, and assemble materials and components; embodied energy in recycled products is captured when they are reused.

Emission Release of gases, liquids, and/or solids from any process; liquid emission is commonly referred to as effluent.

Emission control Mechanism for reduction of emissions into air, water, or soil; the most effective emission control involves the redesign of the process so less waste is produced at the source.

Emission factor Quantity of a substance or substances released from a given area or mass of a material at a set point in time; measured in milligrams per square meter per hour.

Emissions cap Limit on the quantity of greenhouse gases that a company or country can legally emit.

Endangered species Species in danger of extinction throughout all or a significant part of its natural range.

Endocrine disruptors Substances that stop the production or block the transmission of the hormones required to maintain life.

Energy conservation Using energy efficiently or prudently.

Energy efficient Products and systems that use less energy to perform as well or better than standard products and systems; although some have higher up-front costs, energy-efficient products cost less to operate over their lifetime.

Energy Star Federal government program that labels appliances as to energy efficiency; measured in cost of operation per year.

Energy Star rating EPA and the U.S. Department of Energy (DOE) rating to designate appliances and products that exceed federal energy efficiency standards; Energy Star label helps consumers to identify products that will save energy and money.

Engineered lumber Manufactured wood materials; may employ laminated wood chips, strands, and/or finger joints; generally perceived to be stronger, lighter, straighter, and more dimensionally stable than solid sawn lumber.

Environmental footprint Company's environmental impact, determined by the amount of depletable raw materials and nonrenewable resources it consumes to make its products and the quantity of wastes and emissions that are generated in the process.

Environmental impact Any change to the environment, whether adverse or beneficial, wholly or partially resulting from human activity, industry, or natural disasters.

Environmental restoration Act of repairing damage to a site caused by human activity, industry, or natural disasters. The ideal environmental restoration, rarely achieved, is to restore the site to its natural condition before it was disturbed.

Environmental tobacco smoke (ETS) Tobacco smoke from the burning of a tobacco product and exhaled by smokers and inhaled by all; also called second-hand smoke.

Environmentally preferable product Products that have a lesser or reduced effect on human health and the environment when compared with competing products that serve the same purpose; product analysis may consider raw materials acquisition, production, manufacturing, packaging, distribution, operation, maintenance, reuse, and/or disposal.

Environmentally preferable purchasing Federal government requirement that products or services have the least negative effect on the environment and on human health across the life cycle; includes acquisition of raw materials, manufacturing methods, packaging, distribution, operation, maintenance, recyclability, and final disposal.

Eutrophication Process by which a body of water becomes enriched in dissolved nutrients (e.g., phosphates) that stimulate growth of aquatic plant life, resulting in the depletion of dissolved oxygen in the water.

Exposure Amount of radiation or pollutant present in a given environment that represents a potential health threat to living organisms.

F

Factory farming Corporate, large-scale, industrialized agriculture.

Factory ships Ships used for industrialized, large-scale collection and processing of fish.

Fauna Total animal population that inhabits an area.

Federal land Land owned and administered by the federal government, including national parks and national forests.

Fertility Ability to reproduce; in humans, the ability to bear children.

Fertility rates Average number of live births per woman during her reproductive years, for a given population.

Fisheries Established area of water where fish species are cultivated and harvested.

Fissile material (1) Substance that can be easily split by energy neutrons; (2) fissionable nuclear material.

Fission Process whereby the nucleus of a particularly heavy element splits into multiple nuclei of lighter elements, with the spontaneous release of energy.

Flora Total vegetation assemblage that inhabits an area.

Flush out Process to protect indoor air quality in which mechanical systems are operated for a minimum of two weeks, using 100 percent outside air, at the end of construction and prior to building occupancy.

Fly ash Fine, glass-powder produced as a byproduct of burning coal during the production of electricity; when mixed with lime and water, fly ash can be used as a substitute for portland cement in concrete or as a replacement for gypsum in drywall panels.

Forest certification Process of labeling wood that has been harvested from a well-managed forest and tracked as to chain of custody in order to document environmentally responsible production.

Forest Stewardship Council (FSC) Nonprofit organization that created and administers a forestry-certification program to assure the responsible management of the world's forests. www.fsc.org

Formaldehyde (CH$_2$O) Colorless, toxic, carcinogenic, water-soluble gas, derived from methyl alcohol, used primarily in aqueous solution as a disinfectant and preservative and in the manufacture of various resins and plastics.

Fossil fuel Fuel product (e.g., coal, crude oil, natural gas) produced by the decomposition of ancient (fossilized) plants and animals. See *Alternative energy*.

Fungicide Pesticides that are used to control, deter, or destroy fungi.

Fungus (Fungi) Group of organisms, including molds, mildews, yeasts, and mushrooms, that are lacking in chlorophyll and are usually nonmobile and multicellular;

may grow in soil or on decaying material to obtain nutrients; some are pathogens, others stabilize sewage and digest composted waste.

G

Gas chromatography Analytical process by which chemical mixtures are separated into individual components for quantitative and perhaps qualitative analysis.

Gasoline Petroleum fuel used by internal combustion engines.

Geothermal energy Energy obtained when rock and/or water is heated by contact with molten rock deep in the Earth's core (i.e., magma); the heat can be extracted and used for space heating, water heating, or to generate electricity.

Global warming Process that raises the air temperature in the lower atmosphere; can occur as the result of natural influences but is most often applied to the warming that occurs as a result of human activities (i.e., from the emissions of greenhouse gases).

Golden Carrot Incentive program that is designed to transform the market to achieve much greater energy efficiency; trademark of the Consortium for Energy Efficiency. www.cee1.org

Grassroots Local or person-to-person process for implementing change.

Gray water Wastewater captured from washbasins, bathtubs, showers, and clothes washers; can be recycled to flush toilets or for irrigation. See *Captured rainwater* and *Sanitary water*.

Green Blue Institute Nonprofit organization dedicated to speeding the adoption of sustainable, cradle-to-cradle thinking, and therefore impacting the design, manufacture, and use of goods and services; founded by William McDonough. www.greenblue.org/

Green building Building that provides the specified performance requirements while minimizing disturbance to the environment and improving the functioning of local, regional, and global ecosystems both during and after its construction and specified service life.

Green design (1) Micro perspective, design that protects peoples' health, safety, and welfare (e.g., a designer would not specify a product that off-gassed formaldehyde); (2) Design that conforms to environmentally sound principles of construction, material, and energy use.

Green Globes Green-management tool that includes an assessment protocol, rating system, and guide for integrating sustainable design into commercial buildings; includes a third-party certification process. www.greenglobes.com

Green Guide for Health Care (GGHC) Voluntary environmentally responsible design support for the health-care sector to integrate enhanced environmental and health principles and practices into the planning, design, construction, operations, and maintenance of their facilities.

Green Seal Independent, nonprofit organization that strives to achieve a healthier and cleaner environment by identifying and promoting products and services that cause less toxic pollution and waste, that conserve resources and habitats, and that minimize global warming and ozone depletion. www.greenseal.org

GreenGuard Certification Program Independent, third-party, voluntary testing program for low-emitting products and materials that is overseen by the GreenGuard Environmental Institute.

GreenGuard Environmental Institute (GEI) A nonprofit organization whose mission is to improve public health and quality of life through programs that improve indoor air quality. www.greenguard.org

Greenhouse effect (1) Warming of Earth's surface and lower atmosphere as a result of carbon dioxide and water vapor in the atmosphere, which absorb and reradiate infrared radiation; (2) intensification of this warming effect brought about by increased levels of carbon dioxide in the atmosphere, resulting from the burning of fossil fuels.

Greenhouse gas Gas that absorbs infrared radiation in the atmosphere; greenhouse gases include, but are not limited to, water vapor, carbon dioxide (CO_2), methane (CH_4), nitrous oxide (N_2O), chlorofluorocarbons (CFCs), hydrochlorofluorocarbons (HCFCs), ozone (O_3), hydrofluorocarbons (HFCs), perfluorocarbons (PFCs), and sulfur hexafluoride (SF_6).

Greenpeace Nonprofit organization, with a presence in 40 countries across Europe, the Americas, Asia, and the Pacific; focuses on the most crucial worldwide threats to the planet's biodiversity and environment. www.greenpeace.org

GreenSpec Product information service from BuildingGreen that contains detailed listings for more than 2,000 green and/or sustainable building products, with environmental data, manufacturer information, and links to additional resources. www.buildinggreen.com

Greenwash Purposeful dispersion of false or exaggerated information by an organization with the intent of presenting an environmentally responsible public image.

Greenway Undeveloped land, usually in cities, set aside or used for recreation or conservation.

Groundwater Water below the Earth's surface; the water source for wells and springs.

H

Habitat (1) Natural home of an animal or plant; (2) sum of the environmental conditions that determine the existence of a community in a specific place.

Halon Compound consisting of bromine, fluorine, and carbon; production in the U.S. ended in 1993 because it is much more effective at destroying ozone than chlorine.

Harvested rainwater Rainwater captured and used for indoor needs and/or irrigation.

Hazardous waste By-products of society that have physical, chemical, or infectious characteristics that pose hazards to the environment and human health when improperly treated, stored, transported, disposed, or otherwise managed.

Haze Atmospheric condition marked by a slight reduction in atmospheric visibility, resulting from air pollution, radiation of heat from the ground surface, or development of a thin mist.

Healthy Building Network National network of green building professionals, environmental and health activists, socially responsible investment advocates, and others who are interested in promoting healthier building materials as a means of improving public health and preserving the global environment.

High-performance green building Building that includes design features that conserve water and energy; use space, materials, and resources efficiently; minimize construction waste; and create healthy indoor environments.

Holistic Emphasizing the importance of the whole and the interdependence of its parts.

Household hazards Dangerous substances or conditions in human dwellings.

Hydrocarbons (HCs) Chemical compounds that consist entirely of carbon and hydrogen; fossil fuels are made up of hydrocarbons.

Hydrochlorofluorocarbon (HCFC) Fluorocarbons used to replace CFCs (primarily in aerosol cans), because they are less damaging to the ozone layer. Both HCFCs and CFCs are slated to be banned by 2030. See *Chlorofluorocarbon.*

Hydroelectric Relating to electric energy produced by moving water.

Hydrofluorocarbon (HFC) Compound consisting of hydrogen, fluorine, and carbon; HFCs are a class of replacements for CFCs that do not deplete the ozone layer, however some possess global-warming potentials that are thousands of times greater than carbon dioxide (CO_2).

Hydronic heating In-floor heating system in which hot water is pumped through tubing in a thermal-mass floor that absorbs the heat and evenly radiates it over an extended period of time.

Hydrophilic Having a strong affinity for water; attracting, dissolving in, or absorbing water.

Hydrophobic Having a strong aversion to water; repelling water.

Hypersensitivity Exaggerated immune system response to an allergen.

Hypoxia (1) Depletion of dissolved oxygen in water; (2) condition resulting from an overabundance of nutrients that stimulate the growth of algae, which in turn die, and require large amounts of oxygen for decomposition, resulting in low oxygen levels in the water.

I

Indoor Air Quality (IAQ) (1) Assessment of the indoor air to determine levels of molds, bacteria, viruses, dust mites, particulates (e.g., dust), gases (e.g., carbon monoxide), and chemicals produced by off-gassing of construction materials, furnishings, finishes, and equipment used in the building or carried into the building by the HVAC system; (2) ASHRAE defines acceptable indoor air quality as air in which there are no known contaminants at harmful concentrations as determined by cognizant authorities and with which 80 percent or more people exposed do not express dissatisfaction.

Industrialized countries Nations whose economies are based on industrial production and the conversion of raw materials into products and services, mainly with the use of machinery and artificial energy (fossil fuels and nuclear fission); generally located in the Northern and Western Hemispheres (e.g., United States, Japan, and European countries).

Integrated design team All individuals involved in a design project, including the design professionals (architect, engineers, landscape architect, and interior designer); the owner's representatives (investors, developers, building users, facility managers, and maintenance personnel); and the general contractor and subcontractors.

Integrated waste management Complementary use of a variety of practices to handle solid waste safely and effectively. Techniques include source reduction, recycling, composting, combustion, and landfill.

ISO 14001 International standard of an organization's environmental management system to minimize the harmful effects on the environment caused by its activities in order to achieve continual improvement of its environmental performance. www.iso14000-iso14001-environmental-management.com

K

Kyoto Protocol Outcome of a meeting in 1997, in which the developed nations agreed to limit their greenhouse gas emissions relative to the levels emitted in 1990. The United States' target was to reduce emissions from 1990 levels by 7 percent during the period 2008 to 2012, but the U.S. did not ratify the protocol.

L

Landfill (1) Sanitary landfill is a disposal site for nonhazardous solid waste, which is spread in layers, compacted to the smallest practical volume, and covered by material applied at the end of each operating day; (2) Secure chemical landfill is a disposal site for hazardous waste, selected and designed to minimize the chance of release of hazardous substances into the environment.

LCA in Sustainable Architecture (LISA) Software program that is a streamlined life-cycle analysis (LCA) decision-support tool for construction; intended to help identify key environmental issues in construction, to give designers an easy to use tool for evaluating the environmental aspects of building design, and to enable designers and specifiers to make informed choices based on environmental considerations. www.lisa.au.com

Lead Naturally occurring heavy, comparatively soft, malleable, bluish-gray metal; exposure can cause brain and nervous system damage, especially in children.

Lead poisoning Damage to the body (specifically the brain) from absorbing lead through the skin or by ingestion.

Least-cost planning Process for satisfying consumers' demands for energy services at the lowest societal cost.

LEED (Leadership in Energy and Environmental Design) USGBC's self-assessing, rating system for evaluation of new and existing buildings; evaluates environmental performance from a whole-building perspective over a building's life cycle, providing a definitive standard for what constitutes an environmentally responsibly designed building. www.usgbc.org/LEED/

Life-cycle analysis (LCA) Assessment of a product's full environmental costs, from raw material to final disposal, in terms of consumption of resources, energy, and waste.

Life-cycle assessment Examination of the total impact of a product's environmental and economic effects throughout its lifetime, including raw material acquisition, production, shipping, installation, operation, maintenance, and disposal.

Life-cycle cost Amortized annual cost of a product that includes raw-material acquisition, production, shippping, installation, operation, maintenance and disposal costs over the product's lifetime.

Life-cycle inventory (LCI) Accounting of the energy and waste associated with the creation of a new product through raw material acquisition, use, and disposal.

Life cycle of a product Stages of a product's development, from raw material acquisition, production, shipping, installation, operation, maintenance, and disposal.

Light pollution Environmental pollution consisting of harmful or annoying light.

Long life/loose fit Built environments that can be easily adapted to new uses in the future; they conserve the energy embodied in their construction and increase the returns on initial investment.

Low-emission vehicles Vehicles that emit little air pollution compared to conventional internal combustion engines.

Low-energy and high-performance Buildings designed to use as little energy as possible and minimal or no fossil fuel, to be resource efficient, and to incorporate value-added environmentally responsible design principles (e.g., improved indoor environment).

Low-tech Anything that does not incorporate sophisticated electronics or mechanisms.

Low toxic Degree to which a substance is poisonous to people or other living organisms.

Lowest observed adverse effect level (LOAEL) The lowest level of a stressor that causes statistically and biologically significant differences in test samples.

Lung disease Condition that damages the lung or bronchia, such as cancer or emphysema.

Lymphoma Tumor marked by swelling in the lymph nodes.

M

Mass spectrum Characteristic fingerprint of a substance, which makes its identification possible.

Mass transit See *Public transportation*.

Material safety data sheet (MSDS) Product-information sheet that identifies hazardous chemicals and health hazards, including exposure limits and precautions for workers who come into contact with these chemicals.

Material toxicity Toxic effect of materials used in the built environment, ranging from being an irritant to causing severe health problems; such toxins can be delivered through contact, ingestion, or inhalation.

Megalopolis City that is expanding so quickly that city government cannot provide services (such as police and fire protection).

Methane (CH$_4$) Colorless, nonpoisonous, flammable greenhouse gas with a global warming potential estimated at 23 times that of carbon dioxide (CO$_2$); hydrocarbon produced through anaerobic (without oxygen) decomposition of waste in landfills, animal digestion, decomposition of animal wastes, production and distribution of natural gas and petroleum, coal production, and incomplete fossil fuel combustion.

Methyl bromide (CH$_3$Br) Poisonous gas compound used primarily for insect and rodent control that depletes the stratospheric ozone layer.

Microbial growth Multiplication of microorganisms such as bacteria, algae, diatoms, plankton and fungi.

Microbiological organism Broad range of living organisms that can only be observed through a microscope.

Micron Measure of length; 1 millionth of a meter.

Moratorium Legislative action that prevents an entity from taking a specific action.

Mulch Leaves, straw, or compost used to cover growing plants to protect them from the wind or cold and to retain moisture.

Multiple chemical sensitivity (MCS) Illness in which the individual shows extreme sensitivity to very low concentrations of chemicals and other irritants that affect one or more of the body's organ systems.

N

National Ambient Air Quality Standards (NAAQS) Standards established by the EPA that apply to outdoor air throughout the United States.

Natural daylighting Use of daylight and often direct sunlight in a built environment.

Nitric oxide (NO) Gas formed under high temperature and pressure in an internal combustion engine as a by-product of fossil-fuel combustion. See *Nitrogen oxide*.

Nitrogen oxide (NO$_x$) Gas formed from nitric oxide by photochemical reactions that take place in sunlight; major component of smog and a major contributor to acid rain and to the formation of ozone in the lower atmosphere.

No observable adverse effect level (NOAEL) Exposure level at which there are no statistically or biologically significant increases in the frequency or severity of adverse effects in the exposed population.

Noise pollution Environmental pollution created by harmful or annoying noise.

Nonrenewable Does not regenerate after it has been used; not replaceable (e.g. mineral ore).

Nonrenewable energy Energy derived from depletion of fossil fuels (oil, gas, coal) that are created through lengthy geological processes and present in finite quantities on Earth.

Nonrenewable resource Resource that cannot be replaced in the environment (e.g., virgin forest) because it forms at a rate far slower than its consumption.

Nuclear energy Energy or power produced by nuclear reactions (fusion or fission). See *Fission*.

Nuclear reactor Apparatus in which nuclear fission may be initiated, maintained, and controlled to produce energy, conduct research, or produce fissile material for nuclear explosives. See *Fissile material*.

O

Oceanography Study of the ocean and ocean life.

Odor threshold Minimum odor of a water or air sample that can just be detected after successive dilutions with odorless water.

Off-gassing Process of evaporation or chemical decomposition through which vapors are released from materials; also known as "out-gassing".

Oil Mineral, vegetable, animal, or synthetic substance that is generally slippery, combustible, viscous, liquid (or liquefiable) at room temperatures, soluble in organic solvents (e.g., ether) but not in water, and used in a variety of products, especially lubricants and fuels.

Oil spill Harmful release of oil into the environment, usually into water, often killing area's flora and fauna. See *Oil*.

Old-growth forest See *Ancient forest*.

Open-loop recycling Recycling system in which a product made from one type of material is recycled into a different type of product made from the same material (e.g., used newspapers into toilet paper); the product receiving recycled material may or may not be recyclable.

Organic (1) Anything having an interrelationship with living things; (2) anything produced or grown naturally (i.e., without chemical enhancement, artificial ingredients, etc.).

Organic compound Array of substances typically characterized as principally composed of carbon and hydrogen, but which may also contain oxygen, nitrogen, and other elements as structural building blocks.

OSHA (Occupational Safety and Health Administration) Division of the U.S. Department of Labor whose mission is to assure the safety and health of America's workers by setting and enforcing standards; providing training, outreach, and education; establishing partnerships; and encouraging continual improvement in workplace safety and health.

Overdevelopment Expansion or development of land to the point of damage to the environment.

Ozone (O_3) A naturally occurring, highly reactive, irritating gas, formed by recombination of oxygen in the presence of ultraviolet radiation; accumulates in the lower atmosphere as smog pollution; forms a protective layer in the upper atmosphere that shields the Earth and its inhabitants from excessive exposure to damaging ultraviolet radiation.

Ozone depletion Reduction of the protective layer of ozone in the upper atmosphere by chemical pollution that is created by the breakdown of compounds such as CFCs or halons.

Ozone hole Seasonal decrease in the protective layer of ozone in the lower stratosphere over Antarctica caused by oxidation of ozone-depleting substances (ODS) when exposed to sunlight; during the spring, the depth of the ozone layer may decrease by as much as 50 percent.

Ozone layer Protective layer of atmosphere, 15 miles above the ground, that absorbs some of the sun's ultraviolet rays, reducing the amount of potentially harmful radiation reaching the Earth's surface.

P

Particulate Fine dust or minute discrete particles (e.g., smoke or water vapor).

Particulate pollution Pollution made up of small liquid or solid particles suspended in the atmosphere or water supply.

Passive solar (1) Technology of heating and cooling a building naturally, through the use of energy-efficient materials and proper site placement of the structure; (2) using or capturing solar energy (usually to heat water) without any external power.

Pathogen Microorganism (e.g., bacteria, virus, or parasite) that can cause disease in humans, animals, and plants.

Pesticide Chemical agent used to destroy pests, typically spiders and insects.

Petroleum Crude oil or any fraction thereof that is liquid under normal conditions of temperature and pressure; includes petroleum-based substances comprising a complex blend of hydrocarbons derived from crude oil through the process of separation, conversion, upgrading, and finishing, such as motor fuel, lubricants, petroleum solvents, and heating oil.

Photochemical oxidant Air pollutant formed by the action of sunlight on oxides of nitrogen and hydrocarbons.

Photochemical smog Air pollution caused by chemical reactions, in the presence of sunlight, of various pollutants.

Photovoltaic (PV) Capable of producing electricity from radiant energy, typically from the sun.

Plastic Durable and flexible synthetic-based material, typically petroleum based (but agriculture-based plastics are increasingly available); some plastics are difficult to recycle and/or pose problems with toxic properties (e.g., PVC plastic).

Plasticizer Any substance added to plastics or other materials to make or keep them soft or pliable.

PM$_{10}$ Particulate matter less than 10 microns in diameter.

Poison runoff See *Polluted runoff*.

Polluted runoff Precipitation that captures pollution from agricultural lands, urban streets, parking lots, or suburban lawns and transports it to rivers, lakes, or oceans.

Pollution Presence of a substance in the environment that, because of its chemical composition or quantity, prevents the functioning of natural processes and produces undesirable environmental and health effects.

Polyvinyl chloride (PVC) Fine-grained resin produced by combining ethylene (derived from petroleum, natural gas, or coal) and chlorine to form chlorinated vinyl plastic, a durable, flexible material used for vinyl flooring, upholstery, and siding; dioxin, an extremely toxic chemical, is released during production; toxic PVC vapors are off-gassed during installation or when burned as waste.

Postconsumer material Any household or commercial product that is at end of useful life in it's original form and for its intended use.

Postconsumer recycled content Product composition that includes a percentage of material that has been reclaimed from the same or another end use at the conclusion of its former, useful life.

Postconsumer waste Waste collected after the consumer has used and disposed of it (e.g., cardboard shipping box).

Postindustrial or preconsumer content Waste produced during the manufacturing process of virgin material and rerouted from one step in the process to the next. This does not refer to recycled material.

Postindustrial or preconsumer recycled content Product composition that includes some percentage of manufacturing waste material that has been reclaimed from a process generating the same or a similar product.

ppb Parts per billion.

ppm Parts per million.

Preconsumer recycled content See *Postindustrial recycled content*.

Public land Land owned in common by all and managed by the government (town, county, state, or federal).

Public transportation Shared-ride services, including buses, vans, trolleys, and subways that are intended for conveying the public.

Pyrolysis Decomposition of a chemical by extreme heat.

R

Radiant heat Flexible tubing installed under flooring, behind walls, or above the ceiling to circulate warm water as a heat source; in the ceiling, electric wire can be substituted for tubing.

Radioactive Capable of emitting radiation, including alpha particles, nucleons, electrons, and gamma rays.

Radioactive waste By-product of nuclear reactions that emits (usually harmful) radiation.

Radioactivity Spontaneous emission of matter or energy from the nucleus of an unstable atom, usually in the form of alpha or beta particles, gamma rays, or neutrons.

Radon Cancer-causing radioactive gas found in ground water.

Rammed-earth building Building made from wall forms filled with earth instead of poured concrete.

Rapidly renewable Raw materials that are not depleted when used; typically harvested from fast-growing sources that do not require unnecessary chemical support (e.g., bamboo, flax, wheat, wool).

Reclamation Restoration of materials found in the waste stream to a beneficial use that may be other than the original use.

Recyclability Ability of a product or material to be recovered or diverted from the solid-waste stream for the purpose of recycling.

Recycling Process by which materials that would otherwise become solid waste are collected, separated, or processed, and then returned to the economic mainstream to be reused in the form of raw materials or finished goods.

Reduce Act of purchasing or consuming less, so as not to have to reuse or recycle later.

Refrigerants Cooling substances, many of which contain CFCs that are harmful to the Earth's ozone layer.

Relative humidity Ratio of the amount of water vapor in air at a specific temperature to the maximum capacity of the air at that temperature.

Remanufacturing Production of a usable product from an existing product through a cleaning or repairing process.

Renewable resource Materials that can be replenished (e.g., sustainably managed forests) or are virtually inexhaustible (e.g., mud, clay, sand)

Replenishable energy Energy harvested from the sun, wind, or water.

Replenishable resource Materials from renewable sources (e.g., straw or sustainably managed forests) or virtually inexhaustible ones (e.g., mud or sand).

Reservoir Artificial lake created and used for the storage of water.

Resource conservation Practices that protect, preserve, or renew natural resources.

Resource efficiency Practice in which material use begins with the concept of "reduce, reuse, recycle" in descending order of priority; in design, the goal is to reduce the amount of material that is specified; to reuse materials, to recycle products or product waste; to specify products made from recycled materials; and to repair or restore products instead of replacing them.

Respirable Particles or aerosols less than 3 microns in diameter capable of being inhaled deep into the lung.

Reuse Using a material, product, or component of the waste stream in its original form more than once, rather than recycling it into other products.

Riparian Located alongside a watercourse, typically a river.

Risk assessment Measure of the probability of an adverse effect on a population or the environment under a well-defined exposure scenario.

Risk factor Characteristics (e.g., race, gender, age, obesity) or variables (i.e., smoking, occupational exposure level) associated with increased probability of a toxic effect.

Runoff Precipitation that the ground does not absorb and that, ultimately, reaches rivers, lakes, or oceans.

S

Salvage logging The logging of dead or diseased trees to improve overall forest health; sometimes used by timber companies as a rationalization to log otherwise protected areas.

Salvaged material Reusable material from carefully demolished or deconstructed buildings.

Sanitary sewer Underground pipes that carry domestic or industrial waste but not storm water.

Sanitary survey On-site review of the water sources, facilities, equipment, operation, and maintenance of a public water system to evaluate the adequacy of those elements for producing and distributing safe drinking water.

Sanitary water Water discharged from sinks, showers, kitchens, or other nonindustrial operations but not from toilets. Also referred to as "gray water."

Scientific Certification Systems (SCS) Independent, third-party testing and certification organization whose Environmental Claims Certification program validates a wide variety of claims related to environmental achievement in the product manufacturing and natural resource extraction sectors; SCS also certifies Environmentally Preferable Products, which are products or services that can demonstrate a reduced or lessened environmental impact when compared to other products performing the same function. www.scscertified.com/

Second-growth forests Forests that have grown back after being logged.

SERP (Super-Efficient Refrigerator Program) Competition developed by 24 U.S. utilities to produce a refrigerator with at least 25 percent lower energy use and 85 percent lower ozone depletion; Whirlpool produced the winning product which cut energy use by 40 percent in 1995.

Sick building syndrome Illness in a building whose occupants experience acute health and/or comfort effects (e.g., headache; runny nose; inflamed, itchy eyes; cough, etc.) that appear to be linked to time spent therein but where no specific cause can be identified; complaints may be localized in a particular room or zone or may spread throughout the building; symptoms diminish or abate on leaving the building. See *Building-related illness*.

SIP (State Implementation Plan) Mandate for achieving health-based air quality standards.

Smog Dense, discolored fog containing large quantities of soot, ash, and gaseous pollutants, such as sulfur dioxide and carbon dioxide, responsible for human respiratory ailments. Most industrialized nations have implemented legislation to promote the use of smokeless fuel to reduce emission of toxic gases.

Solar energy Energy derived from sunlight.

Solar photovoltaic electricity Electricity produced by silicon solar panels that can be immediately used, stored in batteries, or sold back to the utility grid.

Solar water heating Solar collectors used to convert the sun's energy into heat for hot water, space heating, or industrial processes.

Solid waste Nonliquid, nongaseous category of waste from nontoxic household and commercial sources.

Soot A fine, sticky powder, comprised mostly of carbon, formed by the burning of fossil fuels.

Source reduction (1) Design, manufacture, purchase, or use of materials to reduce the amount or toxicity of waste in order to reduce pollution and conserve resources; (2) practices that reduce the amount of any hazardous substance, pollutant, or contaminant entering a waste stream or otherwise released into the environment.

Stack effect Flow of air resulting from warm air rising, creating a positive-pressure area at the top of a building and negative-pressure area at the bottom, which can overpower the mechanical system and disrupt building ventilation and air circulation.

Sterilizer One of three groups of antimicrobials registered by the EPA for public health use that destroys or eliminates all forms of bacteria, viruses, and fungi and their spores; because spores are considered the most difficult form of microorganism to destroy, the EPA considers the term "sporicide" to be synonymous with "sterilizer."

Stratosphere Upper portion of the atmosphere (approximately 11 km to 50 km above the surface of the Earth).

Straw-bale construction Building walls constructed of stacked and tightly wrapped hay bales coated with mud, plaster, or concrete stucco.

Strip mining Mining technique in which the land and vegetation covering the desired mineral are stripped away by huge machines, usually damaging the land severely and limiting subsequent use.

Sulfur dioxide (SO_2) Colorless, nonflammable, water-soluble, suffocating gas formed when sulfur burns; can be condensed into a clear liquid used to make sulfuric acid; a major source of air pollution in industrial areas.

Surface water Water located above ground (e.g., rivers, lakes).

Sustainability Ability of a system to continue functioning into the future without being forced into decline through exhaustion or overloading of the key resources on which that system depends.

Sustainable Buildings Industry Council (SBIC) A nonprofit organization whose mission is to advance the design, affordability, energy performance, and environmental soundness of residential, institutional, and commercial buildings. www.sbicouncil.org/

Sustainable communities Communities capable of maintaining their present levels of growth without limiting future generations' ability to live in them.

Sustainable design Macro perspective: sustainable design protects Earth's health and welfare (e.g., a designer would not specify a product that contributed to rain forest destruction); design practice that "meets the needs of the present without compromising the ability of future generations to meet their needs" (UN World Commission on Environment and Development 1987, 54). See *Green design*.

Sustainable development Approach to progress that "meets the needs of the present without compromising the ability of future generations to meet their needs" (UN World Commission on Environment and Development 1987, 54).

Sustainable practices Policies and procedures that provide ongoing economic and social benefits without degrading the environment.

Sustainable-yield vs. ecologically sustainable forestry Sustainable-yield forestry requires the same number of trees be planted as are cut down (e.g., clear-cutting with 100 percent of the trees replanted); ecologically sustainable forestry requires the management of a productive forest so that it supports a healthy ecosystem.

T

Tap water Drinking water that is monitored (and often filtered) for protection against contamination and is available for public consumption.

Technical nutrient Material or product that can be retrieved and reused, therefore remaining in a closed-loop system and maintaining its value through many product life cycles; component of the cradle-to-cradle concept credited to William McDonough.

Telecommuting Working with others via telecommunications technologies (e.g., telephones, internet connections, faxes) without physically traveling to an office.

Thermal comfort Appropriate combination of temperature (i.e., air is warmed or cooled) airflow, and humidity that allows an individual to be comfortable within the confines of a building.

Thermal mass Heat-holding capacity of a material; heat is collected and stored (often using masonry or water), then slowly released.

Thermal pollution Addition of sufficient heat to a body of water to change the ecological balance.

Thermonuclear Application of high heat, obtained via fission, to bring about fusion of nuclei.

Threatened species Species of flora or fauna likely to become endangered within the foreseeable future.

Threshold limit value (TLV) Concentration of an airborne substance to which an average person can be repeatedly exposed without adverse effects.

Tipping fee Charge for the unloading or dumping of waste at a recycling facility, composting facility, landfill, transfer station, or waste-to-energy facility.

Total Environmental Impact (TEI) Index Tool developed by INVISTA Antron that includes value recovery of waste materials as well as a measure of societal impact.

Total life-cycle costing Life-cycle analysis that includes social costs and benefits, the ecological impact of the materials, and the recyclability of the components.

Total volatile organic compounds (TVOC) The total mass, typically in milligrams per cubic meter, of the organic compounds held in suspension in the ambient air.

Toxic The ability to cause severe biological harm or death after exposure or dose.

Toxic emissions Poisonous chemicals discharged to air, water, or land.

Toxic off-gassing Vapors produced at room temperature by the drying and curing of construction materials, furnishings, or finish materials that have been shown to cause death (e.g., formaldehyde found in carpets and some manufactured wood; phenol in fiberglass insulation; volatile organic compounds found in paints, adhesives, and plastics).

Toxic sites Land contaminated with toxic pollution, therefore unsuitable for human habitation.

Toxic waste Garbage or waste that can injure, poison, or harm living organisms or be life threatening.

Toxicity The property of a material, or combination of materials, to adversely affect organisms by poisoning them.

U

United States Green Building Council (USGBC) Coalition of leaders from across the building industry working to promote construction of built environments that are environmentally responsible, profitable, and healthy places to live and work. www.USGBC.org

Unsustainable practices Policies and procedures that meet an immediate need but with time deplete or damage natural resources.

Up-cycling Creation of a product with higher intrinsic value, manufactured from a material at the end of its service life that had a lower initial end-use value; up-cycling may be less environmentally responsible if energy used is more than would be used in recycling back to the same product.

Urban planning Science of managing and directing city growth.

Utilities Companies permitted by a government agency to provide important public services (such as electricity, energy, or water) to a region; when utilities are provided with a local monopoly, their prices are regulated by the permitting government agency.

V

Vinyl See *Polyvinyl chloride.*

Virgin forest See *Ancient forest.*

Volatile organic compound (VOC) (1) Organic substances capable of entering the gas phase from either a liquid or solid form; (2) highly evaporative, carbon-based chemical substance that produces noxious fumes; found in many paints, caulks, stains, and adhesives.

W

Waste Items or material discarded or rejected as useless or worthless; trash, rubbish, refuse, and/or garbage.

Waste reduction (1) Preventing or eliminating the amount of waste generated at its source; (2) reducing the amount of toxicity from waste; (3) the reuse of materials.

Waste site Uncontrolled or abandoned place where waste is located, possibly affecting local ecosystems or people; Superfund is the federal government's program to clean up uncontrolled hazardous waste sites.

Waste stream Total flow of solid waste from homes, businesses, institutions, and manufacturing that is recycled, burned, or disposed of in landfills.

Waste to energy Burning of industrial waste to provide steam, heat, or electricity; sometimes referred to as waste-to-fuel process.

Wastewater Water that has been contaminated by being used for washing, bathing, or flushing a toilet, or used in a manufacturing process.

Water filters Substances (such as charcoal) or fine-membrane structures used to remove impurities from water.

Water-quality testing Monitoring water for various contaminants to determine if it is safe for fish protection, drinking, and swimming.

Waterborne contaminant Unhealthy chemical, microorganism (like bacteria), or radiation found in tap water.

Watershed Region or area over which water flows into a particular lake, reservoir, stream, or river.

Wetland Land (marshes or swamps) constantly or recurrently saturated with water; typically conducive to wide biodiversity.

Wilderness area Undeveloped area that Congress has preserved by including it in the National Wilderness Preservation System.

Wildlife refuge Land set aside to protect certain species of fish or wildlife (administered at the federal level in the United States by the Fish and Wildlife Service).

Wind power energy Energy generated through the use of a turbine that collects wind energy and converts it to electricity.

Wise Use Movement A loosely affiliated network of people and organizations throughout the United States in favor of widespread privatization and opposed to environmental regulation; often funded by corporate dollars.

X

Xeriscape Low-maintenance landscaping that conserves water and protects the environment by using soil analysis, mulch, and appropriate plant selection.

Z

Zero-emission vehicles Vehicles (usually powered by electricity) with no direct emissions from tailpipes or fuel evaporation.

Zoning Arrangement or partitioning of land areas for various types of usage in cities, boroughs, or townships.

Bibliography

Adams, W. M. 1990. *Green Development: Environment and Sustainability in the Third World.* London: Routledge.

Adams, C., and L. Elizabeth, eds. 2005. *Alternative Construction: Contemporary Natural Building Methods,* rev. ed. Hoboken, NJ: John Wiley & Sons.

Air Quality Sciences. 2000. *AQSpec List: A Guide to Indoor Environmentally Preferred Products.* Atlanta, GA: Air Quality Sciences.

Allenby, B. 2005. *Reconstructing Earth: Technology and Environment in the Age of Humans.* Washington, DC: Island Press.

Alexander, S., and B. Greber. 1991. *Environmental Ramifications of Various Building Materials Used in Construction and Manufacture in the United States.* Portland, OR: U.S. Dept. of Agriculture, Forest Service, Pacific Northwest Research Station.

American Institute of Architects (AIA). 1991. *Energy, Environment, and Architecture.* Washington, DC: AIA.

————. 1993. *Design and the Environment.* Washington, DC: AIA.

————. Biannual. *Environmental Resource Guide.* Hoboken, NJ: John Wiley & Sons.

Anderson, R. C. 1995. *The Journey from There to Here: The Eco-odyssey of a CEO.* Atlanta, GA: Peregrinzilla Press.

————. 1998. *Mid-Course Correction: Toward a Sustainable Enterprise, The Interface Model.* Atlanta, GA: Peregrinzilla Press.

Anink, D. 1996. *Handbook of Sustainable Building: An Environmental Preference Method for Selection of Materials for Use in Construction and Refurbishment.* London: Earthscan Publications.

Architects for Social Responsibility. n.d. *The Source Book for Sustainable Design: A Guide to Environmentally Responsible Building Materials and Processes.* Cambridge, MA: Architects for Social Responsibility.

Baker, N., and K. Steemers. 2000. *Energy and Environment in Architecture: A Technical Design Guide.* New York: Routledge.

Barnett, D. L., and W. D. Browning. 1998. *A Primer on Sustainable Building.* Snowmass, CO: Rocky Mountain Institute.

Battle, G., and C. McCarthy. 2001. *Sustainable Ecosystems and the Built Environment.* New York: John Wiley & Sons.

Behling, S., and S. Behling. 2000. *Solar Power: The Evaluation of Sustainable Architecture.* New York: Prestel.

Benyus, J. M. 1997. *Biomimicry: Innovation Inspired by Nature.* New York: Perennial.

Bierman-Lytle, P., and J. Marinelli. 1995. *Your Natural Home: A Complete Sourcebook and Design Manual for Creating a Healthy, Beautiful, Environmentally Sensitive House.* Boston: Little, Brown.

Bolini, B., ed. 1986. *The Greenhouse Effect, Climate Change, and Ecosystems.* New York: John Wiley & Sons.

Bonda, P. 2005. *Creating Sustainable Interiors.* Washington, DC: National Council for Interior Design Qualification.

Bonda, P., and K. Sosnowchik. 2006. *Sustainable Commercial Interiors.* Hoboken, NJ: John Wiley & Sons.

Boston Society of Architects. n.d. *Sourcebook for Sustainable Design.* Boston, MA: Boston Society of Architects.

Bower, J. 2000. *Healthy House Building for the New Millennium: A Design and Construction Guide.* Bloomington, IN: The Healthy House Institute.

Bower, J. 2000. *The Healthy House: How To Buy One, How To Build One, How To Cure a Sick One,* 4th ed. New York: Healthy House Institute.

Braungart, M., and W. McDonough. 2002. *Cradle to Cradle: Remaking the Way We Make Things.* New York: North Point Press.

Brown, H. 1999. *High-Performance Building Guidelines.* New York: City of New York Department of Design and Construction.

Browning, W. D., Green Development Services, Rocky Mountain Institute, and D. Lopez Barnett. 1995. *A Primer on Sustainable Building.* Snowmass, CO: The Institute.

Building Design and Construction. 2005. *Building Design and Construction White Paper: Life Cycle Assessment and Sustainability.* Oak Brook, IL: Building Design and Construction.

Buzzelli, D. T., and J. Lash. 1996. *Sustainable America: A New Consensus.* Washington, DC: Government Printing Office.

Carson, R. 1965. *Silent Spring.* New York: Houghton Mifflin.

Chatterjee, P., and M. Finger. 1994. *The Earth Brokers.* London: Routledge.

Chiras, D. D. 2000. *The Natural House: A Complete Guide to Healthy, Energy-Efficient Environmental Homes.* White River Junction, VT: Chelsea Green Publishing Company.

———. 2004. *The New Ecological Home: The Complete Guide to Green Building Options.* White River Junction, VT: Chelsea Green Publishing Company.

Christopher, A. 1979. *The Timeless Way of Building.* New York: Oxford University Press.

Clayton, A., and N. Radcliffe. 1996. *Sustainability: A Systems Approach.* London: Houghton Mifflin.

Colorado State University. n.d. *Institute for the Built Environment* (brochure). Fort Collins, CO: Colorado State University.

Craven, J. 2003. *The Healthy Home: Beautiful Interiors That Enhance the Environment and Your Well-Being.* Gloucester, MA: Quarry Books/Rockport Publishers.

Cronon, W., ed. 1996. *Uncommon Ground: Rethinking the Human Place in Nature.* New York: W. W. Norton.

Crosbie, M. J. 1994. *Green Architecture: A Guide to Sustainable Design.* Rockport, MA: Rockport Publishers.

Croxton Collaborative and National Audubon Society. 1994. *Audubon House: Building the Environmentally Responsible Energy Efficient Office.* New York: John Wiley & Sons.

Dadd-Redalia, D. 1994. *Sustaining the Earth: Choosing Consumer Products that Are Safe for You, Your Family, and the Earth.* New York: Hearst Books.

Daly, H., and J. Cobb. 1989. *For the Common Good: Redirecting the Economy towards Community, the Environment, and a Sustainable Future.* Boston, MA: Beacon.

Dean, A. M. 2003. *Green by Design: Creating a Home for Sustainable Living.* Salt Lake City, UT: Gibbs Smith.

DeSimone, L., and F. Popoff. 1997. *Eco-Efficiency: The Business Link to Sustainable Development.* Cambridge, MA: MIT Press.

Devall, B., ed. 1994. *Clearcut: The Tragedy of Industrial Forestry.* San Francisco: Sierra Books/Earth Island Press.

Dorf, R. C. 2001. *Technology, Humans, and Society: Toward a Sustainable World.* San Diego, CA: Academic Press.

Dresner, S. 2002. *The Principles of Sustainability.* London: Earthscan Publications.

Durning, A. 1992. *How Much Is Enough?* New York: Norton.

Dyson, F. 1992. *From Eros to Gaia.* New York: Pantheon.

Earth Pledge Foundation. 2000. *Sustainable Architecture White Papers.* New York: Earth Pledge Foundation.

Ecotone. 2005. *Who's Green 2006: The Directory of Who's Green in the Design and Construction Field.* Kansas City, MO: Ecotone.

Edwards, A. R. 2005. *The Sustainability Revolution: Portrait of a Paradigm Shift.* Gabriola Island, BC: New Society Publishers.

Edwards, B. 2001. *Green Architecture.* London: John Wiley & Sons.

Ehrlich, P. R., and A. H. Ehrlich. 1991. *The Population Explosion.* New York: Simon & Schuster.

Environmental Protection Agency (EPA). 2002. *Solid Waste Management and Greenhouse Gases: A Life-Cycle Assessment of Emissions and Sinks,* 2nd ed. Washington, DC: EPA.

Envirosense Consortium. 1993. *IAQ management.* Kennesaw, GA: Envirosense Consortium.

Foster, K. 2006. *Sustainable Residential Interiors.* Hoboken, NJ: John Wiley & Sons.

Fiksel. J. 1995. *Design for Environment: Creating Eco-Efficient Products and Processes.* New York: McGraw-Hill.

Frei, A. B. 2005. *Green Office Buildings: A Practical Guide to Development.* Washington, DC: Urban Land Institute.

Fuad-Lake, A. 2002. *Eco Design: The Sourcebook.* San Francisco: Chronicle Books.

Galbraith, J. K. 1958. *The Affluent Society.* New York: New American Library.

Gladwell, M. 2000. *The Tipping Point: How Little Things Can Make a Big Difference.* New York: Little Brown.

Godish, T. 2001. *Indoor Environmental Quality.* New York: Lewis Publishers.

Goldsmith, E., and N. Hildyard. 1990. *The Earth Report: An Essential Guide to Global Ecological Issues.* New York: Price, Stern, Sloan.

Goodland, H., S. Daly, and S. El-Serafy. 1992. *Population, Technology and Lifestyle: The Transition to Sustainability.* Washington, DC: Island Press.

Greenguard Environmental Institute. 2005. *2005 Greenguard Indoor Air Quality Guide.* Atlanta, GA: Greenguard Environmental Institute.

Hawken, P. 1993. *The Ecology of Commerce: A Declaration of Sustainability.* New York: HarperCollins.

Hawken, P., A. Lovins, and L. H. Lovins. 1999. *Natural Capitalism: Creating the Next Industrial Revolution.* New York: Little, Brown.

Hawthorne, C., and A. Stang. 2005. *The Green House: New Directions in Sustainable Architecture.* New York: Princeton Architectural Press; Washington, DC: National Building Museum.

Henshilwood, C., F. d'Errico, R. Yates, Z. Jacobs, C. Tribolo, et al. 2002. "Emergence of Modern Human Behavior: Middle Stone Age Engravings from South Africa. *Science 295* (February 15): 1278–1280.

Hermannsson, J. n.d. *The Green Building Resource Guide.* Newtown, CT: Tauton Press. http://www.greenguide.com.

Hobbs, A. 2003. *The Sick House Survival Guide: Simple Steps to Healthier Homes.* Gabriola Island, BC: New Society Publishers.

Home Energy. 2005. *Home Energy: Advancing Home Performance.* Berkeley, CA: Home Energy.

Huxley, A. 1932. *Brave New World.* London: Chatto & Windus.

Incentive Travel and Meeting Executives Show. 2000. *2000 IT and ME Green Directory.* New York: Incentive Travel and Meeting Executives Show.

Intergovernmental Panel on Climate Change. 2001. *Climate Change 2001.* Geneva: World Meteorological Organization.

International Union for Conservation of Nature and Natural Resources (IUCN). 1980. *World Conservation Strategy: Living Resources Conservation for Sustainable Development.* Gland, Switzerland: IUCN.

Johnston, D., and K. Master. 2004. *Green Remodeling: Changing the World One Room at a Time.* Gabriola Island, BC: New Society Publishers.

Jones, D. L. 1998. *Architecture and the Environment—Contemporary Green Buildings.* Woodstock, NY: Overlook Press.

Kalin Associates. 1996. *GreenSpec: Specifications for Environmental Sustainability.* Newton Centre, MA: Kalin Associates.

Kellert, S. R. 2005. *Building for Life: Designing and Understanding the Human-Nature Connection.* Washington, DC: Island Press.

Kennedy, J. F. 2002. *Art of Natural Building.* Gabriola Island, BC: New Society Publishers.

Kibert, C. J. 1999. *Reshaping the Built Environment: Ecology, Ethics, and Economics.* Washington, DC: Island Press.

———. 2005. *Sustainable Construction: Green Building Design and Delivery.* Hoboken, NJ: John Wiley & Sons.

Kirk, S. J., and A. Dell'Isola. 1995. *Life-Cycle Costing for Design Professionals.* New York: McGraw-Hill.

Krasner, L., ed. 1980. *Environmental Design and Human Behavior: A Psychology of the Individual in Society.* New York: Pergamon Press.

Kunkle, K. R. 2004. "Content Analysis: Sustainable/Green Design Taught in FIDER Accredited Interior Design Programs' Curriculum." Master's thesis, Eastern Michigan University, 2004.

Laporte, P. B., E. Elliott, and J. Banta. 2001. *Prescriptions for a Healthy House: A Practical Guide for Architects, Builders, and Homeowners,* 2nd ed. Gabriola Island, BC: New Society Publishers.

Lerner, S. 1997. *Eco-Pioneers: Practical Visionaries Solving Today's Environmental Problems.* Cambridge, MA: MIT Press.

Lock, J. 1983. *Two Treatises of Government.* London: Everyman.

Lopez-Barnett, D., and W. Browning. 1995. *A Primer on Sustainable Building.* Aspen, CO: Rocky Mountain Institute.

Lovelock, J. 1997. *The Ages of Gaia: A Biography of Our Living Earth.* Oxford: Oxford University Press.

Lovins, H. 2005. *The Next Sustainability Wave: Building Boardroom Buy-In (Conscientious Commerce).* Gabriola Island, BC: New Society Publishers.

Lyons, K. 2000. *Buying for the Future: Contract Management and the Environmental Challenge.* Sterling, VA: Pluto Press.

Maddox, J. 1972. *The Doomsday Syndrome.* London: Macmillan.

Magadi, S. N. 2005. "Perception and Implementation of Sustainable/Green Design in India." Master's thesis, Eastern Michigan University, 2005.

Makower, J. 1993. *The E Factor: The Bottom-Line Approach to Environmentally Responsible Business.* New York: Tilden Press.

Marcus, A. 2002. *Reinventing Environmental Regulation.* Washington, DC: RFF Press.

Marinelli, J., and P. Bierman-Lytle. 1995. *Your Natural Home.* New York: Little Brown and Company.

Marx, K., and F. Engels. 1848. *The Communist Manifesto.*

McDonough, W. 1995. *Textiles: Environmentally Intelligent,* 2nd ed. New York: Designtex.

McDonough, W., and M. Braungart. 2002. *Cradle to Cradle: Remaking the Way We Make Things.* New York: North Point Press.

McGraw-Hill Construction and U.S. Green Building Council (USGBC). 2005. *Green Building Smartmarket Report: 2006 Green Building Issue.* New York: McGraw-Hill Construction and USGBC.

McHarg, I. 1992. *Design with Nature.* New York: John Wiley & Sons.

McLennan, J. F. 2004. *The Philosophy of Sustainable Design.* Kansas City, MO: Ecotone Publishing.

Mendler, S., W. Odell, and M. A. Lazarus. 2006. *The HOK Guidebook to Sustainable Design,* 2nd ed. Hoboken, NJ: John Wiley & Sons.

Merkel, J. 2003. *Radical Simplicity: Small Footprints on a Finite Earth.* Gabriola Island, BC: New Society Publishers.

Metz, D. 2004. *The Big Book of Small House Designs: 75 Award-Winning Plans for Your Dream House, All 1,250 Square Feet or Less.* New York: Black Dog and Leventhal Publishers.

Mumma, T. 1997. *Guide to Resource Efficient Building Elements.* Missoula, MT: National Center for Appropriate Technology, Center for Resourceful Building Technology.

Myers, N., ed. 1984. *Gaia: An Atlas of Planet Management.* Garden City, NJ: Doubleday.

National Association of Home Builders (NAHB) Research Center. 2000. *A Guide to Developing Green Builder Programs.* Washington, DC: NAHB.

National Audubon Society. 1991. *Audubon Headquarters: Building for an Environmental Future.* New York: National Audubon Society.

National Audubon Society and Croxton Collaborative. 1994. *Audubon House: Building the Environmentally Responsible, Energy-Efficient Office.* Hoboken, NJ: John Wiley & Sons.

National Building Museum. 2002. *Big and Green: Toward Sustainable Architecture in the 21st century.* New York: Princeton Architectural Press.

National Park Service, Denver Service Center. 1993. *Guiding Principles of Sustainable Design.* Denver, CO: National Park Service.

National Research Council. 1999. *Our Common Journey.* Washington, DC: National Academy Press.

Nelson, G. 1989. *A Brief History of Earth Day.* Congressional Record April 20, 1990. Washington, DC: Government Printing Office.

Neuzil, M., and W. Kovari. 1996. *Mass Media and Environmental Conflict.* Thousand Oaks, CA: Sage.

Nor, S. A. 2002. "Occupant's Perception of Indoor Air Quality: A Comparison of Green and Conventional Finishes and Furnishings." Master's thesis, Eastern Michigan University, 2002.

Norman, D. 1990. *The Design of Everyday Things.* New York: Doubleday.

Norman, M. E. F. 2003. "Shades of Green: A Sustainable Resource Guide for Interior Designers, Architects, Students, and Educators Committed to Making A Difference." Master's thesis, Eastern Michigan University, 2003.

Orr, D. 1992. *Ecological Literacy: Education and the Transition to a Postmodern World.* Albany, NY: State University of New York Press.

Papanek, V. 1984. *Design for the Real World: Human Ecology and Social Change.* London: Thames and Hudson.

Pearce, D. W., and Moran, D. 1994. *The Economic Value of Biological Diversity.* London: Earthscan.

Pearce, D. W., A. Markandya, and E. Barbier. 1989. *Blueprint for a Green Economy.* London: Earthscan

———. 1990. "Environmental Sustainability and Cost Benefit Analysis?" *Environment and Planning 22*: 1259–1266.

Pearson, D. 1989. *The Natural House Book.* New York: Simon and Schuster.

Peters, R., and T. Lovejoy, eds. 1992. *Global Warming and Biological Diversity.* New Haven, CT: Yale University Press.

Pilatowicz, G. 1995. *Eco-Interiors: A Guide to Environmentally Conscious Interior Design.* New York: John Wiley & Sons.

Ponting, C. 1991. *A Green History of the World: The Environment and the Collapse of Great Civilizations.* New York: Penguin Books

Quinn, D. 1993. *Ishmael.* New York: Bantam Books.

Richard, D. A. J. 1971. *A Theory of Reasons for Action.* Oxford: Clarendon Press.

Rifkin, J. 1990. *The Green Lifestyle Handbook.* New York: Henry Holt.

Riggs, J. R. 2003. *Materials and Components of Interior Architecture.* 6th ed. Englewood Cliffs, NJ: Prentice Hall.

Robert, Karl-Hendrick. 1997. *The Natural Step: A Framework for Achieving Sustainability.* Cambridge, MA: Pegasus.

Rocky Mountain Institute. 1998. *Green Development: Integrating Ecology and Real Estate.* New York: John Wiley & Sons.

Roodman, D. M., and N. Lenssen. 1995. *A Building Revolution: How Ecology and Health Concerns Are Transforming Construction.* Worldwatch Paper 124. Washington, DC: World Watch Institute.

Roome, N., and M. Hinnells. 1993. "Environmental Factors in the Management of New Product Development." *Business Strategy and the Environment 2*: 12–27.

Samuels, R., and D. K. Prasad. 1994. *Global Warming and the Built Environment.* New York: E & FN Spon.

Schomer, V. 1993. *Interior Concerns Resource Guide: A Guide to Sustainable and Healthy Products and Educational Information for Designing and Building.* Mill Valley, CA: Interior Concerns Publications.

Schumacher, B. 2006. *LEED-NC Sample Exam.* Belmont, CA: Professional Publications.

Schumacher, E. F. 1973. *Small Is Beautiful.* New York: Harper & Row.

Scott, A. 1998. *Dimensions of Sustainability.* New York: E & FN Spon.

Seymour, J., and H. Giardet. 1990. *Blueprint for a Green Planet.* Englewood Cliffs, NJ: Prentice-Hall.

Sitarz, D., ed. *Agenda 21: The Earth Summit Strategy to Save Our Planet.* Boulder, CO: Earth Press.

Slessor, C. 2001. *Eco-Tech: Sustainable Architecture and High Technology.* New York: John Linden.

Smart, B. 1992. *Beyond Compliance: A New Industry View of the Environment.* Washington, DC: World Resources Institute.

Smith, P. F. 2005. *Architecture in a Climate of Change: A Guide To Sustainable Design,* 2nd ed. Boston, MA: Elsevier/Architectural Press.

Snell, C., and T. Callahan. 2006. Building Green: A Complete How-To Guide to Alternative Building Methods. New York: Sterling Publishing.

Spiegel, R. 1999. *Green Building Materials: A Guide to Product Selection and Specification.* New York: John Wiley & Sons.

Springer, D. L., and S. Toshach, eds. 1993. *Design and the Environment.* Washington, DC: American Institute of Architects.

Stang, A., and C. Hawthorne. 2005. *The Green House: New Directions in Sustainable Architecture.* New York: Princeton Architectural Press.

Steele, J. 1997. *Sustainable Architecture.* New York: McGraw-Hill.

Steger, W. 1990. *Saving the Earth: A Citizen's Guide to Environmental Action.* New York: Alfred A Knopf.

Steiner, F. R., and G. F. Thompson, eds. 1997. *Ecological Design and Planning.* New York: John Wiley & Sons.

Stitt, F. A., ed. 1999. *Ecological Design Handbook: Sustainable Strategies for Architecture, Landscape Architecture, Interior Design, and Planning.* New York: McGraw-Hill.

Sustainable Buildings Industry Council. 2004. *Green Buildings Guidelines: Meeting the Demand for Low-Energy, Resource-Efficient Homes.* Washington, DC: Sustainable Buildings Industry Council.

Sutton, P. W. 2004. *Nature, Environment, and Society (Sociology for a Changing World).* New York: Palgrave Macmillan.

Svendsen, L. 2003. *Good Green Homes: Creating Better Homes for a Healthier Planet.* Layton, UT: Gibbs Smith.

Thompson, A. 2004. *Homes that Heal (and Those That Don't): How Your Home Could Be Harming Your Family's Health.* Gabriola Island, BC: New Society Publishers.

Thompson, W. I. 1987. *Gaia: A Way of Knowing.* San Francisco: Lindisfarne Press.

Thornton, J. 2002. *Environmental Impacts of Polyvinyl Chloride Building Materials: A Healthy Building Network Report.* Washington, DC: Healthy Building Network.

UN Conference on Environment and Development (UNCED). 1992. *The Rio Declaration on Environment and Development.* Rio de Janeiro, Brazil: UNCED Secretariat.

U.S. Green Building Council (USGBC). 2003. *Building Momentum: National Trends and Prospects for High-Performance Green Buildings.* Washington, DC: USGBC.

———. 2005. *Leadership in Energy and Environmental Design (LEED).* Washington, DC: USGBC.

U.S. Department of Commerce Technology Administration. 1994. *U.S. Green Building Conference.* NIST Special Publication 863. Washington, DC: Government Printing Office.

U.S. Department of the Interior, National Park Service. 1993. *Guiding Principles of Sustainable Design.* Washington, DC: Government Printing Office.

U.S. Office of Technology Assessment. 1992. *Green Products by Design: Choices for a Cleaner Environment.* Washington, DC: U.S. Office of Technology Assessment.

Vale, B., and R. Vale. 1991. *Green Architecture: Design for an Energy-Conscious Future.* Boston: Little, Brown.

Van der Ryn, S. 1993. Sustainable Communities. *Design and the Environment.* Washington, DC: American Institute of Architects.

Vote Hemp. 2002. *The Vote Hemp Report: 2002/2003.* Merrifield, VA: Vote Hemp.

Wackernagel, M., and W. Rees. 1996. *Our Ecological Footprint: Reducing Human Impact on the Earth.* Gabriola Island, BC: New Society Publishers.

Wall, D. 1994. *Green History: A Reader in Environmental Literature, Philosophy, and Politics.* London: Routledge.

Ward, B. 1966. *Spaceship Earth.* New York: Columbia University Press.

Wasowski, A., and S. Wasowski. 2000. *Building Inside Nature's Envelope: How New Construction and Land Preservation Can Work Together.* New York: Oxford University Press.

Wege, P. M. 1998. *Economicology: The Eleventh Commandment.* Grand Rapids, MI: Economicology Press.

Weiner, J. 1994. *The Next Hundred Years: Shaping the Fate of the Living Earth.* New York: Bantam Books.

White House Council on Sustainable Development. 1999. *Sustainable America.* Washington, DC: Government Printing Office.

William McDonough Architects. 1992. *The Hannover Principles: Design for Sustainability.* New York: William McDonough Architects.

Wilson, A. 2006. *Your Green Home.* Gabriola Island, BC: New Society Publishers.

Wilson A., and M. Piepkorn, eds. 2005. *GreenSpec Guide to Residential Building Materials.* Gabriola Island, BC: New Society Publishers

Wilson, A., N. Malin, and M. Piepkorn. n.d. *BuildingGreen Suite: GreenSpec™ Directory* (electronic version). Brattleboro, VT: BuildingGreen.

———. n.d. *Environmental Building News.* Brattleboro, VT: BuildingGreen.

———. 2006. *GreenSpec Directory,* 6th ed. Brattleboro, VT: BuildingGreen.

Wines, J. 2000. *Green Architecture.* Edited by P. Jodidio. New York: Taschen.

Wong, K. 2005. "The Littlest Human." *Scientific American* (February): 40–49.

World Commission on Environment and Development. 1987. *Our Common Future.* Oxford and New York: Oxford University Press.

World Resources Institute with UNEP and UNDP. 1992. *World Resources, 1992–1993.* Oxford: Oxford University Press.

Yeang, K. 1995. *Designing with Nature: The Ecological Basis for Architectural Design.* New York: McGraw-Hill.

———. 1999. *The Green Skyscraper: The Basis for Designing Sustainable Intensive Buildings.* New York: Prestel.

Zeiher, L. C. 1996. *The Ecology of Architecture: A Complete Guide to Creating the Environmentally Conscious Building.* New York: Whitney Library of Design.

Index

Wiley Books on Sustainable Design

For these and other Wiley books on sustainable design, visit www.wiley.com/go/sustainabledesign

Environmental Benefits Statement

This book is printed with soy-based inks on presses with VOC levels that are lower than the standard for the printing industry. The paper, Rolland Enviro 100, is manufactured by Cascades Fine Papers Group and is made from 100 percent post-consumer, de-inked fiber, without chlorine. According to the manufacturer, the use of every ton of Rolland Enviro100 Book paper, switched from virgin paper, helps the environment in the following ways:

Mature trees saved	Waterborne waste not created	Waterflow saved	Atmospheric emissions eliminated	Solid wastes reduced	Natural gas saved by using biogas
17	6.9 lbs.	10,196 gals.	2,098 lbs.	1,081 lbs.	2,478 cubic feet